Induction, Growth
and Trade

SIR ROY HARROD

Induction, Growth and Trade

ESSAYS IN HONOUR OF
SIR ROY HARROD

EDITED BY

W. A. ELTIS   M. FG. SCOTT

J. N. WOLFE

CLARENDON PRESS · OXFORD
1970

Oxford University Press, Ely House, London W.1

GLASGOW NEW YORK TORONTO MELBOURNE WELLINGTON
CAPE TOWN SALISBURY IBADAN NAIROBI DAR ES SALAAM LUSAKA ADDIS ABABA
BOMBAY CALCUTTA MADRAS KARACHI LAHORE DACCA
KUALA LUMPUR SINGAPORE HONG KONG TOKYO

MADE AND PRINTED IN GREAT BRITAIN BY
WILLIAM CLOWES AND SONS, LIMITED
LONDON AND BECCLES

PREFACE

SIR ROY HARROD retired from his Studentship at Christ Church and the Nuffield Readership of International Economics at Oxford in the summer of 1967. Although he is as active as ever, it seemed fitting to mark his formal retirement by presenting him with a volume of essays written by his colleagues, pupils, and fellow economists. The editors wrote to some of them, and this book is the result.

The first essay, by Robert Blake, for many years Sir Roy's colleague at Christ Church, is a fitting tribute by one biographer to another.

Next come three philosophical essays. The first two, by A. J. Ayer and Jacob Marschak, discuss the problem of induction, surely one of the most famous and important of all the problems of philosophy. The third, by Sidney S. Alexander, considers the impersonality of normative judgements. Sir Roy's contributions to philosophy are valued highly. He would say that, in the long view, economics is ephemeral, but philosophy is eternal. It is therefore right that the philosophical essays should come first.

Nevertheless, it is by his contributions to economics that he is best known, and most of the essays in the volume are in this field. It is a wide one, and Sir Roy has not confined himself to any corner of it. This set a problem for the arrangement of the essays, which we have attempted to solve by grouping them as nearly as possible by subject. There are two main groups: growth and development, and international trade; and there is a single essay on the firm. These divisions, however, are by no means absolute and certain subgroups can be discerned among which there is substantial overlapping.

This is particularly true of the first paper, by Trygve Haavelmo, which is appropriately placed next to the philosophical essays since it discusses how the economist's skills can be used to analyse wider issues than those to which they are customarily confined.

The following five essays, by W. A. Eltis, Michal Kalecki, Kenneth K. Kurihara, J. R. Sargent, and Tsukumo Shionoya deal with various aspects of the theory of growth and development, a part of economics to which Sir Roy's own contribution has been especially important, having touched off a whole train of writings by many other economists.

Ragnar Frisch's essay, in which he reviews the present state of econometrics with some disquiet, is followed by essays in applied econometrics by Jere Behrman and L. R. Klein, F. P. R. Brechling and J. N. Wolfe, and Franco Modigliani.

The next three essays exemplify the straddling of different fields mentioned above. J. Tinbergen's brings out the essentials of the two-gap theory of the determinants of growth. One of these is the foreign exchange gap, and so one is led rather naturally to Richard E. Caves's essay on export-led growth. Léon H. Dupriez's discussion of the way in which international price structures change as development proceeds is also concerned with both growth and trade, and it is clear that our allocation of these three essays to growth or trade is arbitrary.

Harry G. Johnson's essay is a particularly notable tribute to Sir Roy since it comes from one who was long persuaded that an increase in the price of gold was not a good way of easing the growing shortage of international liquidity. Sir Roy has advocated such an increase for many years, and Harry Johnson underlines the force of his arguments. The remaining five essays, by Vijay Joshi, Kiyoshi Kojima, Bertil Ohlin, M. FG. Scott, and Jean Weiller, all grouped under international trade, fit clearly into this broad category.

The final essay is William J. Baumol's analysis of the rationale of selling in a market where demand is inelastic, a situation which, at first sight, no profit-maximizing firm should allow to persist; but it does persist, and so an explanation is clearly needed.

The bibliography of Sir Roy's writings completes the volume. This includes all his books and articles in learned journals to date. But Sir Roy has written very much more. With his assistance, a list which includes articles in the daily and weekly press has been drawn up, with a view to depositing copies in three libraries: at the Institute of Economics and Statistics in Oxford, at Yale, and at Pennsylvania. These writings show Sir Roy's extraordinary vigour and his many contributions to contemporary discussion on a wide range of subjects. Attention should in particular be drawn to his pre-war letters and articles in the *Times* and other newspapers. These were influential, in some respects anticipated Keynes's *General Theory*, and may have prompted Schumpeter to write 'Mr. Harrod may have been moving independently toward a goal not far from that of Keynes, though he unselfishly joined the latter's standard after it had been raised. Justice imposes this remark. For that eminent economist is in some danger of losing the place in the history of economics that is his by right, both in respect to Keynesianism and in respect to Imperfect Competition.'[1] Because of their importance, these pre-war letters and articles are listed at the end of the bibliography.

One has only to glance down the list of contents, which we have briefly outlined, to see how the contributions have come in from the four corners of the globe and how they cover a vast range of subjects. Only one thread connects them all—Sir Roy's life and work.

M. FG. S.

W. A. E.

J. N. W.

[1] 'John Maynard Keynes 1883–1946', *American Economic Review* Vol. XXXVI (1946), p. 509. See also J. A. Schumpeter, *History of Economic Analysis*, New York, 1954, pp. 1152 and 1172.

CONTENTS

International Trade

The Firm

LIST OF PLATES

1

A PERSONAL MEMOIR

ROBERT BLAKE

SIR ROY HARROD was a don at Christ Church—'Student of Christ Church' is the somewhat misleading title—for forty-five years. He was elected in 1922 after a brilliant academic career at Westminster and at New College where he obtained a first in Greats and, after one year's work, a first in Modern History. His answers in the latter school are said to have been remarkable for their brevity and compression. At first sight the examiners were sceptical but on reflection decided that he had said all that needed to be said without a superfluous word, and what more could one ask? It would be wrong, however, to imagine that Sir Roy Harrod carried this practice of brevity on into later life. He used to make the unusual complaint that speeches at college feasts and the like were not long enough. I remember how he once adjured me before the Censors' Dinner, an important college occasion at which I was one of the hosts that year, 'Do not, I beg you, my dear Censor, imitate your colleagues and make a *short* speech.' And suiting practice to precept he explained to me at some length the disadvantages of brevity. The advice was no doubt flattering but I thought I would be unwise to act on it. Sir Roy himself was, however, an admirable after-dinner speaker with a splendid command of wit and anecdote and eloquence, nor do I remember that he ever went on too long for me.

Harrod was elected to teach in the new school of philosophy, politics and economics then called 'Modern Greats'. In latter days the general mania for initials has substituted P.P.E. for the older title. To the end of his time Sir Roy would never make any concession to this usage either in speech or writing, and would from time to time mildy rebuke junior colleagues who lapsed. Since he knew little or nothing about economics when he was first elected, the college wisely gave him leave of absence to learn what he was to teach. He spent two terms (Michaelmas 1922 and Hilary 1923) sitting at the feet of Maynard Keynes at King's and writing weekly essays for him. This was the beginning of a life-long friendship, and after Keynes's death Roy Harrod was chosen by the executors to write his official biography—to the mortification of one or two Cambridge economists who considered that the life of such a quintessential Cambridge figure should not have been entrusted to an Oxford man. Whether any of them would have written a better book than Sir Roy Harrod's must be a matter of speculation. What is certain is that Sir Roy wrote a very good book and on its appearance in 1951 it was widely acclaimed as such. But of that more later.

As a young don Harrod was disappointed with the conversation in Common Room. It was not sufficiently intellectual. He would often recall what he maintained was the only remark even vaguely referring to such matters, made on his first evening. The Steward (Domestic Bursar in other colleges), a robust *ancien militaire*, was warming himself in front of the fire and observed apropos of nothing in particular: 'A pity about that feller, Oscar Wilde. A great pity. He was clever as paint, you know, clever as paint.' But there was no follow-up to this intriguing opening. As an undergraduate at New College, Harrod enjoyed to the full the endless opportunities for discussion, moral, philosophical, literary, and artistic. He had been brought up in a highly cultivated home 'in which the tradition was that conversation was by far the greatest pleasure, if not the prime object of life'.[1] Undergraduate life in Oxford had suited him ideally, and he believed to the end of his career in Christ Church that young men learn more from each other than anyone else.

'Dons have always struck me, lifelong don although I have been myself, as playing a subsidiary role in Oxford and Cambridge. They provide a certain background of quiet culture, and they supply standards of precision and self-discipline in research, so that the young men can get a glimpse, an inkling, of the exacting nature of the pursuit of truth. I dissent violently from the view that the main service of the University is in the provision of courses and examinations, and in the insistence on the desirability of obtaining high classes; I frankly view the tendency of the dons to encroach upon the life and time and energy of undergraduates with suspicion.'[2]

This philosophy did not imply that Roy Harrod in any way neglected his pupils or failed to do his best for them. He was an energetic and stimulating tutor. He was also still young enough to enjoy the parties and the company of undergraduates, especially the gay circle which centred around Harold Acton; but there is inevitably something of a gap between even a young don and undergraduates however sophisticated, and so, if he had a spare morning, he would go round to New College and talk about the universe with Lord David Cecil. 'He took this as the most natural thing in the world. My Christ Church colleagues would have thought that I must be mad, had I invaded their rooms at such a time.'[3] There has been perhaps no more agreeable existence in recent times than that of a bachelor college fellow in his twenties in the nineteen-twenties. The stipend was adequate. Life was remarkably

---

[1] Harrod, 1959, p. 40. This fascinating study of the late Lord Cherwell also contains much autobiography. I have freely drawn upon it in this essay.
[2] Ibid., p. 41.   [3] Ibid., p. 43.

cheap. There was a high standard of food, wine, and service. Christ Church itself, curious amalgam between a cathedral close and a great country mansion, mixture of Barchester and Blenheim, was an ideal habitat for one who enjoyed the grand as well as the intellectual world. It was leisurely and civilized and if occasionally the night would be shattered by, to quote Evelyn Waugh's immortal words, the noise of the English aristocracy 'baying for broken glass', this was a merely temporary interruption of an otherwise placid style of life. Lord Cherwell used to repeat with pleasure one of Roy Harrod's first remarks when he arrived new to the Christ Church Common Room: 'I *cannot* work hard'[4]—though Sir Roy himself has no memory of making it. What Lord Cherwell particularly enjoyed was the authoritative tone in which the new arrival imparted this interesting piece of information to his senior colleagues. Whether or not it was true when he said it, it certainly was not true later. I have never known anyone who worked harder than Roy Harrod in the twenty years after the second world war when I had the honour to be one of his junior colleagues in the teaching of Modern Greats in Christ Church. Nor can I believe that this was a sudden change. A man who is lazy till his forties does not usually become galvanized with energy overnight.

It naturally took a little time before Harrod got into his stride as a contributor to his chosen field. His first two articles in learned journals appeared early in 1927. Then there was a pause till the end of 1930 before he published anything more. But during that time he occupied one of the most important offices in the college, and one whose occupants have seldom found much time to write or research. This was the post of Senior Censor, which combined the functions filled by the Senior Tutor and the Tutor for Admissions in other colleges, together with half the disciplinary work of the college—the other half falls to the Junior Censor—and some at least of the duties carried out elsewhere by the head of the college. In those days it was the usage that the two Censors should be bachelors living in college, and it was customary to hold the two offices successively for an inclusive period of five years, three as junior and two as senior or vice versa according to the tenures of the previous incumbents. The post of Junior Censor was not, and is not, arduous. It is by way of being an apprenticeship for the more onerous position.[5]

The Senior Censor's was, however, a much bigger job. He largely controlled admissions. He sat on nearly all the key committees of the college *ex officio*. It was part of his duty to know all the undergraduates and to be ready to deal with those of their problems which for one reason or another

---

[4] Ibid., p. 159.

[5] The Senior Censor is a very busy man to this day, but some of his labours were taken off his shoulders a few years ago by the appointment of a separate Tutor for Admissions. The burden of administration in Oxford colleges has greatly increased since the inter-war years, although it is fair to say that assistance to cope with it has also increased. In Harrod's day there was no College Secretary and all letters had to be answered by hand.

were not within the scope of their tutors. A system which gives to relatively junior members of the college for a short period such heavy responsibilities has not been without its critics in latter days. Indeed, but for historical reasons peculiar to Christ Church, it would probably never have been invented in the first place. However, it seems to work, and it certainly gave a young don who had the prudence not to plunge into premature matrimony an opportunity which did not come so readily in other colleges.

Harrod was Junior Censor from 1927 to 1929 and became Senior Censor at the beginning of 1930, strictly on Christmas Day 1929. For some reason the Censorship, unlike most university and college offices, changes with the calendar year. In 1929 he was also elected at the exceptionally early age of twenty-nine to membership of Hebdomadal Council, which is the governing body, in so far as there is one at all, of the University. As a strong left wing Liberal he was regarded both in the college and the University as something of a radical in university politics; but curiously enough the battles which brought him into conflict with 'the Establishment' resulted from an alliance with one who was anything but liberal, and whose politics Harrod himself described as exhibiting an 'acrid conservatism'. This was the head of the Clarendon Laboratory, Professor Lindemann, later Lord Cherwell, intimate friend of Churchill, and one of the most striking characters in Oxford. At this time he was regarded not only as striking but as highly controversial both in the University and in Christ Church where he occupied the anomalous position of a Student not on the Governing Body. Harrod fought vigorously on his behalf in Hebdomadal Council when the question arose of the right of the Radcliffe Trustees, who had received a large benefaction, to site a new giant telescope in Pretoria rather than Oxford. Lindemann argued that the University had a moral claim on the money to be used for the benefit of astronomy in Oxford. But it seems hardly surprising that the courts—for the parties went to law on the matter—decided in favour of Pretoria. The University's case was legally thin, and common sense suggests that the endemic miasma of the Thames valley does not make Oxford the ideal place from which to observe the stars.

Scarcely had the echoes of this battle died away than Harrod, again allied with Lindemann, was engaged in an even more serious struggle, this time within Christ Church. The question was whether a research Studentship in science financed by Lindemann's friend, the Duke of Westminster, should or should not carry with it membership of the Governing Body. Lindemann considered this to be a test case for the status of science in Oxford. Harrod took the same view and indeed regarded it as exemplifying an even wider issue—the importance to be attributed by colleges to research as such. What may be called the college's 'Establishment', its nine weightiest, most influential and best known tutors were strongly opposed to this proposal. They argued, a little speciously perhaps, that the Duke of Westminster Student would get on with his research better if he were not on the Governing Body, more speciously that there was no room for an extra member on the Governing Body (it has doubled since then without notable inconvenience). A better argument was that under the terms of the Duke's covenant Lindemann had an effective veto on their choice.

Harrod plunged into the fray with a zest and enthusiasm which has always been one of his most engaging qualities but which his seniors deemed to be improper in the holder of his office. He bombarded his colleagues with long and eloquent memoranda—a technique which he continued to employ with varying degrees of effectiveness to the end of his time in Christ Church. I still possess the powerful appeal which he addressed to us all on the perhaps not very vital question of the brass chandelier in the Senior Common Room, and I can well imagine the vigour with which he prosecuted the cause of the Duke of Westminster Studentship. The account of what followed should be read in *The Prof.*[6]: how he discovered that the Establishment was meeting the night before the crucial vote in secret cabal unprecedently excluding the Senior Censor; how he decided that if defeated he must resign the Censorship; how he consoled himself in advance by a dinner to which Sir Maurice Bowra and two of the gayest Christ Church undergraduates were invited; how after the consumption of much champagne one of the young men was sent to listen at the keyhole of the room where the cabal was supposed to be deliberating, only to find it empty; how Lindemann 'nobbled' the Dean by playing on his partiality to Dukes; how on the great day Roy Harrod himself made a speech of flowing eloquence; and how—contrary to all expectation—the quiet inconspicuous members of the Governing Body voted in just sufficient numbers to defeat the Establishment.

And so the Duke of Westminster Student became a member of the Governing Body and Harrod did not have to resign the Senior Censorship. It is a splendid story, although it is only fair to add that some of the other participants who remember the episode are by no means in agreement with Harrod's version. Indeed, I have heard some very emphatic language on the point but it is better not repeated in these pages. R. H. Dundas, the most influential of the ex-Censors who by custom nominate to the Censorship, had indicated at one time to Harrod that he might be asked to continue for a third year.

'I should have liked that but now it was utterly out of the question. One of the nine had me to lunch shortly afterwards alone with him. He said that under my Senior Censorship the college had been raised to a pitch of domestic strife such as he could not recall during his long period of service there; everyone was angry at the way in which the Dean had been 'nobbled'. For all these disturbances he held me to blame.'[7]

[6] pp. 145–59.   [7] Ibid., p.158.

No doubt this was very unfair, but people are apt to judge by results, and there seems little doubt that, whoever was to blame, dissension reached a high point in the college during those years.

The early 1930s saw Harrod beginning to make his name in the field of economics. He did not believe in being merely theoretical. It was the custom for dons living in college to act in turn as caterer for a term with responsibility for the High Table. These were the days of the great slump. Harrod in accordance with Keynes's heterodox views held that the right thing to do was to inject as much purchasing power as possible into the economy. He, therefore, to the surprise, but not one assumes wholly to the displeasure, of his colleagues ordered particularly lavish meals during his term. He was succeeded by the Law Tutor, a rigid Conservative. The doctrines of the May Committee replaced those of Keynes, and the gourmets, as they looked glumly at the dismal dishes which appeared at the High Table, reflected with nostalgia upon the reign of Harrod.

Politically throughout these years Harrod continued to adhere to the Liberal party and was active in speaking and writing on its behalf. In the 1920s he was a friend of Asquith and a regular guest at The Wharf. He was vigorous in promoting Asquith's candidature for the Chancellorship, though the attempt failed. He was also on close terms with Gilbert Murray and acted as his election agent on the many occasions when he unsuccessfully stood for the university seat. In the elections of 1931 and 1935 he strongly opposed the National Government and even spoke on Labour platforms in constituencies where there was no Liberal candidate. He went so far to the left as to join the Oxford Pink Lunch Club whose members were nearly all avowed supporters of socialism.

The rise of Hitler posed a painful dilemma to all those who, whatever their party affiliation, held 'liberal' views. To them it had long been an article of faith that Germany had been unjustly treated at Versailles—the theme on which Keynes had been so eloquent; that British foreign policy ought to be based on the League of Nations; that we should work hard for an agreement on disarmament, if necessary setting an example by unilateral action; and that the just grievances of the defeated powers should be remedied with a view to achieving a *détente* in Europe. These ideas were far from being confined to the Liberal or Labour parties. They penetrated the top echelons of the Conservative party too, and constituted the intellectual background to the policy of appeasement which culminated in the Munich Agreement. But as that dismal decade wore on it became more and more doubtful to thinking persons whether the liberal remedies could possibly cope with a megalomaniac nationalist dictator whose ambitions seemed limitless and who was rearming with sinister rapidity.

To the more *simpliste* Conservatives of the right, there was no dilemma. They did not care a hang about liberal principles. The danger was that they

SIR ROY HARROD, TAKEN IN THE MIDDLE 'THIRTIES

might be pro-Hitler precisely because he was so illiberal and because fascism might seem to be a bulwark not only against communism but against social democracy. However, this attitude, epitomized in France by the slogan 'Better Hitler than Blum', was mercifully rare in England. The right wing of the Conservative party on the whole took the view that all would be well as long as Britain and France kept up their armaments, and that German grievances were irrelevant when the question of the balance of power in Europe was at stake. This was the attitude of Churchill echoed naturally by his friend Lindemann.

Harrod had of course been a strong adherent of the 'liberal' line in the 'twenties, but he became increasingly doubtful about it in the 'thirties. He describes how he made a strong speech in 1935 on a Labour platform in support of tough action against Mussolini. To his dismay the candidate, the present Lady Longford, followed with a passionate speech in favour of disarmament. He protested afterwards. '"But we ought to disarm", she said, "as an example to others." "You think our example will cause Hitler and Mussolini to disarm?" I asked. "Oh, Roy," she said, "have you lost all your idealism?" I am afraid that, confronted by the spectacle of Hitler, I had.' In terms of Oxford politics Harrod thus found himself again in the same camp as Lindemann, despite their very divergent political faiths. He already knew Churchill, whose son had been up at Christ Church, and he stayed from time to time at Chartwell to talk over these problems. As a Liberal he could, however, do little to assist Lindemann's ill-starred attempts, strongly backed by Churchill, to get himself elected as one of the Burgesses for the University. It was essentially an intra-Conservative party struggle and an outsider's activities would have been what is now called 'counter-productive'.

By 1938 Harrod had become such a convinced anti-appeaser that on the news of Munich he took to his bed for a day or two, thus refuting Dr. Johnson's dictum that 'public affairs vex no one'. But he soon recovered and played a considerable part in the effort to put up an independent anti-Munich candidate at the impending by-election in Oxford City. Quintin Hogg was the Conservative candidate campaigning on the slogan that a vote for him was a vote for Mr. Chamberlain. The Labour candidate was Harrod's colleague, Patrick Gordon-Walker, and there was a Liberal also. The first task of the anti-appeasers was to induce the two to stand down in favour of the independent, A. D. Lindsay, the Master of Balliol. Harrod was chairman of the committee charged with this ungrateful task. It could not be achieved painlessly, and inevitably some degree of resentment was left behind. Harrod then became chairman of Lindsay's committee. After a stiff contest Quintin Hogg was victorious, though by a much reduced majority compared with the general election of 1935.

At the outbreak of war Lindemann at once became a sort of statistical-cum-scientific adviser to Churchill at the Admiralty. Harrod helped him to staff this new and anomalous organization known as S Branch. One of his most successful suggestions was the name of G. D. A. (now Sir Donald) MacDougall. 'I regard my choice of man on that occasion as a stroke of genius, and my best contribution to the defeat of Hitler.'[8] Undoubtedly MacDougall's acute statistical mind and high degree of tact were precisely what was needed to ensure the success of the Branch. On 1 January 1940 Harrod himself after repeated entreaties joined S Branch. He found the work highly congenial at first, and he gives a most interesting account of it in *The Prof*.[9] But he was less happy about his own position after May 1940. He had expected that when Churchill became Prime Minister the need for this special branch would disappear. Surely it was only invented to meet the peculiar circumstances of a First Lord of the Admiralty who saw himself rightly as the next Prime Minister at no distant date and therefore wished to be informed about a large number of matters which had little connection with the Admiralty. As soon as he actually became Prime Minister he would have all the resources of the governmental machine at his command. Harrod assumed and hoped that the position of S Branch would be regularized and that it would be merged into some kind of Economic General Staff.

Nothing of the sort occurred. Churchill, like Lloyd George in the first world war, was determined to have his private advisers as watch dogs on the figures and facts put forward by the great departments of state. S Branch, transformed and enlarged as 'the Prime Minister's Statistical Section', became, though far more sophisticated, Churchill's equivalent of Lloyd George's 'garden suburb'. Harrod did not wish to dispute Churchill's and Lindemann's decision but he felt that this was not what he himself had bargained for. Moreover, as the war went on he felt a certain uneasiness about the extent to which he might have to subordinate his own views on post-war economic policy to those of Lindemann: 'I was not prepared to accept the Prof. as an authority on these economic problems superior to myself.' Both in the University and in Christ Church he had had experience of the way in which Lindemann's persuasiveness could in some mysterious way land his allies in positions where they never expected to find themselves.

'And then there was the Prof.'s tendency to lead one along further than one had originally intended to go, of which I had had twenty years of intimate experience. On the first engagement one might have a slight qualm, yet not think the difference material enough not to be willing to join forces with him. Then before one knew where one was one had become involved in a further engagement, about which one's doubts were much more grave; and then in another engagement, and so on.'

In the spring of 1942 Harrod decided to resign and return to his teaching work in Christ Church, but there was not much to do, and it all seemed rather

---

[8] Harrod, 1959, p. 181.   [9] Ibid., pp. 187–224.

small beer in wartime. On the other hand further employment was not easy to secure, despite his recognized eminence as an economist. S Branch had made itself intensely unpopular. Lindemann, now Lord Cherwell and a Minister, was one of the best-hated figures in Whitehall as far as the Civil Service was concerned. Anyone who had served him was regarded with suspicion. Harrod goes so far as to say that, 'From a worldly point of view it was certainly a fatal error.' Eventually he was offered a post by Admiral Boyd, the Fifth Sea Lord, who wanted someone with statistical experience to present the requirements of the Fleet Air Arm which, as Harrod observes in *The Prof.*, 'was clearly a respectable institution'. 'I felt that there could be no one in the country better qualified than I for this particular task.' He insisted, however, that it should be on a half-time basis so that he could continue his work in Oxford. The Fleet Air Arm's case had recently been heavily mauled by none other than Cherwell himself, and Harrod found himself in a paradoxical position. 'I had spent the early years of the war writing minutes on behalf of the Prof., and now I had unwittingly been engaged to write minutes against him.' Fortunately, though by no means predictably, Cherwell did not appear to mind—at least not much.

In the last years of the war Harrod took a keen interest in post-war economic policy, in particular co-operation with America in obtaining a freer flow of international trade, and he was very anxious to ensure the full implementation of Article 7 of the Mutual Aid Agreement. He discussed the matter in detail with Mr. Harcourt Johnstone, who was the member of the Liberal Shadow Cabinet concerned with post-war planning. Harcourt Johnstone hoped to combine emphasis on Article 7 with the traditional Liberal policy of free trade put into a Keynesian framework. He strongly urged Harrod to stand for Parliament. Unfortunately he died suddenly and unexpectedly before the general election, but Harrod decided none the less to stand and was adopted as candidate for Huddersfield. He had to fight a somewhat lonely battle, for Sir Archibald Sinclair was not *au fait* with the latest Anglo-American negotiations in this field, and Sir William Beveridge was far more interested in his own plans for social security. However, he attracted enough attention for Churchill to send a message to the electors of Huddersfield adjuring them to ignore his 'mischievous' allegations.

Harrod did not succeed in getting in. For a time he remained high in Liberal counsels and was even a member of their Shadow Cabinet, but he could not persuade them to take much interest in Article 7 and he found them divided over many issues. In the late 'forties he joined the Conservative party. I well remember what I believe was his first public declaration of conversion. He appeared in the Oxford Town Hall on the same platform as Quintin Hogg. His old Liberal habits had not yet been eradicated. He dwelt upon the parlous state to which the Labour Government had reduced British Government Securities on the New York Stock Exchange and asked: 'What would Mr.

Gladstone have said?' Then he paused for a moment. 'What, indeed, would Mr. Disraeli have said, if the Funds had sunk so low . . . ?' At this stage he had by no means abandoned the idea of entering Parliament, and Churchill, with whom cordial relations had soon been restored, sent messages of support for his candidature to various Conservative constituency associations. But the power even of the leader is limited in these matters, and competition was keen. Although at one stage the prospect seemed sufficiently imminent for the Governing Body to agree, not without misgiving, to an arrangement whereby Harrod would combine reduced teaching duties with membership of the House of Commons, nothing came of it in the end.

In some ways he moved further to the right as the years passed. He was a strong supporter of Anthony Eden's policy during the Suez crisis of 1956. He approved of the Vietnam War and had no sympathy with the usual liberal and left-wing criticisms. But he did not fit into any easily identifiable political slot. He was an opponent of the Common Market partly on economic grounds but also because he thought it was merely a rich man's club and would discourage aid for under-developed countries of Asia and Africa, which is not on the whole a right-wing cause. Yet in spite of a Liberal past he had no great feeling about racialism. He did not of course approve of *apartheid* but it did not excite him to tremendous indignation; likewise the Rhodesian declaration of independence.

Perhaps this is partly a matter of age group. As a very rough generalization the passion for equality, racial or otherwise, seems to be in inverse proportion to age, the great divide being between those who are old enough to have served in the last war and those who are not. I do not presume to explain the sociological reason for this gap. Harrod may not be quite what Gladstone declared himself to be, 'an out and out inequalitarian', but he has always been in his own words 'a great believer . . . in the importance of the varieties of (hereditary) stock'. He was not opposed to the widest possible ladder for educational advancement, but he believed that dependence on examinations as the sole measure of fitness for responsible positions would be a grave error: it is too chancy and often quite irrelevant.

'The only known principle by which we can supplement the examination system is to give advantages to those whose forebears have proved themselves. It is thus important that we should retain the system now threatened, by which parents can buy their children a better education, and not at top level only.'[10]

For this reason he was opposed to swingeing death duties, and always looked with a kindly eye on candidates for Christ Church who were scions of famous families or descended from persons of great distinction. These are very unfashionable views today, but not for that reason to be despised or regarded as incapable of revival.

[10] Harrod, 1959, p. 81.

To revert to politics, he appeared to grow increasingly out of sympathy with the Conservative party after 1959. He certainly condemned the policy of stop-go in no uncertain terms and being on friendly terms with Mr. Macmillan tried hard to persuade him to over-rule the Treasury in 1960–1. I seem to recall that he told me that he decided to abstain from voting in the election of 1964. I do not know whether he felt the same way in 1966.

In 1938 Harrod had married Wilhelmine ('Billa') Creswell. But marriage did not, as it does with some dons, separate him from the college or create the 'nine to five' mentality which is so much to be deplored in the academic world, however necessary it may be for commuters from Kent. They lived in a delightful house belonging to, and a very modest stone's throw from Christ Church. Furnished and decorated with admirable taste by Billa it became a social centre for the more amusing undergraduates and the less dull dons. There must be a host of people to whom it brings back memories of gay parties, excellent food, and memorable conversation. During the vacations the Harrods would normally depart to their house in Norfolk, Billa's home county. But in term Christ Church saw almost as much of Roy Harrod as it did in his bachelor days.

I first came to know him when in 1946, rather to my surprise, I was elected as Politics Tutor in succession to Frank Pakenham (now the Earl of Longford), who had exchanged academic for real politics and had become a Lord-in-Waiting in the Labour Government. Although my academic career had been respectable, I had never moved in the upper intellectual circles of the under-graduate world, and six years in the Army had made me forget almost every-thing I knew. Roy Harrod seemed to me frighteningly sophisticated and at first a bit aloof, although that quickly changed and we soon came on terms of easy friendship. Even from the beginning he was invariably most kind, and, although he never dreamed of acting as a preceptor, I learned a great deal from him in conversation and by example. His attitude to undergraduates seemed—and seems—to me entirely right. He would take an infinity of trouble about anyone in difficulties. He was perhaps over-inclined to perceive psychological malaise where some of us saw mere lead-swinging, but this is surely an error on the right side. With the ordinary undergraduate he did not lose much sleep. He listened to their essays, criticized particular points of fact, style, presentation, logic, and discoursed on some theme arising out of them, often with personal reminiscences of people and episodes. His pupils did not get what too many expect and, alas, nowadays too often receive; a potted lecturette, covering the principal aspects of the topic together with hints on how to answer a question in the Schools. But the more perceptive among them left his spacious room in Kilcannon feeling that they had been in contact with a brilliant, many-sided intellect and often that they had had a glimpse of the great world where decisions were taken and policies framed.

Roy Harrod was a firm advocate of the view that tutorial fellows were appointed just as much to research and advance knowledge as to teach and lecture. He always encouraged his junior colleagues in this direction, and urged them on no account to degenerate into mere teaching hacks. He himself was certainly in no danger of doing so. On the contrary he published a great deal. His contribution to Economics will no doubt remain his principal claim to academic fame. I will merely observe that to those like myself who were not in the inner ring of the Economics Faculty it seemed extraordinary that he was never elected to an Oxford chair, but it was perhaps some consolation that he should have been knighted in 1959—a most unusual honour for someone who was still a 'mere college tutor', for knighthoods tend to go only to selected members of the upper academic hierarchy.

Others deal elsewhere with his contribution to economics, but this is an appropriate place to discuss his contribution to the art of biography. Roy Harrod wrote two biographies of very different types. The only thing in common is that they were about people very recently dead when he wrote, and that both subjects were intimately known to the author. *The Life of John Maynard Keynes* was first published in 1951. It belongs to the genus known a little forbiddingly as 'official biography', that is to say Harrod was invited to write it by the owner of the copyright in Keynes's papers, his brother Dr. Geoffrey Keynes, and he was the first person to be given access to those papers for that purpose.

The Prof., published in 1959, was in no sense an official biography; in fact very much the reverse. It occasioned what was, I like to believe, one of the very few serious disagreements that I ever had with Roy Harrod. As one of Lord Cherwell's executors I had played some part in arranging with his brother, Brigadier Charles Lindemann, that the official biography should be written by Lord Birkenhead who knew Cherwell well and whose father, the famous 'F. E.', had been Cherwell's close friend in the 1920s. Harrod had made it quite clear that he did not personally wish to write the official biography. I was, therefore, slightly disturbed when I was told that he contemplated producing a sort of pen portrait or memoir of Cherwell to appear in a collection of such portraits which he was bringing out. It was certain to be published long before Lord Birkenhead's official life. I was much more disturbed when it transpired that the memoir was going to be a book on its own of considerable length.

My fear was in a sense flattering. I would not have minded if I had expected it to be a bad book, for then there would be no danger of stealing Birkenhead's thunder. But it seemed far more likely that it would be a rather good book, as indeed turned out to be the case. Of course Roy Harrod was entirely within his rights. No one can have a monopoly in a subject. If he was prepared to write a personal memoir without any access to Cherwell's papers he could not be stopped. Nevertheless . . . was it really fair on Lord Birkenhead? Harrod argued that there would be no competition, that the scope of the two books would be wholly different, that the appearance of his would even help the official life by stimulating interest in the subject. I was not convinced at the time, nor am I now, that these contentions had much validity. Had I been the official biographer, I would have found, as did Lord Birkenhead, both the prospect and the fact of such a book appearing before mine annoying, vexatious, and confusing. Roy Harrod never appeared to see this point. Reviewing *The Prof.* in the *Daily Telegraph* I mentioned the forthcoming official life and went on, 'Meanwhile Sir Roy Harrod has stepped nimbly in...'. He wrote me a long letter protesting at the word 'nimbly'. What exactly did I mean? How could this apply? I have an impression that I did not answer.

The *Life* of Keynes is a major work of scholarship. Harrod had a deeply sympathetic subject whose views on most of the important issues in life he fully shared; the love of art and literature, the economic outlook, the optimistic liberalism, the broad faith in humanity and progress. Not all of the book is easy reading. The sections on Keynes's economic thought are presented as lucidly as they can be but it is the professional economist who will understand them best. The layman is more likely to wish to know about Keynes's personality and background and the great national issues with which he was concerned. In these matters he will not be disappointed. The account of Keynes's *Economic Consequences of the Peace* is masterly, an admirable statement of the case for and against Keynes's famous polemic, ending with a surely irrefutable vindication. Nor does he forget the literary quality of Keynes's book:

'The book is seldom read nowadays. People feel that they know what it says and have nothing to learn from it. .... This is a mistake. There are a number of matters—the evils of inflation and price control—which continue to be of live interest. The German problem is still with us. But, beyond all this, there is the pleasure to be obtained from it as a work of art. We still read Pascal's *Provincial Letters*, although not many still regard the distinction between efficacious and sufficient grace as a live issue.'

The personal portrait of Keynes is admirably drawn. The reader by the end feels the charm, the wit, the sheer intellectual power of one of the most remarkable figures of the twentieth century. The portrait is built up gradually and wholly convincingly. The development from the Eton Scholar gratified by his election to 'Pop' to the negotiator of the American loan in 1945 is natural, coherent, inevitable. Roy Harrod is equally good on Keynes's background, the circles in which he moved, the society in which he dwelt. One of the most interesting sections is the digression on Bloomsbury in Chapter V. The author has known most of the personalities concerned, and he has preserved the Bloomsbury world, its accents, its style, its taste, its gestures, crystallized for posterity. To read it makes one regret that the flavour of other intellectual coteries no less famous—'The Souls' for example—has vanished, for want of an observer to record these apparently trivial matters which give flesh and blood to the dry bones of history.

There is one matter on which Roy Harrod, as behoved a biographer writing so soon after the death of his subject, was discreet. He touched only lightly on the liberal or, as some would say, lax sexual morality of 'the Apostles' and of Bloomsbury. Michael Holroyd in his recent life of Lytton Strachey, whose career was much mixed up with that of Keynes, was the first person to disclose this aspect of that world in any detail. There are some hints in *Keynes* but little more. It is perfectly possible to approve of Harrod's reticence without condemning Holroyd's frankness. Taste and usage in these matters have changed since 1951. In any case Holroyd was writing about a man who had been dead for over thirty years, whereas Harrod's subject had died less than five years before the biography was published.

Keynes is undoubtedly a most important biography. Its only defect is a tendency to be rather verbose in places, but this may be because, as the author himself told me, much of it was dictated. One can hardly imagine it being superseded in the foreseeable future, and, although time will inevitably change perspectives, whoever writes again on Keynes will have to depend heavily upon Roy Harrod's work. Of its genre—the life written by one with close personal knowledge of the subject—it is surely one of the best in the last twenty years. Indeed apart from Lord Birkenhead's life of Lord Halifax I cannot think of anything comparable. Too often such books are written by members of the family who with the best will in the world can seldom achieve the necessary detachment.

The Prof. does not, and was not intended to, have the solidity, scholarship, judiciousness of *Keynes*. It is based on no research; it is written from memory, and without documentation; it is exactly what its subtitle says, 'a personal memoir'. As such it is most enjoyable; a vivid yet subtle portrait of Lindemann himself, and a highly entertaining account of the Christ Church Common Room in the inter-war years. It is also full of autobiographical information. *The Prof.* is written with a greater economy of words than *Keynes*, and is extremely easy to read.

My memories of the Prof. would not quite accord with Harrod's, but I knew him only when success, general acceptance, and a peerage had much mellowed him. I find it a little fanciful to suppose that his famous bowler was psychologically a helmet to protect him from being pelted by the proletariat, and his conservatism though very strong did not strike me as 'acrid'. But then I did not meet him before the war, and I was never a Liberal. He was certainly a most interesting and extraordinary mixture. The combination of immense intellectual power with utter philistinism in everything to do with literature, and art, except music, was in itself remarkable; and Harrod does it full justice. The warts are not omitted from the portrait: Prof.'s tendency to mumble tortuous insults, his unfortunate penchant for anti-semitic jokes, his long memory for anything that he regarded as an injury or slight. But his virtues are there too—above all his formidable mind, his devastating ability to argue. 'Keynes might be described as, of all his generation, the greatest apostle of sweet reason. The Prof. was an apostle of remorseless reason.'

Harrod brings out something else which is often forgotten: the sheer fun of the Prof.'s company. I can remember quite early in my time in Christ Church being allied with him in what some might stigmatize as 'an intrigue' in a matter of college politics, whose details there is no point in resuscitating now. Although on a less important subject, it must have been rather like the battle over the Duke of Westminster Studentship. There was a good deal of 'nobbling', much discussion of the potential vote. It was all very enjoyable. No less enjoyable was the great row about the road through Christ Church Meadow—a proposal which the Prof. would have detested anyway but which he detested the more because it was advocated by Duncan Sandys—one of his *bêtes noires*.

The Prof. managed somehow to cast a sort of magic spell of gaiety and absurdity over these things. Harrod puts it admirably:

'His special form of humour, however, arose out of the way in which he saw things; through his vision the sundry stupidities of mankind became droll, ridiculous, laughable. It was part of his idea of the way in which life should be conducted that in conversation there should be a constant byplay with fun and jokes. Indeed his attitude was a sort of challenge to oneself. If one had a ponderous point to make to him, one thought it a good plan to dress it up in an amusing guise. Thus everything was kept gay and light . . . he was in every respect the opposite of a bore. The Prof. is no longer with us. I often catch myself thinking when something is said or done, "that would amuse the Prof.". And then one has a rueful thought that one cannot think of anyone else whom that particular slant, that particular aspect, would amuse. I suppose that the funny in things is just as objective as those qualities that produce sensations of warmth and colour; but like those it requires a percipient mind. The Prof. made one see all sorts of funny things in the world which, without his guidance, we are unable to see. Do they still have a real existence? Or has all that gay spangle ceased to exist along with him?'

There are factual inaccuracies in *The Prof.*—inevitably in a book written from memory. No one should read it as a proper biography which it never claims to be. Important aspects of Lindemann's career and personality are scarcely mentioned. For example Lord Birkenhead does much more justice to the secret benevolence which was such a surprising aspect of his character, and which Harrod probably did not encounter. But as a personal memoir it is brilliant. Incidentally it makes one hope that some day Roy Harrod will give us his reminiscences of the other aspects of his own career in addition to those prompted by his memories of the Prof.

Roy Harrod was deeply devoted to Christ Church. He was a 'college man' in the best sense of the words. That is to say he believed strongly in the independence and autonomy of colleges in general, and in the superiority of his own in particular. He considered that colleges should be much in the forefront of new developments and not leave them to the University. 'You made one of the most atrocious remarks I have ever heard in this Common Room', he said to one of his colleagues who quickly but vainly racked his brain to recall what indiscretion or insult he might unwittingly have perpetrated. 'You said that the University rather than colleges ought to provide seminar rooms.' His colleague was so relieved that he laughed heartily—a reaction which had by no means a placatory effect.

I do not think Roy Harrod would have left Christ Church at all readily to move to another academic body; perhaps the offer of the Drummond Chair of Political Economy which is tied to All Souls would have drawn him away, but it is hard to imagine anything else. For the last few years of his time he was what is called Curator of Common Room, the man who presides over the port and dessert and who, more importantly perhaps, is responsible for the finance, administration, and efficient running of that vital institution which in Christ Church has always had a rather special independent status not quite paralleled elsewhere. He once said that he regarded the Curatorship in Christ Church as a greater honour than the headship of any other college. He was a most delightful host in the evenings and particularly agreeable to the many guests who come to the Christ Church High Table. He took great trouble over the *placement* at the ladies' dinners, and much pride in his skill. In this matter there are two schools—those who favour 'doing good' and those who encourage what might be called 'the economy of nature'. Roy Harrod was an emphatic adherent of the latter school; he always made a point of putting the bores next to each other, and separating them from the more lively and interesting guests.

Not that he was in any way personally intolerant of bores. Indeed he was something of a connoisseur of the species, and used to say that he rather enjoyed bringing a really ripe specimen in to dinner. This was all very well if one was forewarned and it was for a single evening. The college was not so happy when on his recommendation it elected for a whole year as a member of High Table a visiting professor who was, we were told—ominously as it seems in retrospect—the thirteenth most distinguished economist in America. He is dead now and I can safely say that he was without exception the most grinding and remorseless bore I have ever met—an opinion which was shared by the whole Common Room.

There was therefore consternation when the professor, whose home university not surprisingly found that it could spare him for a bit longer, announced his intention of staying for another year. It was impossible for us to refuse to re-elect him, but one or two of the younger members of the Governing Body put up a show of doing so if only for the fun of extracting some sort of apology from his sponsor. I recall that Roy Harrod, who was not usually slow to utter, began very late in the debate with the words: 'Mr. Dean, I fear that on this occasion I must appear in a white sheet. . . .' But he rather marred his penitence by saying later on that, although the professor was indeed a bore of the first magnitude, he preferred his company to that of some members of the college. It was the end of the summer term, and the Gaudy was imminent. For college as opposed to Common Room dinners the Senior Censor and the Steward control the *placement*. I was Senior Censor at the time and it seemed poetic justice to put Harrod next to the professor. The Steward, I remember, had doubts about this jest—and he was right. Unfortunately Harrod looked in at the Steward's office a few days beforehand and saw the proof of the seating plan. He came round to my rooms where I was conducting, as befits a hot afternoon, a rather dozy tutorial on some such subject as the Reform Act of 1867. It would be a *meiosis* to say that he was cross. It was not too late to change the seating. We did.

Roy Harrod was always worth hearing on the Governing Body. Meetings in Christ Church are rather more formal than in some colleges. The number of Students (Fellows), though not the largest in Oxford, is on the large side. There is an opportunity for set speeches. Harrod was skilled in this art, and his voice always commanded attention. He is, incidentally, an excellent elocutionist and his reading of the lesson in Cathedral at the Prof.'s funeral service was a memorable and moving performance. Not for nothing is he a nephew of the famous actor manager, Forbes Robertson.

On the Governing Body his long experience enabled him to cite precedents and episodes of which his audience only knew by hearsay if at all. Some will recall how he suddenly reverted to what must have been an older usage, and instead of referring to the Canon/Professors as 'Dr. X', 'Professor Y', or 'the Archdeacon', he alluded to them by the number of their canonical stall: e.g. 'As the Fourth Stall has correctly observed . . .' or 'I cannot agree with the comments of the Second Stall . . .'. Since most of us had forgotten, if we ever knew, who was who under this nomenclature, the effect was bewildering.

He often brought an agreeable echo from the great world into our parochial affairs. On one occasion we were discussing a matter of redecoration—ever a bone of contention in colleges—and the opinion of someone connected rather indirectly with the Ministry of Works had been cited: 'But, Mr. Dean, *everyone* knows how atrocious the new décor of Number Ten is.' Everyone, I wondered as I looked round the room. . . . Everyone?

In all that appertained to the interests of Christ Church he was most assiduous. For some years he was Curator of Pictures, and he took an infinity of trouble over both the arrangement of the old pictures and the commissioning of new ones. He must have spent many days, even weeks of his time, trying to find a suitable portrait painter for Anthony Eden, and he made the Pictures Committee work hard too. He was always a great enthusiast, plunging with zealous energy into any cause that he took up. He believed much in the efficacy of the written word, and if a crisis in college politics was imminent, he was apt to shower his colleagues with letters. One or two found this rather trying and seemed to share the sentiments of Lord Liverpool on Canning: 'I have not the strength and nerves to bear Mr. Canning's notes. He sends me a dozen a day. . . . Some people whose nerves are less irritable might not mind it but I cannot bear it.' Personally, I felt no such irritation. Indeed I rather enjoyed a morning mail which might include several notes written at intervals during the previous night, with times recorded up to the small hours; rather like medical bulletins on a sinking monarch, or—perhaps a better simile—situation reports from a hard fought nocturnal battle front.

If Roy Harrod has been very much a 'college man', he has never suffered from the defects of the species. There has never been anything complacent or parochial about him. He did not think in terms of academic 'league tables', nor worry about the position of the first Eight. He could never have declined into a mere repository of college customs, an old man, to vary Lord Randolph Churchill's phrase, crooning round the fire of Christ Church Common Room. On the contrary he was critical of much established usage. He considered that the traditional private hour could not survive in its existing form and that it wasted too much of dons' time. I quote from a memorandum which he circulated to his colleagues in 1964:

'By their wonderful buildings and amenities Oxford colleges are able to attract the best brains in the country, and by their system of work they largely sterilize those brains. It is unhappy for the men themselves and bad for the country. We cannot afford this wastage, especially with the "brain drain", which is a real thing, proceeding.

'I do not personally believe that the private hour system can survive *in its present form*. The burden is too great. I hasten to add that I regard it as imperative that it should survive in some form. It is the greatest glory of Oxford (and Cambridge) and is one reason why those two universities continue to be held in high esteem. But I have observed with some sadness that Oxford and Cambridge have lost standing somewhat in world esteem during my lifetime. When I first came here they could probably be ranked as the two greatest universities in the world; that is no longer so. They can easily slip down much further, unless they alter their ways in some respects.

'I believe that the system of the private hour has itself become in a certain sense degraded. The original idea was that the hour with a distinguished scholar should be taken up mainly with correcting points of style, presentation, logic, modes of criticizing the authorities studied, etc. It was not regarded as an occasion when the pupil should be fed with information likely to be needed for the Schools. It has now become a system of spoon feeding. Once the private hour is regarded as an occasion where one gains necessary information, the tutor inevitably has to go over the same ground, parrot-wise, with successive pupils over and over again. This is not a fitting task for anyone who has real promise in his own line of study. It is a waste of time.

'What I suggest is that the privilege of having a private hour once a week with a distinguished scholar should be restricted to, say, two terms out of nine. This should be supplemented by classes, say, of ten. All the instruction, i.e. matter required for Schools, should be done in the classes. These should be very conscientiously prepared, and might entail quite a lot of once over work, if the new system was started.

'It is said that an inter-college concordat would be needed for the inception of such a system. That may be so. But if, as I believe, the combined system of much rarer private hours and classes covering the whole ground was more effective in preparing men for their Schools, there would be no need to wait for action by other colleges. If we succeeded, we

> 'Might serve as model for the mighty world
> And be the fair beginning of a time.'"

The college not unreasonably did nothing about this then, for the Franks Commission was about to begin its inquiries. Nor have colleges in general tried since to achieve such a concordat. No doubt the proposal is controversial, but I believe that, as the years go by, its wisdom will seem more and more obvious, and something of the sort, possibly in a modified form, will prevail in the end.

Roy Harrod is a supremely Oxford figure. Some dons do not appear particularly donnish: they might, if one did not know, be lawyers, civil servants, occasionally even business executives. But he could never have been mistaken for anyone but a don—and an Oxford don at that. Naturally he was a very well known Oxford 'name'. But he also moved much in other circles. He was often in London and to be seen at rather grand parties of a mixed social and intellectual sort. Both Evelyn Waugh and Nancy Mitford are said to have put him in novels, though I must confess that I could never see the slightest resemblance to the fictitious characters supposed to represent him. One portrait is kindly, one is less so. Neither is in the least like him.

He is much loved by his pupils. In March 1968 a dinner in his honour given by them and arranged by Mr. Peter Jay took place in the House of Commons, and the large number who attended testified to the admiration and respect with which he is regarded by those whom he taught. His colleagues on the Governing Body had already shown their appreciation by electing him to an Honorary Studentship immediately upon his retirement in October 1967—a very unusual, possibly unprecedented, step for the college to take. It was, however, an appropriate and deserved recognition of one of the most devoted and intellectually distinguished figures to have served Christ Church during the last half century.

REFERENCES

HARROD, R. F., *The Life of John Maynard Keynes* (London, 1951).
——, *The Prof.: a Personal Memoir of Lord Cherwell* (London, 1959).

2

HAS HARROD ANSWERED HUME?

A. J. AYER

SIR ROY HARROD's book on the *Foundations of Inductive Logic*[1] has not attracted the attention which it deserves. A great deal has been written on this subject since 1956, when Harrod's book was published, but I have found very few references to it in the literature and hardly any serious attempt to evaluate its conclusions. Yet there is no doubt that if these conclusions are sound they are, as Harrod claims, of great philosophical importance. For reasons which I shall give, I do not think that he does make his main contention good, but his argument is highly ingenious and his fidelity to the empiricist standpoint, which I share with him, is admirably consistent. Even if his claim to have solved one of the most intractable problems of philosophy is not acceptable, it calls for serious consideration.

Harrod describes his book in the preface as the refutation of Hume. Starting from Hume's basic principles, he professes to rebut his sceptical conclusions. Hume had argued, first, that inductive reasoning was not demonstrative; secondly, that there was no relation of non-logical necessity by which distinct events could be connected; and thirdly, that there was no valid means of showing that the conclusions of inductive arguments were even probable. For a judgement of probability has to have some basis: this basis can lie only in our past experience, but the legitimacy of arguing from past to future experience is just what is in question. Neither can we meet the difficulty by making some factual assumption about the uniformity of nature: for the assumption itself will need to be justified. It cannot be logically necessary: and since all probable argument will have to be founded on it, to ascribe any probability to it would be to reason in a circle. Consequently, Hume concludes that inductive reasoning has no justification. It is a natural habit; and that is the most that can be said for it.

Harrod rightly accepts the first two stages in Hume's argument, but he dissents from the third. He agrees that if we had to make special assumptions about the constitution of nature in order to validate our judgements of probability, inductive reasoning would not be justifiable; and he rightly scorns the device of assigning to empirical propositions an initial probability. Besides the

---

[1] Harrod, 1956 (for all subsequent references in this paper).

fact that he is not one to accept what Russell has called 'the advantages of theft over honest toil', it is not clear to him, any more than it is to me, what 'initial probability', in this usage, can be understood to mean. He is, therefore, at one with Hume in holding that any judgement of probability which relates to a matter of fact requires to be supported by empirical evidence. But whereas Hume maintained that in cases where two empirical propositions did not stand in any relation of logical entailment it was only in virtue of some factual assumptions that one could count as evidence in favour of the other, Harrod thinks himself able to show that, in certain crucial instances, the relation of 'being evidence in favour of' is a logical relation. His idea is that even when it is granted to Hume that propositions which refer to distinct events are logically independent, it is still permissible for one to entail that another is probable.

The view that probability, in the sense which is here in question, is a logical relation has been held by other writers, including Keynes and Carnap, but Harrod's version of it is original. He ascribes probability to events, rather than to propositions, but his definition can easily be made to apply to propositions. One has only to substitute for the reference to an event a reference to the proposition which states that the event exists. Since it is propositions and not events that are logically related, this would be the more correct formulation; but I prefer to reproduce Harrod's definition in the form in which he gives it.

His first step is to introduce the concept of 'evidential value'. An event is said by him 'to have evidential value if it belongs to a class of events all having a certain character in common, which we may call A. This character A is such that it does not often happen that an event having that character occurs and some other event of a kind determined by the specific nature of the A event does not occur.'[2] What Harrod means by this is not, as one would at first suppose, that there is a high positive correlation between the incidence of the class which is specified by A and that of some other class, but rather that each member of the A class has a co-ordinate in the other class which accompanies it on most occasions. He should, therefore, have made it clear that the events of which he speaks are not individuals but types. An individual event occurs or fails to occur; it is only of a type, or kind, of event that one can significantly say that it occurs in such and such a proportion of cases. At this stage in his exposition Harrod does not refer to these proportions in numerical terms. A little later on, however, he gives it as his opinion that 'observations giving valid grounds for probability judgements always entail a precise number'.[3] If, as very often happens, we are unable to specify the number, it is because we have not been in a position, or not thought it worth while, to make the count. This being his opinion, it is surprising that Harrod should stipulate in his definition of evidential value that it applies only to cases where the

[2] p. 29.   [3] p. 35.

positive correlation is high. It would appear more natural to allow that any established frequency, however small, has its corresponding evidential value. And this is, in fact, how he usually proceeds.

To say, then, that an individual event E is probable to a degree m/n is, on Harrod's view, to say that there is some actual event f such that events of the kind F have the evidential value m/n with respect to events of the kind E. It is, however, not sufficient, in his opinion, that the Fs and Es should actually occur together with the designated frequency: if the occurrence of an F is to be evidence for the occurrence of an E, it is necessary also that their connection should be known. But the only way in which it can be known, on the assumption that we have not run through all the instances, or at any rate do not know that we have, is by its having a logical basis. Harrod, therefore, adds the requirement that the Fs should be of such a nature as to have, by definition, the character A, their possession of which logically entails that Es accompany them with the frequency in question.

This is a very strong requirement; so strong indeed that it is not at all obvious that anything satisfies it, once we go beyond the purely mathematical calculus of chances into the domain of empirical fact. If it were written into the definition of probability, as Harrod seems to be proposing, the range of true ascriptions of probability would at best be extremely small. In fact, Harrod does not himself adhere to this proposal. He repeatedly speaks of probability in cases where the frequency of the type of event to which the probability is ascribed is certainly not deducible from the evidence with respect to which the probability is assessed. What he requires of these judgements of probability is only that they be justifiable in a roundabout way on the basis of judgements of probability which do satisfy his logical condition.

That Harrod does not, in general, conceive of an ascription of probability as following logically from the evidence with respect to which the probability is assessed is shown by his refusing to adopt the axiom that if the probability that an event e will occur, on evidence f, is m/n, the probability, on the same evidence, that e will not occur must be $1 - m/n$. His reason for this refusal is that it can very easily happen that we have weak evidence in favour of e, without its being the case that we have strong evidence, or indeed any evidence at all, in favour of not-e. Even if the evidence we have is all in favour of e, it may still be weak because it is slender. 'In these circumstances', he concludes, 'it would be grossly fallacious to argue that there is a high probability that the hypothesis is false.'[4] But while this is a perfectly good argument, the cases to which it applies are just those that do not satisfy Harrod's logical condition. In any case in which the evidence logically entailed that the frequency of the occurrences of events of type E was m/n, it would also entail that the frequency of their non-occurrence was $1 - m/n$. And in fact this applies, as we shall see,

---

[4] p. 34.

to the single example which Harrod offers of a class of cases in which his logical condition is satisfied.

The only axiom which Harrod adopts at this stage is the following: 'If it is the case that B is true if, and only if, A is true, whatever probability pertains to A pertains to B also.'[5] Since he regards this axiom as being of the utmost importance for the development of his system, it is unfortunate that he should have failed to say what meaning he attaches to it. He can hardly have intended his 'if and only if' to be the relation of material implication, since this would have the ridiculous consequence that all true propositions, and likewise all false propositions, had the same probability. A more plausible interpretation would be to take the bi-conditional as stating that A and B were necessary and sufficient for one another, but even so the axiom would be unacceptable. Indeed, the only case in which it would clearly hold would be that in which the proposition that B was necessary and sufficient for A was itself part of the evidence, and there is certainly no reason to suppose that this would always be so. A third possibility is that Harrod was taking A and B to be logically equivalent, and in that case I think that the axiom should be accepted, though even here it leads to difficulties, in the well-known example of 'the infamous ravens',[6] which Harrod does not discuss.

Having given his definition of probability, Harrod then sets out to prove that it is satisfied. He undertakes to show that even on the assumption that 'we are starting from a condition of total nescience',[7] our experience provides us with instances of his character A; that is, a character which is such that from the fact that it is exemplified it follows logically that some other character X, which is not comprised in A, is also exemplified with some determinate frequency. As I said before, it is not at all obvious that any such character is to be found; but Harrod devises a most ingenious example.

What he does is to introduce the notion of a journey which is defined as 'the continuation of a specific uniform feature—colour, pattern or what not'.[8] He then invites us to consider the case of a man who is embarked on such a journey, in the sense that he is experiencing such a continuity. The man has to know enough to have acquired the concept of the past and future, but he need not be credited with any factual knowledge, beyond the knowledge that he is having the experience in question and has been having it for such and such a length of time. He then forms the hypothesis that the journey will continue for at least $1/x^{th}$ of the time that it has already lasted. If he believes this throughout the journey he is bound to be right x times for every one that he is wrong. But this means, according to Harrod, that the probability of this being right on any given occasion is $x/x+1$. If x is given the value 10, this probability comes to 10/11. So Harrod is able to cast for his character A the property of being in the course of such a journey and for x the property of having

[5] p. 48.   [6] cf. C. Hempel. Studies in the Logic of Confirmation, *Mind* 1945.
[7] p. 52.   [8] p. 53.

it continue for at least $1/x^{\text{th}}$ of the time it has already lasted. Alternatively, A could be identified with the property of being a continuity and x with its continuance, or, better still, one could speak of the proposition that there is a continuity of the requisite kind as entailing the proposition that there is such and such a probability that it will continue for such and such a fraction of its existing length.

There is no doubt that this reasoning is mathematically correct. For instance, let us assume that the continuity in question persists for just 11 seconds. Then throughout the first 10 seconds of its duration, the proportion of the time for which it will still endure is always more than $1/10^{\text{th}}$ of the time for which it has endured already. If it is represented as a line which is divided into eleven segments, it is only in the last segment that the proportion becomes less. Admittedly, this is on the assumption that the line is infinitely divisible. If we believe, as Harrod does, in the existence of *minima sensibilia*, we must recognize that his formula breaks down in the case of any continuity which lasts only so long as a *minimum sensible*; for the question whether the continuity will persist for a fraction of a *minimum sensible* is not significant: there are here only two possibilities; either the continuity will persist for at least as long as it has already lasted, or it will come to an end. Harrod acknowledges this, but fails to see that his formula breaks down also in the case of longer continuities if the length represented by the fraction '$1/x^{\text{th}}$ of the period already traversed' is less than that of a *minimum sensible*. This places a restriction on the values that can be given to x as well as on the shortness of the continuities, but both these restrictions are slight. They do not seriously impair the generality of Harrod's argument.

Subject, then, to these provisos, we are supposed to be able to infer with certainty, in any case in which we know that a continuity has lasted for a period n, that there is a probability $x/x+1$ that it will persist for a further period $1/x^{\text{th}}$ of n. From this two interesting points emerge. The first is that the smaller the extrapolation, the larger the probability. The probability that the continuity will persist for a further $1/10^{\text{th}}$ of its existing length is 10/11, the probability that it will persist for a further $1/100^{\text{th}}$ is 100/101, for a further $1/1000^{\text{th}}$, 1000/1001, and so on. The second is that since the probability that the continuity will persist for any given fraction of its existing length remains constant, the longer the continuity has lasted, the greater the period that there is a given probability of its persisting. Thus, if it has endured for 10 units of time there is a probability of 10/11 that it will persist for one further unit, but if it has endured for 100 units, there is the same probability that it will persist for a further 10, if for a 1000, for a further 100, and so on. This is a simple consequence of the mathematical truism that $1/10^{\text{th}}$ of 10 is 1, $1/10^{\text{th}}$ of 100 is 10, $1/10^{\text{th}}$ of 1000 is 100, and in general that the larger a number is, the larger a given fraction of it will be.

That there should be a probability as high as 10/11 that a continuity which has lasted for a thousand temporal should persist for a further hundred may seem a very important result. At least it would be important if we were entitled to interpret the probability, in the way that Harrod wishes, as implying that the person who is experiencing the continuity is justified in expecting it to persist for the specified period with the corresponding degree of belief. There are, however, difficulties in the way of this interpretation. To illustrate one of them, let us take up Harrod's simile of the traveller along the line. Ignoring the complication of *minima sensibilia*, we find that the question which he is supposed to be continually asking himself, 'Shall I be able to continue my journey for $1/x^{th}$ of the distance that I have already travelled?', receives an affirmative answer in all but the last $1/x+1^{th}$ section of the line. It is from this that the probability $x/x+1$ is derived. Now the fact that the traveller does not know his position on the line, in the sense that so long as his journey continues he never knows what proportion of its total length he has already traversed, makes no difference to the probability of his receiving an affirmative answer to his question, since wherever he happens to be this probability remains the same. It does, however, make a difference from the point of view of the traveller. Given that his journey is of a certain minimal length, that the value which he gives to x is not too small, and that he asks his question uniformly from the start, the traveller knows *a priori* that the total of affirmative answers to it will exceed the total of negative answers by a calculable amount, but this knowledge is of no interest to him. It tells him only that no matter when the negative answers start coming in their number will be less than that of the affirmative answers which he has already stockpiled. But what he wants to know is when it is likely that the negative answers will start coming in. To put it more precisely, he is interested in the ratio of future affirmative to negative answers from the point which he currently occupies, and to the answer to this question it would seem that nothing in his previous experience of the journey gives him any clue at all. So long as he cannot know what proportion of the total line it represents, the distance which he has already covered becomes irrelevant.

Harrod acknowledges this difficulty, but believes that he has found a way of overcoming it. His method is to represent the total series of answers, that is to say predictions that the journey will continue for at least $1/x^{th}$ of the distance already covered, by a straight line of $x+1$ units. Going from left to right, the x units embody the true answers and the 1 unit those that are false. In principle, each of the units has to be multiplied by a coefficient n, representing the uniform rate at which the answers are being given, but since n cancels out it can be ignored. The next step is to consider the answers from every point of view, that is, from the point of view of every position on the line. This is effected by constructing a square on the original line, as in Figure 1.

The horizontal line AB, which now forms the base of the square, continues to represent the series of answers. The vertical line AC represents the number of times this series has to be surveyed if it is surveyed from every point of the journey. Now draw the diagonal AD and let p be a point on AC at a distance Y from A. From p draw a line ps parallel to AB and intersecting the diagonal at q. Then pq measures the answers already past and qs those that are future when the traveller has gone the distance Y. This may be done for all values of Y from 0 to $x+1$. Consequently, the area to the left of the diagonal represents the answers which are past at the various stages of the journey, and the area to the right of the diagonal those that are future. Now we know that it is only in the last $1/x+1^{th}$ part of the journey that the answers become false. So if we shade the rectangle formed by drawing a vertical line parallel to the sides of the square from the point at which the false answers begin, we can take the shaded area as representing the false answers, and the remainder of the square the true answers. What we now have to calculate is the ratio of true to false answers, given that we take no account of past answers at every stage. This

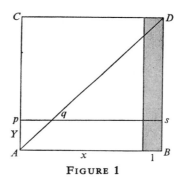

FIGURE 1

result is yielded by taking the ratio of true to false answers on the right-hand side of the diagonal, and this can easily be seen to be $x^2/(x+1)^2$.

Here then we have the probability at any stage of the journey that it will be prolonged for at least $1/x^{th}$ of the distance already traversed, leaving out of account any stockpiling of answers from the past. It is, indeed, a lower probability than our original $x/x+1$, but it can be made to approach certainty the larger we take x to be, and so the smaller the extent of the extrapolation represented by $1/x$. And even though we are not taking any account of past answers, it still remains true that the longer we have travelled the greater is the further distance for which there is a constant probability $x^2/(x+1)^2$ that we shall be able to continue.

Harrod remarks, correctly, that his formula does not require any assumption about the distribution of continuities in our experience. Neither does it presuppose the principle of indifference in its classical form. The traveller does not need to assume that the line on which he is travelling is as likely to be of any one length as of any other. Whatever its length, provided that it exceeds the requisite minimum, the formula applies equally well. On the other hand, I shall argue that the very fact that the formula holds independently not only of the length of the line but also of the traveller's position on it does introduce the principle of indifference in another guise. How serious this consequence is for Harrod's theory I shall consider later on.

Harrod refers to his conclusion that there is a probability $x^2/(x+1)^2$ that any continuity will persist for at least $1/x^{th}$ of its existing length as the Principle of Experience. It is on this principle that he takes what he calls simple induction to be founded, and it is on the validity of simple induction that all our factual reasoning, in his view, ultimately depends. As we shall see, the principle of experience is indirectly used to justify the ascription of probability to hypotheses which range over the past and present states of the universe; it plays what Harrod calls a primary part in his attempt to justify our trust in memory, and it directly sustains the conjectures that we make about the future.

That Harrod should rely on the principle of experience to justify our trust in memory might be thought to involve him in a circle, since it would appear at first sight that he has to assume the reliability of memory in order to establish the existence of the continuities on which the principle operates. He meets this difficulty by setting himself to show that our trust in memory can be justified merely on the basis of continuities that fall within the specious present. His argument is that in itself the occurrence of any given content of a specious present is very improbable indeed. It is improbable just in the sense that any particular combination of data would be only one out of an enormous number of combinations that were logically possible. On the other hand, if these data were known to be the prolongation of past continuities, they would acquire probability from the principle of experience. But in very many cases, we seem to remember that these past continuities have in fact obtained. We rely on these apparent memories to make predictions that turn out to be successful within the specious present. Since the success of these predictions would be so very improbable if our memory-beliefs were false, there is a high probability that they are true. It is, indeed, only a narrow class of memories that can be vindicated in this manner. We have, however, a way of extending it, if the experiences of which they are memories themselves include predictions which are successful within their specious presents. By this means we can build up a respectable sample of memories which are very likely to be veridical: and then by the use of a principle of fair sampling, which, as will presently be seen, itself is made to depend on the principle of experience, we can secure high probability for a substantial proportion of our memory-beliefs.

I have two comments to make on this argument. The first is that it requires the notion of a continuity to be taken in a much wider sense than that which Harrod originally gave it. If we adhered to the model of our uniform expanse of colour, the only conclusion that we could reach on the basis of the principle of experience would be that the immediate past was exactly like the present. In so far as our apparent memories suggested to us that it was in any way different, the correct inference would be that they were probably delusive. Harrod avoids this unwelcome conclusion, which would make it difficult for him to establish any high probability for the truthfulness of memory in general, by including among his continuities not only the persistence of sensory qualities but also processes of change, and indeed any constant conjunction of disparate events. Thus among his examples of predictions within the specious present that are supposed to supply material for the principle of experience are the prediction that a path will end in a lake and the prediction that when the hands of Harrod's watch point to 9.5 p.m. the bell in Tom Tower will begin to toll. But this is to extend the notion of a continuity so far that it now looks as if any hypothesis which is in tune with past observation can be taken as founding a continuity. Since a 'continuity' is in any case a term of art for Harrod, we cannot object to his using it as he pleases. The difficulty, as we shall see, is just that he may have made it so elastic that it ceases to serve his purpose.

The second point to which I wish to draw attention is that when Harrod speaks of the improbability of our being able to make the successful predictions that we do, if our memories were not veridical, he is not using the term 'probable' in the sense in which he defined it. There is no question here of the existence of any *de facto* correlation between different classes of events, or even of there being such a relation between two different classes of events as logically to entail that their members are correlated with such and such a determinate frequency. The sense of probability which Harrod now brings into play is indeed logical, but it has nothing to do with any actual frequencies. As in the calculus of classes, it relates only to the enumeration of *a priori* possibilities. To say, in this sense, that a state of affairs is probable to the degree $1/n$ is just to say that it is one of n states of affairs which are logically possible. How, in the case of the contents of some present experience, the range of the logical possibilities is to be determined is a question into which Harrod does not enter. The reason why he does not enter into it may be that he has not noticed that his argument requires that it be answered. We have, indeed, already remarked that one of the claims which he makes for his general theory is that it avoids the dubious assumption of initial prior probability. We shall see in a moment that when he engages in the manœuvre of 'reversing the consequents' he replaces this assumption, on which the classical treatment of inverse probability depends, by invoking our knowledge of the ratio of the occurrences of certain kinds of samples. It is, however, obvious that this device will not serve him in the present instance, since we have to rely upon memory at some point in order to determine at what rate samples are occurring. Consequently, the attempt to justify our trust in memory in terms of an estimate of probability which depended on this knowledge would be circular.

If initial prior probabilities are to be admitted, the principle which Harrod's argument requires is that when an event *e* has a low initial probability but a high probability given some hypothesis *h*, the occurrence of *e* bestows a high probability upon *h*. But now it seems to me that this principle itself is open to question. It involves a tacit passage from the premiss that *e* is only one of many logically possible alternatives to the conclusion that *e* is antecedently unlikely to happen: and in the absence of any special assumptions about the constitution of nature, it is not clear why this inference should be thought to be valid, or even what the conclusion is supposed to mean. Neither is it clear what is meant by saying that *h* is probable, unless this is just a way of issuing us with a licence to accept it. Surely, this is not a probability that can be analysed in terms of any actual frequencies.

Can anything be done to salvage Harrod's justification of the claims of memory, if, in conformity with his declared intention, we refuse to admit initial prior probabilities? The obvious course would be simply to drop the premiss that *e* is improbable in the absence of *h*. Then the principle at work would have to be that if an event *e*, which is not otherwise susceptible of a probability judgement, is highly probable given *h*, the occurrence of *e* bestows a high probability upon *h*. But, apart from the fact that there will still be a problem of interpreting the ascription of probability to *h*, the condition that *e* is not otherwise susceptible of a probability judgement is not going to be satisfied. We can imagine any number of past continuities which, in combination with the principle of experience, will yield various probabilities for *e*. Admittedly, there will be only one set of these continuities of which it is true that we seem to remember that they occurred. But that is no reason to favour them, unless we assume that our seeming to remember something is of evidential value in itself. And this is an assumption which Harrod was trying to avoid.

The main source of these difficulties, it seems to me, is that Harrod is trying to employ what amounts to an argument of inverse probability under conditions where it is not applicable. An argument of this kind depends on our being able to collect samples which may be taken as reflecting the composition of the larger population from which they are drawn. But the contents of a single specious present do not provide any such samples: in the state of total nescience, in which Harrod places us, we are not even entitled to assume that the larger population exists. Even if we were to take the reliability of memory for granted, we should hardly be able to compile from this source alone a stock of samples from which we could extrapolate with any degree of confidence. One needs the further evidence which is obtained by drawing on the testimony of others and on historical records. This illustrates the general difficulty which besets those who look to the theory of probability to justify induction. They have to use inductive processes in gathering the material on which the theory of probability can be put to work. Harrod is more keenly aware than most of the threat of this circle, but I do not think that he entirely succeeds in avoiding it. I do not see, indeed, how it can be avoided.

Let us, however, set this difficulty aside. Let it be assumed that we have a respectable amount of trustworthy information about the results of observations which have been made up to the present time. We can then look to arguments of inverse probability to supply us with probable conclusions about the general characteristics of the things on which these observations bear. Harrod confines these conclusions to the period of time which the observations cover, leaving it to the principle of experience to buttress any conjectures that we make about the future. There is, however, no reason in logic why the scope of the conclusions should be restricted in this way. The reason which Harrod gives, that the future is outside our range of observation, is not cogent, since our range of observation is limited, in any given instance, by the position which we occupy in space as well as by the position which we occupy in time. The point of resorting to inverse probability is that it carries us beyond these limits: and this applies to an extension in time no less than to an extension in space.

The principle on which arguments of inverse probability depend is that of the Law of Large Numbers. The upshot of this law, which is mathematically demonstrable, is that in the case of any sample which is drawn from a larger population, the probability that the distribution of any given character within the sample approximately matches its distribution within the parent population tends towards unity as the size of the sample increases. This being a theorem in the calculus of chances, the reference to probability is to be construed in terms of the incidence of logical possibilities. To say that if the sample is sufficiently large, it is highly probable that it approximately matches the parent population with respect to the distribution of any given character is just a way of saying that if we take all possible selections from the parent population which yield a sample of this size, we shall find that those which roughly match the parent population in the relevant respect very greatly outnumber those which do not. In short, deviant samples are untypical, and become more untypical, the larger the sample.

The operation of this law is quite general. Whatever the frequency with which the given character is distributed in our sample, it determines the probability, in the sense just explained, that the character occurs with approximately the same frequency in the parent population. Harrod, however, chooses to concentrate exclusively on cases in which the character for which he is sampling occurs in the sample with a frequency of 100 per cent. His reason for this is that owing, as he puts it, to the fact that 'the frequency curve has a sharp declivity when it approaches all or none'[9] he is able in this way to

9 p. 105.

obtain higher probabilities on the basis of smaller samples. Thus he calculates that given a population which may be as large as one pleases, in which 95 per cent of P's have the property q, a probability that in a sample of 540 members all the P's have q is 1/1,080,000,000,000. That is to say, there are over a billion possible samples in which at least one P lacks q for every one in which all P's have q. Harrod characterizes this fact by saying that in relation to the hypothesis that only 95 per cent of P's have q a sample of 540 in which all P's have q is a billion-fold deceptive, and accordingly that it is a billion-fold suggestive in relation to the hypothesis that the proportion of P's which have q in the total population of P's is higher than 95 per cent.

Does it follow that we have good reason to believe that the proportion of P's which have q in the total population of P's really is higher than 95 per cent? What we know is that if it is not higher, our sample is very untypical, in the sense that it belongs to a very small minority, not necessarily of actually recorded samples, but of all possible samples of its own size. But why should it not be untypical in this sense? What assurance do we have that our actual samples are not deviant?

Harrod meets this difficulty by introducing a postulate of fair sampling. He does so on the assumption that it can later be shown to be unnecessary, so that the part which it plays in his system is that of what he calls a tool of thought. His postulate is not the simple but implausible one that any given sample is fair but rather, as he puts it, that 'on a long run of experience our sample of samples is fair'.[10]

This assures us that, 'If we are confronted with many populations in which 95 per cent of P's have q, we shall only come across a sample of 540 in which all P's have q once for every billion times that we come across a sample of 540 in which at least one P lacks q.'[11] Now suppose that we are able to ascertain the rate at which such billion-fold suggestive samples are in fact occurring in our experience. For the sake of the argument, let us take this rate to be once per 1000 samples. Then the fair-sampling postulate guarantees that, 'If we believe a hypothesis supported by evidence of this kind we shall be right 1000 million times for every once that we are wrong.'[12]

The reference to many populations and to our being right a given proportion of times shows that Harrod's postulate is more complex than might at first appear. He is not assuming that if we have a sufficiently numerous set of samples which are drawn from a given population, the average distribution of the character throughout the samples approximately matches its distribution in the population as a whole. His samples do not all relate to the same hypothesis: if they did, they would be drawn from one population, not from many, and there would be no question of our being sometimes right and sometimes wrong. If the hypothesis in question were true, we should be right all the time,

---

[10] p. 89.   [11] p. 90.   [12] p. 93.

and if it were false we should be wrong all the time. The samples, therefore, relate to different hypotheses, and what the fair-sampling principle is meant to ensure is that the rate at which 100 per cent samples of whatever kind occur throughout the whole of our experience corresponds to the distribution of the logical possibilities. What Harrod is in fact doing is to treat 100 per cent samples which conform to different hypotheses as if they conformed to the same hypothesis, and then apply the law of large numbers.

The advantage of this procedure is that it supplies us with a more numerous set of samples than we could in practice obtain by confining our selections to a single class of objects, but there are serious objections to it. Harrod himself admits that it appears paradoxical that 'the evidential value of a specific piece of evidence for a specific hypothesis depends on the rate of occurrence of pieces of evidence that have no specific bearing on the hypothesis at all',[13] but argues that this sense of paradox should not survive closer scrutiny. If part of what we mean by saying that a conclusion is probable is that 'it does not often happen *both* to have evidence of the kind that is before us *and* for the conclusion to which it points not to be the case',[14] we are in any case referring to evidence which is not specifically of the kind that is before us but only of the same logical structure. In fact, this does not follow. We should satisfy the definition if we argued from the fact that the last n A's we had observed were B, to the probability that the next A to come to our notice would be B, without taking account of any other sort of evidence than the frequency with which a series of n AB's had been followed by an $n+1^{th}$. What is true is that if we ascribe probability in this sense to a universal hypothesis, we must be taking account of a wider range of evidence for the reason, which I have already mentioned, that it makes no sense to speak of a specific hypothesis of this kind as being often or seldom the case; it is only when we view it as a member of a class of hypotheses that the notion of truth-frequency becomes applicable to it. This might be taken as vindicating Harrod's approach, but it also might be taken as showing that his definition broke down when it came to the probability of universal hypotheses: that it properly applied only to conclusions which referred to types of particular events.

I myself should be inclined to take the second course, but I do not want to press the argument here. My main objection to Harrod's procedure is that, in the absence of any ruling as to what samples are admissible, its working is almost entirely arbitrary. It is clear from his talk of P's and q's that what Harrod means by a sample is a set of individuals which have been selected on the basis of their having some character, or set of characters, P, in common: the question then is whether they also have in common some other character q. But now if no restriction is going to be placed upon the choice of q, it is clear that this question can always be answered in the affirmative. Even if we

---

[13] p. 100.   [14] Ibid.

make the stipulation, which Harrod presumably intends, that q should be logically independent of P, we can still make practically sure of getting a positive answer by fixing on some pervasive property, like that of being more than ten miles from the fixed stars. It can then be contrived that 100 per cent samples occur at the rate of 100 per cent, with the result that all our judgements of probability of the sort in question will, by Harrod's procedure, be ridiculously inflated. Of course there will still be any number of properties the distribution of which throughout a given sample is found to be less than 100 per cent, but if we are going to require for anything to be a 100 per cent sample that its constituents have all their properties in common, we pass to the opposite extreme: the rate at which 100 per cent samples occur in our experience will then be 0 per cent, and in the resulting deflation none of our so-called suggestive samples will count for anything at all. Clearly what Harrod has in mind is something between these two extremes, but he does not say how it is to be arrived at. One possibility would be to confine ourselves to what Peirce called 'pre-designated' characters. This would mean that the only samples of which we took account would be those that were related to the relative incidence of characters which we had already decided to investigate. We could still artificially increase probabilities by choosing to investigate characters which were obviously pervasive, but it could perhaps be assumed that we should not do this, that it would not be regarded as playing the game. It would, indeed, appear from other things that Harrod says that he would consider this limitation to be too restrictive, but it is not easy to see what he could substitute for it. Until this point is decided, the value of this principle of fair-sampling must remain in doubt.

This is not, however, a very serious consequence for Harrod, if he is able to show that his principle of fair-sampling plays no greater role in his system than that of a dispensable tool of thought. The argument which he offers for its being dispensable is very simple. Either the apparent stability and uniformity which our observations have revealed to us reflect the constitution of the universe, or there has been a very great systematic bias in our sampling. If there has been a bias we can infer by the principle of experience that it is likely to continue. Accordingly, whether our sample of samples is fair or not, the extrapolation of our evidence to further instances, is likely to be successful; and this is the only assurance that we need.

A weakness in this argument is that it assumes that we have a way of determining the degree of regularity that has so far been displayed by the phenomena which have come under our observation. To the extent that this remains arbitrary, as I have argued that it does under Harrod's treatment, it will be correspondingly unclear what future expectations we are entitled to cherish. It would therefore seem preferable to apply the principle of experience, not to anything so general and vague as the apparent order of nature, but directly to the specific hypotheses that we want to project. This also has the advantage that we are spared the dubious step of treating the apparent order of nature as being yet another sort of continuity.

Everything, then, depends on the principle of experience. We have seen that the mathematical certainty on which this principle rests is that if a quantity y is divisible into $x+1$ equal units, then for any number n which is less than y but greater than 1, $y-[(y-n)/x]$ is greater than $y-[(y-1)/x]$. In the special case in which y represents the length of a line, this simple truism has the consequence that if the line is traversed from left to right it is only in the last $1/x+1^{th}$ part of the line that the remainder becomes less than $1/x^{th}$ of the distance already covered. We have, however, also seen that even if we allow this fact to be expressed by saying that, for a traveller along the line, there is a constant probability $x/x+1$ that his journey will continue for $1/x^{th}$ of its existing length, we cannot take this probability to be the measure of the traveller's rational expectation. What concerns the traveller is the proportion of future positive answers, whereas, on the assumption that the question is continuously asked, the formula $x/x+1$ gives the proportion of all positive answers, past and future. It was to avoid this objection that Harrod substituted the formula $x^2/(x+1)^2$ which is obtained, as we have seen, by a process of discounting past successes.

Does this second formula meet the difficulty? I do not think that it does. It does not discount the past in the way that is required. What the formula yields is the result of neglecting past successes from the point of view of every position on the line: what it does not yield is the result of neglecting past successes from any given point of view. But this makes it useless to the traveller. It is of no interest to him to know that the ratio of future successes to failures in general is $x^2/(x+1)^2$. He wants to know what the proportion of his future successes will be, from the position which he actually occupies, and this the formula does not tell him. Since it treats his position as an unknown factor, it is not to be expected that it should.

It would appear, then, that the principle of indifference, in the form of the assumption that the traveller is as likely on any given occasion to be at any one point in the line as at any other, is required after all. Harrod dismisses this as the triviality that the traveller spends an equal period of time in every equal portion of the line; which is, indeed, a triviality, if we think of the traveller as experiencing a temporal continuity. But here he underestimates the difficulty. Let us suppose that the question, in concrete terms, is whether a specified conjunction of properties, which has hitherto obtained in our experience, will hold good in the future. The proposition on which Harrod relies is that, even if there is a counter-example to the hypothesis that the properties in question are universally conjoined, it is unlikely to occur in the immediate future. In the terms of his simile, it is unlikely that the traveller is near the end of the line. But what is the ground for this proposition? Certainly not the simple tautology that equal periods of time are equal. Its only basis is the fact that positions near the end of the line amount to only a small fraction of the number of positions that the traveller could occupy. But clearly this is insufficient, unless we assume that his occupation of any of these positions is antecedently equi-probable: and this is just the sort of assumption that Harrod was trying to avoid. We again find him in the situation of tacitly depending on a notion to which he officially, and in my opinion rightly, denies any meaning.

A postulate which would meet the case is that which Harrod himself puts forward as justifying what he calls conditional simple induction. In the case of unconditional simple induction, it is assumed that the answers to the question whether the continuity will persist for at least $1/x^{th}$ of its existing length are given continuously throughout: the induction is said to be conditional when this assumption is dropped. The postulate, which is made necessary by the admission that the question may be raised sporadically, is that, 'If a man makes a great many enquiries concerning the continuance of continuities, these will be equi-proportionally dispersed among the sectors of the various continuities.'[15] Harrod says of this postulate that 'it is not a postulate about nature; it is concerned only with the distribution of enquiries about nature',[16] but this distinction must appear tenuous when we see that to ask when the enquiry is made is equivalent to asking at what point in the continuity the traveller makes it, and that this is equivalent to asking how long the continuity has still to run. In effect, Harrod's postulate assigns equiprobability to the traveller's being in any equal section of any given continuity; and this entails the requisite conclusion that he is unlikely to be near the end.

Harrod describes this consequence of his postulate as a weak form of it and claims that it can be justified on the ground that our experience supports it. 'We have not found, as a matter of plain fact, that no sooner do we notice some continuity than it presently comes to an end.'[17] He realizes that this argument itself rests on the inductive assumption that the 'fact' in question can be extrapolated to the future, but he thinks that he can meet the difficulty by treating his postulate in its weak form as a continuity and then appealing to unconditional simple induction. 'By unconditional simple induction', he says, 'we are not likely to be on the extreme edge of such an experience.'[18] But for this argument to succeed, it is essential that unconditional simple induction should do the work required of it, without the assistance of any such postulate. If I am right in thinking that this is not possible, Harrod's argument fails.

Finally, I think it has to be said that even if the objections which I have brought against the principle of experience could be overcome, its yield would be much smaller than might at first appear. The reason for this is that we should still be left with what Professor Goodman has called the new riddle of

[15] p. 65.   [16] p. 66.   [17] p. 7.   [18] p. 77.

induction.[19] The source of the difficulty is that if we put no restriction on the form of our hypotheses, we shall find that any evidence which confirms a given hypothesis h will equally confirm some other hypothesis h^1 which entails not-h. In Harrod's terms, any path that we traverse will be common to a number of different possible continuities: and any justification that we may have for projecting it in one way will be equally a justification for projecting it in another. This is obvious in the case of quantitative hypotheses; it is a generalization of the fact that any number of lines can be found to pass through the same finite series of points. For qualitative hypotheses, Goodman obtains the same result by introducing artificial predicates. If the predicate 'grue' is taken to apply to all things examined before time T just in case they are green, but to other things just in case they are blue, then any evidence, obtained before T, which supports such a hypothesis as that all emeralds are green would equally support the incompatible hypothesis that all emeralds are 'grue'. Efforts have been made to show that predicates like 'grue' are illegitimate, but whatever sympathy one may have with them, they seem to me to miss the main point. What Goodman is in effect doing is to cast a hypothesis which we should naturally state in the form 'Some A is B and some A is not B' into the form 'All A is C.' This ministers to our preference for universal hypotheses, but it serves no logical purpose. The logical point at issue can be illustrated by the example of drawing balls from a bag. If there are a hundred balls in the bag and ninety-nine of them have been drawn and found to be blue, we may think that the hypothesis that all of them are blue has been very strongly confirmed. The fact is, however, that in default of any other information, we have no more reason to expect the hundredth ball to be blue than we have to expect it to be any other colour. It might be argued that only if the hundredth ball were blue would the sequence form a continuity, but even to say this would be arbitrary. In an experiment in which we went through a series of bags, a sequence in which one ball in every bag was of a different colour from the others would be just as much a continuity as one in which each bag contained only balls of the same colour.

It might be thought that Harrod had dealt with this objection in his attempt to justify our preference for simple laws. Following Professor Jeffreys, he assumes that laws can be ranked in order of complexity, possibly in terms of 'the number of adjustable parameters' which are required for the expression of the laws. Then he argues that we are right to prefer simple laws on the ground that the odds against getting a set of observations which conform to a simple law are greater than those against getting a set of observations which conform to a more complex law; from which it follows, by inverse probability, that the observations favouring the simple law have greater evidential value. Accordingly, he advances, as a first principle of induction, the proposition

[19] Goodman, 1954, pp. 73 ff.

that: 'A set of observations conforming to a law has a cogency in establishing the truth of that law that is in inverse ratio to the number of sets of observations which would occur in the absence of any law and conform to *any law of equal simplicity ranking* with that to which the observed set conforms.'[20]

This is an ingenious suggestion; but once again it depends on the forbidden assumption of prior probabilities. Simple laws are supposed to derive their greater probability from the mathematical fact that out of all the sets of *n* observations that could possibly be made the number of sets that conform to a simple law is smaller than the number of those that conform to a more complex law. In other words, sets which conform to a simple law are comparatively rare, and their comparative rarity increases with the increase of *n*. But, quite apart from the difficulty of specifying the totality of possible observations, this mathematical fact supplies no basis for a judgement of probability unless it is assumed that all these observations are antecedently equi-probable, in the sense that each has an equal chance of being made; and again this is a proposition to which, on his own correct principles, Harrod is unable to attach any meaning.

I conclude that Harrod has not found the answer to Hume. He has made a most valiant attempt to justify induction on no other basis than that of the necessary propositions of formal logic and pure mathematics, but his materials are insufficient for the task. If his theory fails, I think that the moral to be drawn is that no theory of this logical type is going to be successful.

REFERENCES

GOODMAN, Nelson, *Fact, Fiction and Forecast* (London, 1954 and 1965).
HARROD, R. F., *Foundations of Inductive Logic* (London, 1956).
HEMPEL, C. Studies in the Logic of Confirmation, *Mind*, 1945.

[20] p. 185.

3

THE ECONOMIC MAN'S LOGIC

JACOB MARSCHAK*

1

THE contributors to this volume want to honour an economist. He is also the author of *Foundations of Inductive Logic*.[1] I shall relate induction to the making of decisions under uncertainty. This will be recognized by economists as a natural extension of the problem facing a producer, consumer, investor (or, for that matter, a government agency) under uncertainty. It is also in the spirit of some modern logicians. Ramsey (1926, 1928) and von Wright (1963) have, in a sense, extended deductive logic by adding axioms of preference. Ramsey has used these axioms as the very foundations of probabilities and thus, presumably, of induction. Harrod, whose preface acknowledged Ramsey's moral support, has gone on to discoveries of his own. But I shall ask later whether Harrod's fundamental principle of 'continuity' of experience is at all related to De Finetti's (1937) 'exchangeability'. This concept is used by some of those working in Ramsey's spirit, in order to understand the relation between the probabilities that the maker of decisions (including predictions) uses, and the frequencies he has observed. Harrod refers at length and, on balance, critically to Carnap's duality of 'probability$_1$' and 'probability$_2$'. The latter is defined as a frequency. The former is closer to, or identical with, the concept to be presented here. This closeness is more evident now than it was at the time of Harrod's writing. For in 1962 Carnap explained some changes in his views, starting with a statement that will be acclaimed by those approaching probabilities via the logic of decisions.[2]

* Acknowledgements to the National Science Foundation and the Office of Naval Research for the support of the Western Management Science Institute, University of California at Los Angeles; and to James MacQueen for criticisms.

[1] Harrod, 1956, for all subsequent citations of his work.

[2] Here is the statement from Carnap, 1962, p. XV:

'A. *The meaning of logical probability* (probability$_1$) was informally explained in ... several ways: (a) as the degree to which a hypothesis *h* is confirmed or supported by the evidence *e*; (b) as a fair betting quotient; and (c) as an estimate of relative frequency. Even at that time I regarded (a) as less satisfactory than (b) or (c); today I would avoid formulations of the kind (a) because of their ambiguity. ...'

'Although the concept of logical probability in the sense here intended is a purely logical concept, I think that the meaning of statements like "the probability of *h* with respect to *e* is 2/3" can best be characterized by explaining their use, *in combination with the concept of utility, in the rule for the determination of rational decisions* (my emphasis,

2

Both logicians and economists are wont to distinguish between prescribing and describing. Logic prescribes. Psychology describes. So do other 'behavioural sciences.' To illustrate: if objects x and y are identical, and objects y and z are also identical, the *homo logicus*, obeying the formal norms (consistency rules) of ordinary logic, will recognize x and z as identical too. But the 'brain-twister' puzzle at the end of the weekly paper will present these three objects in such a way that even a well-rested, college-educated reader may fail to recognize the identity between x and z; let alone a tired or sick man, a child, a drunk. And how often does a political speaker conclude in good faith that A implies B when his sole premiss was that A is a necessary condition for B; and how often, and how many people go along with his reasoning! Cognitive psychology[3] or, for that matter, anthropology may study the frequency of such aberrations among subjects with given physical and cultural characteristics, given the type of objects ('stimuli') considered.

Similarly, the consistent decision maker, the *homo economicus*, is not the actual, real man. For example: just like the non-logical (yet real) man may fail to obey the norm of transitivity of the identity relation between objects, the non-economic (yet real) man may fail to conform with the norm of transitivity of the indifference relation between actions: though indifferent between actions a and b, and between b and c, he may prefer a to c, say. And the empirical study may usefully occupy itself with recording the frequency of such behaviour, and its dependence on the characteristics of the man as well as of the actions considered. I say 'usefully' because such records can lead to predictions of practical importance.

It is of some consequence to extend our example of intransitive identity and indifference relations from man to an electronic computer. Because of its limited memory, or its limited speed (and a limited amount of available time), the computer must round off the results of its additions and multiplications. It will happen therefore, from time to time, that although the numbers x and y, and the numbers y and z are defined as pairwise equal, yet the computer's print-out will show x and z as not equal.[4]

J.M.). . . . The explanation of probability as a betting quotient is a simplified special case of this rule.'

See also Carnap, 1962a. Carnap's student Jeffrey (1965) proceeded to systematize the approach characteristic of Ramsey (rather than that of De Finetti, or of Savage (1954), which I shall mostly follow here).

[3] Abelson and Rosenberg, 1958.

[4] Hamming, 1965; Rothstein, 1965. In application to human decisions see Kramer, 1968, and, of course, Simon, 1957, 1959. In application to probabilities, see many passages in Harrod's book. For example on p. 35: 'The reason why we cannot specify . . . [a precise probability number] is simply that we have not had time, nor, perhaps, inclination, to make the count that would be required for [its] evaluation. . . .' See also his numerous remarks on feasible limits of tolerance.

Thus, an economic question arises, which I shall not try to answer here. The question applies, in fact, to men and machines alike. How much rationality, consistency, precision can one afford? What price logic? It was Ramsey (1926) who pointed to the 'reluctance to bother about trifles'. Indeed, we are free to proclaim weaker or stricter systems of consistency norms. Some of those which are weaker and which bother less 'about trifles' may turn out to be more 'rational'[5] if, as befits us economists, we take account of cost and limited resources, appropriately defined. The boundary between prescriptive and descriptive studies of human thought and decision is thus fluid.

Whatever this boundary, the study of the choice between conclusions from premises is usually regarded as the business of the logician (if prescriptive) or as the business of the cognitive psychologist (if descriptive).[6] The *description* of choices between actions (or decisions) is also usually regarded as the business of psychologists with their experiments,[7] but also of other students of human behaviour: anthropologists and sociologists with their interviews and questionnaires, economists with their attempts to estimate statistically the effect of various factors upon the (individual or aggregate) demands for goods, securities, foreign currencies. . . .

But what about the *prescriptive* norms, the consistency rules for choices between decisions? In general, action must be decided upon under uncertainty about its results. Or, in an equivalent formulation, under uncertainty about the state of the world, which will affect the action's result. We are led to discussing something called 'probabilities', to be assigned by the decision-maker to the several possible results of a given action of his, in a manner consistent, in some formal sense, with his preferences between actions. Or, in an equivalent formulation, he is thought to assign appropriate probabilities to the several possible events, each being a set of states of the world that determine the results of actions. In short, we discuss formal consistency rules that lead to judgements which are themselves not judgements about formal consistency but about material truth. And this, I suppose, is the proper domain of inductive logic. But note that, presented here in its relation with decision making, this logic involves, in addition to 'probability judgements' that the decider makes about the world, also his preferences between, his 'utility judgements' about, the compared actions and their results. (Thus both truth and goodness seem to be involved, and the post-Aristotelian wall between logic and ethics seems to be breached. Was not, in Socrates' eyes, the wise and the virtuous the same man?)

---

[5] Indeed, some recent thinking about decision norms (in particular, some yet unpublished work of P. Fishburn and of A. K. Sen) has stated important implications of depriving the economists' indifference relation of the transitivity property usually ascribed to it. This is the very reason why I chose to discuss this property as an example for the (moving) boundary between prescriptive and descriptive theory.

[6] Bruner *et al.*, 1956.

[7] Edwards and Tversky, editors, 1967.

3

A set of decision norms or axioms, shaped up by De Finetti and by Savage (1954), is equivalent to the 'expected utility theorem'. We shall give the theorem as a purely mathematical statement. This will be followed by its interpretation, (viz., by translating symbols into corresponding entities relevant to decision making) and by the statement of the axioms.

Define a set A of functions a from the set $X = \{x\}$ to the set $C = \{c\}$. If the binary relation $\succcurlyeq$ on A satisfies axioms 1, 2,..., then, and only then, there exists a probability measure P on X and there exists a real-valued function u on C, such that, for any a_1, a_2 in A,

$$a_1 \succcurlyeq a_2 \quad \text{if and only if} \quad w(a_1) \geq w(a_2);$$

where, by definition,

$$w(a) = \sum_c u(c)p_a(c),$$

$$p_a(c) = P\{x: a(x) = c\}.$$

(X assumed here finite for convenience). This is a purely mathematical statement, and so are the axioms 1, 2, ... But before we talk about the axioms, let us give the *interpretations* for the symbols, and some names:

A = set of *actions* a; X = set of *states* x; C = set of *consequences* (results) c. Thus typically $c = a(x)$: given the state, the action determines the consequence.

$a_1 \succcurlyeq a_2$ reads 'a_1 *is not worse than* a_2'. Depending on whether it is or is not the case that, in addition, also $a_2 \succcurlyeq a_1$, we write, respectively, $a_1 \sim a_2$ ('equally desirable', 'indifferent') or $a_1 \succ a_2$ ('better', 'preferred').

$u(c)$ is called the *utility* of c. P is a *measure* on X, in the usual sense. That is (roughly), P is a real-valued function on the set of subsets Z of X (called events) which is (1) non-negative, (2) additive, i.e., for any disjoint Z_1, Z_2, $P(Z_1 \text{ or } Z_2) = P(Z_1) + P(Z_2)$. Moreover the function P is a *probability measure*, for, in addition to the properties (1) and (2) it has the property (3), $P(X) = 1$.

$p_a(c)$, as defined above, is then the probability assigned to the set of all states which make action a result in consequence c; and $w(a)$, as defined above, is the expectation (i.e., the average) of utilities of consequences of action a; in a rather unfortunate abbreviation, $w(a)$ is called *expected utility* of a.

This is, then, the theorem's interpretation. Utilities of consequences and probabilities of events are defined, for a given decision-maker, as numerical variables whose sum of products he maximizes, given the set of actions (decisions) available to him. But these variables exist if, and only if, he is 'consistent', in the sense that his preferences between all conceivable actions (i.e., all functions from the set of states to the set of consequences) satisfy certain axioms.

These axioms need to be stated only because the theorem as just interpreted in terms of decisions may appear less plausible, convincing, 'transparent' (an expression used in just such a context by Von Neumann and Morgenstern, 1947, p. 25) than those simple axioms, similarly interpreted. Mathematically, they are jointly equivalent to the theorem. To a god who sees this equivalence immediately, there is no virtue in the axioms' greater 'transparency': a psychological rather than logical category, a tribute to human weakness. Elsewhere,[8] I have tried to assemble fragmentary evidence on the extent to which responses of some men conform with Savage's axioms, at least when the subject is trained to 'stop and think' (Ramsey, 1928, p. 201): to 'untwist', e.g., to tabulate a verbally confused decision problem. This was followed by a rough outline of the proof (less rigorous than that of Savage, 1954) that the axioms do imply the theorem (the converse is rather obvious); and, again, by a proposed test of compliance with the theorem itself.

Axiom 1 asserts that the relation 'not worse than' completely orders the set A of conceivable actions. The economists' well-known partitioning of the set of conceivable commodity bundles, *under certainty*, into equivalence sets called 'indifference surfaces' is a special case. Clearly, there is a 1–1 correspondence between the set C of consequences and that subset of A consisting of 'sure actions' only (i.e., such that $a(x) = c$ is a constant). Hence C itself can be said to be completely ordered by the relation 'not worse than'.

This permits a brief statement of *Axiom 2*: if $a(x)$ is not worse than $a'(x)$ for all x, and is better than $a'(x)$ for some x, then a is better than a'. This principle of 'inadmissibility of dominated actions' has guided statisticians long since (see, e.g., Wald, 1950). As a matter of sheer common sense it surely has guided all practical people who 'stopped to think'.

Axiom 3 can be interpreted as 'irrelevance of consequences that are not affected by the choice between two actions': if, for all x in the subset Z of X, $a_1(x) = a_2(x)$ and also $a'_1(x) = a'_2(x)$, and if, for all x not in Z, $a_1(x) = a'_1(x)$ and also $a_2(x) = a'_2(x)$, then a'_1 is not worse than a'_2, provided a_1 is not worse than a_2. I submit that an attentive reader who would care to tabulate a simple example of the premiss of this axiom (with Z and non-Z each consisting just of two elements) might 'convince' himself of the conclusion.[9]

Axiom 4 can be interpreted as 'independence of beliefs on rewards'. Let $a(x) = c = a'(x')$ for all x in Z, x' in Z'; let $a(x) = \bar{c} = a'(x')$ for all x in non-Z, x' in non-Z'; and let c be better than $\bar{c}$. Thus a and a' can be interpreted as two bets, with the same prizes, on the two events Z and Z', respectively. It is a remarkable feature of ordinary English that, when asked why he

---

[8] Marschak, 1968. See also Luce and Suppes, 1965; Edwards and Tversky, 1967.
[9] See, for example, Koopmans, 1957, pp. 157–9.

prefers to bet on Z rather than Z', many a subject says 'because Z is more probable'; and he says this regardless of whether those events are or are not repeatable. Now, Axiom 4 says that this 'belief' (as revealed by preferring a to a', say) remains unchanged when the pair of prizes ('rewards') $c \succcurlyeq \bar{c}$ is replaced by some other pair, $d \succcurlyeq \bar{d}$, say.

The proof of the existence of the numerical utility function $u(.)$ on the set C of consequences is of less interest to us here, than the existence of a probability measure P on X, underlying the 'expected utility' of each action. In fact, Axiom 4 makes it possible to discuss probabilities of events while considering just two consequences, c and $\bar{c}$ ('success' and 'failure'), with utilities 1 and 0 attached to them arbitrarily and with no loss of generality. Then the expected utility $w(a)$ becomes simply equal to the probability with which action a will result in success. In particular, the discussion may be, and is often, confined to the case when the action consists in predicting; its success is 'correct prediction' and its failure is 'wrong prediction'.

This may be also the place to remark that some authors have confined the set of considered consequences to monetary gains and losses only. By tacitly assuming, in addition, a constant marginal utility of money wealth they were able to identify probability with a 'fair betting coefficient'. This is the case with many passages of Carnap and with the original treatment by De Finetti.[10] It seems to me that this approach goes as far back as the Rev. T. Bayes himself![11] The sophistication about marginal utility of money, unleashed by Bayes's contemporary Daniel Bernoulli and taken up by economists, makes the 'fair bets' an insufficient device to reveal the probabilities that guide bettors. A more complicated device, Borel's dial, will be presented in Section 5.

4

Our axioms suffice to prove the existence of a probability measure P on X, such that $P(Z) \geq P(Z')$ whenever a bet on Z is judged as not worse than a bet on Z'. Familiar properties such as 'if Z contains Z' then $P(Z) \geq P(Z')$' and '$P(Z) + P(\text{non-}Z) = 1$' are then guaranteed.

It is important to note that the axioms also imply corresponding properties of 'conditional probabilities', written $P(Z_1 \mid Z_2)$, read 'probability of Z_1, given Z_2', and defined by considering 'conditional bets'. Such a bet is called off if Z_2 does not occur; and the bet yields c or $\bar{c}$ (where, as before, c is better than $\bar{c}$), according to whether 'Z_2 and Z_1' happens. A conditional bet on Z_1

---

[10] But Carnap's rule R_5 is more general: see the last sentence in the extensive quotation given by me in an earlier footnote. And De Finetti provides the necessary corrective note, with due reference to Ramsey, in his later, English edition: Kyburg and Smokler, 1963, p. 102, note (a).

[11] Bayes (1764), Definition 5 and Proposition 2. See their interpretation in Marschak, 1954, pp. 169–70.

given Z_2 is not worse than one on Z'_1 given Z_2 if and only if $P(Z_1 \mid Z_2) \geq P(Z'_1 \mid Z_2)$. For a fixed Z_2, the function $P(Z_1 \mid Z_2)$ has again the three properties of a probability measure. Moreover, the axioms entail the following relation between the 'joint probability' $P(Z_1 \text{ and } Z_2)$ (which we shall assume non-zero) and the conditional and non-conditional probabilities:

$$P(Z_1 \text{ and } Z_2) = P(Z_2).P(Z_1 \mid Z_2) = P(Z_1).P(Z_2 \mid Z_1).$$

Consequently

$$P(Z_2 \mid Z_1) = P(Z_2).P(Z_1 \mid Z_2)/P(Z_1);$$

and similarly, replacing Z_2 by some other event, Z'_2,

$$P(Z'_2 \mid Z_1) = P(Z'_2).P(Z_1 \mid Z'_2)/P(Z_1).$$

Dividing the last equation by the preceding one (no zeros are involved!),

$$\frac{P(Z_2 \mid Z_1)}{P(Z'_2 \mid Z_1)} = \frac{P(Z_2)}{P(Z'_2)} \cdot \frac{P(Z_1 \mid Z_2)}{P(Z_1 \mid Z'_2)}.$$

Sometimes the events Z_2 and Z'_2 are interpreted as two mutually exclusive 'hypotheses', and the event Z_1 as 'evidence'. For later use it will be convenient to denote the latter by E and the two hypotheses by H and H' (replacing Z_2 and Z'_2). We have then

$$\frac{P(H \mid E)}{P(H' \mid E)} = \frac{P(H)}{P(H')} \cdot \frac{P(E \mid H)}{P(E \mid H')}.$$

In this equation, a convenient form of the Bayes Theorem,[12] the ratio on the left-hand side is called 'posterior odds' and is, thus, equal to the product of so-called 'prior odds' to the 'likelihood ratio with respect to evidence E'. If you are consistent and if you assign constant marginal utility to money in the range of the prizes considered, these three ratios, as constrained by the above equation, represent the least favourable odds at which you will accept each of the following three bets: (1) the conditional bet on H given E, against H' given E; (2) the bet on H against H'; and (3) the conditional bet on E given H against E given H'. If constant marginal utility of money is not assumed, the 'Borel dial' to be described in the next section would reveal, as precisely as it can, that you assign to the six events in question just the probabilities consistent with the equation.

The theorem of Bayes, understood in this manner is, then, along with the expected utility theorem, entailed by the axioms of consistent decision making. The theorem will help us to explain why the consistent decision-maker whose evidence consists of a (properly defined) 'large sample' will (almost) maximize

---

[12] In the notation of Harrod (p. 15 footnote), $P(H) = p$, $P(H') = p_2$, $P(E \mid H) = q_1$, $P(E \mid H') = q_2$. If, as is assumed in his example, the two hypotheses are exhaustive, then $P(H \mid E) + P(H' \mid E) = 1$, hence $P(H \mid E) = p_1 q_1/(p_1 q_1 + p_2 q_2)$; the formula he uses.

his expected utility if he assigns to a hypothesis a posterior probability equal to the relative frequency of certain observations.

I shall reason on lines consistent with Savage and De Finetti, I believe; and also with Carnap's treatment of the 'estimation' of his 'probability$_1$' (which is logically derived, not from frequencies but from betting decisions), given the observed frequencies. This approach seems to be different from Harrod's for whom (p. 47) 'The probability relation is ... essentially and by definition a relation of frequency', although he does not regard 'probability numbers as derived from or reflections of statistical frequencies in nature.' The difference between the two approaches will turn out to depend on the difference, if any, between Harrod's principle of 'continuity' (Chapter III) and the 'exchangeability' concept which we shall now present.

5

Although I had each axiom accompanied by its interpretation in terms of decisions, they, and the consequent existence of a probability measure on X, can be regarded as purely mathematical propositions about a binary relation called 'not worse than'. Now, the properties defining a probability measure form only the beginning of the calculus of probabilities. As pointed out by De Finetti (1937), a further premiss for the body of that calculus is the existence of 'exchangeable' subsets (events) of the set on which the probability measure is defined. For example, let X be partitioned into subsets Z and non-Z such that the decision-maker is indifferent between betting on either: each of these two actions is 'not worse than' the other. The two events are then 'exchangeable' and the partition itself, i.e., the pair 'Z, non-Z' is sometimes called a 'fair coin' (with Z and non-Z then called 'heads' and 'tails'). It corresponds to the gross physical reality of minted coins only in the same way in which the straight line of pure geometry corresponds to the edge of the paper page now facing you, my reader. There may or may not be agreement between people as to how closely this page approximates the ideal rectangle; and similarly, whether one should be indeed indifferent between betting on a particular physical coin's falling heads or falling tails up; or between betting on any of the 52 cards of a given (not necessarily well-shuffled) deck. But if you are indeed indifferent between those 52 bets, and, in addition, obey the consistency axioms, you will be also indifferent between betting on any of the four suits, and on either of the two colours. The probabilities of success in each of these three sets of equally desirable bets will, then, respectively be: $\frac{1}{52}$, $\frac{1}{4}$, $\frac{1}{2}$. It will also follow that you should be indifferent between betting on any specified set of (say) seven cards, the probability of success of any such bet being $\frac{7}{52}$.

Probabilities as revealed by preferences between bets with the same pairs of prizes (c, $\bar{c}$ of our Axiom 4), were so described already by Borel (1924) in his review of Keynes (1921). Accordingly, I would like to call a 'Borel dial' the following device, designed to elicit a man's estimate of the probability of 'rain tomorrow', say. First, ascertain that the subject is indifferent between receiving 10 dollars if the twirled arrow stops within one or another of any two equal sectors of the dial. (This is, itself, an induction on the observer's part, in a sense which will become clear.) Then let him choose between receiving $10 if it rains tomorrow (and receiving nothing if it does not), and receiving $10 if the arrow stops between the noon position and the four o'clock position on the dial (and receiving nothing if it does not). If he prefers the former bet, we say that the probability he assigns to tomorrow's rain exceeds $\frac{1}{3}$. We then ask him to choose between receiving $10 only if it rains tomorrow, and receiving $10 only if the arrow stops between the noon and the six o'clock position. If he now prefers the latter bet, his 'personal probability' of rain tomorrow is between $\frac{1}{3}$ and $\frac{1}{2}$. This method of evaluation of probabilities, says Borel (who by the way, uses dice, not a continuous dial) 'has exactly the same characteristics as the evaluation of prices. . . . If one desires to know the price of a ton of coal, it suffices to offer greater and greater prices to the person who possesses the coal; at a certain price he will decide to sell it.' Economists are aware, of course, that price theory and Walras's '*prix criés . . . dans le marché*' idealize gross reality. So does Borel's device, idealizing the consistency of bettors.

6

Is there any relation between probabilities as revealed by a Borel dial applied to a consistent bettor, and the frequencies of observations in statistical samples, the very heart of scientific induction? To answer this, let us first add another case of exchangeability as a property of certain subsets ('events') of the set X (of 'states' x), on which a probability measure is defined. We shall consider the case called 'repeated and independent trials,' viewed again as a mathematical, not physical object. This case will prove to be much more important than that typified by the mathematical objects called 'fair coin', 'well-shuffled deck', etc. In their physical interpretation the latter objects are those illustrating the 'Principle of Indifference', and I agree with Harrod that it is of little consequence for the understanding of induction. By contrast, the exchangeability of 'repeated and independent trials', should its physical interpretation prove justifiable, would indeed entail important consequences for the problem of induction; and I believe it would correspond to Harrod's[13] weighty 'fair sampling postulate'.

---

[13] To quote: 'The Principle of Indifference makes an assumption about nature. . . . If one defines probability by frequency, this implies that nature manifests each alternative an equal number of times. By contrast, the sampling postulate has nothing to do with the composition of nature, but is concerned only with our investigation of nature. It makes

Let, then, the generic element of the set X of states be the sequence (temporal or no, no matter) $x = (x_1, x_2, \ldots)$. Define the set T_i to consist of subsequences in which the component x_i is omitted. For simplicity let each component in each sequence or subsequence have just two possible values, denoted conveniently by 1 ('success') or 0 ('failure'). Define the event Z_i as the set of all those sequences x in which the ith component is a success: $Z_i = \{x : x_i = 1\}$. Suppose a consistent man's indifference between conditional bets (as explained in Section 4) reveals that the conditional probability $P(Z_i \mid T_i)$ is the same for all T_i and all i, so that we can write $P(Z_i \mid T_i) = P(Z_i) = p$, say. Then X is called a set of sequences of repeated and independent trials: the same probability is assigned to each trial, and this regardless of whether any other trial results in success or in failure.

Again, it may be a matter of disagreement whether a particular physical phenomenon has approximately the properties of such a set of sequences: whether, for example, successive experiments performed or to be performed in a certain laboratory under assertedly 'controlled conditions' do indeed possess the property that $P(Z_i \mid T_i)$ is the same for all i, and for all subsequences in T_i. Will everybody be indifferent between betting on a particular outcome of the first such experiment, given all others, and of the tenth, given all others?

We are now ready to establish a relation between probabilities assigned to given events by a consistent decision maker and the frequencies of those events he has observed. Let the states x in X be sequences he believes (as is revealed by his bets) to be sequences of repeated independent trials. That is, his assignment of probability of success, if evaluated on a Borel dial, will be the same for all trials, $i = 1, 2, \ldots$, whether observed or not, and each independently of the outcomes of other trials. Now denote by $Z^{(p)}$ and $Z^{(p')}$, respectively, two subsets of X, each consisting of all sequences x such that, for all i, $P(Z_i \mid T_i) = P(Z_i) = p$ or $= p'$ (where $p \neq p'$). In the present context, $Z^{(p)}$ and $Z^{(p')}$ are two rival hypotheses corresponding to the H, H' of the Bayes theorem as formulated in our Section 4. If one of them, say $Z^{(p)}$, is accepted by the decision-maker, we say that his estimate of $P(Z_i)$ is p for all trials, viz., for all the (n, say) observed ones as well as for the non-observed ones, $i = n + 1, \ldots$. This will be revealed by his betting behaviour; he will be indifferent between betting on the $(n + 1)$th trial being a success, and betting on a fraction p of the circumference of the Borel dial. [Moreover, if

the assumption that the relative frequencies of our observations bear a relation to the relative frequencies of different kinds of observables; this requirement entails no assumption regarding the composition of nature itself' (pp. 102–3). This passage is introduced by Harrod's observing 'that the Bayes-type argument would require, *in addition* [his italics; J.M.] to some such assumption as the Principle of Indifference, a sampling postulate'. If so, the argument that will follow in my text is not 'Bayes type'. It will use Bayes's theorem and a premiss akin to Harrod's sampling postulate but it will not use the Principle of Indifference since it will nowhere assume 'equal prior probabilities'.

the marginal utility of money were, for him, constant over the range of prizes considered, he would also accept a bet with odds $p: (1 - p)$ or better.]

We shall now define that subset of X [i.e., that set of sequences $x = (x_1, \ldots, x_n)$] which will play the role of 'evidence'. First denote by $f_n = (x_1 + \cdots + x_n)/n$ the relative frequency of 'successes' (i.e. of 1s rather than 0s). Now consider the set of all sequences $x = (x_1, \ldots, x_n, x_{n+1}, \ldots)$ such that f_n is within a distance δ from p. We can denote this set by

$$Z^{(p,\delta,f_n)} = \{x: p - \delta < f_n < p + \delta\}.$$

The set, $Z^{(p,\delta,f_n)}$, will play the role of evidence, E, in the Bayes theorem which we can now rewrite, for our present purposes, thus:

$$\frac{P(Z^{(p)} \mid Z^{(p,\delta,f_n)})}{P(Z^{(p')} \mid Z^{(p,\delta,f_n)})} = \frac{P(Z^{(p)})}{P(Z^{(p')})} \cdot \frac{P(Z^{(p,\delta,f_n)} \mid Z^{(p)})}{P(Z^{(p,\delta,f_n)} \mid Z^{(p')})}.$$

We shall consider the last of these three ratios: the likelihood ratio of the two hypotheses, $Z^{(p)}$ and $Z^{(p')}$ with respect to the evidence $Z(p, \delta, f_n)$; and shall apply to it the ('weak') 'law of large numbers'. This latter is a purely mathematical theorem. Its premises are the three properties defining any probability measure on any set, combined with the definition of a set of infinitely long sequences, each component of a given sequence having the same probability distribution of its values. The theorem is therefore valid independently of any particular interpretation of the probability concept in terms of natural (including human) phenomena.[14] This theorem says that, for any positive number δ,

$$P(Z^{(p,\delta,f_n)} \mid Z^{(p)}) \to 1$$

as n increases. That is: given that the probability of success in each of the indefinitely long sequence of trials is p, the conditional probability of the average number's f_n of successes in n trials being within an arbitrarily small distance δ of p tends towards certainty as n increases.[15]

Now, the conditional probability just specified is the numerator of the *likelihood ratio* we have proposed to consider. It follows from the theorem just stated that this ratio increases beyond all bounds (that is, towards $1:0$) as n increases. What, then, about the *posterior odds*? Provided that the prior $P(Z^{(p)})$ is not zero, which, roughly, means that $Z^{(p)}$ is not impossible—the

---

[14] Therefore the theorem called here (and in textbooks on mathematical probability) the Law of Large Numbers cannot be identical with what Harrod (p. 74) calls the Law of Large Numbers and which he 'cannot regard as a universal law of nature *a priori*'. For the mathematical theorem does not claim to describe nature. It is another matter whether or not a particular interpretation of the theorem's premiss and conclusion, i.e., their translation into terms of natural phenomena, can be accepted with any degree of approximation. The same distinction will be made regarding the theorem we are going to discuss now, about estimating posterior probabilities by frequencies.

[15] The proof given in essence 200 years ago is based on combinatorial arithmetic such as that used by Harrod in a similar context (p. 88, footnote).

Bayes theorem as last rewritten and the property of our likelihood ratio as just stated imply that the posterior odds of $Z^{(p)}$ against $Z^{(p')}$ will also increase beyond all bounds. In words (roughly): if, as the number of observations increases, the relative frequency of successes is found to remain close to the number p, then the odds in favour of the hypothesis that this number is the probability of successes in each of the indefinite sequence of trials increase beyond all bounds; provided this hypothesis was not judged impossible to begin with. With this proviso, the effect of prior odds will be 'washed out', 'swamped' by the increasing likelihood ratio derived from observations. On the other hand, zero prior odds will never be overcome.[16]

It must be recalled that we interpret the odds in terms of decision-making. Indeed, one can derive from our premises directly that, for any δ, choices between bets, if based on the estimate $P(Z_{n+1}) = f_n \pm \delta$ will yield, as the number n of observations increases, an increasingly higher expected utility relative to other choices between the same bets; where, it will be recalled, $P(Z_{n+1})$ is the probability that the $(n + 1)$th trial will yield a success, i.e., that $x_{n+1} = 1$.[17] This holds not only for the special case when the decision-maker is a 'predictor' (with utility $= 1$ if right, $= 0$ if wrong), but also in the general case, with utility depending on x_{n+1} and an action in any manner whatsoever. As before, in the limiting case where a certain value of the success probability is *a priori* impossible, it remains so *a posteriori*.

In addition to the proviso of non-zero prior odds, we must remind the reader most emphatically of a more important one: it has been assumed throughout that all of the indefinitely long sequence of trials have the same probability of success. Without this premiss of 'repeated independent trials' the conclusion of the Law of Large Numbers does not obtain, nor does therefore the conclusion about posterior odds of the considered hypothesis against an alternative.

Let me conclude this section with a side issue which, however, will help us, in the next section, to ask questions about Harrod's position compared with the present one. He rightly declares (p. 59) that the so-called Law of Succession[18] 'is derived from assigning equal prior probabilities' and notes

'that the gross and flagrant fallacies to which the application of the Law of Succession leads, all arise . . . in the case of short runs. . . . If the principles by which the Law of Succession is derived were correct, then it ought to apply to

---

[16] The latter is the case of Pigou (1929) and the Archbishop of Canterbury, whom Pigou would maintain to be honest even if the Archbishop had dealt himself in one evening three hands each containing four aces, four kings, and four queens. I owe this reference to W. A. Wallis (1942, p. 236).

[17] See also Marschak and Radner, 1969, Ch. II, Sections 8–11.

[18] The premiss of this ancient theorem is, more precisely, the uniform prior distribution on the set of all values of the probability of success, i.e., on the interval between 0 and 1. One of its conclusions is that, in our notation, $P(Z_{n+1}) = (1 + nf_n)/(2 + n)$. This, of course, approaches f_n as n increases. See, e.g. Uspensky, 1937, p. 69.

very short runs, as well as to longer runs; no one, to my knowledge, has shown why on these principles this should not be so.'

Harrod remarks that his approach, too, 'does not apply to short runs' and that it has 'some family resemblance to the much abused Law of Succession' although its logical basis is quite different.

Now, we have seen that in the 'long run', that is, with a large number of observations, the effect of *any* prior probabilities, whether assumed equal or not, tends to be 'swamped' by the effects of observed frequencies. Thus the position presented here is consistent with the fact, observed by Harrod, that the applications of the Law of Succession, so flagrantly fallacious in the case of short runs, are less so for long runs.

7

The reader will have noted that the emphasis on short *versus* long runs when it comes to estimating from observations is common to the present position and to that of Harrod. Now, mark our important provision: the decision-maker was made to assume that the many trials he has observed are 'exchangeable', both among themselves and with future trials. Harrod, on the other hand describes his Principle of Experience (Chapter III) as one of 'continuity' of a path partly traversed and still to be journeyed on. Is there a family resemblance between 'continuity' in Harrod's sense and our (and De Finetti's) 'exchangeability'? At any rate: what is the relation between these two concepts?

To me, this is the most important of all the numerous questions that I would have to answer before being sure that I have understood Harrod's book. Even if I had answered them I could not convey to the reader of this essay the depth, the vigour, and the beauty of Harrod's thought. As one can see by comparing the literature cited in the book and in this essay, the backgrounds are different even though we are both economists. Perhaps just this difference of backgrounds makes a comparison of the two approaches, and thus my main question as just stated, not altogether useless.

For better understanding, it is worth remarking that in most though not all of Harrod's reasoning, the relative frequency of successes in observed trials (f_n in my notation above) is, in effect, equal to 1. See, for example, the description of the continuous journey in the important Chapter III on the Principle of Experience.[19] I do not believe that this concentration on a special case weakens Harrod's argument. What is essential for Harrod is that

---

[19] Or, at the beginning of Chapter IV, on Inverse Probability: 'If property Q is not in fact almost always conjoined with property P, is it not a very curious thing that out of all the thousands, perhaps hundreds of thousands, of times that P has been seen, it has *always* [J.M.'s emphasis] been seen in conjunction with Q?' (p. 79).

some features observed during the journey are likely to be observed as the journey continues; the more likely the longer you have travelled.

Nor is it a matter of consequence (it seems to be more a matter of nomenclature) that, like Einstein, Harrod seems disinclined to believe that God plays dice. When Harrod says (p. 242) that 'Most of induction . . . is not concerned to establish statistical frequencies, but to establish uniformities, laws or particular facts', I infer from the context that he has in mind deterministic laws and that, while he is indeed concerned with evaluating probabilities of hypotheses, these hypotheses are not themselves probability distributions. Modern statistics as a tool of inductive inference, and much of modern decision theory, takes a more general view. One does assign a posterior probability, for example, to the statement that this person has such and such probability of dying within a year if not operated upon, and a different probability if a particular operation is performed. And this may be more useful to the decision-making surgeon than the statement 'the patient has cancer for sure'. I said this approach is more general because 'probability $=1$ for a certain value of the variable' is a special case of a probability distribution. Thus, statisticians are apt to use distribution parameters to describe the 'state of the world'. Again, I do not believe that Harrod's 'deterministic' nomenclature makes a decisive difference.

Mostly, the hypotheses considered by Harrod are statements of the type 'If P is the case, then Q is the case' rather than simply 'Q is the case'. Again, this is not essential for our comparison of the two approaches. Harrod's interest in the conjoint occurrence of two events can be taken care of, in the other approach, by considering some conditional probability of Q, given P, as the hypothesis, and testing it by recording the conditional frequency of observed Q, given observed P.

In trying to establish a relation between Harrod's 'continuity' and the 'exchangeability of repeated independent trials' defined here, it is not decisive, either, that Harrod first proposes (pp. 89–90) a 'sampling postulate' (also called 'fair sampling postulate'), then shows it to be unnecessary for induction, replacing it by a proposition on the properties of our observations, not of nature itself (pp. 116–17). For both interpretations are consistent with the definition of repeated independent trials (observed as well as not yet observed) by stating:

$$P(Z_i) \text{ is the same for } i = 1, \ldots, n, n + 1, \ldots$$

where $P(Z_i)$ is the probability of success in the ith trial and n is the number of observations already performed.

Nor does it seem to me that the emphasis on decision separates us Ramseyites from Harrod (and, in this respect, from most of traditional literature on logic) in a really important manner. As already pointed out, prediction is a special case of decision. Harrod's book is full of references to the usefulness of correct predictions, for cavemen and others. To be sure there may be disagreement about utilities in detail but hardly any about the need to survive. Moreover, it is presumed (or alleged) for the case of pure scientists that in their case there is intersubjective agreement about the two-valued utility of prediction (e.g., 1 if right, 0 if wrong). This makes expected utility identical with the probability of correct prediction so that, again, induction logic reveals itself as a special case of decision logic.

What does then make the difference, if any, between the two approaches? In Section 2, I pointed out that the boundary between prescription and description is fluid. How relaxed, or how restricted shall be the prescriptive norms of logic including the logic of decision? I have mentioned, for example (in Section 2) those who relax the norms by denying transitivity of indifference (between actions, or between their consequences). Others have restricted the norms by prescribing, for example, aversion to risk. As far as I know, even some logicians of deduction are more 'relativistic' than others; although less so than the students of ethics, among whom Natural Right and the self-evident truths of 1776 are in disrepute, merited or not. But this is precisely why Harrod's ideas are so attractive. It is impossible not to share his aversion against 'defeatism' and 'escapism' (p. 20). There must be a fixed point somewhere!

The mathematical deductions—from premises to conclusions—of De Finetti and others are without blemish. If a given sequence consists of repeated and independent trials, relative frequency approaches probability, and actions should be chosen accordingly. Here the sequences, and the actions themselves, are mathematical objects. But how do we know that a given sequence of actual observations, performed and to be performed in the world of phenomena, can be assumed, albeit approximately, to consist of repeated and independent components? How can we establish intersubjective agreement on these matters (even though agreement on other matters such as prior probabilities is not needed when the sample is large)? Or, in Harrod's language, how do we know that, with respect to a particular physical characteristic of events, we are on a continuous path? In the language of statisticians: how do we know that this and this and another item belong 'to the same population'? Who tells us that, in estimating the mortality rate, separation by age and sex is important but separation by alphabet is less so?

True, Harrod does not answer specific questions like these. But remember: he has not set out to write a treatise for practising statisticians. He has asked the philosopher's question: how has it been, how is it, possible to discover laws of nature? His answer: because the world (or our observation of the world) has regular, 'non-Heraclitean' features—although admittedly it is another matter to specify those features. In another language: yes, indeed, there are sequences sufficiently close to be treated as repeated and independent.

Harrod deplores 'shallow doctrines of a pragmatic kind'. If to be pragmatic is to relate truth to action, the adjective is, to me, a compliment. Separating prediction from decision only makes our thinking more special and thus poorer in results. But 'shallow' is another matter. When Harrod searches for grounds for induction (and thus for decision) he searches in depth.

REFERENCES

ABELSON, R. P. and ROSENBERG, M. J., 'Symbolic Psycho-logic', *Behavioral Science*, 1958, Vol. 3, pp. 1–13.

BAYES, TH., 'An Essay towards solving a Problem in the Doctrine of Chances', 1764, now in *Biometrika*, Vol. 45, pp. 296–315.

BOREL, E., 'Apropos of a Treatise on Probability', 1924, reproduced in Kyburg and Smokler, 1964.

BRUNER, J. S., GOODNOW, J. J. and AUSTIN, G. A., *A Study of Thinking* (New York, 1956).

CARNAP, R., *Logical Foundations of Probability* (Second Edition, Chicago, 1962).

——, 'The Aim of Inductive Logic', 1962a, in Nagel, E. *et al.*, editors, *Logic, Methodology and Philosophy of Science* (Stanford, 1962), pp. 303–18.

DE FINETTI, B., 'Foresight: Its Logical Laws, its Subjective Sources', 1937. Translated from the French and provided with some additional notes of the author, in Kyburg and Smokler, 1964.

EDWARDS, W. and TVERSKY, A., editors, *Decision Making: Selected Readings* (Penguin Books, 1967).

HAMMING, R. W., 'Numerical Analysis vs. Mathematics', *Science*, 1965, pp. 473–5.

HARROD, R., *Foundations of Inductive Logic* (London, 1956).

JEFFREY, R. C., *The Logic of Decision* (New York, 1965).

KOOPMANS, T. C., *Three Essays on the State of Economic Science* (New York, 1957).

KRAMER, G. H., 'An Impossibility Result concerning the Theory of Decision-making', in Bernd, J. L., ed. *Mathematical Applications in Political Science* (University of Virginia Press, 1968), Vol. III, pp. 39–51.

KYBURG, H. E. and SMOKLER, M. E., *Studies in Subjective Probability* (New York, 1964).

LUCE, R. D. and SUPPES, P., 'Preference, Utility, and Subjective Probability', in *Handbook of Mathematical Psychology*, Luce, R. D. *et al.*, editors (New York, 1965), Vol. 3, pp. 249–410.

MARSCHAK, J., 'Probabilities in the Social Sciences', in *Mathematical Thinking in Social Sciences*, Lazarsfeld, P., editor (The Free Press, Glencoe, Illinois, 1954), pp. 166–215.

——, 'Decision-making: Economic Aspects', in *International Encyclopedia of the Social Sciences*, Sills, D. L., editor (New York, 1968), Vol. 4, pp. 42–55.

——, and RADNER, R., *Economic Theory of Teams* (Yale University Press, 1970).

PIGOU, A. C., 'The Function of Economic Analysis', Sidney Ball Lecture, reprinted in Pigou, A. C. and Robertson, D. H., *Economic Essays and Addresses* (London, 1931).

RAMSEY, F. P., 'Truth and Probability', 1926. 'Further Considerations', 1928. Both papers in *The Foundations of Mathematics and Other Logical Essays*, ed. R. B. Braithwaite (New York, 1950). The paper of 1926 also reproduced in Kyburg and Smokler, 1964.

ROTHSTEIN, J., 'Numerical Analysis: Pure or Applied Mathematics?', *Science*, 1965, pp. 1049–50.

SAVAGE, L. J., *The Foundations of Statistics* (New York, 1954).

SIMON, H. A., *Models of Man* (New York, 1957).

——, 'Theories of Decision-making in Economics and Behavioral Sciences', *American Economic Review*, Vol. 49, pp. 253–83.

USPENSKY, J. V., *Introduction to Mathematical Probability* (New York and London, 1937).

VON NEUMANN, J. and MORGENSTERN, O., *Theory of Games and Economic Behavior* (Princeton, 1947).

WALD, A., *Statistical Decision Functions* (New York, 1950).

WALLIS, A. W., 'Compounding Probabilities from Independent Significance Tests', *Econometrica*, 1942, pp. 229–48.

WRIGHT, G. H. VON, *The Logic of Preference* (Edinburgh, 1963).

4

THE IMPERSONALITY OF NORMATIVE JUDGEMENTS

SIDNEY S. ALEXANDER

WHEN young Lionel Robbins, as he then was, returned to the London School from the Vienna of the twenties with his head stuffed with positivism, he administered a shock to Anglo-Saxon economics from which it has not yet recovered. The contemporary showpieces of economic reasoning for policy guidance were, after all, the demonstration of the welfare losses from protection and the argument for progressive taxation based on diminishing marginal utility. 'Invalid!' cried young Robbins and the spirit of the age was with him. In spite of an avuncular demurral from his old teacher, Cannan,[1] and the more philosophically sophisticated attempts at refutation by Fraser[2] and Souter,[3] positivism carried the day.

Interpersonal comparisons of utility were out and Pareto optimality, given an elegant presentation by the Samuelson of 1937, was in.[4] Today the elementary textbooks authoritatively tell us that economics is limited to the investigation of the consequences of economic actions. Whether the consequences are good or bad is a matter for the citizen to decide—not for the economist. How such a judgement is arrived at, the textbooks do not say. It clearly cannot properly be derived from a study of the consequences of economic actions.

Robbins supported his positivist thesis by two different arguments. The first was the absence of an operational measure of utility valid for comparisons either of the levels of utility or of differences of utility experienced by different people. 'There is no way of comparing the satisfactions of different people.'[5] Nevertheless, he recognized that we talk all the time as if we can make such comparisons, and I think it can fairly be said that we do make them. How then could he claim that we cannot do what we in fact do? Clearly Robbins is making a normative judgement that we cannot *properly* make such comparisons.

Robbins further argued that even if there were some properly positive way of making these interpersonal utility comparisons, and if on the basis of these

---

[1] Cannan, 1932. [2] Fraser, 1932. [3] Souter, 1933.
[4] Samuelson, 1947. [5] Robbins, 1935, p. 140.
5—I.G.T.

'we had succeeded in showing that certain policies *had the effect* of increasing "social utility", even so it would be totally illegitimate to argue that such a conclusion by itself warranted the inference that these policies *ought* to be carried out. For such an inference would beg the whole question whether the increase of satisfaction in this sense was socially obligatory. . . . Propositions involving "ought" are on an entirely different plane from propositions involving "is"' (pp. 142–3). 'Unfortunately it doesn't seem logically possible to associate the two studies' (economics and ethics) 'in any form but mere juxtaposition. Economics deals with ascertainable facts; ethics with evaluation and obligations. . . . The propositions involving the verb "ought" are different in kind from propositions involving "is". And it is difficult to see what possible good can be served by not keeping them separate or failing to recognize their essential difference' (pp. 148–9). Similarly, when Samuelson came to endorse Robbins's position, it was sufficient to state in support of the expulsion of the normative from economics that 'Wishful thinking is a powerful deterrent of good analysis and description, and ethical conclusions cannot be derived in the same way that scientific hypotheses are inferred or verified.'[6] That economics should be scientific and that science implies only the verification of hypotheses about matters of descriptive fact were taken for granted as major premises of the positivist argument that normative judgements are to be excluded from economics.

Harrod, was, on the whole, ready to join the positivists[7] but that superb intuition of his suggested reservations, which are the entering wedge of what will some day come to be accepted as the correct position—an anti-positivist one.

Harrod departed from both branches of Robbins's positivist position, which, incidentally, was neither original with Robbins nor peculiar to him even in England, as Robbins was the first to declare. In the first place, Harrod argued, it is the business of the economist to make normative judgements of at least one restricted type—those that can be based on a normative principle that he called *the economic criterion*: 'defined dogmatically as follows: If an individual prefers a commodity or service X to Y, it is economically better that he should have it. . . . The economic good is thus the preferred' (p. 389).

Harrod was a little careless, however, in presenting his criterion as a definition. If he meant that literally he would be guilty of the so-called naturalistic fallacy, provided further that what is so named is indeed a fallacy. For to *define* 'the better' as 'the preferred' would deprive 'the better' of all normative content and reduce it to an operationally descriptive term. But if we take what Harrod advanced as a definition to be rather a specification,[8] we do, I think, come closer to what he meant. For a definition is, in strict logic, a state-

---

[6] Samuelson, 1947, p. 220.   [7] Harrod, 1938.
[8] See Alexander, 1968, for the distinction between a 'verbal' definition and a specification.

ment in the meta-language of the equivalence of two terms of the object language. A specification, as I call it, is a statement of substance in the object language connecting, as a matter of life and not of logic, two terms that have otherwise distinct semantic linkages to non-linguistic objects. In this case, the non-linguistic 'objects' are the states of being preferred and of being better respectively. One of these states is descriptive and hence positively operational; the other is normative and presumably non-operational. So, as Harrod clearly recognized, this criterion furnishes a standard of good and bad.

This criterion has been adopted almost universally in welfare economics as the one normative principle to which an economist can subscribe without losing his licence to practice. It is imbedded in the very expression 'Pareto optimality' which is only recently beginning to be called 'Pareto efficiency' to remove the taint of the normative. To call a Pareto efficient point Pareto optimal is implicitly to adopt Harrod's normative criterion—to use a positive condition, preference or satisfaction, as a test of a normative condition, welfare. Even more unquestionably accepted is a corollary of the criterion: 'The larger the income the better'. Harrod's criterion itself is relevant principally to the micro-economic study of general equilibrium under perfect competition, the corollary gives normative value to macro-economic inquiry into how to increase the national income.

Economists have not offered any thoroughgoing reconciliation of the universal adoption of the normative judgement embodied in Pareto optimality and cost-benefit analysis with the general exclusion of the normative from economics that stands in the elementary textbooks. Implicit in their theoretical discussions, and explicit in Little's[9] is the consideration that 'most people' would accept the normative judgement embodied in Pareto optimality. I shall argue that this is an inappropriate basis for the adoption of a normative principle, an argument for which I claim no originality, however.[10]

Harrod's second departure from Robbins' positivist position was his contention that interpersonal comparisons of utility should be allowed—at least in a rough common sense way (pp. 395–6). Indeed, he went farther and argued that 'some sort of assumption about the equality of men in regard to their needs' must be made, although it is not to be pressed too far (p. 396). And it is to be used as a *prima facie* standard to be 'carefully framed and used with great caution always subject to the proviso "unless the contrary can be shown"' (p. 397). Furthermore, another consideration appeared to Harrod to have greater weight: the distribution of income is intimately connected with the balance of social and political forces, the study of which is outside the economist's province (p. 397).

Two different methodological questions are entangled here, which we

[9] Little, 1950 and 1957.
[10] For a systematic basis for this position, cf. Pole, 1961.

would do well to disentangle: What kind of judgement, positive or normative, are we making:

(1) If we judge one man to be happier than another, or a given increment of income to make a greater difference to one man than to another?
(2) If we judge that the happiness of all men should be given equal consideration in social policy?

The second question is clearly normative. The first, although widely believed by economists, Robbins in particular, to be normative, can be seen on closer examination to be positive. It does not ask what ought to be the case, but what is the case. It seems to lack objectivity because of the difficulty of making the required judgements, but those judgements are judgements of descriptive fact. They are required indeed for a normative judgement of social arrangements, just as the presence or absence of a worm in an apple is required for the normative judgement of its quality. Difficulties in attaining precision in the comparison of the happiness of different people may make difficult and imprecise normative judgements dependent on such comparisons, but those difficulties are in the positive realm not the normative. Here Aristotle's dictum, quoted by Harrod, that we should not demand more precision than the subject warrants, would seem to cover the question adequately.

Little further muddied the waters by claiming that the proposition that aggregate real income would be maximized by equality is analytic, i.e. true as a consequence of the meaning of the terms involved. His argument depends on the contention that we mean the same thing if we say:

(1) A has a real income equal to B's.
(2) The marginal utility of income to A is the same as to B.

In fact, I believe, we are not involved in a contradiction in saying 'A has greater real income than B, but B has a lower marginal utility of income than A.' But there is no space to pursue this argument here. Our principal concern is with the exclusion of the normative, rather than with the positive, synthetic character of comparative judgements of happiness.

From one point of view the objections to interpersonal comparisons of happiness and to the making of normative judgements both spring from a common basis—the lack of agreement to be expected among judgements made by different people. This was explicitly Robbins' position—that Gandhi, Buddha, Lenin and the President of U.S. Steel could agree on the effects of charging interest on loans, but not on its ethical propriety. In fact when we find differences of opinion on social policy, they are more likely to hinge on differences of appraisal of positive facts than on differences in our normative ends. The truth of this is sometimes clouded by a tendency to vest normative commitment in a means rather than in an end—to be 'for' democracy or even for Democrats, rather than being for the general welfare of all concerned. This tendency may be called 'the fallacy of misplaced values'. Certainly the argument between capitalism and Communism, when carried forward on a rational plane, primarily involves positive questions of how the systems operate, rather than the normative question posed by Robbins of whether the fact that a policy increases the happiness of all concerned implies that it should be carried out. The classic attack on the injection of values into the social sciences, Max Weber's, was directed primarily against such a partisan investment of normative values in instruments. The attack itself could only be based on some higher level values.

But even if it be granted that we should find greater agreement on values than on descriptive facts, once we have overcome the fallacy of misplaced values, that would not settle the question of the place of the normative in economics. Truth is no more to be determined by counting noses than by breaking heads. The validity of the findings of natural science is not based on how many people believe them, but on evidence such that all right-thinking investigators ought to believe them. It is the capability of rightly justifying assent, rather than the fact of somehow or other having gained assent, that entitles them to their acceptance. So, even if most of us agree that social policy should serve human happiness, we are not justified in incorporating that normative judgement into economics, unless we are right in that belief.

Robbins' position could of course be that the question is an improper one, that one cannot be said to be right or wrong in a normative belief. One has the belief or one does not, but there is no question of being right or wrong about it. For, if someone denies a law of thermodynamics, he has physics to contend with as well as physicists, but if he denies the principle of utility, he has only the utilitarians to contend with—nothing beyond.

A positive finding of a science makes the claim that if other qualified observers look into the matter, they will find the same thing. A normative finding would be justified if it could make the same claim, but the positivists and their fellow travellers claim that this cannot be done, so there is no room for the normative in interpersonally valid inquiry. I claim the contrary and shall try to outline the basis of my position. Perhaps the reader will be grateful that space will permit only the briefest sketch of that argument.

I have the advantage over my positivist opponent that it is a normative question under consideration—should the normative have a place in economic inquiry—and on his own principles, this is a meaningless question—though it is the positivists that have raised it and proposed the negative answer that is universally accepted in economics—in theory though fortunately not in practice. The direct answer to the positivists' arguments can be made simply, though it will not get us very far because their position is not really based on their arguments. In the case of Wittgenstein of the *Tractatus*, aside from his own subsequent abandonment of the position, we can note that he claimed only to be talking nonsense which might have the therapeutic value of bringing the reader to the proper viewpoint. Ayer, on the other hand, tried to prove the verification principle by hanky-panky with the *a priori*.[11] Since a normative statement claims to be other than analytic and empirical, it must be *a priori* synthetic. Ayer and other positivists then tampered with the notion of the synthetic, switching it from Kant's notion of 'not analytic' to the notion of being empirical (p. 78, 2nd ed.). In this manner, if we take the *a priori* to be non-empirical, as it is generally taken, the *a priori* synthetic becomes a contradiction in terms.

We need not linger longer over these dogmatic methods of ruling out of meaningful discourse statements which are not empirical and not analytic, such as normative statements. We who speak the language know that '*A* should be done' is a meaningful expression. It takes its meaning in a context in which it is presumed that there are reasons why some actions may be the right or wrong things to do, and it says that in this case these reasons indicate that it is *A* that is rightly to be done.

So the normative is not to be ruled out by linguistic considerations. But there is a deeper problem which is, I think, the real basis for the views of those who would exclude the normative from the social studies. It is that judgements of the reasons for doing things are personal in nature and the apparently impersonal claim of a normative statement is fraudulent. A statement can properly claim impersonal validity in a context in which it is based on considerations such that others would rightly agree with it if they were well informed, competent judges. Our problem then boils down to the question of whether such a context ever exists for normative statements, particularly for those evaluating social institutions. An affirmative answer is to be based on our commitment to the normative in general, not to any particular normative commitment, nor to utilitarianism, but to a more general commitment to do what is right, whatever it is. That is the basic commitment of a moral man. Among people so committed, a normative judgement can have interpersonal validity. Whether any particular normative judgement is true or false in its context will usually depend on descriptive facts. Whether this is a good apple or not depends on its size, flavour and freedom from blemishes and worms. What is a blemish is another normative question, although what is a worm is not. Clearly, our judgement of a good apple depends on our taste but we have come to that taste collectively, so that I mean something more, in calling it a good apple, than that I personally like it. Indeed the notion of taste has been developed to mark off one basis for evaluative judgement from others, and it is contrary to our linguistic usage to describe our judgement that a sadistic act is evil as a distaste for the torture of children.

We do have a body of normative beliefs, or rather a collection of ways of

[11] Ayer, 1936 and 1946.

making normative judgements. If any of those ways of making normative, or for that matter, positive, judgements is called into question, we have our ways of attacking that problem too, so that the process of inquiry is embedded in a network of infinite regresses, an open system. At each point of the process the level of inquiry can be escalated by a challenge to the basis of the procedure, like the question whether an apple should be free of worms in order to be a good apple. To reject the process because of its open texture would, of course, lead to the rejection of natural science as well.

The open regress of our system of inquiry is all we have. We must keep it while we try to improve it. And what is to count as an improvement must itself depend on the system we have. This is the point of Peirce's dictum that we must proceed from where we are, or Neurath's image, often quoted by Quine, that we are like sailors engaged in rebuilding our boat as we sail in it. While we do then, in our normative as in our positive inquiry, take a large number of things for granted, these things are not the unalterable boundary conditions of the inquiry, but are only temporarily exempt from questioning until we find reason to question them.

We have, in our society, come to hold certain values, such as the utilitarian principle Robbins threw into question, that human institutions should serve human welfare. We would do well to proceed on that basis, unless we have reason to question it. If we do have reason to question it, that inquiry can be based only on the other things we have come to believe. We have come to believe them together, however, even if not unanimously, and it is that joint-ness of belief and inquiry that justifies the introduction of normative inquiry into the social studies. (I shall refrain from calling them social sciences in order not to raise unnecessary issues of nomenclature.)

When I argue then that 'A should be done', I am arguing that considerations that are rightly to be taken to govern acts of this sort indicate that A is to be done. The term 'rightly', applied at the next level above that of the judgement immediately at issue, does, of course, open the door to the infinite regress. Admittedly, the standards which I am using are derived from our social nexus, but these are public, not personal standards, and they too are open to question, and the answer must be at each stage, not that they are widely held, but that viewed from the next higher normative level, they are rightly held, a question to be judged in turn by standards rightly to be applied. These standards, at every level, do not represent arbitrary choices of mine, but claim to be the standards rightly to be used in this context by any reasonable moral man.

From this point of view, we may possibly judge that it is better to keep the normative out of academic inquiry, itself a normative judgement. But rather, I would agree with Harrod, and with Cannan before him, that some, perhaps limited, normative judgements should be allowed; that it is better for some-one who knows something about a process and its ramifications to judge it normatively than for someone ignorant of the process. If then it is argued that most students of economic processes are likely to be poor judges of how they serve human welfare, I must reply that this implies some defect in their upbringing—possibly in the study and teaching of economics. The notion is questionable that it requires rigorous training to identify the consequences of an economic action, but any fool can judge whether those consequences are good or bad. Casual empiricism is derided, casual normativism prescribed.

The prohibition of the normative in economics, has, I am sure, many deleterious effects. Unlimited and undisciplined indulgence of normative judgements based on personal preferences would be worse. But there may be some degree of temperate indulgence in the normative, especially if attended with scholarly criticism, that would be optimal.

We would have the worst of the two worlds if the normative were to be reintroduced into social studies as personal preference. Then we might witness again the scandalous performance of a Treitschke that inspired Max Weber's strictures. But once standards are recognized for responsible impersonal procedures in normative inquiry, that inquiry might go forward with some modest hopes of finding some improvements in our social arrangements. Indeed, the practice of economists too long belied their methodological strictures, and concern for human welfare has inspired much of their thought and action. But that concern has been shunted into a relatively unexamined portion of their work—since it was largely taken to represent a personal rather than a professional concern. Why should it not have to encounter the same critical process as other aspects of economic study? Most of that, incidentally is not really the rigorous hypothesis testing of the textbooks, but rather the elaboration of intuitively guided descriptions of how the world might behave if it resembled one model or another.

My contention boils down to this. Suppose a social scientist can show that social action A will lead to a state of the world that would be preferred to that consequent on social action B by any reasonable man completely informed as to all the facts, on condition that he is to take the place of anyone concerned with equal probability. This is a positive finding, not a normative. The investigator is justified in saying that A is better than B, and if it is a question of doing either A or B, A should be done. That is a normative judgement, not a positive, but based on the positive finding judged to be valid. Some improvements may be made in this specification. Suppose they are made. Then what are the arguments against the social scientist's making the statement, as a social scientist, that A should be done? We can agree with Robbins, Samuelson, *et al.* that this 'should' statement is different from the 'is' statement on which it is based. But why should not the 'should' statement be made? Someone else might believe that some other aspect of the states consequent on the action was relevant and governing. Should that make a difference irrespective of the basis of the alternative opinion? Suppose some people persist in believing the earth to be flat?

It is a subterfuge to say that the social scientist should limit his statement to the positive report that the test-man would prefer A. For, out of the infinity of questions that might be asked, why ask that one? The principal role of the normative in economics, in particular, and in the social studies in general, is to guide the investigator in the questions to be asked. If the normative is brought in explicitly, there will be a better chance to subject that guidance to the process of inquiry.

The practice current in the past thirty years has been to say that 'some people' assume that social institutions should serve human welfare, that 'numerous individuals find it of interest to specialize the form' of the welfare function.[12] The welfare function is not properly a matter of assumption or postulation, but of what is better or worse, right or wrong. And that is something to be found out, not assumed. Admittedly, it is to be found out by a process different from that by which we find out the atomic weight of copper. But we are bound at any time by the current state of our first order normative beliefs, and over time, by the current state of our higher normative beliefs about the right way to alter our normative beliefs. We are embedded in such a system, open though it may be, and we do wrong to regard it as a set of arbitrary assumptions or wilful preferences.

When we are inquiring into matters related to the normative, we are not exercising arbitrary acts of will and deciding what we shall decree to be better or worse. We are, if we are proceeding rightly, inquiring what *is* better or worse, seeking the answer usually in the positive facts against the entire structure of our beliefs, positive and normative, which we hold because we judge them to be right. And that judgement claims to be valid for others than ourselves, if it is arrived at by the appropriate procedures, because they jointly participate in the process, drawing from our common stock of beliefs as to how to proceed rightly in both normative and positive inquiry. It is not a personal process. If then we treat our normative judgements as personal, we shall not be making them responsibly. The injection of such personally based judgements into scientific inquiry is indeed objectionable. But if we think we have made the judgements impersonally, we are justified in offering them as such, though we may be wrong in that belief. We can be rightly judged to be wrong only on the basis of other judgements also respecting these requirements of the process. This is, admittedly, a difficult business, but to carry it on otherwise is worse.

It is long past time for economists to break out of the trap of Pareto optimality. Even more important is to overcome the limitations of a naive hedonism that identifies a man's welfare with his consumption of goods and services.

[12] Samuelson, 1947, p. 222.

The most important argument for egalitarianism is not the difference in marginal utility of consumption between the rich man and the poor. It is the impact on the quality of our lives that is made by inequality of opportunity for a good life. This is so easily recognized as to be trite, but economists can be trained to overlook it in their attempt to be scientific. As citizens, they are probably more aware than most that the importance of income redistribution lies in the consequent transformation of society rather than the increment of aggregate pleasure from the consumption transferred from a rich man to a poor. But the discipline roots out of those trained in economics any tendency to attack these problems systematically within the authorized system of thought. The expulsion of the normative is based on an unfounded belief in the inherently personal nature of a normative judgement. A closer examination of the nature of normative beliefs would lead to their readmission into the social studies, but subject to the constraints appropriate for impersonally valid judgements.

REFERENCES

ALEXANDER, S. S., 'Public Television and the Ought of Public Policy', *Washington University Law Quarterly*, Vol. 1968, No. 1, pp. 35–70, reprinted in *The Radio Spectrum: Its Use and Regulation* (Brookings Institution, Washington D.C., 1968).

AYER, A. J., *Language, Truth and Logic* (London, 1936, and London and New York, 1946).

CANNAN, E., review of Robbins's *Essay*, *Economic Journal*, Vol. XLII, September 1932, pp. 424–7.

FRASER, L. M., 'How Do We Want Economists to Behave?', *Economic Journal*, Vol. XLII, December 1932, pp. 555–70.

HARROD, R. F., 'Scope and Method of Economics', *Economic Journal*, Vol. XLVIII, September 1938, pp. 383–412 (Presidential Address before Section F of the British Association, Cambridge, August 1938).

LITTLE, I. M. D., *A Critique of Welfare Economics* (Oxford, 1950 and 1957).

POLE, D., *Conditions of Rational Inquiry* (London, 1961).

ROBBINS, L., *An Essay on the Nature and Significance of Economic Science* (Second ed., London, 1935).

SAMUELSON, P. A., *Foundations of Economic Analysis* (Cambridge, Mass., 1947) ('conceived and written primarily in 1937', p. vii).

SOUTER, R. W., "'The Nature and Significance of Economic Science' in Recent Discussion", *Quarterly Journal of Economics*, May 1933, pp. 377–413.

5

SOME OBSERVATIONS ON WELFARE AND ECONOMIC GROWTH*

TRYGVE HAAVELMO

1. *Are Economists too Materialistic in their View on Human Progress?*

SUPPOSE it were true that economists tend to think only in terms of goods and services. Would that necessarily be something to be ashamed of? Even in scientific activity specialization is recognized as a highly respectable approach. But the question is not that simple. Because *applied* economics is not correspondingly specialized. Voluntarily or involuntarily, the science of economics and the expert advisers it breeds have an influence on policy decisions that seems to go far beyond what the theoretical framework could justify. If policy decisions are guided mainly by the kind of indices of growth and development that economists talk about, there is good reason for being concerned. It may lead to a rather artificial distinction between 'main effects' on the one hand and 'side effects' on the other, depending somewhat arbitrarily on which kind of research has the most money to collect data and the most advanced analytical technique for handling information.

What is the responsibility of the economist in this connection? Should he warn the policy makers that they should not listen so much to him? Or should he try to widen his field of competence into the more general branches of social science? I doubt that the first would—or should—have much appeal while the second may sound pretentious, if not frightening. We may, of course, be hopeful that somebody comes up with a revolutionary idea on how to deal with this trouble. In the meantime I should like to suggest that we do something more modest, but nevertheless often very useful in such cases, viz. to take a second look at what we already have at hand in the way of theoretical tools and how we have utilized their capacity. It is my contention that the analytical power of existing concepts and tools in economic theory, when it comes to dealing with so-called non-economic aspects of human life and development, is *grossly underestimated*. This is due partly to the very narrow

* I owe thanks to my colleagues, Eivind Bjøntegård, Leif Johansen, and Jan Serck-Hanssen, for stimulating discussions and helpful suggestions. (The manuscript for the present article was completed in October 1968.)

verbal interpretation given to the existing theoretical apparatus in standard textbooks, partly to the historically important close association between economic theory and a particular market economy. To support this view I shall reproduce some well-known models from welfare economics and confront them with some equally familiar statements concerning 'non-economic' aspects of growth and development.

2. *A Hard-boiled Theorem concerning Economic Growth*

Let me begin by a model which gives very strong conclusions as far as progress is concerned, but which many people would say represents the worst kind of materialism. I shall present the theorem in its simplest possible version, although the result could very easily be generalized to fit a more diversified economy than the one considered here. The simple version will suffice to illustrate the line of thought.

Consider a community where all individuals are alike, as far as preferences, economic resources, etc., are concerned. Let x denote a measure (e.g. some kind of index) of the totality of goods and services that, to the individual, represents something by itself advantageous. And let y denote a measure of the effort or work, taken in a very wide sense, which the individual must perform to obtain x. In other words, there is a budget constraint on x, which we shall assume is

$$(2.1) \qquad\qquad x \leqq g(y, t),$$

where t is time, and where g is a function *given* to the individual and possessing first partial derivatives such that $\partial g/\partial y > 0$. If growth is taken to mean improvement of economic opportunities it seems reasonable to say that there is growth when

$$(2.2) \qquad\qquad \frac{\partial g}{\partial t} > 0.$$

Assume that the individual has a preference function

$$(2.3) \qquad\qquad u(x, y),$$

which has first-order derivatives and such that $\partial u/\partial x > 0$, $\partial u/\partial y < 0$.

Consider an arbitrarily chosen point of time t_0, and let x_0, y_0 represent the situation at that point of time. This situation may have been reached, e.g., by the individual maximizing u with respect to x and y under the constraint (2.1) at time t_0. But it is not necessary to assume that this is the way x_0, y_0 were chosen. All we need to remember is that, by assumption, $\partial u/\partial x$ is > 0 for $x = x_0, y = y_0$.

We now pose the following question: Is it an advantage to the individual that $\partial g/\partial t$ at $t = t_0$ is positive? We take this to mean that we are asking whether it is possible that du/dt at $t = t_0$ can be positive *regardless of the situation* x_0, y_0. If this is true, it will be possible for the individual to move on, with time, to a situation which is *better* than x_0, y_0. That this is true follows simply from the budget constraint (2.1). Assume that, as a particular case y is chosen to be a constant $= y_0$ from $t = t_0$ to $t = t_0 + dt$. Then x could increase and therefore also u could increase, as $\partial u/\partial x > 0$. We are, therefore, sure that the individual *can* reach a higher level of u, and if we assume that this is what the individual wants, a higher u *will* actually be reached.

I should like to indicate two kinds of conclusions that suggest themselves on the basis of the simple result above.

One conclusion is that if one accepts the rather general definition of growth and the likewise fairly general definition of 'better' or 'worse' implied by the model above, then all talk about the possibility of growth being harmful to welfare is unfounded.

Suppose we start from another angle. Suppose we accept (as I think we should) that all the doubt we hear and read about, concerning the blessings of growth, is more than just idle talk. Then it is certain that the concern must be about something that is *not included* in the model above; but the interesting thing is that the model need not be scrapped. It can be repaired, at rather low cost, in ways that will give it explanatory power reaching far into the field of general sociology. It is also fairly obvious what *kind* of repair work we should think of. We can do much of the repair work simply by digging a little deeper down in the tool kit that economics already has on hand.

To see this let us start from the tentative assumption that the repair work can be done by preserving essentially the same general notions of growth and of preferences as those in the model above, but that there is need for including more variables, more factors that could have additional positive or negative effects on the 'welfare level' u. The problem of generalizing the model under these conditions could perhaps be approached along one of the following three lines of thought.

The first and most obvious (but also the least interesting) expansion of the model would be to assume that, concurrently with growth as defined in the simple model, there are independent evolutionary factors which affect the level of welfare u. This idea could perhaps in certain cases be sufficient to simulate the content of such statements as 'in spite of a better economy we are less happy than in the old days'. But this kind of model would not be relevant to the discussion of what economic growth as such has done to the level of welfare. I shall, therefore, not follow up this line here.

A second approach could be to introduce elements of individual ignorance, or failure of the individual to take account of relevant accessible information. There are, essentially, two possible ways of thinking in this connection. One idea could be that if people say they are not sure of the blessings of economic growth, this simply means that it is growth as defined by some economic expert or policy maker that they do not wholly approve of. The fundamental assumption of the strong theorem above was, of course, that the model represented the individuals' own way of feeling and not that of an onlooker or a policy maker in power. It is obviously possible to define economic growth in such a way that a given particular group of people will not deem it a good thing. It is, nevertheless, possible that part of the popular complaints about certain negative effects of economic growth are due simply to the fact that a particular kind of economic growth has been *imposed* by some authority, either because this authority does not know what people want, or is unwilling to be guided by individual preferences. The other idea could be that the individuals themselves choose on the basis of a wrong model, so to speak. That is, we do not know or do not pay sufficient attention to all consequences of our own decisions even when it would, in point of principle, be practically possible for us to do so in our own individual process of choice. Hence, the possibility of regret, but perhaps also the possibility of learning. I shall consider these ideas a little more in detail in the next section.

There is, however, a third way of expanding the model which I think is the more important, from a theoretical point of view and for the purpose of expanding the explanatory power. This approach is based on the well-known ideas of *collective* (or '*external*') *economies or diseconomies*. The leading idea here is that people may be fully aware of the additional consequences that individual decisions may have when they are added up for the whole community, and yet it is not possible or rational for the individual to try to do something about the matter. The main reason why I think that this way of expanding the model is the more important is that here we have a possibility of explaining why people could choose, in cold blood so to speak, a kind of economic progress which they do not really want, without having to refer to such factors as stupidity or ignorance. In Section 4 I shall explore such possibilities a little further.

Besides these three ideas of generalization one could, of course, also take the somewhat negative point of view that people's tastes change in an unpredictable way over time so that it has little sense to ask whether things get better or worse. More interesting is the possibility that people's taste could change in a systematic way as a gradual consequence of their own decisions and their adjustment to a certain way of living. This brings in the possibility of disappointment as it shows up in statements like 'economic progress has not made us as happy as we thought it would'. I shall make further comments on this idea in Section 5.

3. *Effects of Misinformation and Bad Choice*

Assume that $x_1, x_2, \ldots, x_m$ is a fairly comprehensive set of variables that people may take into account in evaluating whether their welfare improves or deteriorates. Let x be some index based on the set of m variables x_i, and let $u(x)$ be a welfare indicator, such that u increases with x. Here two important problems arise at once. First, there is the question of whether the preferences of people could be represented by such an aggregated function even if all people were alike. Secondly, there is the question of individual differences as far as preferences are concerned. These 'index problems' we shall neglect in what follows, because the points we want to make are not primarily connected with these problems. Consequently, we shall assume that people are all alike and that $u(x)$ is a true representation of their way of evaluating growth.

Suppose now that the policy makers in power, or some 'experts' who represent the official view on what growth is, base their judgement on an index x^* that may be different from x, for reasons of misinformation or special ideas regarding what people 'ought to like'. It is obvious that there need not exist any unique function $u^*(x^*)$ which represents peoples evaluation of an increase in x^*. But even if such a function should exist, there is no reason to assume that u^* would necessarily increase with x^*.

Thus, when people sometimes say that growth has not made them any happier, the explanation may simply be that people feel there has not been growth, it is only the politicians or the index makers who say so.

More interesting, perhaps, are the mistakes that people themselves make in choosing what they think is growth in a positive sense, only to find out that the result was not so good after all (or, as a happy alternative, was better than they had hoped for). The explanation may be that people have only rather hazy ideas about what is a good index x or about the $u(x)$ that represents their real feelings. Lacking information about possible systematic biases in these respects there is not much more that can be said about the matter. If, however, some information is available on such biases, it may be possible to give meaning to the paradoxical idea that people should sometimes freely choose what they do not like. By way of an illustration I should like to indicate a line of thought that may perhaps be relevant in this connection.

One quite often hears people praise the greater abundance of goods and services that economic growth has made it possible for them to buy, but at the same time complain that life has become more strenuous and restless. New gadgets for the house may save time and give more opportunity for leisure, but the effect may also be the opposite. To illustrate, suppose that y_1 represents work hours in the usual meaning while y_2 represents 'consumption time' in the sense of time which is in itself not enjoyable but which reduces the part of the day that is 'really free' time. Let this latter part of the day be y_3. Suppose that the true preference function is $u(x, y_1, y_3)$ or, which is the same, $u(x, y_1, 24 - y_1 - y_2)$ with partial derivatives $\partial u/\partial x > 0$, $\partial u/\partial y_1 < 0$, and $\partial u/\partial y_3 > 0$. Suppose now that 'consumption time' y_2 is actually tied to the level of consumption x by a function $y_2 = h(x)$, where $\partial h/\partial x > 0$. And let the income function $x = g(y_1, t)$ be as in the previous section. Consider a given situation x^0, y_1^0, y_2^0, y_3^0 at time t_0. Is it an advantage to the individual that $\partial g/\partial t$ at t_0 is positive? The answer is still 'yes', because it becomes possible, for example, to keep x (and thereby y_2) constant and to reduce y_1, hence increase y_3. But it now also becomes possible to make a bad choice by an understandable mistake. Suppose that people in their adjustment to the growing potential of goods and services x 'forget' the variable y_2. Suppose, for example, that the choice is to keep work hours constant and to raise x. Then, depending on the function h, there comes an additional utility effect via the change in consumption time y_2.

Turning the argument above in a different direction we get another possible effect which actually belongs to the subject matter of our next section. Indeed, suppose that the main effect of y_2 is not so much that it steals from my own y_3 but that it reduces the time I can find to be helpful to others (free of charge). Then the really important effect in this connection may not be that I myself get less time for others but rather that others get less time for me! In other words, the average amount of leisure hours y_3 for people in the community may be a variable in my own utility indicator. Partially, my own influence on this average may be infinitesimal, but, nevertheless, the total effect on the average of y_3 of all the individual changes in y_3 is of course of the same order of magnitude as that of my own change. It is, however, misleading to classify such average effects under the heading of this section, because the choice of the individual in this case may be perfectly informed and rational, even when the total effect for the community as a whole adds up to a situation that is not wanted. As I have said, this leads us right into the subject matter of the next section.

4. *Collective Economies and Diseconomies*

Is it possible that people, without being uninformed, irrational, or inconsistent, can choose an economic development which is inferior to an alternative open to them? Is it contrary to a maximizing behaviour that people should choose more material growth than what they actually prefer? Should the answer be that 'maybe so, but these are not proper problems for respectable economic theory'? The fact is, however, that the analytical apparatus for dealing precisely with such questions is already well developed in the classical theory of economic welfare. This apparatus builds on the notions of collective (or 'external') economies and diseconomies.

The well-known general idea, to restate it very briefly, is this: In the utility or welfare function of the individual there are three different types of parameter. First, there are those which it is the primary business of the individual to adjust according to his own taste. Secondly, there are the collective parameters that are in fact determined by individual choices but which are such that the *partial* effect of the actions of a particular individual is very small. Thirdly, there are parameters that are data, not subject to choice.

As far as the second kind of parameters is concerned the point is *not* whether the individual actually takes into account his small partial influence or neglects it. The crucial point is whether or not each individual has the assurance that all the other individuals will follow suit if he himself should choose to influence such collective parameters.

To illustrate the use of this analytical framework in the present context we shall consider a very simple model. Let x and y have the same meaning as in Section 2 and let $\bar{x}$ denote the arithmetical average of all the (n) individual x's. As we shall continue to assume that all individuals are equal, the value of $\bar{x}$ will of course have the same value as x for each individual. Suppose now that the utility function of the individual can be represented by a function

$$(4.1) \qquad\qquad u(x, y, \bar{x}),$$

where we assume that $\partial u/\partial x > 0$, $\partial u/\partial y < 0$ while the sign of $\partial u/\partial \bar{x}$ is more problematic. The effect of $\bar{x}$ upon u could embrace at least the following two kinds of influence.

(1) The effect, upon the feeling of welfare, of the scale of production activity as such, that is, more production, more noise and smoke, less untouched nature, etc. There could, of course, also be positive effects. Many people undoubtedly prefer to be where there is life and activity also as far as production is concerned.

(2) The effect upon individual welfare of the general level of real income $\bar{x}$. Here again the effect has many different components. One of these may be the (positive) benefit of being surrounded by neighbours with a high standard of living and, therefore, presumably also with some cultural assets. Another effect may be one of envy, calling forth a struggle to keep up with the others. There may even be the effect of bad conscience by having more than one's fellow neighbour.

Leaving the question of the net effect of all these influences aside for the moment, let us consider the possible consequences of individual rational behaviour in maximizing (4.1) with respect to x and y and subject to a constraint of the type (2.1) with the equality sign assumed, i.e., maximization of the Lagrange expression

$$(4.2) \qquad\qquad u(x, y, \bar{x}) - \lambda[x - g(y, t)].$$

As $\partial \bar{x}/\partial x = 1/n$ we obtain the necessary condition

$$(4.3) \qquad\qquad \frac{\partial u}{\partial y} + \left(\frac{\partial u}{\partial x} + \frac{1}{n}\frac{\partial u}{\partial \bar{x}}\right)\frac{\partial g}{\partial y} = 0.$$

If n is large the individual may safely neglect the second term of the parenthesis which gives us

$$(4.4) \qquad\qquad \frac{\partial u}{\partial y} + \frac{\partial u}{\partial x}\frac{\partial g}{\partial y} = 0.$$

What will now be the sign of du/dt if $\partial g/\partial t > 0$? From the equality in (2.1), together with (4.4), and the definition of $\bar{x}$ we get

(4.5)
$$\frac{du}{dt} = \frac{\partial u}{\partial x}\frac{\partial g}{\partial t} + \frac{\partial u}{\partial \bar{x}}\left(\frac{\partial g}{\partial y}\frac{dy}{dt} + \frac{\partial g}{\partial t}\right).$$

If $\partial u/\partial \bar{x} < 0$, that is, if $\bar{x}$ causes disutility, the expression to the right in (4.5) is not necessarily positive even when $\partial g/\partial t$ is positive. This is easy to demonstrate by means of a simple example.

Consider for this purpose the special utility function

(4.1.a)
$$u = u_1(x - \bar{x}) + u_2(y),$$

and let the 'income equation' be

(2.1.a)
$$x = wy,$$

where the 'wage level' w is subject to positive growth over time, but is a *datum* to the individual at any time. We then have

(4.4.a)
$$\frac{\partial u_2}{\partial y} + \frac{\partial u_1}{\partial x}w = 0,$$

(4.5.a)
$$\frac{du}{dt} = -\frac{\partial u_1}{\partial x}w\frac{dy}{dt}.$$

From (4.4.a) we see that if there is increasing disutility of labour and w increases while, as here, $\partial u_1/\partial x$ remains a constant (>0), y must increase. Consequently, the expression to the right in (4.5.a) must be negative. It should be noted that there is no reason even in this particular case to assume that the individual 'maximum' satisfying (2.1.a) and (4.4.a) should not be stable.

If all the individuals simultaneously would adjust themselves to the situation in a *co-operative* fashion, taking account of the effects of $\bar{x}$, the situation would be quite different. Instead of (4.4) we should then have

(4.6)
$$\frac{\partial u}{\partial y} + \left(\frac{\partial u}{\partial x} + \frac{\partial u}{\partial \bar{x}}\right)\frac{\partial g}{\partial y} = 0.$$

And instead of (4.5) we obtain

(4.7)
$$\frac{du}{dt} = \left(\frac{\partial u}{\partial x} + \frac{\partial u}{\partial \bar{x}}\right)\frac{\partial g}{\partial t}.$$

If there is disutility of labour and positive marginal productivity of labour in equilibrium, the parenthesis to the right in (4.7) is necessarily positive. That is, growth is always an advantage.

The special example used above in studying the sign of du/dt in (4.5) could perhaps be interpreted as follows. Suppose everybody tries to get ahead of everybody else and that this is all that matters as far as improving the standard of living is concerned. Then growth may make everybody work harder to achieve the same as before. Disappointment concerning the assumed blessings of growth would then be understandable.

The model above could be varied in innumerable ways that could simulate many common arguments concerning the goods or bads of economic growth. One could, for example, consider the effect upon the individuals' disutility of labour of the amount of work that one's fellow neighbour is doing. Or one could consider the efficiency of taxes and subsidies to force the individuals automatically to take account of indirect, collective factors. However, the simple examples already given are probably sufficient to illustrate the general idea that we wanted to bring out.

5. *Irreversibility*

We have seen that people, acting individually in their own best interest, may be forced to choose a non-optimal process of growth because a co-ordinating policy to take account of side effects is lacking. Another possibility leading to similar effects is that a growth process, in retrospect, may turn out to be different from what was expected *a priori*. A case in point—although not the most interesting from a theoretical point of view—is that of wrong expectations about future facts, or careless planning. In other words, there is always the chance of mistakes and of subsequent *regret*. Sometimes the mistakes may have a learning effect so that the decisions will gradually improve. In other cases it may simply be too late, over and over again. The reason that I would say that such non-optimal processes are less interesting is that they simply show the normal imperfections of human activities in practice as compared to the ideal.

There is another possibility of irreversibility which is more interesting in this connection, namely effects of what could be called *unforeseeable* events. This may be a controversial philosophical concept, but what I have in mind is not quite as mysterious as it may appear. The idea can be illustrated by the following simple model.

Let $X(t, t - \omega)$ denote the *time shape* of the flow of goods and services that the individual has experienced in the past, from time $t - \omega$ to present time t. Suppose that the utility function of the individual is of the form

$$(5.1) \qquad u[x(t), y(t), X(t, t - \omega)],$$

i.e., u is a *functional*. As an illustration $X(t, t - \omega)$ may be a weighted integral over $x(\tau)$ from $\tau = t - \omega$ to $\tau = t$. We shall assume that $x(t)$ has an infinitesimal effect on $X(t, t - \omega)$. For simplicity assume that ω is a constant.

Suppose that at each 'present' point of time t the individual can choose $x(t)$ and $y(t)$ subject to, for example, the constraint (2.1.a). If we assume that the individual knows the development of the wage rate, w, over time, there is the possibility that he could maximize his utility taking account of the gradual effect on $X(t, t - \omega)$ that his choice of $x(t)$ will have. Suppose, however, that he has no basis for doing this. In other words, suppose that $X(t, t - \omega)$ simply represents a given parameter at each point of time indicating all that he could possibly know about his desires for $x(t)$. $X(t, t - \omega)$ is then, as it were, an index of the 'personality' of the consumer as it has been formed by experience in the past. The decision of the individual at any moment could then be the result of maximizing (5.1) with respect to $x(t)$ and $y(t)$ subject to $x(t) = w(t)y(t)$ with $w(t)$ and $X(t, t - \omega)$ as given magnitudes. (This means that there is no 'learning effect' of X.) We should then have the necessary condition

$$(5.2) \qquad\qquad w\frac{\partial u}{\partial x} + \frac{\partial u}{\partial y} = 0,$$

where u is now the function (5.1).

Suppose that $\partial u/\partial X$ and dX/dt exist as proper derivatives. What could be the development of u over time, especially, how could du/dt be? We have, when u is constantly maximized as indicated above,

$$(5.3) \qquad \frac{du}{dt} = \frac{\partial u}{\partial x}\frac{dx}{dt} + \frac{\partial u}{\partial y}\frac{dy}{dt} + \frac{\partial u}{\partial X}\frac{dX}{dt} = \frac{\partial u}{\partial x}y\frac{dw}{dt} + \frac{\partial u}{\partial X}\frac{dX}{dt}.$$

We see here that the first term to the right represents the normal positive effect that was discussed in Section 2. But the second term could well be negative if $\partial u/\partial X < 0$.

It is tempting to interpret the scheme above as simulating the following phenomenon. Suppose that $\partial u/\partial X$ is negative, and that X is the higher the higher x has been in the past. Then X in (5.1) could represent the effect of taking for granted what was originally appreciated as a novelty. This could mean that a certain increase in x at a time when X has grown large is less appreciated than the individual thought it would be at an earlier time when X was smaller. At the same time, looking back at an earlier lower level of x, that level may now look even more austere than it did at the time it was experienced. But this is only one of many possible developments that could be described by the model.

The reasoning above, as well as in the preceding sections, is of course rather drastic in its assumptions concerning the existence of cardinal utility. However I do not see that such assumptions should become less drastic merely by dealing with these matters under the headings of sociology or social psychology.

6. Conclusions

The starting point of this paper was the proposition that the tools of economic theory have a much wider range of applicability than that for which they were originally constructed. I should, of course, like to be able to conclude that my analysis in the preceding sections shows the truth of this proposition; but the reader may find that quite a bit more is required to substantiate such a claim. Let me, therefore, draw two conclusions of a more conditional nature.

The first of these conclusions concerns the future content of economic theory. Suppose it is true, as many people think, that the nature of human preferences becomes more and more influenced by social environment as society grows richer. In other words, suppose that models of the kind we have discussed simulate central features of modern economic life rather than oddities. Is it then wise use of our analytical tools to continue teaching economics as if the basic features of economic life could be represented by a model of Robinson Crusoes trading with each other? Are the 'curious cases' of interdependent preferences a subject matter only for footnotes and appendices? I think this may be a bad approach if we are looking for a first approximation that would deserve that name. If we have to admit that important collective economies and diseconomies are the rule rather than the exception, the effects upon the findings that economists ought to teach may be quite profound. We need only think of the usual textbook theorems concerning what is right and what is wrong in the use of excise taxes or subsidies.

The second conclusion concerns possible implications for the kind of statistical data we ought to collect in order to do econometric research or to make policy decisions. If collective economies and diseconomies are really important, we may want statistical measurements of a new and different kind. We may find that such measures of welfare as the national income or the value of total consumption are even more dubious than many people have already argued. In general, we may find that the idea of observed choice representing revealed preferences is very misleading because the choice may be based on partial or conjectural constraints that do not tell the individual what he is actually choosing. This could mean that 'facts' in the way of data showing answers to hypothetical questions may become very important as a supplement to figures showing present status, or the history of the market.

6

THE ACHIEVEMENT OF STABLE GROWTH AT THE NATURAL RATE

W. A. ELTIS

IN this paper, the problems involved in achieving stable growth at the 'natural' rate will be analysed. The circumstances where this will occur without government intervention will be analysed first, and the manner in which the government can intervene to achieve it where these conditions do not obtain will then be considered.

It will be seen that the analysis owes much to Sir Roy Harrod's growth model which has evolved continuously from 1939 to 1964. The model differs from the Harrod model in a number of respects, and there is a considerable debt to Professor Kaldor's trade cycle model of 1940. There are particular departures from the Harrod model in the assumptions made about investment decisions, and the determination of G, the actual rate of growth.

In the Harrod model, the determination of the rate of investment is only defined to a limited extent. It is posited that investment will rise if C, the actual capital coefficient, is less than C_r, the capital coefficient entrepreneurs wish to maintain, and that it will fall if C exceeds C_r, and in his most recent article, Sir Roy Harrod has pointed out that any rate of investment is possible where C equals C_r.[1] In the model outlined in this paper, planned investment will depend on three factors, the degree of capacity working of the 'representative' firm, the rate of profit, and growth expectations.

First, in the spirit (but not the letter) of the C and C_r relationship, it will be assumed that planned investment varies (as a share of value-added) with the degree of capacity working of the 'representative' firm. With a rigid acceleration principle, the sensitivity of investment to the degree of capacity working is implausibly great. With 1 per cent excess capacity there is no net investment at all, and there is twice as much net investment with 2 per cent overcapacity working as there is with 1 per cent overcapacity working. This would lead to much greater fluctuations in investment than those experienced in developed economies since 1945, but there must be some kind of relation between the degree of capacity working and planned investment.

---

[1] Harrod, 1964, pp. 906–7.

Hence, it will merely be assumed that planned investment is higher where the degree of capacity working is greater.[2]

The rate of profit will be a further factor influencing planned investment. Its effect has been partly allowed for already, for both investment and the rate of profit will be higher where the degree of capacity working is higher, but this does not allow for the full effect of the rate of profit on investment. Two economies may have the same degree of capacity working, and different rates of profit, and in this case, the economy with a higher rate of profit will have a higher share of planned investment (*ceteris paribus*). Its higher rate of profit will provide more potential internal finance for investment (since (investment/capital) can be higher if a given proportion of profits is invested and (profits/capital) is higher); it will allow more potential investments to fulfil any given pay-off requirement; and it will allow more potential investments to fulfil *d.c.f.* requirements if the profit rate is higher in relation to the marginal cost of finance. Hence, it will be assumed that with a given degree of capacity working, planned investment will be higher where the rate of profit is higher.

A further factor which will influence planned investment is the growth expectation of businessmen. An economy with the same rate of profit and the same degree of capacity working as another will have a higher share of planned investment if its businessmen expect a faster rate of growth. It will be assumed that the expected rate of growth will tend towards *any* actual rate of growth which is steadily maintained, so that the expected rate of growth will equal the actual rate of growth in equilibrium. Where the rate of growth fluctuates, however, there may be considerable differences between the expected rate of growth 'and the actual rate, and the expected rate will then independently influence investment decisions.

Thus planned investment will be assumed to depend on (i) the degree of capacity working of the 'representative' firm, (ii) the rate of profit at a given degree of capacity working, and (iii) growth expectations. These assumptions can be expressed quite simply diagrammatically, but before this is done, something must be said about the 'natural' rate of growth.

In this paper, a slightly modified version of Sir Roy Harrod's definition will be used. The 'natural' rate of growth, G_n, will be defined as 'the rate of growth made possible by technical progress and population increase at a constant rate of profit'. A precise share of investment will be needed to raise productive capacity at rate G_n. With a higher share of investment than this, and continuous normal capacity working, the extra investment will cause the growth rate to exceed G_n, at least for a time, and it will also lead to a falling rate of profit (while the growth rate exceeds G_n) because of diminishing returns to the extra capital stock. With a lower share of investment, the growth rate will be less than G_n, and the rate of profit will be rising. Hence there is a most

[2] cf. Kaldor, 1940.

important relationship. At any given degree of capacity working, the rate of profit will be rising if investment is insufficient to raise productive capacity at rate G_n, and it will be falling if investment is more than that needed for G_n.

The assumptions made about investment decisions will now be shown diagrammatically in Figure 1. The horizontal axis shows the degree of capacity working of the representative firm. At 100, it has what it judges to be the ideal capacity to produce current output, and this corresponds (but not precisely) to the Harrod situation where C equals C_r. If it is producing at 99 (which corresponds to C greater than C_r) it has 1 per cent excess capacity. The vertical axis shows investment by the representative firm expressed as a share of

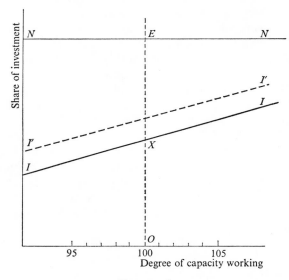

FIGURE 1

value-added. II shows investment by the representative firm at different degrees of capacity working, and NN shows the investment needed for the 'natural' rate of growth.

The first assumption made about investment is that this is higher at a higher degree of capacity working. This is shown by drawing II sloping upwards from left to right.

The second assumption is that at any given degree of capacity working, investment will be higher at a higher rate of profit. If capacity is worked at a point where II is below NN, investment will be insufficient for the 'natural' rate of growth. This will lead to a rising rate of profit at any given degree of capacity working, and because investment is related to the rate of profit, a rising II line (for instance, from II to $I'I'$). If II is above NN, investment will exceed that needed for G_n, the rate of profit will be falling, and the II line will be falling.

It is also assumed that investment will depend on the growth expectations of entrepreneurs. These are shown by the relation between X and E. At 100 (i.e., at normal capacity working), the II line shows that the representative firm will invest OX while OE needs to be invested to raise productive capacity at the 'natural' rate of growth. If growth expectations are insufficient for growth at the 'natural' rate, X will be below E, and it will be above E if expectations are more than sufficient.

The next step in the argument is to show (with the help of Figure 2) how the actual degree of capacity working is determined at any time. The whole economy is represented in Figure 2, and not simply the representative firm, so

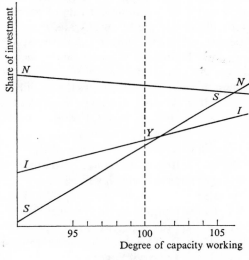

FIGURE 2

II shows planned investment (as a share of the National Product) in relation to the degree of capacity working in the economy as a whole. SS shows planned saving (as a share of the National Product) at different degrees of capacity working, and it slopes upward from left to right, partly because the share of profits is normally higher at higher degrees of capacity working, and the share of saving is likely to vary with the share of profits,[3] and partly because some people will dissave at the low levels of income associated with a low degree of capacity working, while saving will be high because of 'windfall' incomes at a high degree of capacity working. For simplicity, it will be assumed that SS, the relationship between the share of saving and the degree

[3] Kaldor, 1955–6.

of capacity working, does not shift through time. Thus planned saving will be a constant fraction of income at each degree of capacity working, and it will be a higher fraction of income at a higher degree of capacity working.

II and SS cut at Y which shows the degree of capacity working where planned saving equals planned investment. Y will show the equilibrium degree of capacity working at any time. The equilibrium at Y is stable if SS is steeper than II, and it is unstable if II is steeper than SS.[4]

The conditions for steady and stable growth at the 'natural' rate can now be outlined. For G, the actual rate of growth to continuously equal G_n, four conditions must be satisfied. First, productive capacity must grow at the 'natural' rate. Second, output must grow at the 'natural' rate, i.e., at the same rate as capacity. This condition will be satisfied if capacity grows at the 'natural' rate, and the degree of capacity working is constant. Third, the expected rate of growth must equal the actual rate of growth, so it must be expected that output will grow at the 'natural' rate. Fourth, there must be a stable equilibrium degree of capacity working at all times. The circumstances where these conditions will be fulfilled will now be outlined.

The first condition is that productive capacity grows at the 'natural' rate. This condition will be satisfied if Y, which shows the equilibrium where II and SS cut is always on NN. If Y is below NN, investment and the rate of growth of capacity will be insufficient for the 'natural' rate of growth, while investment will be more than that needed if Y is above NN.

The second condition is that output must grow at the 'natural' rate. This condition will be satisfied if capacity grows at the 'natural' rate, and the degree of capacity working is constant, which will be achieved if the investment and saving functions intersect at a given point on NN. For this, II and SS must intersect on NN, and there must be no tendency for II and SS to shift.

The third condition is that the expected rate of growth must equal the actual and the 'natural' rates. This condition will only be satisfied if II passes through E in Figure 1, i.e., if investment is just sufficient for the 'natural' rate of growth at a degree of capacity working of 100. Where II is below E, the expected rate of growth is less than the 'natural' rate, while it exceeds the 'natural' rate where II is above E.

The fourth condition for steady stable growth at the 'natural' rate is that the equilibrium at Y must be stable. This condition will be satisfied if SS is steeper than II. If II is steeper than SS, any chance disturbance will lead to unlimited expansion or contraction.

---

[4] If SS is steeper than II, planned saving will exceed planned investment to the right of Y causing the degree of capacity working to fall towards that at Y, and planned investment will exceed planned saving to the left of Y, causing the degree of capacity working to rise. Hence, the equilibrium at Y is stable. It is unstable if II is steeper than SS because the degree of capacity working would always move further away from Y if it was at all away from that at Y. (See Kaldor, 1940.)

The effect of these conditions is shown on Figure 3. *SS* and *II* both pass through *E* where investment is just sufficient for the 'natural' rate of growth, the degree of capacity working is 100, and *SS* is steeper than *II*. At *E* growth will continue at the 'natural' rate. Capacity will grow at the 'natural' rate. There will be no tendency for the degree of capacity working to alter, for *SS* will continue to pass through *E*, and with a constant rate of profit, and exactly the rate of growth which entrepreneurs expect, and exactly the degree of capacity working which they desire, *II* will not alter through time, so it will continue to pass through *E*. Moreover, the equilibrium at *E* is stable.

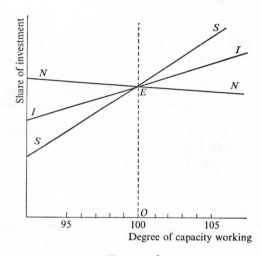

FIGURE 3

Some of these conditions are equivalent to the conditions for growth at the 'natural' rate in Sir Roy Harrod's argument. The condition that *SS* must pass through *E*, i.e., that planned saving at normal capacity working must just equal the investment needed for the 'natural' rate of growth is equivalent to the condition that the 'natural' rate of growth must equal the 'warranted' rate of growth. The condition that *II* should pass through *E*, i.e., that planned investment at normal capacity working must just equal the investment needed for the 'natural' rate of growth is equivalent to the condition he was concerned with in 1964, that investment should be just sufficient for the 'natural' rate of growth where C equals C_r. The condition that *SS* should be steeper than *II* is one which Professor Kaldor has considered important,[5] but it is the opposite of the normal situation in the Harrod model. In the latter, a departure from equilibrium, i.e., a departure of G from G_w, leads to a greater rise (or fall) in

[5] Kaldor, 1940 and 1957.

planned investment than in planned saving, with consequently unlimited expansion or contraction.

It is to be noted that much more is needed for growth at the 'natural' rate than equality between G_w and G_n. These will only be equal by chance, but even if they are equal, II must pass through E, i.e., growth expectations, etc., must be appropriate to the 'natural' rate of growth, and SS must be steeper than II if any kind of comfortable progress is to be possible. It is almost inconceivable that an economy could arrive at this fortunate situation without government intervention, and the remainder of the argument will be concerned with how the government can solve the problems raised by the need to fulfil these conditions.

It is generally accepted that the government has sufficient policy tools to control the *level* of SS. With control over personal and company taxation, and control over public expenditure on current account, it can influence the proportion of the National Income which is consumed—and therefore the proportion which is saved. The effects of changes in taxation and public expenditure on consumption may not be precisely those predicted, and there may be unpredictable changes in consumption due to shifts in the consumption function, but such effects can be largely corrected for subsequently. It is arguable that the principal difficulties involved in the control of the economy are not those associated with control of the *level* of SS. It will therefore be assumed that the government can control the level of SS through changes in taxation and public expenditure.

Control over the slope of SS is more difficult. This is influenced by the progressiveness of the tax system, and a limit is set to this by the view a society takes of social justice and necessary incentives. If there is a limit to the progressiveness of the tax system due to such considerations, the government cannot prevent the increased incomes associated with a rise in the degree of capacity working from leading to a moderate increase in consumption, and it cannot prevent the lower incomes (and unemployment) associated with a low degree of capacity working from leading to a fall in consumption. The government cannot then increase the steepness of SS beyond a certain point. The assumptions which will be made about SS are then that its level can be whatever the government wishes, and that its steepness is limited.

Investment depends on the degree of capacity working, the rate of profit, and growth expectations. To control investment, the government must influence one or more of these. Initially, it will be assumed that the government's only control over investment is through the degree of capacity working (which it can influence through its control over SS). Whether this will be sufficient for the achievement of stable growth at the 'natural' rate will now be analysed.

In the absence of government intervention, there is no guarantee that II will be such that investment will be sufficient for G_n at normal capacity working. Investment may well be less than this, and the II line will then cut the vertical line showing a degree of capacity working of 100 below E, as in Figure 4. Here investment is OX at a degree of capacity working of 100, which is insufficient for G_n, and it will only be sufficient for G_n if the degree of capacity working is 104. Alternatively, the II line could be the much higher $I'I'$, in which case investment would be OX' at 100, which would be more than that needed for G_n.

If the government continuously adjusts SS so that a degree of capacity working of 100 is maintained, a growth rate of capacity of G_n will eventually be achieved from either of these situations. Consider first the situation where investment is insufficient for G_n at normal capacity working. By continuously maintaining the degree of capacity working at 100, the government ensures

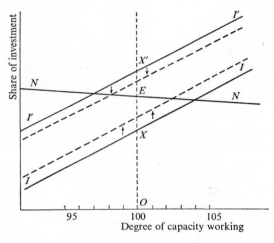

FIGURE 4

that output will grow at precisely the same rate as capacity, but this grows at a slower rate than G_n because investment is less than OE. However, because investment is insufficient for G_n, the rate of profit will be rising, and this will have a favourable effect on II. The II line will rise steadily from period to period as the rate of profit rises, and, as the rates of growth of capacity and output tend towards the 'natural' rate, the expected rate of growth will also tend towards the 'natural' rate which will raise II further, until X and E coincide, and investment is just sufficient for G_n. Once X and E coincide, there will be no further tendency for the rate of profit to rise, II will rise no further, and growth at rate G_n can be maintained at normal capacity working from then onwards. Similarly, starting from the much higher $I'I'$ where X' is above E, capacity and output will rise at a faster rate than G_n at a degree of capacity working of 100, but this will cause the rate of profit to fall continuously until

X' and E coincide. The actual and expected growth rates will then fall steadily towards the 'natural' rate.

The government can therefore achieve growth at the 'natural' rate in the fullness of time, if it is prepared to use its control over the level of SS to maintain continuous normal capacity working. The rate of profit will provide the adjusting mechanism to investment. Where the rate of growth is less than G_n, the rising rate of profit will raise investment steadily, and therefore the growth rate which will lead to improved expectations which will raise investment further. Where the rate of growth exceeds G_n, the falling rate of profit will reduce investment, etc. This process for the achievement of growth at the 'natural' rate may, however, be a very lengthy one, particularly if X is some way below E and investment is not very elastic with respect to the rate of profit. Indeed, the rise in II due to a rising rate of profit could be so gradual that G_n would only be achieved in the course of decades, which would make this strategy for raising the growth rate to G_n somewhat unattractive. There is no reason why reducing the growth rate slowly to G_n where X' is above E should cause problems; but where investment is insufficient for G_n because X is below E, an alternative to a slow rise in II because of the rising rate of profit which is associated with growth at less than the 'natural' rate must be found.

Working still with the assumption that control over the degree of capacity working via control over SS is the government's only method of control, there is an alternative line of policy for the achievement of G_n. The degree of capacity working can be made such that investment will be just sufficient for G_n. In Figure 5, the II line cuts NN at a degree of capacity working of 104. If the government causes SS to pass through Y, the equilibrium degree of capacity working will be 104, and investment will be just sufficient for G_n. If taxation and public expenditure are so adjusted that SS continues to pass through Y, growth at the 'natural' rate will be maintained in the absence of changing expectations. With the maintenance of Y on NN, capacity will grow at the 'natural' rate which will keep the rate of profit constant, and with a constant degree of capacity working, output will grow at the same rate as capacity, i.e., at the 'natural' rate. However, if growth is maintained at the 'natural' rate for some time in this way, the expected rate of growth will rise towards the 'natural' rate which will raise II towards $I'I'$. As II rises towards $I'I'$, the degree of overcapacity working can be gradually reduced (by shifting SS towards $S'S'$), and the economy can be so managed that it will tend from Y towards E, as the expected rate of growth tends towards the 'natural' rate. Where this method of taking the economy towards E is used, capacity grows at the 'natural' rate throughout the adjustment process, and the rate of growth of output is continuously close to the 'natural' rate. It is then apparently preferable to use this method to achieve stable growth at the 'natural' rate, rather than the method of maintaining a continuous degree of capacity working of 100 which was outlined above.

However, the process of adjustment where the economy shifts from Y towards E may not be entirely comfortable, or even tolerable. The degree of capacity working may be little more than 100 during the period of adjustment, but this will be the degree of capacity working of the *representative* firm. A number of firms are likely to have 10 to 15 per cent less capacity than they consider to be ideal to produce current output where the representative firm has 3 to 4 per cent less, and there will be delayed deliveries in these sectors of the economy, and probably quite heavy importing of goods which would not be imported at a degree of capacity working of 100. Moreover, if overcapacity working is associated (as is likely) with labour scarcity, econometric studies by

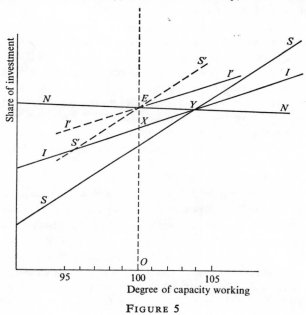

FIGURE 5

Dow and Dicks-Mireaux (1959) suggest that wages may well rise rather quickly, for they find that in the United Kingdom from 1946 to 1956, an excess of vacancies over unemployment of 1 per cent of the labour force was associated with a faster rise in earnings of about $2\frac{3}{4}$ per cent per annum. This would lead to faster cost inflation, for overcapacity working cannot increase the growth rate as much as this for more than a transient period—for the growth rate will only exceed G_n (where investment is just sufficient for G_n) to the extent that the degree of capacity working is *rising*. Hence, overcapacity working is likely to damage the balance of payments, both because cost inflation is likely to be faster if it is at all prolonged, and because some sectors of the economy will be so short of capacity that the goods they cannot produce (without long delivery delays) will be imported. These adverse effects on the balance of payments will not necessarily lead to a deficit. If they lead to a deficit (and this might well be the case), using up reserves, borrowing, or special measures to limit imports may well make it possible for the policy to be persisted with until the expected rate of growth rises to G_n. The economy can then run close to E with little overcapacity working, and less adverse pressure on the balance of payments. However, it is possible that the effects of overcapacity working on the balance of payments may be so unfavourable (and methods of dealing with the consequent deficit limited by various constraints) that the maintenance of continuous overcapacity working might prove to be impracticable. In that case, an alternative method of achieving growth at the 'natural' rate would be needed.

Continuous undercapacity working, as advocated by Professor F. W. Paish (1962) is hardly a satisfactory solution to the problem, for if II is below E at normal capacity working, investment will be insufficient for the 'natural' rate of growth to an even greater extent with excess capacity working.

If overcapacity working has to be ruled out because of its adverse effect on the balance of payments, and undercapacity working is ruled out because of its adverse effect on investment, it follows that the government must maintain continuous normal capacity working via its control over SS, and it will be assumed in what follows that the government maintains normal capacity working, via control over SS.

It is to be noted that there may be a problem in addition to those so far discussed. If II is steeper than SS, no equilibrium will be stable, and any sort of orderly progress will be impossible. Any expansion will be associated with an excess of planned investment over planned saving which will lead to *pure demand inflation*, and inevitable balance of payments difficulties. This *pure demand inflation* must be distinguished from the situation discussed above where planned investment *equals* planned saving at a degree of capacity working of more than 100. There may then be shortages of some goods but the situation need not be unmanageable. Where II is steeper than SS, the situation is almost certain to be unmanageable, and it must be a prime aim of policy to make SS steeper or II less steep. It will be assumed in what follows that SS is made steeper than II so that the problems of an unstable equilibrium do not arise. SS may well be steeper than II in any case (as Professor Kaldor supposes [6]) so that intervention may not be needed to achieve this result.

With government control over SS to maintain a stable degree of capacity working of 100, the problem which needs to be solved is how the 'natural' rate of growth is to be achieved where investment is insufficient for this at normal capacity working. Where investment is more than sufficient, there is no problem, for the growth rate will fall slowly to G_n, and the fact that it falls slowly is no disadvantage. It is where investment is insufficient that there is a

[6] Kaldor, 1957.

problem, for here the growth rate will only rise to the 'natural' rate slowly in the absence of further intervention, and more than this is likely to be desired.

Apart from the degree of capacity working (which it may be inexpedient to use to achieve faster growth) investment is influenced by growth expectations and the rate of profit. Writing in 1964, Sir Roy Harrod took the view that growth expectations could be induced by 'indicative' planning. The present author argued the same view in 1966. The abandonment of *The National Plan* in the United Kingdom must have done much to undermine the view that II can be raised so that it passes through E (or in Sir Roy Harrod's terminology, so that investment is sufficient for G_n where $C = C_r$) by the publication of official documents, sold to the general public at 8*s*. 6*d*.[7] or £1 10*s*.[8] If the view that making investment sufficient for G_n through the effect of 'indicative' planning on expectations has to be abandoned, the only method of influencing business investment which remains is to influence it through the rate of profit.

A government can have little influence over the rate of profit before tax (at a given degree of capacity working) for this will be determined by technical factors and entrepreneural pricing policies which are not easily subject to government influence in the short run. However, investment decisions are likely to be much more influenced by the rate of profit net of tax. This is what will influence the internal finance available for investment, and it will also determine the period over which the capital committed to a project is recovered, so where investment decisions are based on pay-back criteria, more investment projects will be acceptable with a higher rate of profit net of tax. It then appears that the government could have an immediately favourable effect on II (in so far as its level depends on the rate of profit) by reducing the rate at which profits are taxed, provided that the benefits from lower profits taxation were not entirely passed on to consumers through lower prices.

An objection to this line of policy is that the taxation of profits is a method of reducing inequality. If profits need to be taxed at low rates to ensure that investment is sufficient for G_n, egalitarian policies will suffer. On the other hand, it is arguable that business must be taxed lightly where growth expectations are weak, and a balance of payments constraint prevents the correction of these weak expectations through overcapacity working. Where growth expectations are stronger, a society may be able to take more from business without frustrating growth.

Where growth expectations are weak, the conflict between equality and growth may not be quite as great as the argument of the last paragraph has suggested, for there are methods of stimulating investment which do not involve taxing all profits at low rates. One possibility here is a move towards 'free-depreciation', or the permitted write-off of the whole cost of an investment

[7] National Economic Development Council, *The Growth of the Economy*, H.M.S.O., 1964.
[8] *The National Plan*, H.M.S.O., 1965.

against taxation in the year the investment is made. This should precisely cancel out the effect of taxation on investment decisions, for with 'free-depreciation', the post-tax rate of return from investment is precisely the same as the rate of return before tax, to a company with more profits than investment.[9] Moreover, a business which always invested its entire profits would never pay tax, for its investment would be precisely offset against its entire profits in every year, reducing its taxable profits to zero. On the other hand, a business which invested nothing would pay the full rate of profits tax on its entire profits. Thus, with 'free-depreciation', profits taxation would further equality to the extent that profits were earned, and not immediately reinvested.

However, it would be wrong to think that a combination of high profits taxation and 'free-depreciation' would lead to as efficient a pattern of investment as a low overall rate of profits taxation. 'Free depreciation' makes internal finance (which can grow within a company without any payment of tax so long as profits earned from it are continuously reinvested) much cheaper than external finance, and this must impede the transfer of capital between sectors of the economy, and frustrate the growth of companies which require external finance.[10, 11]

[9] Suppose a company invests C in a project which is expected to yield gross profits of P_1 in its first year, P_2 in its second year, . . . and P_n in its nth year. With profits taxation (at a proportional rate of T) and 'free depreciation', the investment would reduce the company's tax bill by $C \cdot T$ in the year the investment was made, so the initial cost of the project (net of tax) would be $C(1 - T)$. The expected profits net of tax would all be $(1 - T)$ times the gross profits before tax (since no further depreciation allowances could be offset against them), so these would be $P_1(1 - T)$, $P_2(1 - T) \ldots . P_n(1 - T)$. Then profits taxation combined with 'free-depreciation' would reduce the cost of an investment and all gross profits earned from it in the same proportion $(1 - T) : 1$, so the expected rate of return from the project, i.e., the discount rate which equated the expected returns to the cost of the project, would be unaffected by T.

[10] If company A invests £1 million in its own operations, the £1 million can grow without any tax payments until the accumulated profits cease to be reinvested in its own operations. If it does not have an obvious outlet for the £1 million in its own operations and pays it out in dividends to its shareholders who subscribe what they receive to a new issue made by company B, what B will receive is £1 million net of corporation tax and the shareholders' income tax, or £321,750 with corporation tax at 45 per cent, and the standard rate of income tax at $41\frac{1}{2}$ per cent. It will then be in the shareholders' interests that A should reinvest the £1 million unless B can earn a very much higher rate of return. With no taxation of profits or dividends, B could receive £1 million where A decided not to invest £1 million, so it would be in the shareholders' interests that capital should be invested where it was expected to earn the highest returns.

[11] The minority report of the *Royal Commission on the Taxation of Profits and Incomes* (1955) which Mr. N. Kaldor signed puts the case against reliance on internal finance very strongly. 'It can be argued also that the system of financing capital expenditure so largely out of the undistributed profits of companies does not ensure the best use of the community's savings. It makes it more difficult for fast expanding firms to raise funds in the capital market; it strengthens the monopolistic tendencies in the economy, and it encourages wasteful expenditure on behalf of those firms who have more money than they can use and who are yet prevented (by custom and tradition as well as by the instruments of public control) from channelling those funds to their most profitable potential use' (pp. 387–8).

An alternative method of stimulating investment while at the same time taxing profits which are not invested at high rates for redistributional purposes is for the government effectively to pay part of the cost of investment through investment grants, investment allowances, or tax credits. These suffer from the defect that certain investments which actually have the effect of reducing the growth rate will become profitable to business if the government pays part of the cost of investment. For instance, with cash grants for investment at 20 per cent, the rate ruling in the United Kingdom in 1970 for investment (outside development areas) in new plant and machinery, an investment which cost £1,000 and earned gross profits of £984 over three years would produce a net post tax rate of return on capital of 10 per cent.[12] However the investment of £1,000 which produces aggregate gross profits of £984 will most probably *reduce* the United Kingdom's growth rate, for £1,000 worth of plant and machinery is put into the economy and only £984 is obtained from this; less than sufficient to maintain capital intact and earn zero profits.

Hence, any attempt to stimulate investment by raising the post-tax rate of return on capital other than a straightforward reduction in the overall rate of profits taxation will only stimulate investment at the cost of a reduction in the overall growth effectiveness of investment. With accelerated depreciation (and 'free-depreciation' is the extreme form of this), investment will be stimulated, but it will be made predominantly out of retained earnings by businesses currently earning high profits. The transfer of capital between businesses and between different sectors of the economy will be prohibitively expensive. With investment grants, etc., investment will be stimulated, but a part of investment will consist of projects which make little positive contribution to growth, and possibly reduce it.

Hence, governments which seek to achieve growth at the 'natural' rate where business invests too little for this at normal capacity working face a most cruel set of alternatives. If they maintain continuous normal capacity working, growth at the 'natural' rate may not be achieved for a great many years. If they permit overcapacity working, investment will be sufficient for the 'natural' rate, but the period during which the expected rate of growth adjusts to the 'natural' rate is likely to be exceedingly uncomfortable so far as the balance of payments and price inflation are concerned. If they wish to use the tax system to stimulate investment and to redistribute incomes against profits at the same time, they will get more investment, but some of it will be rather ineffective investment. On the other hand, if they cut overall profits

---

[12] Discounting at 10 per cent per annum, the first year's gross profits of £328 (one-third of £984) have a 'present value' of £295 the second year's gross profits have a 'present value' of £265 10s., and the third year's of £239. The 'present value' of the total gross profits of £984, discounted at 10 per cent per annum, is the sum of these, or £799 10s., which equals approximately the £1,000 cost of the investment less a £200 cash grant—so approximately 10 per cent net will be earned on the original £800.

taxation, they should get more investment, and effective investment, but the distribution of incomes after tax may differ significantly from the distribution a society desires.

Governments in economies where business is prepared to invest enough for growth at the 'natural' rate at normal capacity working are most fortunate, for they do not need to choose between these alternatives.

Once the problem of achieving stable growth at the 'natural' rate has been solved, there will be a basis for the solution of further problems which have not been considered in this paper. There are a series of possible 'natural' rate growth paths, and while the rate of profit will be constant on each of these, some will have a lower rate of profit and higher consumption per worker than others. It may be an ultimate object of policy to achieve the 'natural' rate growth path where consumption per worker will be maximised. Before this objective can be approached, the basic problem of achieving growth at the 'natural' rate along one of the possible paths must be solved.

REFERENCES

DICKS-MIREAUX, L. A. and DOW, J. C. R. 'The Determinants of Wage Inflation in the United Kingdom, 1946–56', *Journal of the Royal Statistical Society*, 1959.
ELTIS, W. A., *Economic Growth* (London, 1966).
HARROD, R. F., 'An Essay in Dynamic Economics', *Economic Journal*, 1939.
——, *Towards a Dynamic Economics* (London, 1948).
——, 'Supplement on Dynamic Theory', *Economic Essays* (London, 1952), no. 14.
——, 'Second Essay in Dynamic Theory', *Economic Journal*, 1960.
——, 'Are Monetary and Fiscal Policies Enough?', *Economic Journal*, 1964.
KALDOR, N. 'A Model of the Trade Cycle', *Economic Journal*, 1940.
——, 'Alternative Theories of Distribution', *Review of Economic Studies*, 1955–6.
——, 'A Model of Economic Growth', *Economic Journal*, 1957.
PAISH, F. W., *Studies in an Inflationary Economy* (London, 1962).

Official Papers

Final Report of the Royal Commission on the Taxation of Profits and Income (Cmnd. 9474), H.M.S.O., June 1955.
National Economic Development Council, *The Growth of the Economy*, H.M.S.O., March 1964.
The National Plan (Cmnd. 2764), H.M.S.O., September 1965.

7

PROBLEMS OF FINANCING ECONOMIC DEVELOPMENT IN A MIXED ECONOMY

MICHAL KALECKI*

1. THE argument presented in this paper is based to a considerable extent on a distinction between two types of consumer goods: necessities and non-essentials. By necessities are meant goods which constitute a major part of the consumption of broad masses of the population. On the other hand non-essentials are consumed mainly by richer strata of the population. The chief items in necessities are staple foods.[1]

We make the following two assumptions on the financial aspects of economic development:

(a) There must be no inflationary price increases of necessities, in particular staple foods.

(b) No taxes should be levied on lower-income groups or necessities so that restraining of consumer demand must be effected through raising direct taxes on higher-income groups or indirect taxes on non-essentials.

It will be seen that these two assumptions are of considerable significance for the course of economic development because they make it dependent to a great extent on the rate of increase of the supply of necessities.

2. Let us now consider a development plan for a medium period, say, five to ten years. Let us denote the average rate of growth of the national income by r. We shall try to show that the rate of increase of the supply of necessities required in order to warrant the growth of the national income at a rate r without infringing upon our two basic postulates is a definite increasing function of r.

Let us assume for the moment that aggregate personal consumption increases proportionately to the national income, i.e., at a rate r, and that there are no major changes in the distribution of personal incomes between various classes of the population, such as, e.g., those caused by the increase in the prices of necessities or by changes in taxation. Then to the rate of growth of

---

* Michal Kalecki died in April 1970. At his widow's request, the proofs of this essay were kindly corrected by Professor Wlodzimierz Brus.

[1] It follows from this definition that the list of necessities will widen with the long-run increase in the standard of living.

the national income r there corresponds a definite rate of increase of demand for necessities c_n. If the rate of growth of national income and thus of total consumption r is equal to the rate of increase of population q, so that per capita consumption remains unaltered, the rate of increase of demand for necessities is equal to q as well: $r = q = c_n$. If, however, the rate of growth r is higher than the rate of increase of population q then per capita consumption will increase (approximately) at a rate $r - q$ and the rate of increase of per capita demand for necessities will be $c_n - q$ which will in general be lower than $r - q$. If we denote the average income elasticity of demand for necessities by e we can say that:

$$c_n - q = e(r - q)$$

where e is in general less than one. From this we derive

$$c_n = q + e(r - q).$$

The average income elasticity of demand for necessities e depends on such elasticities for various classes of the population and on income distribution between these classes.

We also should take into consideration that, strictly speaking, e changes within the period considered. Indeed, as per capita consumption increases the income elasticity of demand for necessities tends to decline. This effect is the more pronounced the higher the rate of growth r, so that e should be really assumed a declining function of r. But as r is in fact a rather low percentage and the period encompassed not very long the influence of r upon e is of no great importance and may be neglected.

Thus e in the above equation may be considered a constant so that c_n appears to be a linear function of r. This is shown diagrammatically in Figure 1. The straight line inclined less than $45°$ ($e < 1$) passes through the point B for which both the abscissa and the ordinate are equal to the rate of increase in population q. This point stands for the situation where there is no increase in total per capita consumption and thus the demand for necessities increases at a rate q as well. If $r = OM$ is higher than q, then the same is true of $c_n = MN$; however, c_n is less than r, the point N being situated below the $45°$ line OQ.

3. We assumed in the preceding paragraph that total consumption changes proportionately to the national income. This, however, was intended merely to simplify a stage in our argument. In fact it may be necessary, as will be seen below, to restrain consumption in order to allow for a more rapid increase in investment than that of national income. In such a case consumption will have to be restrained by taxation. According to our rules of the game this will consist of raising taxes on higher-income groups and on non-essentials. The question arises here whether this will not upset the functional relations between c_n and r arrived at above.

It should be noted, however, that the taxation of higher-income groups or non-essentials will hardly affect significantly the consumption of necessities by the well-to-do. Thus the relation between the rate of increase of demand for necessities corresponding to the rate of growth of national income will continue to be represented with a fair approximation by the above equation or Figure 1. Hence c_n can be considered the approximate value of the rate of increase of supply of necessities which warrants the rate of growth of national income at a rate of r without infringing our basic assumptions.

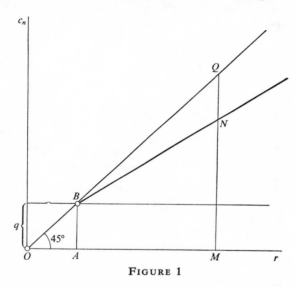

FIGURE 1

4. The relation between the rate of growth c of total consumption and that of the national income r is of an entirely different character from that between c_n and r considered above. In order to sustain the growth of the national income at a rate r a part of this income must be, of course, devoted to investment. Now the higher the rate of growth the higher the relative share of investment in the national income. Indeed, the higher the increment of the national income at its given level the higher the investment required in order to achieve it. Thus the higher the ratio of the increment of the national income to its level—or the higher the rate of growth—the higher the ratio of investment to the national income.

Imagine that we start from a position characterized by a rate of growth, r_0, to which corresponds a certain relative share of investment in the national income. If this rate of growth is continued the relative share of investment in the national income is maintained (unless, of course, there is a change in the capital-output ratio). But if the average rate of growth envisaged in the plan is higher so will be the average relative share of investment in the national income. This means that the relative share of investment in the national income will be increasing from the beginning to the end of the plan. (For instance, it may be 14 per cent at the beginning of a five-year plan, 20 per cent at its end, and 17 per cent on the average.) The relative share of consumption in the national income will be correspondingly falling. In other words the average rate of growth of consumption c will be lower than that of the national income r. The difference, $r - c$, will be the higher the greater is the average rate of growth of the national income r in relation to r_0; because where r is higher the acceleration of the rate of growth as compared with the initial position will be greater and thus the increase in the relative share of investment in the national income will be greater in the period considered.

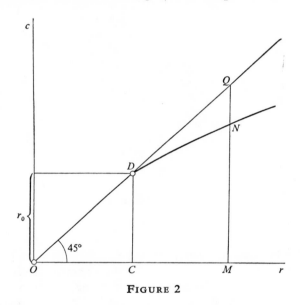

FIGURE 2

The relation between c and r is represented on Figure 2 by the curve DN. The point D represents the initial position at which the rate of growth equals $r_0 = OC$. If this is the rate adopted in the plan consumption need not increase more slowly than the national income; i.e. $c = CD = r_0$. Thus the point D is situated on a 45° line OQ.

If, however, the average rate of growth of the national income $r = OM$ envisaged in the plan is higher than r_0 the rate of growth of consumption $c = MN$ is lower than r and thus is below the 45° line OQ, the difference $r - c = NQ$ being more marked the higher is r.

The rate of growth of consumption c as determined by the curve DN shows how much it is possible to increase consumption after a sufficient allowance has been made for investment required to sustain the growth of the national income at a rate r. If r is higher than the rate of growth in the initial position r_0, the increase in consumption will have to be restrained by taxation to provide for the rise in the relative share of investment in the national income. (In case this rise is effected through expansion of private investment the revenue from the additional taxation serves to create an 'offsetting' budget surplus.)

As already mentioned above, according to our basic postulates additional taxes will have to be levied on higher income groups or non-essentials. Thus the curve DN indicates what is the task of the government in checking the increase in consumption at a given rate of growth of national income, r, by means of this type of taxation.

5. Let us now consider the interrelation between the three rates, c_n, r, and c. We shall consider the case where the capital-output ratio does not increase over the level at the initial position; however, all our subsequent argument applies fully also to the case where such an increase does take place.

Let us combine Figure 1 and Figure 2 in Figure 3 (the letters of Figure 2 are now put in brackets to avoid confusion). It will be noticed that $r_0 = (O)(C)$ is greater than $q = OA$. Thus the rate of growth of national income in the initial position is assumed here to be higher than the rate of increase of population.

It is clear that of the three rates of growth in question c_n, c, r our diagram determines two if one is given. Now in underdeveloped mixed economies it is c_n, the rate of increase of supply of necessities that can be considered as given. The increase in production of necessities, especially of staple food, is limited by institutional factors, such as feudal land ownership and domination of peasants by merchants and money lenders. As a result c_n the average rate of increase in the supply of necessities over the planning period is kept down to a rather low level. It is true that supply of necessities is not identical with their production because they can be procured through foreign trade. We shall consider this problem at a later stage; for the time being we shall abstract from it, so that c_n is directly affected by the institutional barriers to the development of agriculture.

From the ceiling of the average rate of increase of supply of necessities which we denote by $c_{n \ max}$ we can determine by means of our diagram the rate of growth of the national income r and that of total consumption c. We draw a horizontal line at the level OE, find the point of intersection F with the straight line BN, project this point downwards and thus obtain $r = (O)(G)$ and $c = (G)(H)$.

In other words the rate of increase of supply of necessities $c_{n \ max}$, as fixed by institutional barriers to the development of agriculture, determines the rate of growth of national income r which is warranted without infringing our basic postulates. Next is determined the rate of growth of total consumption c which makes a sufficient allowance for investment required for the

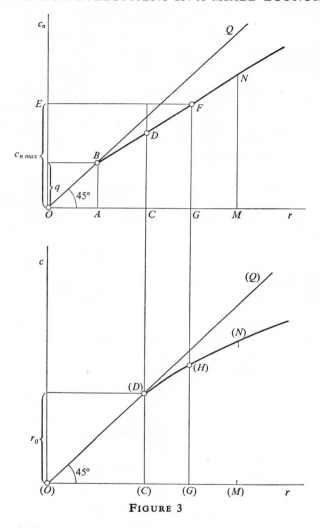

FIGURE 3

expansion of the national income at a rate r. In order to restrain the increase in total consumption to the rate c appropriate taxation of higher income groups and non-essentials must be devised. This seems to me the gist of the problem of financing economic development in a mixed economy.

According to this conception the main 'financial' problem of development is that of adequate agricultural production. The key to 'financing' a more rapid growth is the removal of obstacles to the expansion of agriculture, such as feudal land-ownership and domination of peasants by money lenders and merchants.

The other strictly financial problem of levying taxes on higher-income groups and non-essentials is also very grave because of the influence of vested interests upon the government and because of the difficulty of overcoming tax evasion. However, the main bottleneck in the balanced growth of a mixed economy seems usually to be the low rate of expansion of agriculture resulting from agrarian conditions. Indeed, the rate of growth of the national income determined by it in the way described above will not usually be so high as to present an insuperable problem of financing investment by taxation in such a way as not to affect low-income groups or the prices of necessities. However, if the problem of the inadequate increase of agricultural production were solved by means of agrarian reform, etc., so as to warrant a higher rate of balanced growth, a parallel effort would have to be made in the fiscal sphere in order to achieve an increase in taxation of high-income groups and non-essentials.

6. What happens, however, if the rate of growth of national income exceeds the level warranted by the rate of increase of supply of necessities? Let us assume that $r = OM$ is higher than OG (see Figure 3). Then c_n equals MN instead of GF. As the supplies of necessities forthcoming are inadequate to meet demand their prices rise.

Equilibrium is restored through a fall in the real income of the broad masses of the population while the extra profits of the capitalists do not increase the demand for necessities since they are spent on non-essentials or accumulated. Such extra accumulation reduces the need for taxation in order to finance investment. This is a reflection of the fact that the consumption of necessities and thus total consumption is restrained by the increase in their prices. It is true that this is partly offset by the extra consumption of non-essentials; but to the extent to which extra profits are accumulated, total consumption is on balance restrained.

Thus this type of growth involving inflationary price increases of necessities —against the first of our basic postulates—is definitely to the advantage of the upper classes. A relatively high rate of growth is secured without resorting to a radical reform of the agrarian conditions and with lower taxation of these classes than would be necessary if growth at this rate were balanced.

The aggregate consumption of the broad masses of the population is the same as it would be if the growth of national income were at a rate warranted by the actual rate of increase in the supply of necessities, i.e., it is the same at a rate of growth OM as at a rate of growth OG; employment is higher when $r = OM$, but real wages are correspondingly lower as a result of the increase in the prices of necessities. The higher relative share of investment which is necessary to increase the rate of growth from OG to OM is achieved at least in part at the expense of this fall in real wages.

Imagine that the planned rate of growth of the national income is OM.

Allowing for the investment necessary to implement that plan the planned rate of increase in consumption is $(M)(N)$. This plan will be fulfilled but the rate of increase in supply of necessities will be GF and not MN and the rate of increase in the consumption of non-essentials will accordingly be higher. A corresponding shift will occur in the structure of investment: the development of industries producing luxury goods will be emphasized. The rate of growth will indeed be higher than OG but growth itself will be lopsided.

7. We have so far disregarded foreign trade. However, for some countries it is a serious omission because they are able to purchase necessities abroad in exchange for exports, especially in the case where they are endowed with rich natural resources (e.g. the oil-producing countries). We shall try now, therefore, to introduce foreign trade into our model.

The rate of increase of supply of necessities c_n stood for the rate of production of necessities when foreign trade was disregarded and it was on this assumption that the argument in section 6 was based. If we introduce foreign trade, however, the straight line BN in Figure 3 ceases to represent the rate of increase of *production* of necessities p_n. If imports of necessities can be increased, more rapidly than their home production, the rate of increase of the latter is lower than that of the total supply of necessities.

Imagine that such is the case where $r = r_0$; i.e., where the rate of growth of the national income adopted in the plan is equal to the rate of growth in the initial position. Then where $r = r_0 = OC$ the curve IP (see Figure 4) relating the rate of increase in *home production* of necessities, p_n, to the rate of growth of national income, r, which it can warrant without infringing our basic postulates, will be situated below the straight line BN (which shows the rate of increase in the supply of necessities which is needed at different growth rates). The gap between BN and IP is made good through foreign trade.

However, as r becomes higher than r_0, the difference $c_n - p_n$ between the ordinates of the curves BN and IP will become smaller. Indeed, the higher the rate of growth, r, the more rapidly will the demand for imports other than necessities rise, and in particular the demand for investment goods. In general it will be increasingly difficult to balance imports by a rise in exports because of certain limitations either of supplies of export goods or of foreign markets. Thus it will become increasingly difficult to increase imports of necessities at a rate which permits the increase in their domestic production to lag behind demand requirements. Finally at the rate of growth corresponding to the point of intersection of the curves BN and IP home production and imports of necessities rise *pari passu*, c_n being equal to p_n. If the rate of growth of national income is pushed beyond that point, it appears that, in order to provide adequate imports of items other than necessities the rate of growth of the domestic production of necessities would have to be higher than that of the required supply.

Figure 4 shows the influence of foreign trade upon the rate of balanced growth. Let us draw, as in Figure 3, a horizontal line at the level OE of the maximum rate of growth of production of necessities $p_{n\ max}$. (We denoted this rate $c_{n\ max}$ in section 5 because $c_{n\ max} = p_{n\ max}$ if there is no foreign trade.) But now it will be the point of intersection of this line with the curve IP rather

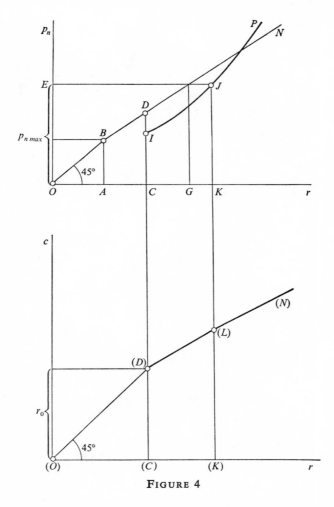

FIGURE 4

than with the curve BN that determines the rate of balanced growth. This rate of growth of the national income OK is higher than OG that would prevail without the contribution of foreign trade to the acceleration of the increase in the supply of necessities. Such will be, for instance, the position in the oil-producing countries.

If, however, the foreign trade situation is less favourable, so that the difference $c_n - p_n$ at the lower ranges of r is smaller than in Figure 4, the contribution of foreign trade to the achievement of a higher rate of balanced growth may be nil (see Figure 5). The horizontal line at the level OE here passes through the point of intersection of the curve IP with the straight line BN.

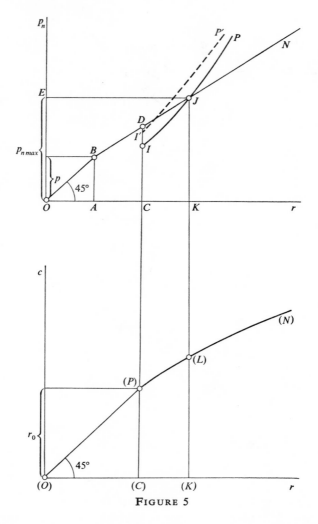

FIGURE 5

Indeed, the position may even be reversed. Foreign trade may affect the rate of balanced growth adversely by aggravating rather than relieving the problem of the adequate increase of the supply of necessities. Such will be, for instance, the case if the relation between p_n and r is as represented by the dotted curve $I'P'$.

In the case where a favourable foreign trade position may permit a given rate of increase of production of necessities p_n to warrant a higher rate of balanced growth r the purely financial problem of adequate taxation of higher-income groups and non-essentials will, of course, grow in relative importance.

8. We assumed tacitly in the preceding section that imports are fully covered by exports thus disregarding possible capital imports. We shall now consider the case where foreign credits are available to the government concerned

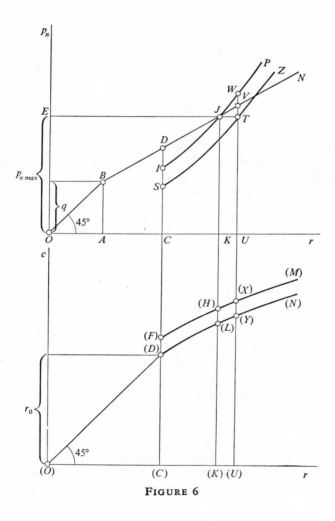

FIGURE 6

for the period encompassed by the plan (which was not the case prior to that period). This eases the position of the economy with regard to the supply of necessities and thus makes possible a higher rate of non-inflationary growth. This is illustrated by Figure 6.

As a situation which would exist if no foreign credits were forthcoming we choose the case where foreign trade does not contribute to the achievement of a higher rate of growth; the horizontal line at the level OE representing the rate of increase in the actual production of necessities; the straight line BN representing the rate of increase in the supply of necessities which warrants the rate of non-inflationary growth of the national income r; and finally the curve IP representing the respective rate of increase of required home-produced necessities—all three intersecting at point J. As a result of the availability of foreign credits the rate of increase in the supply of home produced necessities which warrants the rate of non-inflationary growth r will be represented by the curve SZ situated below the curve IP. In consequence the rate of non-inflationary growth will now be determined by the point of intersection T of the curve SZ and the horizontal drawn at the level OE. Since this point is to the right of J, the rate of non-inflationary growth OU is higher than OK which could have been realized in the absence of the import of capital.

It will be seen that, if there were no foreign credits, the rate of growth OU would require a rate of increase in the supply of necessities UV higher than UT and a still higher rate of increase in the *production* of necessities UW in order to cover the gap in foreign trade in other commodities. Foreign credits make it possible to reduce the rate of increase in the production of necessities for internal consumption to UT and to cover the gap in foreign trade in other commodities reflected in the discrepancy WV. Thus foreign credits will be used not only to supplement the home supplies of necessities but to make possible the required higher imports of other goods such as machinery or raw materials.

9. Foreign credits affect, however, not only the problem of the supply of necessities and the balancing of foreign trade in other commodities, but also the problem of financing investment and thus they reduce the need for taxation of non-essentials and higher income groups which is required in order to restrain the consumption of non-essentials.

Or to put it more precisely: as a result of foreign credits the total supply of goods will increase in the period considered more rapidly than the national income. However, the relative share of investment in the national income depending on the rate of growth of the latter will not be affected. Thus at a given rate of growth of the national income, the time-curve of investment will be the same as in the absence of foreign credits. It follows that total consumption will grow at a higher rate than it would have done at the same rate of growth of the national income if no foreign credits had been available. Since the rate of increase in the required supply of necessities (home produced or imported) corresponding to a given rate of growth remains the same, it is the consumption of non-essentials that will benefit and the need for restraining this will be accordingly reduced.

In the lower part of Figure 6 the higher permissible rate of increase in total consumption is now represented by the curve $(F)(M)$ which is situated above the curve $(D)(N)$. To the rate of growth OU based on availability of foreign credits thus corresponds the rate of increase in total consumption $(U)(X)$ which is higher than $(U)(Y)$ that would correspond to $r = (O)(U)$ if no foreign credits were forthcoming. Since the required rate of increase in the supply of necessities corresponding to $r = (O)(U)$ is UV with or without foreign credits, it is the rate of increase in the consumption of non-essentials that will benefit from $(U)(X)$ being higher than $(U)(Y)$.

10. It will be seen that when the import of capital is used to raise the rate of non-inflationary growth by supplementing the home supplies of necessities— the reduction of the taxes required to finance investment appears merely as a by-product of the process involved. However, it is perfectly feasible that capital imports may be used solely for budgetary purposes. The rate of non-inflationary growth remains at the level OK while taxation of non-essentials and higher incomes is reduced. As a result the rate of increase of total consumption is $(K)(H)$ and not $(K)(L)$, the consumption of non-essentials rising correspondingly faster. If the increased demand is directed towards foreign non-essentials it is reflected in their imports. In the case where home produced non-essentials are the object of this demand the production of investment goods has to be kept down by the authorities if inflationary pressures on necessities are to be avoided and thus investment requirements have to be to this extent satisfied by imports. In either case foreign credits are directly or indirectly wasted on non-essentials while economic growth is not accelerated, although in the second case foreign credits seem to be used 'productively'.

It should be noticed that even in the case where foreign credits *are* used to raise the rate of growth of the national income it is by no means *necessary* to reduce the taxation of non-essentials and higher incomes which permits a relatively faster increase in the consumption of non-essentials in the period encompassed by the plan. Indeed, the relief in the financing of investment which is a by-product of capital imports may be used for an expansion of government expenditure for such purposes as low cost housing, health and education.

At this point the question may arise how it is that capital imports manage to benefit the country considered in two ways. This, however, follows clearly from the two functions that capital imports perform: first, the availability of a certain amount of foreign exchange enables the country concerned to modify its *structure* of home supplies, e.g., to increase the supply of necessities; second, by raising the *volume* of home supplies without creating new incomes foreign credits contribute to the economic surplus and thus they reduce *pro tanto* the need for domestic savings.

8

THE GAP BETWEEN ACTUAL AND POTENTIAL OUTPUT IN GROWING ADVANCED ECONOMIES

KENNETH K. KURIHARA

1. *Preliminary Remarks*

THIS essay is broadly intended to implement Sir Roy Harrod's fundamental concept of 'the welfare optimum'[1] against the background of Keynes's allusion to a growing affluent society's widening 'gap between its actual and its potential production'.[2] My specific purpose, however, is to analyse the paradox of affluence on different structural assumptions from those made by Harrod (and Keynes before him), with an ultimate view to indicating the technical condition to be satisfied by design for securing 'the welfare optimum' in Harrod's sense.

Many writers have observed and lamented over the anomalous fact that the economic growth of mature capital-rich countries is lagging not only relatively to that of maturing capital-rich countries but also relatively to their own growth potential.[3] Harrod has himself noted the secular tendency of the American economy, for example, to grow at an actual rate lower than 'the maximum sustainable rate of progress . . . having regard to technical progress and population'.[4] He has attributed the failure of a mature capital-rich

---

[1] Harrod, 1966, p. 297. As far as I know, Sir Roy used the expression 'the welfare optimum' in that writing for the first time to characterize his 'natural' rate of growth. The welfare content of this latter will be made clear a little later.

[2] 'The richer the community,' warned Keynes, 'the wider will tend to be the gap between its actual and potential production; and therefore the more obvious and outrageous the defects of the economic system.' He explained this 'paradox of poverty in the midst of plenty' by reference to a wealthy community's greater need 'to discover much ampler opportunities for investment if the saving propensities of its wealthier members are to be compatible with the employment of its poorer members', an investment need that is seldom fulfilled in peace-time and in conditions mainly of *laissez-faire*. See Keynes, 1936, p. 31.

[3] See, e.g., Hansen, 1962; American Bankers Association, *A Symposium on Economic Growth* (including such participants as P. A. Samuelson, R. M. Solow, R. R. Nathan, and Per Jacobsson); and National Commission on Technology, Automation, and Economic Growth, *Technology and the American Economy* (the Commission being headed by H. R. Bowen and including R. M. Solow among its members).

[4] Harrod, 1966, p. 303.

economy to attain 'the welfare optimum' (in his sense) to the persistent tendency of its 'warranted' growth rate to be above its 'natural' growth rate.[5] The essence of his argument seems to be this: If the rate of capital accumulation 'warranted' by the economy's saving persistently exceeds the 'natural' rate of output expansion allowed by its population growth and technological advance, the economy will, *cet. par.*, stagnate eventually and chronically for lack of labour to man a growing stock of capital (when the full-employment ceiling is reached) or because of the depressing impact of excessive capital on further investment (even before full employment).[6]

Harrod's 'dynamized version of the stagnation thesis',[7] as such, sounds like a sophisticated variant of Marx's 'breakdown theory' which runs in terms of self-destroying contradictions of capitalism.[8] Be that as it may, Harrod seems fairly optimistic about the ability of a modern mixed economy to achieve 'the welfare optimum' in his sense. Otherwise he would not have added: 'The target of policy should be to bring the warranted rate as near as possible to the natural rate.'[9] Thus Harrod's juxtaposition of the 'warranted' and the 'natural' growth rate represents at once a helpful starting point and a useful point of departure for further theoretical explorations and practical experiments in the arena of economic dynamics. The present essay owes its inspiration to Sir Roy Harrod's seminal insights,[10] and is hopefully designed to help push the frontiers of dynamic economics further along the lines of *structural* analysis and *conscious* policy.

2. *The Harrodian Concept of 'The Welfare Optimum'*

To Harrod 'the welfare optimum' is a proxy for the 'natural' rate of growth of output defined by him as 'the rate of advance which the increase of population and technological improvements allow'.[11] He seems to regard the 'natural' rate thus defined as 'the welfare optimum' presumably because it would, if realized, guarantee fuller employment and better living on a continuous basis. Thus his 'natural' rate is a *potential maximand* to be achieved within the technical limits set by the fundamental forces of population growth

[5] Ibid., pp. 300–1.
[6] Harrod, 1948, especially where he states: 'the relation of G_n (natural rate) to G_w (warranted rate) is clearly of crucial importance in determining whether the economy over a term of years is likely to be preponderatingly lively or depressed' (pp. 87–8).
[7] Harrod, 1966, p. 298. For the *original* 'stagnation thesis', see Keynes, 1936, Ch. 16, and 1937; and Hansen, 1938.
[8] Tsuru, 1954 (especially where he compares Harrod and Marx, pp. 328–30). Also see Steindl, 1952.
[9] Harrod, 1966, p. 298.
[10] Harrod's 'An Essay in Dynamic Theory' (1939) and *Towards a Dynamic Economics* (1948) have, I think, definitely established him as *the* father of an *operationally significant* dynamic economics in the *modern* history of economic thought.
[11] Harrod, 1948, p. 87.

and technological advance, as well as a *social optimand* to be desired for the long-run welfare of a growing labour force with an increasing productivity.[12] As such, Harrod's 'natural' growth rate is to be considered more fundamental and general than his 'warranted' rate.[13] For the 'natural' rate of growth, when rigorously determined, would serve as an indispensable guide-post for the target-setting and policy-making of *any* growing economy, *irrespective of* economic organization and political ideology.

We may approximate Harrod's concept of 'the welfare optimum' as follows. Let the *potential* output obtainable by fully employing the available labour force equipped with the given stock of capital take the dynamic form[14]

$$(1.1) \qquad Y^p{}_t = N_t\, Z_t \qquad (t = 0, \ldots, n)$$

where Y^p is potential productive capacity, N the demographically given labour force when fully employed, Z the technologically given productivity of labour (reciprocal of the labour–output ratio), and t time. The independent variables of equation (1.1) can be specified in the exponential forms

$$(1.2) \qquad N_t = N_0 e^{\lambda t} \qquad (t = 0, \ldots, n)$$

$$(1.3) \qquad Z_t = Z_0\, e^{\pi t} \qquad (t = 0, \ldots, n)$$

where N_0 and Z_0 are the initial conditions, while λ and π are respectively the average annual rate of increase in the labour force and that in labour productivity. Taking equations (1.1)–(1.3) into account, we have

$$(1.4) \qquad Y^p{}_t = Y^p{}_0\, e^{(\pi + \lambda)t} \qquad (t = 0, \ldots, n)$$

and where g^p is the average annual rate of growth of potential output:

$$(1.5) \qquad g^p = \lambda + \pi$$

Thus the *average annual rate of growth of potential output* comes to the sum of the rate of growth of the fully-employed labour force (λ) and the rate of growth of labour productivity (π). This g^p given by equation (1.5) would, *if realized*, guarantee not only continuous full employment of labour but also a rising standard of living (due to $\pi > 0$) *pari passu* with population growth and

---

[12] Compare Kurihara, 1959, Ch. 3.

[13] A separate and detailed discussion of the 'warranted' rate will be found in the next section of this essay.

[14] This is the reduced form of the production function applicable to the case where labour is the limiting factor of production, and where factor specificity technically prevents capital from being readily substituted for labour regardless of relative input prices. Thus in a capital-rich economy the usual production function $Y = f(N, K)$ must be replaced by $Y = N/v$, where Y is output, N labour–input, K capital–input, and v the labour–output ratio. This latter production function presupposes the general form $Y = \min(N/v, K/b)$ implying that $Y = N/v$ when $N/v < K/b$ as in a capital-rich economy. In words, output cannot exceed labour–input divided by the labour–output ratio regardless of the quantity of capital–input available.

technological advance. It is the rigorous version of Harrod's intuitively defined 'natural' rate of growth and at the same time the formal representation of his 'welfare optimum'. Since the rate of growth of the labour force (λ) and that of labour productivity (π) are measurable and predictable, the above derivation by means of (1.1)–(1.5) transforms Harrod's 'welfare optimum' into an operational target to aim at in any foreseeable future.

The optimal–maximal line of steady advance expressed by equation (1.5) could be attained and maintained *only if* demand and capital grew at the same rate, g^p. But the basic difficulty with capital-rich economies in general is that the richer they become, the wider will tend to be the gap between their rate of growth of *actual* output from demand and capital and their rate of growth of *potential* output from full employment and technological improvements, to dynamize Keynes' aforementioned warning. I propose in the subsequent sections to discuss the *modus operandi* of this paradox of affluence in a dynamic setting. The next logical step to take, therefore, is a *closer* examination of Harrod's concept of the 'warranted' growth rate in the light of post-Keynesian theoretical developments.

3. *The Derivation and Dual Meaning of the 'Warranted Rate'*

We have learned from Keynes that in given conditions of supply *actual* output is determined by *effective demand*, that is, by the interaction of investment and saving. More recently Harrod has told us: 'My warranted rate is simply the dynamized version of Keynes' excess or deficiency of aggregate effective demand in relation to what is required for full employment.'[15] Since Harrod has not himself shown in detail how exactly his 'warranted rate' represents 'the dynamized version' of Keynes' static 'Principle of Effective Demand',[16] it seem useful to work out the derivation of Harrod's demand-oriented 'warranted' rate of growth (in my own symbolism).

Let the capital-rich economy's supply–demand equilibrium condition to be satisfied take the basic form

$$(2.1) \qquad Y^a_t = C_t + I_t; \qquad I_t = S_t,$$

where Y^a is actual output, C consumption expenditure, I net investment-demand, S net saving, and t time. As is well known, (2.1) expresses Keynes' *macrostatic* equilibrium condition in two equivalent forms. Now enters Harrod to specify the investment and saving variables of (2.1) respectively as

$$(2.2) \qquad I_t = b \, \Delta Y^a_t, \qquad (b = \text{const.})$$

$$(2.3) \qquad S_t = s Y^a_t, \qquad (s = \text{const.})$$

where b is the marginal ratio of investment-demand to actual output and

---

[15] Harrod, 1966, p. 298.   [16] Keynes, 1936, Ch. 3.

identical with Harrod's 'required capital coefficient' (C_r), while s is the average saving ratio in Harrod's sense of 'the reciprocal of the multiplier' (also s in his notation; $s = 1/k$, where k is the Keynesian investment multiplier).[17] The parenthetical constancy assumptions about b and s, while necessary for Harrod's case for 'steady advance', nevertheless will be relaxed in our later analysis of structural factors affecting their secular behaviour. Meanwhile we are getting closer to Harrod's 'dynamized version' of Keynes' investment-saving theory, especially by virtue of the former's 'acceleration principle' expressed by equation (2.2).

Taking equations (2.2) and (2.3) into account, the investment–saving equilibrium condition expressed by (2.1) can be rewritten as

$$(2.4) \qquad b\,\varDelta Y^a_t = s Y^a_t,$$

dividing which equation through by Y^a_t gives

$$(2.5) \qquad b\frac{\varDelta Y^a_t}{Y^a_t} = s; \qquad \frac{I_t}{\varDelta Y^a_t}\frac{\varDelta Y^a_t}{Y^a_t} = \frac{I_t}{Y^a_t} = \frac{S_t}{Y^a_t}.$$

Equation (2.5) is Harrod's condition for 'entrepreneurial equilibrium', which dynamic investment-saving equilibrium condition in terms of *ratios* represents a highly important step beyond the more familiar static Keynesian condition expressed by equation (2.1). For Harrod's investment *ratio* is the joint product of the accelerator (b) times the *rate of growth* of actual output ($\varDelta Y^a/Y^a$) as equation (2.5) clearly demonstrates, whereas Keynes' autonomous investment in terms of levels ($I = \bar{I}$) is definitionally independent of such a rate of growth of output.

Dividing equation (2.4) through by $b Y^a_t$ yields the *rate of growth of actual output* (g^a):

$$(2.6) \qquad g^a \equiv \frac{\varDelta Y^a_t}{Y^a_t} = \frac{s}{b},$$

which is synonymous with Harrod's 'warranted' growth rate (G_w) given as the transpose of his $G_w C_r = s$ expressing 'the equilibrium of a steady advance'.[18] Equation (2.6) shows the possibility of the rate of growth of actual output varying directly with the saving ratio and inversely with the accelerator. A seeming paradox is involved here, for Harrod's 'warranted' growth equation (in the transposed form $G_w = s/C_r$) indicates saving as a force tending to *increase* effective demand (s being the *numerator*) while Keynes' multiplier

---

[17] Since the saving ratio involved in Keynes' multiplier theory runs in marginal terms, Harrod's s as 'the reciprocal of the multiplier' logically presupposes a long-run saving function with a zero intercept that renders the marginal and the average saving ratio equal. Such a presupposition is also essential to any meaningful comparison of Harrod and Domar, as will be shown presently.

[18] Harrod, 1948, p. 81.

equation shows saving as a force tending to *decrease* it (s being the *denominator* in $\Delta Y = \Delta I/s = 1/s(\Delta I) = k\,\Delta I$). However, a moment's reflection would dispel any misgivings about such a paradox, for Harrod's 'warranted' growth rate G_w (or our g^a) is the rate of actual output expansion *required to induce enough investment-demand* to absorb saving in terms of ratios when the accelerator C_r (or our b) remains constant.

Thus equation (2.6) should, in conjunction with equation (2.5), be interpreted as signifying and establishing the dynamic theorems (a) that the higher is s (as in the maturing stage of economic development), the higher also will g^a (rate of growth of actual output *demanded*) have to be in order to bring investment into equality with saving (in terms of ratios) when b remains unaltered, and (b) that the lower is b (as in the capital-saving stage of technological advance), the higher will g^a have to be for the same purpose of equating the investment and the saving ratio when s remains unchanged. The exponential growth of actual output implicit in equation (2.6) is expressible in the form

$$(2.7) \qquad Y^a_t = Y^a_0\, e^{g^a t} \quad \text{or} \quad Y^a_t = Y^a_0\, e^{(s/b)t} \qquad (t = 0, \ldots, n).$$

This actual output Y^a given by (2.7) will be found to possess anomalous dynamic properties for reasons to be specified in the next section. Meanwhile it is important to look at Harrod's 'warranted rate' from the *supply* side of net investment.

Equation (2.6) carries with it the often neglected implication that the economy growing at the rate g^a (or at Harrod's G_w) is thereby capable of *accumulating capital* at the same rate. Such a capability is explicit in Domar's 'sigma effect'[19] and implicit in Harrod's admission that Domar's marginal productivity of capital is formally the reciprocal of his own capital coefficient ($\sigma = 1/C_r$ in Harrod's notation[20] or $b = \sigma^{-1}$ in ours, where σ is Domar's 'potential social average productivity of investment'[21]).[22] We may see that implication, as follows:

$$(2.8) \qquad\qquad I_t = K_{t+1} - K_t = \Delta K_t,$$

$$(2.9) \qquad K_t = b\, Y^a_t, \qquad \Delta K_t = b\,\Delta Y^a_t, \qquad (b = \text{const.})$$

[19] Domar, 1957, p. 98.

[20] Formal identification of Harrod's C_r as the reciprocal of Domar's σ presupposes at least (a) that the former's 'warranted' output admittedly associated with Keynesian underemployment (Harrod, 1948, p. 87) is equated to his 'natural' output from full employment and hence to the latter's explicitly postulated full-employment output (Domar, 1957, p. 87); and (b) that the former's capital (inclusive of inventories) is equated to the latter's capital (exclusive of inventories) via conceptual and statistical adjustments. Otherwise $\sigma \neq 1/C_r$.

[21] Domar, 1957, p. 89.

[22] When discussing the capacity-increasing aspect of net investment, 'the capital–output ratio' in the technological sense of that term seems to be a more perspicuous expression to use than 'the accelerator' in the usual trade-cycle sense.

$$(2.10) \qquad I_t = S_t = sY^a{}_t, \qquad (s = \text{const.})$$

$$(2.11) \qquad g^k \equiv \frac{\Delta K_t}{K_t} = \frac{I_t}{K_t} = \frac{S_t}{K_t} = \frac{sY^a{}_t}{bY^a{}_t} = \frac{s}{b}.$$

Here K is the stock of capital when fully utilized, b the average and marginal capital-output ratio technologically predetermined (relevant to the capacity-increasing effect of net investment), g^k the *rate of growth of fully utilized capital*, all other variables being the same as before. Equation (2.8) defines net investment as an increment of capital from the present to the next period. Equation (2.9) shows the technological relation of capital and output in average and marginal terms; the parenthetical constancy assumption makes for $b = K/Y^a = \Delta K/\Delta Y^a$. Equation (2.10) is the familiar investment-saving equilibrium condition to be satisfied; the parenthesized constancy assumption makes for $s = S/Y^a = \Delta S/\Delta Y^a$ (as in the case of a long-run saving function with a zero intercept). Equation (2.11), which is derived from (2.8)–(2.10), shows the possibility of capital growing at the same rate (g^k) as the rate at which actual output is growing ($g^a = s/b$). Implicit in equation (2.11) is the exponential growth of fully utilized capital:

$$(2.12) \qquad K_t = K_0 \, e^{g^k t} \quad \text{or} \quad K_t = K_0 \, e^{(s/b)t}, \qquad (t = 0, \ldots, n)$$

which is the *supply* counterpart of the growth of *demand* equation expressed by (2.7), owing to the *capacity-increasing* effect of net investment (as distinguished from its demand-generating effect). For the economy accumulating capital at the rate g^k can increase its productive capacity (actual output *supplied* by fully utilizing the existing stock of capital manned by the constant labour force) at the same rate:

$$(2.13) \qquad \frac{\Delta Y^c{}_t}{Y^c{}_t} = \frac{b\,\Delta K_t}{bK_t} = \frac{\Delta K_t}{K_t} \equiv g^k$$

where $\Delta Y^c{}_t/Y^c{}_t$ is the *rate of growth of productive capacity* representing the supply side of a growing economy *more directly* than the g^k of equation (2.11) does. This rate of growth of productive capacity given by equation (2.13) or the rate of growth of capital given by (2.11) is of crucial importance to capital-scarce *underdeveloped* economies.[23] But here we are interested in emphasizing the point that the demand side of net investment described by equations (2.1)–(2.7) and its supply side depicted by (2.8)–(2.13) jointly make it possible for us to think of Harrod's 'warranted rate' in interchangeable terms of

---

[23] Having regard to this capacity-increasing aspect of net investment, a spokesman for the United Nations Economic Commission for Asia and the Far East states: 'Since capital is the most scarce factor in most under-developed economies, the model which suits our purpose best is the Harrod–Domar model.' (See Ichimura, 1960, p. 81.)

demand and capital, especially in the present context of a capital-rich economy *subject to the deficiency of demand and the under-utilization of capital.*

4. *The Growth of Actual Output with an Inflection Point*

Let us in this section ponder the paradox of affluence in the light of the preceding section on the 'warranted rate', and in relation to 'the welfare optimum' discussed in section 2. The rate of growth of *actual* output given by equation (2.6) would, if realized, guarantee *full utilization of capital,* but not full employment of labour—unless it happened to coincide with the rate of growth of *potential* output given by equation (1.5). Since there is no reason to suppose that g^a should coincide with g^p except by chance or by design, it will be argued that g^a tends to exceed g^p during the *maturing* stage of economic development to entail unemployment due to insufficient demand (or to over-saving) but that during the *mature* stage g^a tends to lag behind g^p to cause structural unemployment due to insufficient capital. This section purports to discuss the whys and hows of the inequality of g^a and g^p by reference to the structural determinants of g^a in the course of economic development.

In contra-distinction to Harrod's constancy assumption about the saving and the capital–output ratio ($s, b = s_t, b_t = $ const., $t = 0, \ldots, n, n = \infty$), the following behavioural-structural assumptions about those basic determinants of the rate of growth of actual output will be made in the *transitional* context of a capital-rich economy undergoing the *maturing* and the *mature* stage of its development:

$$(3.1) \qquad \frac{d (\log s_{t-n})}{dt} > \frac{d (\log b_{t-n})}{dt} \quad before \quad t$$

$$(3.2) \qquad \frac{d (\log s_{t+n})}{dt} < \frac{d (\log b_{t+n})}{dt} \quad after \quad t$$

The first of these assumptions expressed by (3.1) means that during the *rapidly maturing* phase of a capital-rich economy's development (such as Japan and West Germany are now undergoing, and as Britain and America historically underwent) the saving ratio representing the community's thriftiness tends to increase faster than the capital–output ratio representing its capital requirements. The second assumption expressed by (3.2) signifies that during the *fully mature* phase of a capital-rich economy's development (such as Britain and America are now undergoing, and Japan and Germany will undergo in the decades ahead) the saving ratio tends to increase more *slowly* than the capital–output ratio. The exact length of time it takes a real capital-rich economy to experience the transition from assumption (3.1) to assumption (3.2) of course differs from one concrete case to another. It is to be noted that these behavioural-structural assumptions[24] expressed by (3.1) and (3.2) are fundamentally different from the Keynes–Harrod assumptions whereby a high propensity to save is unqualifiedly linked to a high-income community and a high productivity of capital (or a low capital-output ratio) inferentially associated with a technologically advanced economy—*without having regard to the stage of economic development.*

The economically meaningful interpretation of assumptions (3.1) and (3.2) is in order. During the $t - n$ *maturing* phase of economic development the traditional 'abstinence of the rich' doctrine is in full swing even at the cost of great income–wealth disparities. To borrow Keynes' dramatic phrase 'to save and to invest' become 'at once the duty and the delight of a large class', and 'the morals, the politics, the literature, and the religion of the age' join in 'a grand conspiracy for the promotion of savings'.[25] During that phase the capital–output ratio, on the other hand, tends to increase more slowly than the saving ratio, partly because by that time such capital-requiring bases of industrialization as roads, harbours, and transportation-communications facilities have already been constructed, and partly because the propensity to innovate tends to be so strong as to reduce progressively the amount of capital required per unit of output (or, what is tantamount to the same, to increase the productivity of capital). These structural reasons make it plausible to assume that s tends to grow faster than b during the $t - n$ phase.

During the $t + n$ *fully mature* phase, by contrast, an already affluent economy is likely to experience the reverse situation characterized by assumption (3.2). For by the time such an economy reaches t (demarcation point of time in the present context) all sorts of institutional, psychological, and technological changes will have occurred to weaken the propensity to save as well as to reintensify capital requirements. Extensive social-security programmes and consumer credit systems tend to render traditional saving 'for a rainy day' virtually superfluous; income equalization via progressive income taxa-

---

[24] The empirical plausibility of these assumptions can be inferred from the following data:

International Comparison of s and b for 1951–1957[a]

Country	Saving Ratio (s)[b]	Capital–Output Ratio (b)[c]
Japan	28·8	2·53
West Germany	23·3	2·77
U.S.	18·0	5·67
U.K.	15·9	5·61

[a] The data are based on U.N. and other international and national publications, as cited in Nakayama, 1960, pp. 13 and 26.

[b] The s variable here refers to the *gross* saving ratio $(S/G.N.P.)$ and so differs from our s which runs in *net* terms. Moreover, the s figures here include individual, corporate, and budgetary savings.

[c] The b variable here denotes the marginal ratio of capital to *gross* output $(\Delta K/\Delta G.N.P.)$, whereas our b runs in *net* terms.

[25] Keynes, 1923, pp. 9–10.

tion and negative taxes for the poor (autonomous transfer payments, such as are exemplified by the American 'anti-poverty' programme) tends to de-emphasize the traditional 'abstinence of the rich' doctrine; mounting TV commercialism and other forms of mass advertising tend to increase the propensity to consume at the expense of saving; long-term credit extensions through the capital market and the banking system for investment in plant and equipment tend to obviate excessive reliance on corporate saving; deficit financing for full employment and rapid growth becomes so generally acceptable as to render less necessary strict adherence to budget balancing and austerity measures to achieve budgetary saving;[26] increasing urbanization and suburban living tend to expand the scope for 'the demonstration effect' and 'conspicuous consumption' at the expense of saving; and so on. Is it any wonder that America and Britain save a smaller fraction of the G.N.P. than Japan and Germany (see n. 24)? But the latter countries may sooner or later follow the former in this respect, for their institutional–psychological complexes seem to be rapidly changing in the direction of more spending and less saving.

During the $t + n$ phase the capital–output ratio seems to attain a relatively high level for such reasons as Bronfenbrenner has attributed to the American economy, i.e., the practice of rapid depreciation and obsolescence under market pressures (irrespective of physical wear and tear) and concentration on cost-reducing investment (*vis-à-vis* output-increasing investment).[27] One might add the lagging productivity of labour in the tertiary or service sector (which sector expands *pari passu* with industrialization in general and democratic welfare-statecraft in particular) as a major explanation for the high level of the capital–output ratio during the $t + n$ phase of economic development.[28] It is no wonder, either, that America and Britain have a much higher level of the capital–output ratio than Japan and Germany (also see n. 24). The latter countries need not but may follow the former in this respect, too.

For these economic reasons behind the assumptions expressed by (3.1) and (3.2) we should expect that, during the $t - n$ phase, when s is growing faster than b and so g^a is increasing, g^a comes to exceed g^p and exceeds it by more and more until time t. At that point there is a switch due to the change in the institutional-technological complex affecting s and b so that, from then onwards, s grows more slowly than b, and so g^a decreases. There is therefore a *kink* in g^a at t. As g^a falls, it eventually becomes less than g^p at, let us say, time T. The *dynamic* behaviour of g^a and g^p is (as explicit functions of time) illustrated in Figure 1.

---

[26] cf., Hansen, 1957, and also Heller, 1967.

[27] Bronfenbrenner, 1965.

[28] It is well to recall that the capital–output ratio tends to vary directly with the capital–labour ratio (K/N) and inversely with the productivity of labour (Y/N): $b = K/Y = (K/N)/(Y/N)$.

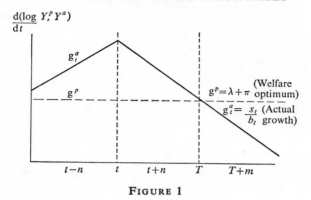

FIGURE 1

This behaviour of g^a signifies that the actual output growth curve (in Figure 2) possesses the dynamic properties

(3.3)
$$\frac{d(\log Y^a)}{dt} > 0, \qquad \frac{d^2(\log Y^a)}{dt^2} > 0 \quad \text{at} \quad t - n;$$

$$\frac{d(\log Y^a)}{dt} = \text{max}, \qquad \frac{d^2(\log Y^a)}{dt^2} = 0 \quad \text{at} \quad t;$$

$$\frac{d(\log Y^a)}{dt} > 0, \qquad \frac{d^2(\log Y^a)}{dt^2} < 0 \quad \text{at} \quad t + n.$$

The dynamic behaviour of $\log Y^a$ is illustrated in Figure 2. Up to t it increases at an *increasing* rate and beyond t it increases at a *decreasing* rate. It follows that the output growth curve has an inflexion point at t, when the curvature of the curve changes from concavity (from above) to convexity (from above). Figure 2 brings out the *paradox of affluence* in bold relief, for the actual growth curve (*solid* $\log Y^a$ line) has a steeper gradient than the potential growth curve (*broken* $\log Y^p$) up to T, intersects the latter curve at T (given the way Figure 2 is drawn), and then tapers down beyond T. Here

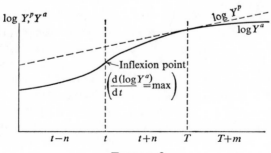

FIGURE 2

we see clearly that a rapidly maturing capital-rich economy sooner or later finds itself paradoxically growing at a lower rate than that which is consistent with full employment of growing labour population with an increasing productivity, the *turning point* of time being T.

Three things deserve special attention here. *First*, the position (as distinguished from the gradient) of the log Y^a curve (in Figure 2) is lower than that of the log Y^p curve except at time T, thus revealing Keynesian–Harrodian under-employment equilibrium as the rule rather than as an exception. *Second*, contrary to Harrod's interpretation,[29] the g^a curve (in Figure 1) gets its kink at t, not because of the 'full-employment ceiling' (such as represented by the log Y^p curve) acting as an exogenous shock, but because of structural changes in the endogenous determinants of g^a itself (that is, in s and b). In fact, the kink in the g^a curve occurs *before* the full employment ceiling is reached at T. This implies that the ceiling might, indeed, never be reached since the institutional-technological complex affecting s and b might make log Y^a start to taper down before log $Y^a = $ log Y^p (contrary to what Figure 2 depicts notionally), or it might change in such a way as to enable log Y^a to creep along the log Y^p curve *for a while* (i.e., $T + 1, T + 2 \ldots$). *Third*, the log Y^a curve, while tapering down beyond T, nevertheless is still positively inclined during the $T + m$ low-gear phase, contrary to what the Keynes–Hansen 'stagnation thesis' or the Marxian 'breakdown theory' would have us expect.

Thus viewed, the observed or observable slow growth of mature capital-rich economies relative to 'the welfare optimum' (in Harrod's sense) owes its *fundamental* explanation to (a) the low trend value of the saving ratio to necessitate only a low rate of growth of actual output to induce an offsetting investment ratio, and (b) the high trend value of the capital–output ratio to obviate a high rate of growth of actual output as an investment inducer relatively to an already lower saving ratio.

5. *Policy Implications of the Harrodian Welfare Optimum*

Let us in this concluding section explore the concrete implications of Harrod's general policy suggestion (to repeat): 'The target of policy should be to bring the warranted rate as near as possible to the natural rate'—for the *optimal* growth of a fully mature *mixed-open* economy in the $t + n$ stage of development. It is presumed that such an economy has a highly developed fiscal system, a sophisticated central banking apparatus, and enlightened policy-making agencies as well as a flexible import-control mechanism. In terms of the preceding analysis such an economy is confronted with the secular tendency of the actual growth rate to lag behind the potential growth rate ($g^a < g^p$). Our problem therefore is to make $g^a = g^p$ at some future time

---

[29] Harrod, pp. 300 ff.

$T + 1$ through 'State action . . . as a balancing factor,' to borrow Keynes' phraseology.[30] Harrod himself included the export, the import, and autonomous government investment ratio (public works) in his seminal determination of the 'warranted' growth rate.[31]

Considering the potential rate of growth as the fixed target given by equation (1.5), let us combine a set of *manipulative policy parameters* and a set of *structural parameters* so as to determine a policy-influenced g^a:

$$(4.1) \qquad g = \bar{G}_{t+1}/Y_{t+1}^a,$$

$$(4.2) \qquad \gamma = \bar{I}_{t+1}^g/\bar{G}_{t+1},$$

$$(4.3) \qquad \tau = T_{t+1}/Y_{t+1}^a,$$

$$(4.4) \qquad \delta = \bar{D}_{t+1}/Y_{t+1}^a,$$

$$(4.5) \qquad v = \bar{I}_{t+1}/Y_{t+1}^a,$$

$$(4.6) \qquad e = \bar{X}_{t+1}/Y_{t+1}^a,$$

$$(4.7) \qquad m' = \mu(M_{t+1}/Y_{t+1}^a) = \mu m, \qquad (\mu \gtrless 1)$$

$$(4.8) \qquad s' = \xi(S_{t+1}/Y_{t+1}^a) = \xi s, \qquad (\xi \gtrless 1)$$

$$(4.9) \qquad b' = \varepsilon(I_{t+1}/Y_{t+1}^a) = \varepsilon b. \qquad (\varepsilon \gtrless 1)$$

Here g is the ratio of autonomous government expenditure to actual output, γ the ratio of autonomous government investment to total government expenditure, τ the ratio of general taxes (direct and indirect) to output, δ the ratio of autonomous investor credit (as distinguished from consumer credit) to output, v the ratio of autonomous private investment to output, e the ratio of autonomous exports to output, m' the ratio of imports to output after the imposition of a shift parameter (μ), s' the saving ratio including a shift parameter (ξ), and b' the capital-output ratio including a shift parameter (ε). Here g, γ, and τ are manipulative *fiscal-policy* parameters,[32] while ξ is a similar *monetary-policy* parameter.[33] Here, also, m', s', and b' are *flexible policy* parameters, whereas m, s, and b are *fixed structural* parameters. Finally, μ, ξ, and ε are *controllable shift parameters*[34] (e.g., $\mu = 1$ denoting no change from the base period, $\xi = 1.2$, a 20 per cent increase, and $\varepsilon = 0.85$, a 15 per cent decrease—through appropriate measures).

The 'investment-saving' equilibrium condition to be satisfied in the present context of a *mixed-open* economy takes the expanded form

$$(4.10) \quad I_{t+1} + \bar{I}_{t+1} + \bar{I}_{t+1}^g + \bar{X}_{t+1} = S_{t+1} + T_{t+1} + \bar{D}_{t+1} + M_{t+1},$$

[30] Keynes, 1936, p. 220.   [31] Harrod, 1939.

[32] For some such fiscal-policy parameters see Musgrave, 1960; and Peacock, 1959.

[33] For monetary and other policy parameters see Kurihara, 1963 as well as 1959.

[34] For programming suggestions about controllable shift parameters see Ichimura, 1960.

the left-hand side of which roughly represents the composite demand for 'investment', while the right-hand side likewise represents the composite supply of 'saving'.[35] Taking (4.1)–(4.9) into account, equation (4.10) can be rewritten as

$$(4.11) \quad \varepsilon b \, \Delta Y_{t+1}^a = \xi s Y_{t+1}^a + \tau Y_{t+1}^a + \delta Y_{t+1}^a + \mu m Y_{t+1}^a \\ - v Y_{t+1}^a - \gamma g Y_{t+1}^a - e \, Y_{t+1}^a,$$

dividing which through by $\varepsilon b Y_{t+1}^a$ yields

$$(4.12) \qquad g'^{a}_{t+1} \equiv \frac{\Delta Y_{t+1}^a}{Y_{t+1}^a} = \frac{\xi s + \tau + \delta + \mu m - v - \gamma g - e}{\varepsilon b}$$

This g'^a given by equation (4.12) is the *new* rate of growth of actual output including the policy parameters. Equation (4.12) indicates the theoretical possibility of the rate of growth of actual output at time $t + 1$ being positively influenced by s, τ, δ, m, ξ, and μ and negatively influenced by v, γ, g, e, b, and ε.

It follows, therefore that the *optimal dynamic equilibrium condition* to be satisfied is given by

$$(4.13) \quad g'^{a}_{t+1} - g^{p}_{t+1} = 0; \qquad \frac{\xi s + \tau + \delta + \mu m - v - \gamma g - e}{\varepsilon b} = \lambda + \pi,$$

which expresses an ideal situation where Harrod's 'entrepreneurial equilibrium' (equality of the investment and the saving ratio expressed in g'^a) happily coincides with 'the welfare optimum': in his sense (g^p), albeit *by design*. It is also what Joan Robinson colourfully calls a 'golden age' equilibrium condition in which the economy grows with both full employment of labour and full utilization of capital.[36]

Equation (4.13) implies that if and when a fully mature capital-rich economy finds itself on a divergent growth path characterized by $g^a < g^p$ as in the $t + n$ stage, it would be possible and desirable to get up on the optimal growth path characterized by $g'^a = g^p$ via appropriate *increases* in s', m', τ, and δ as well as through appropriate *decreases* in g, γ, v, e, and b'. Then *actual* output would grow at the same rate as the rate of growth of *potential* output consistent with population growth and technological advance ($G_w = G_n$ in Harrod's notation).

Thus Harrod's concept of 'the welfare optimum' provides a general frame of reference for the policy-makers concerned with continuous full utilization of human resources and material capital, while his concept of 'the warranted

---

[35] Here, 'saving' has the special meaning given to it by equation (4.10).

[36] Robinson, 1956, p. 99. She regards a 'golden age' equilibrium as 'a mythical state of affairs not likely to obtain in any actual economy'. Her scepticism might be justifiable as far as *laissez-faire* economies are concerned, but would not apply to the sort of policy-oriented economy discussed above.

rate of growth' lays a theoretical basis for a conscious growth policy to implement that concern with 'the welfare optimum'. Thus, too, Harrod's twin concepts of the 'natural' and the 'warranted' growth rate have stirred the imagination of the growth-conscious generation and opened up vast vistas for generations of macro-dynamic welfare economists to come. The present essay may have made some contribution to the forwarding of Sir Roy Harrod's epochal dynamic theory in this welfare-sensitive, policy-oriented post-Keynesian age.

REFERENCES

AMERICAN BANKERS ASSOCIATION, *A Symposium on Economic Growth*, 1963.

BRONFENBRENNER, M., 'Economic Miracles and Japan's Income-Doubling Plan', in Lockwood, W. W. (ed.), *The State and Economic Enterprise in Japan* (1965).

DOMAR, E. D., 'Expansion and Employment', *American Economic Review*, March 1947; reprinted in his *Essays in the Theory of Economic Growth* (1957).

HANSEN, A. H., *Full Recovery or Stagnation* (1938).

——, *The American Economy* (1957).

——, 'We Must Grow—Or We Sink', *New York Times Magazine*, 18 March 1962.

HARROD, R. F., 'An Essay in Dynamic Theory', *Economic Journal*, March 1939.

——, *Towards a Dynamic Economics* (1948).

——, 'Domar and Dynamic Economics', *Economic Journal*, September 1959; reprinted in Mueller, M.G. (ed.), *Readings in Macroeconomics* (1966).

HELLER, W., *New Dimensions of Political Economy* (1967).

ICHIMURA, S., "Macro-Economic Models', in United Nations, *Programming Techniques for Economic Development* (1960).

KEYNES, J. M., *Monetary Reform* (1923), reprinted in *Essays in Persuasion* (Rupert Hart-Davis, 1952).

——, *The General Theory of Employment, Interest, and Money* (1936).

——, 'Some Economic Consequences of a Declining Population', *Eugenic Review*, April 1937.

KURIHARA, K. K., *The Keynesian Theory of Economic Development* (1959).

——, *Applied Dynamic Economics* (1963).

——, *Macroeconomics and Programming* (1964).

MUSGRAVE, R., *The Theory of Public Finance* (1960).

NAKAYAMA, I. (ed.), *Nihon Keizai no Seicho* (The Growth of the Japanese Economy) (1960).

NATIONAL COMMISSION ON TECHNOLOGY, AUTOMATION, AND ECONOMIC GROWTH, *Technology and the American Economy*, Vol. 1 (1966).

PEACOCK, A. T., 'The Public Sector and the Theory of Economic Growth', *Scottish Journal of Political Economy*, February 1959.

ROBINSON, JOAN, *The Accumulation of Capital* (1956).

STEINDL, J., *Maturity and Stagnation in American Capitalism* (1952).

TSURU, S., 'Keynes versus Marx: The Methodology of Aggregates', in Kurihara, K. K. (ed.), *Post-Keynesian Economics* (1954).

9

ECONOMIC GROWTH: THEORY AND POLICY FORMATION

J. R. SARGENT

F ROM time to time every science experiences a moment at which a key concept is formed and lifts it to an altogether higher level of enquiry. One such moment in economics occurred when Roy Harrod arrived at the concept of 'warranted' or equilibrium growth. The energy which this released has been devoted rather more to establishing the theoretical possibility of equilibrium in the growth process, and rather less to analysing the practical consequences of disequilibrium, than Roy, with his keen sense of the public relevance of economic theory, would probably have wished. This paper is intended to lend whatever weight it may have to correcting this bias. Its object is to ask and answer the question whether inferences can be drawn from the observable macroeconomic behaviour of a closed economy about the existence of certain disequilibria in the growth process and about the policy changes concerning investment and technical change which are required to remove them.

It did not take long for economists dedicated to the pursuit of equilibrium to remove the original Harrodian dichotomy between the warranted and the natural rates of growth and to subordinate the former to the latter. Various mechanisms have been suggested by which the warranted rate could come into line with the natural: by neo-classical authors a variable capital-output ratio; by Kaldor a variable savings ratio; by devotees of the vintage approach to capital theory, a variable age at which assets are retired. But although the dichotomy of natural and warranted can be eliminated in one way or another, the possibility of steady growth at the natural rate usually turns out to require the rate of exogenous technical progress to have a particular property, the absence of which implies the emergence of one-way trends in one or another of the ratios of capital to output, investment to output, and profits to capital, and in vintage models in the average age of capital assets. The existence of such one-way trends must call in question the possibility of maintaining steady growth at the natural rate in the long run. The property of technical progress required to remove this difficulty is usually identified as Harrod-neutrality. A somewhat different property emerges from the model used in this paper, and the first part of the argument is concerned with deriving what it is. But it still remains the case that for steady growth to be possible, with constancy of the key macroeconomic ratios, technical progress must be constrained in a particular way, which at first sight there is no reason to expect. The second part of the paper discusses why, at second sight, technical progress might adapt itself as required. But the ideas here are derived from writers such as Kennedy and Phelps, who have developed theories of induced technical progress, and the discussion will be brief.

The third and final part of the paper is concerned with what happens if technical progress is not in fact constrained in the manner required to produce steady growth with the key ratios constant. The economy can evidently live with changes in at least one of these ratios for quite long periods. Matthews's series for the capital–output ratio in the U.K. show it to have been on a falling trend between 1850 and 1900 and again from 1920 to 1950.[1] Between 1900 and 1920 and since 1950 the falling tendency appears to have been reversed. This raises the interesting historical question how these trends were both generated and accommodated; and a possible answer is that they sprung from disequilibria created in the growth process when technical progress was not constrained in the way which would have removed them. This poses the formidable task of grafting on to the growth model a set of expressions which describe the reactions of its variables to these disequilibria. I do not attempt this, and the model cannot be used in the form proposed for the interpretation of macroeconomic history. Its object is forward—rather than backward—looking. It assumes that the government acts to maintain equilibrium in the labour market (which may be interpreted to mean full employment) and in the product market—or in other words to eliminate the most pressing of the possible disequilibria—and with this assumption it asks how much can be learned from the subsequent macroeconomic behaviour of the economy about the necessity for policies designed to correct disequilibria due to the nature of technical progress and the rate of investment. The aim is a policy-orientated piece of economic theory, appropriate to the spirit in which Roy Harrod has so signally advanced the study of economics.

The building-blocks of the theory are not particularly novel. Suppose that technical progress is experienced entirely through gross investment in the equipment which embodies it; and that gross investment, $I(t)$, in any period t is entirely in equipment of the latest vintage. Equipment of any given vintage is technically more advanced than that of earlier vintages in two ways: it yields more output and it needs less labour to man it, for a given scale of investment in real terms. But the output and the labour requirement do not necessarily vary proportionately with the scale of investment. These assumptions are summed up, writing $y(v)$ for total output in real terms from all equipment of vintage v and $n(v)$ for its labour requirement, as follows:

[1] Matthews, 1964.

(1a)
$$y(v): \mu I(v)^a \, e^{\beta v},$$

(1b)
$$n(v): \lambda I(v)^b \, e^{-\alpha v}.$$

We assume that these relationships remain unchanged for periods subsequent to v, unaffected by physical depreciation or by disembodied technical progress. The aggregate output of the economy ($Y(t)$) and its aggregate labour requirement ($N(t)$) can be evaluated from (1a) and (1b) if we know the past history of investment and the age of the oldest equipment in use. Assume that the former is a history of steady growth at rate g, so that

(2)
$$I(v) = I(0) \, e^{gv}.$$

The age of the oldest equipment in use (T) can then be found by calling in the vintage equivalent of the marginal productivity principle, namely

(3)
$$n(t - T)w(t) = y(t - T).$$

That is, the oldest equipment in use is that which just covers the cost of the labour required to operate it,[2] since this is presumably what it has to be paid. (The current wage $w(t)$ is a real wage in terms of the product, so that for an individual industry it would in most cases differ from what the workers would think of as their real wage, measured in terms of consumption goods in general.) If the current real wage, $w(t)$, is known, the relationships (1a), (1b) (2), and (3) enable us to find T and so to evaluate:

$$Y(t) = \int_{v=t-T}^{v=t} y(v) \, dv$$

$$= \int_{v=t-T}^{v=t} \mu(I(0) \, e^{gv})^a \, e^{\beta v} \, dv$$

(4)
$$= \mu I(0)^a \, e^{(ag+\beta)t} \frac{1 - e^{-(ag+\beta)T}}{ag + \beta}$$

and

$$N(t) = \int_{v=t-T}^{v=t} n(v) \, dv$$

$$= \int_{v=t-T}^{v=t} \lambda(I(0) \, e^{gv})^b \, e^{-\alpha v} \, dv$$

(5)
$$= \lambda I(0)^b \, e^{(bg-\alpha)t} \frac{1 - e^{-(bg-\alpha)T}}{bg - \alpha}$$

These expressions do no more than spell out what total output and its associated labour requirement will be if investment grows steadily at rate g. They say nothing about total demand and the labour supply. But steady

---

[2] y is evaluated at constant *value-added* prices.

growth is not likely to be maintainable (at least in a market economy) unless it is consistent with equilibrium in both product and labour markets.

Let total demand in the product market be:

$$D(t) = I(t) + (1 - s) Y(t),$$

where s is a constant average and marginal propensity to save. Then equilibrium requires:

$$I(t) = s Y(t)$$

or

(6) $$I(0) \, e^{gt} = s\mu I(0)^a \, e^{(ag + \beta)t} \frac{1 - e^{-(ag + \beta)T}}{ag + \beta}.$$

In the labour market, let the labour supply be:

$$N_s(t) = N_s(0) \, e^{nt}.$$

Then equilibrium in the labour market requires:

(7) $$N_s(0) \, e^{nt} = \lambda I(0)^b \, e^{(bg - \alpha)t} \frac{1 - e^{-(bg - \alpha)T}}{bg - \alpha}.$$

Provided that it has a solution initially,[3] equation (7) may perfectly well be satisfied continuously with T changing over time at a certain rate, i.e., if

(8) $$\frac{dT}{dt} = (n + \alpha - bg) \frac{e^{(bg - \alpha)T} - 1}{bg - \alpha}.$$

Similarly, equilibrium in the product market may be maintained continuously if:

(9) $$\frac{dT}{dt} = (g(1 - a) - \beta) \frac{e^{(ag + \beta)T} - 1}{ag + \beta}.$$

But it is fairly obvious[4] that the same rate of change of T over time will not satisfy both (8) and (9) simultaneously unless it is zero. Simultaneous equilibrium in both product and labour markets therefore requires both of the following conditions:

[3] See Annex for a discussion on the conditions for this.
[4] Under certain conditions a value of T may exist at which

$$(n + \alpha - bg) \frac{(e^{(bg - \alpha)T} - 1)}{bg - \alpha} = (g(1 - a) - \beta) \frac{(e^{(ag + \beta)T} - 1)}{ag + \beta}$$

But if the two functions of T intersect at a value of T such that $dT/dt \neq 0$, that value of T cannot be maintained and will give place to a value at which the above equality is not satisfied. There is also a special case, $g = n = (\beta + \alpha)/(b + a)$, in which the two functions are identical, but they can yield $dT/dt = 0$ only if $T = 0$.

(10)
$$g = \frac{n + \alpha}{b}$$

and

(11)
$$g = \frac{\beta}{1 - a}$$

so that

(12)
$$\frac{n + \alpha}{b} = \frac{\beta}{1 - a}.$$

In other words the maintenance of steady growth requires not merely a certain growth rate of investment, but also a certain relationship between the two parameters of technical change.

It can quickly be shown that, if these conditions hold, steady growth is consistent not only with constant s and T, but also with a constant share of wages in the national income and a constant rate of profit. The real wage, determined by (2) and (3), is:

(13)
$$w(t) = \frac{\mu}{\lambda} I(0)^{a-b} e^{((a-b)g + \beta + \alpha)(t - T)};$$

and if (10) and (11) hold, it increases at the rate $[(n + \alpha)/b] - n$. The real wage bill (Nw) therefore increases at the rate $(n + \alpha)/b$. Real income (Y) from (4), increases at the rate $\beta/(1 - a) = (n + \alpha)/b$. So the share of wages is constant. Aggregate profits also increase at the rate $(n + \alpha)/b$, but the capital on which they are earned can be valued either at its historical cost:

$$K(t) = \int_{v=t-T}^{v=t} I(v)\, dv$$

or at its current market value:

$$K'(t) = \int_{v=t-T}^{v=t} \int_{\tau=t}^{\tau=v+T} (y(v) - n(v)w(\tau))\, e^{-\delta(\tau - t)}\, d\tau\, dv$$

where τ refers to future periods in which assets are in use. But with T constant, and expected to remain so, both of these increase over time at the rate $(n + \alpha)/b$,[5] and on either measure the capital–output ratio is constant. Hence the rate of profit on capital is constant.

The possibility of steady growth, however, when technical progress has both β and α positive, requires us to place certain restrictions on a and b. Conditions (10) and (11) above cannot both be satisfied by the same positive g

---

[5] For the current market value of capital to increase at this rate, it is necessary to assume that T is expected to remain constant at its going value, and that the growth of real wages over the remaining life of the assets in the capital stock is expected to be the same as in the past. This is needed in order to evaluate the future flow of profits from the assets until their future retirement.

unless we have $a < 1$, $b > 0$. Furthermore, if the level of investment is to be determinate, in the sense that there is to be one and only one level which is more profitable than all others,[6] we also have to assume that $b < a$. So we can state the requirements of the model generally as $1 > a > b > 0$. We might describe them as 'diminishing returns'.

We must be cautious, however, because the sort of question which is asked under the heading of 'returns to scale' cannot be asked of this model. The model does not let us double the number of new machines, and double the number of men manning new machines, and observe the effect on the output from new machines.[7] The number of new machines determines the number of men required to man them at the same time as it determines the output from them. We are not in a world of entirely fixed coefficients, because the two effects of investment in new machines differ according to the scale of investment. There is a special case, $a = b = 1$, when doubling investment has the effect of doubling both the output and the manning requirement of the new machines, and to this we might stretch the title of 'constant returns'. It is clearly inconsistent in this model with steady growth. It is also highly unrealistic, because it requires us to suppose that output per man employed on new machines is independent of the scale of investment in them. One would prefer to suppose that output per man rises, or in other words that $a > b$. But should we exclude the possibility that $a \geq 1$, or that doubling investment in new machines at least doubles the output obtainable from them?

It seems to me that in the context of embodied technical progress we should exclude this possibility. Living no longer in a world of homogeneous capital, what we are adding to the capital stock through investment is something different in kind—a new vintage, which has to operate within constraints imposed by the continued existence of old vintages. A certain amount of the new vintage may yield an output which is impressive compared with that of the same scale of investment in older vintages. But without substantial adaptation of the older vintages, which are after all still profitable to operate as they are without spending money adapting them, the output yield of the newest vintage is unlikely to rise proportionately with the scale of investment in it. The yield

---

[6] That is to say, if there is to exist a maximum to the present value of expected future profits of current investment, $I(t)$, i.e. to:

$$\Pi(t) = \int_{\tau=t}^{\tau=t+T} (y(t)p(\tau) - n(t)w(\tau)) \, e^{-\delta(\tau-t)} \, d\tau$$

when $p(\tau)$, $w(\tau)$ are expected prices and money wages, T the expected life of the investment and δ the entrepreneurial discount rate; or alternatively if there is to exist a maximum to the *immediate* rate of return on current investment, $y(t)p(t) - n(t)w(t)$.

[7] We could observe the effect on *aggregate output*, $Y(t)$, of equi-proportionate increases in $I(t)$ and the *total labour force*, $N(t)$, because any labour not required to man $I(t)$ could be applied to the oldest machines on the scrapping margin; or if there were not enough labour from the proportionate increase in $N(t)$ to man the same proportionate increase in $I(t)$, it could be found by scrapping more old machines. But this is a different matter.

of a new motorway is limited by the existing pattern of feeder roads and the bottlenecks created by them; the yield of plant producing a new synthetic fibre by the number of existing looms capable of weaving it; the yield of a plant producing new building materials by the number of builders with the equipment capable of manipulating it into position. The adaptation which is required to make full use of the output potential of new machines may be not only that of old equipment complementary to them but also that of old knowledge and skills. To meet this possibility we should really write y as a function of t as well as of v, allowing for an element of learning or disembodied progress; but even if this allows constant or even increasing output per unit of investment *in the long run* as investment increases, it supports the presumption that it will be decreasing *in the short run*—that is, in the period in which the investment is made. Further support for this presumption is obtained if we think of the yield of investment as the ratio to the cost of the new equipment of the market price of its output. For even if the number of physical units of output per new machine is invariant to the number of new machines, it is not likely that the product of the new machine can be sold in increasing quantity without reducing its price relative to the cost of the new machine. As something new and less than perfectly substitutable for the products of old machines, it will have to carve itself out a market at the expense of worsening terms of trade between the price of the product and the price of the new equipment which produces it. We can reasonably interpret the requirement that $a < 1$ in this sense.

In point of fact the requirements of the model—that $0 < b < a < 1$—correspond closely to those which are normally imposed upon the neo-classical aggregate production function for the case of variable proportions. In the neo-classical function, an increased capital stock results in increased labour productivity and decreased capital productivity. In our model, increased investment in new equipment raises labour productivity and lowers capital productivity on new equipment. We cannot freely vary the proportions between capital and labour, even on new equipment, as we can in the neo-classical case; for having chosen the level of investment, we have chosen the amount of labour to be applied to it. But by varying the level of investment we are varying the proportions between new and old types of capital. To the declining productivity of capital, which occurs in the neo-classical case as the capital worked by the labour force increases, there is a direct analogy in our case in the form of the declining productivity of investment in new equipment, which occurs as more of it is brought into use alongside the existing stock of older equipment. We conclude, therefore, that the 'diminishing returns' property, which our model requires for steady growth, is not merely reasonable but apt.

It is of some interest to note that this property positively excludes the possibility of steady growth when technical progress is of the Harrod-neutral kind. Harrod-neutrality requires that $\beta = 0$ and $\alpha > 0$. Condition (12) cannot be satisfied if this is the case, and $1 > a > b > 0$, unless $n = -\alpha$, in which case income is constant and the labour force falling. Steadily growing income with a steadily growing labour force is not possible. It can be made possible only if we are prepared to entertain the special case in which $a = b = 1$, and the condition for its existence is then that $g = n + \alpha$. This allows condition (8) to be satisfied for $dT/dt = 0$. Condition (9) in this special case is satisfied for $dT/dt = 0$ by any g whatsoever. This suggests that there is something odd about the special case. In fact it leaves the level of investment undetermined; for if doubling investment in new machines doubles both their output and their labour requirement, the profitability of investment is invariant to the scale on which it takes place. We have already rejected the special case on these and other grounds.

The fact that for steady growth the model actually requires the absence of Harrod-neutrality (except in the implausible special case) might make us distrust it, if there were compelling intuitive reasons for expecting that in reality technical progress would be of the Harrod-neutral sort. But this is not the case. To me at any rate it is more appealing to suppose that the normal characteristic of technical progress is that it is simultaneously both increasing the output obtainable from a given scale of investment and decreasing the amount of labour required to operate it; or in other words, that both $\beta > 0$ and $\alpha > 0$. We may note in passing that the model is consistent with Hicks-neutrality, in which $\alpha = 0$, $\beta > 0$, and with Solow-neutrality, in which $\beta > 0, \alpha = -\beta$.

Having resolved this issue, we turn to the question whether there is any reason to expect technical progress to adapt itself to the particular conjuncture required for steady growth: that is, to the condition that:

$$\frac{\beta}{1 - a} = \frac{n + \alpha}{b}.$$

What if this is not the case? Equations (6) to (9) above show that there must then be a developing disequilibrium in at least one of the two markets, for labour or for products, given constant T and s. One way of tracing the results of this would be to suppose that money wages and/or prices respond in some appropriate way, probably with time-lags, to the disequilibria which develop. Rather than this, we shall adopt the assumption that we are concerned with a managed economy in which full employment is the aim and budgetary policy the instrument. As equation (8) shows, full employment can be continually maintained provided that T changes appropriately over time. If $g > (n + \alpha)/b$, T must be falling in order to release enough men from old equipment to man the rapidly growing amount of new; and if $g < (n + \alpha)/b$, older and older equipment must be kept in use to keep men employed. But how can the authorities managing the economy affect T? They can do this by varying the rate of growth of output, through the management of demand, in such a way as to cause the change in T required for the maintenance of full employment. The rate of change of output, from equation (4), is

$$\frac{\mathrm{d}\,Y(t)}{\mathrm{d}t} = (ag + \beta)\,Y(t) + \frac{ag + \beta}{e^{(ag+\beta)T} - 1}\,Y(t)\frac{\mathrm{d}T}{\mathrm{d}t}$$

$$(14) \qquad = (ag + \beta)\,Y(t) + y(t - T)\frac{\mathrm{d}T}{\mathrm{d}t}.$$

That is, output increases at the rate determined by technical progress and investment, plus or minus the effect at the margin of changes in the age at which equipment is scrapped.

For the maintenance of full-employment, we require from (8):

$$\frac{\mathrm{d}T}{\mathrm{d}t} = (n + \alpha - bg)\,\frac{e^{(bg-\alpha)T} - 1}{bg - \alpha}$$

$$(15) \qquad = (n + \alpha - bg)\,\frac{N(t)}{n(t - T)}.$$

Substituting (15) into (14) we find the full-employment rate of growth of output:

$$\frac{\mathrm{d}\,Y(t)}{\mathrm{d}t} = (ag + \beta)\,Y(t) + \frac{y(t - T)}{n(t - T)}\,N(t)(n + \alpha - bg).$$

But if this rate of growth of output is maintained,

$$(16) \qquad \frac{\mathrm{d}(I(t)/Y(t))}{\mathrm{d}t} = \frac{I(t)}{Y(t)}\left(g(1 - a) - \beta - \frac{w(t)N(t)}{Y(t)}(n + \alpha - bg)\right)$$

which is only zero if $g = \beta/(1 - a) = (n + \alpha)/b$. Thus the maintenance of full employment, when this condition is not fulfilled, demands a growth rate of output which involves some change in the savings ratio if it is to be compatible with equilibrium in the product market. Our assumption is that the authorities effect the necessary change in the savings ratio by means of some appropriate combination of fiscal and monetary policy.

In consequence of their actions designed to maintain both full employment and product-market equilibrium, the distribution of income and the capital output ratio also change over time. Since:

$$\frac{w(t)N(t)}{Y(t)} = \frac{ag + \beta}{bg - \alpha}\frac{e^{(bg-\alpha)T} - 1}{e^{(ag+\beta)T} - 1}$$

$$(17) \qquad \frac{\mathrm{d}}{\mathrm{d}t}\left(\frac{w(t)N(t)}{Y(t)}\right) = \frac{y(t)}{Y(t)}\,w(t)\left(\frac{n(t)}{y(t)} - \frac{N(t)}{Y(t)}\right)\frac{\mathrm{d}T}{\mathrm{d}t}.$$

Since the number of men per unit of output is smaller on new machines than for the average of all machines in the capital stock, the share of wages in the national income rises as T falls and falls as T rises. Similarly, valuing the capital stock at its historical cost, we have:

$$\frac{K(t)}{Y(t)} = \frac{1}{\mu} I(0)^{1-a} \, e^{(g(1-a)-\beta)t} \frac{ag+\beta}{g} \frac{1-e^{-gT}}{1-e^{-(ag+\beta)T}}$$

$$\therefore \frac{d}{dt}\left(\frac{K(t)}{Y(t)}\right) = \frac{K(t)}{Y(t)}\left[g(1-a)-\beta+\left(\frac{g}{e^{gT}-1}-\frac{ag+\beta}{e^{(ag+\beta)T}-1}\right)\frac{dT}{dt}\right]$$

$$(18) \qquad = \frac{K(t)}{Y(t)}\left[g(1-a)-\beta+\left(\frac{I(t-T)}{K(t)}-\frac{y(t-T)}{Y(t)}\right)\frac{dT}{dt}\right].$$

It is obvious from (18) that the capital–output ratio does not change if $g = \beta/(1-a)$; for then $g = ag+\beta$. Furthermore, the coefficient of dT/dt is positive or negative according as g is less than or greater than $\beta/(1-a)$. That is, if g is large in the sense of being greater than $\beta/(1-a)$, the capital–output ratio is being forced up by the effect of diminishing returns to investment, provided that T is not increasing to offset this; for since a large g makes output per unit of investment greatest on old equipment, the effect of including older and older equipment in the capital stock (by increasing the age of retirement) is to lower the average ratio of capital to output. Inserting into (17) and (18) the value of dT/dt required to maintain full employment, we find the following consequences for the behaviour of the share of wages and the capital–output ratio:

$$(19) \quad \frac{d}{dt}\left(\frac{w(t)N(t)}{Y(t)}\right) = \frac{y(t)}{n(t-T)}\frac{w(t)N(t)}{Y(t)}\left(\frac{n(t)}{y(t)}-\frac{N(t)}{Y(t)}\right)(n+\alpha-bg)$$

$$\frac{d}{dt}\left(\frac{K(t)}{Y(t)}\right) = \frac{K(t)}{Y(t)}\left[g(1-a)-\beta\right.$$

$$(20) \qquad \left.+\left(\frac{I(t-T)}{y(t-T)}-\frac{K(t)}{Y(t)}\right)\frac{y(t-T)}{K(t)}\frac{N(t)}{n(t-T)}(n-\alpha-bg)\right].$$

Now let us suppose that technical progress is maladjusted in the sense that $(n+\alpha)/b > \beta/(1-a)$; or in other words that it has a labour-saving bias. If g is at the lower of these two values, the capital–output ratio is constant but the share of wages is falling; and if g is at the higher of the two, the capital–output ratio is rising and the share of wages is constant. Intuitively, if g lies between an upper limit of $(n+\alpha)/b$ and a lower limit of $\beta/(1-a)$, we shall have the capital–output ratio tending to rise and the share of wages tending to fall. Since capital is increasing in importance and labour decreasing in importance as a factor of production, we might well expect that this would exert an influence on technical progress making it less labour-saving and more capital saving, so that the gap between $(n + \alpha)/b$ and $\beta/(1 - a)$ would close.[8] Similarly, if technical progress has a capital-saving bias, so that $(n + \alpha)/b <$ $\beta/(1 - a)$, the share of wages is either constant or rising when g is at or between these values, and the capital–output ratio seems likely to be either falling or constant. In these circumstances, we might expect the increasing relative importance of labour to bring about a shift in the nature of technical progress, making it more labour-saving and less capital-saving, and again the gap between $(n + \alpha)/b$ and $\beta/(1 - a)$ would close. Thus it is possible to justify the theoretical existence of a mechanism, analogous to the one more rigorously propounded by Kennedy, Phelps, and others, by which technical progress may in the long run conform to what is required of it in the interests of maintainable growth.

Whether this actually occurs, however, we shall all be dead before we have discovered; and I now turn to the final question of this paper. This is whether the behaviour of the major macroeconomic variables—the share of investment in the national income, the share of wages in the national income, and the capital–output ratio—is sufficient to enable the authorities to recognize the presence and to identify the nature of disequilibria in the growth process. These disequilibria include the maladjustment of technical progress already mentioned; but there is another which must now be included, and which concerns g, the rate of growth of investment itself. We may distinguish four cases:

(1) where g is greater than either $(n + \alpha)/b$ or $\beta/(1 - a)$; this is the case of absolute over-investment;

(2) where

$$\frac{n + \alpha}{b} > g > \frac{\beta}{1 - a};$$

this is the case of a labour-saving bias in technical progress;

[8] I have not proved rigorously that the square bracket in (20) is positive for

$$\frac{n + \alpha}{b} > g > \frac{\beta}{1 - a}.$$

Obviously it is zero when $g = \beta/(1 - a)$. If g is slightly greater than $\beta/(1 - a)$, the terms in the square bracket are:

$$[(+) + (-)(+)]$$

But as g is made larger, the $(-)$ term, although itself becoming larger absolutely, is multiplied by a $(+)$ which diminishes to zero as g reaches $(n + \alpha)/b$. Similar considerations suggest that the square bracket in (20) is negative for

$$\frac{n + \alpha}{b} < g < \frac{\beta}{1 - a}.$$

(3) where

$$\frac{n + \alpha}{b} < g < \frac{\beta}{1 - a};$$

this is the case of a capital-saving bias in technical progress;

(4) where g is smaller than either $(n + \alpha)/b$ or $\beta/(1 - a)$; this is the case of absolute under-investment.

We continue to assume that the authorities pursue a policy of full employment, or at least of maintaining equilibrium in the labour market, taking whatever steps this implies for the maintenance of equilibrium in the product market by the appropriate fiscal or monetary policies for adjusting the ratio of savings to national income. We do not, however, assume that investment and its growth rate are determined in any particular way; only that its growth rate is constant. This is methodologically convenient, because in a model of the type used here it eases the problem of constructing by integration the observable aggregates in which we are interested. But apart from this it is preferable to imposing a particular theory of investment on the model, when we are trying to say something about an economy in which much investment is in fact autonomous, and for the rest the authorities are apt to have a view about its adequacy or inadequacy, which they attempt to enforce through various inducements to invest. Nevertheless the assumption of a constant growth rate of investment is a limitation, which means, for example, that if we identify the behaviour of the economy as that of absolute over-investment, i.e., of case (1), we must strictly mean that what it is doing is what it would have done if it had constantly maintained a growth rate of investment in excess of either of the rates permitted by technical progress.

We shall assume first that we are confined to observations of the share of wages in the national income, $[w(t)N(t)]/[Y(t)]$, and of the share of investment in the national income, $I(t)/Y(t)$. Observations of the capital–output ratio, $K(t)/Y(t)$, are either unavailable or unbelievable. From equation (19), it is evident that if the share of wages is observed rising, it must be the case that

$$g > \frac{n + \alpha}{b}, \quad \text{and if falling,} \quad g < \frac{n + \alpha}{b}.$$

For on the assumption made that $a > b$, and that α, β and g are all positive, $n(t)/y(t)$ is smaller than $N(t)/Y(t)$ always. So the behaviour of the share of wages establishes whether g is above or below what we may now label the 'natural' rate. But what of the 'warranted' rate? Take the case where the share of wages is observed rising, so that we infer $g > (n + \alpha)/b$ from equation (19), and refer to equation (16). If the share of investment is observed falling, this necessarily requires that $g < \beta/(1 - a)$; otherwise the right-hand side of (16) cannot be negative. So a combination of rising share of wages and falling share of investment must mean:

$$\frac{\beta}{1-a} > g > \frac{n+\alpha}{b}$$

That is, we are in the presence of case (3) above, in which technical progress is not labour-saving enough; or to apply the Harrodian terms, the 'warranted' rate exceeds the 'natural' rate and the actual rate lies between them.

However, no such clear-cut identification can be made when observation of a rising share of wages is associated with observation of a rising share of investment. The last term of the right-hand side of (16),

$$-\frac{w(t)N(t)}{Y(t)}(n+\alpha-bg),$$

is positive, and a positive value for the whole of the right-hand side is consistent with either

$$g > \frac{\beta}{1-a} \quad \text{or with} \quad g < \frac{\beta}{1-a}.$$

All that we can conclude is that either technical progress is not labour-saving enough (case (3)) or that we have absolute over-investment (case (1)). The larger the absolute size of the observed rate of rise of the share of investment, the more likely it is that we are in the presence of large g and case (1); but further than this we cannot go.

Similarly, if the share of wages is falling, so that we infer $g < (n+\alpha)/b$, it is only if the share of investment is rising that we can unequivocally state that $g > \beta/(1-a)$; for $g < \beta/(1-a)$ will not generate the required observations of a rising share of investment. We can thus unequivocally identify a rising share of investment and a falling share of wages as case (2), in which technical progress has a labour-saving bias and is inadequately capital-saving. But if the falling share of wages is observed to go with a falling share of investment, then either

$$g > \frac{\beta}{1-a} \quad \text{or} \quad g < \frac{\beta}{1-a}$$

is possible, and we have either case (2) or case (4), between which we cannot further discriminate.

The results so far are summarised in Table I opposite.

Is it possible to remove the uncertainty over the interpretation of observations (ii) and (iv) by bringing in observations of the behaviour of the capital–output ratio, $K(t)/Y(t)$? We have left these out of account so far because of obvious defects in the statistical series which exist for measurement of the capital stock. Quite apart from problems of the valuation of capital assets installed

TABLE I

Observations	Inference
(i) $\dfrac{w(t)N(t)}{Y(t)}$ rising $\dfrac{I(t)}{Y(t)}$ falling	$\dfrac{\beta}{1-a} > g > \dfrac{n+\alpha}{b}$; technical progress too little labour-saving; case (3).
(ii) $\dfrac{w(t)N(t)}{Y(t)}$ rising $\dfrac{I(t)}{Y(t)}$ rising	$g > \dfrac{n+\alpha}{b}$, but g either $>$ or $< \dfrac{\beta}{1-a}$; either case (3) or case (1).
(iii) $\dfrac{w(t)N(t)}{Y(t)}$ falling $\dfrac{I(t)}{Y(t)}$ rising	$\dfrac{n+\alpha}{b} > g > \dfrac{\beta}{1-a}$; technical progress too little capital-saving; case (2).
(iv) $\dfrac{w(t)N(t)}{Y(t)}$ falling $\dfrac{I(t)}{Y(t)}$ falling	$g < \dfrac{n+\alpha}{b}$, but g either $>$ or $< \dfrac{\beta}{1-a}$; either case (2) or case (4).

in the past, for which in the majority of cases there is no second-hand market, there is the problem of what assets invested in past periods are still alive and well and living in the current stock of capital. The perpetual inventory method of estimating the capital stock is based on assumptions of specific lives in terms of years for specific types of asset, and it is very doubtful whether these assumptions are sensitive enough to the changes which actually occur in the ages at which assets are retired. These changes are reflected in the expression set out in equation (18) for changes in the capital–output ratio, but we cannot be confident that they are also reflected in the statistical series for this ratio which we have to use in practice. The statistical series might be improved if it were important enough to do so—for example, by organizing a regular census of capital in use—and the importance of this depends on the extent to which it could help us to infer more precisely the underlying causes of the economy's observed behaviour. If we could know more reliably what the capital–output ratio was doing, would it help?

Consider (ii) in Table I, where the share of wages and the share of investment are both rising, and no unequivocal inference can yet be made. Looking at the right-hand side of equation (18), since $g > (n + \alpha)/b$, $dT/dt < 0$. If $g > \beta/(1 - a)$, it follows[9] that

$$\frac{g}{e^{gT} - 1} < \frac{ag + \beta}{e^{(ag + \beta)T} - 1}$$

[9] Since $\dfrac{g}{e^{gT} - 1} \approx \dfrac{1}{T + \dfrac{gT^2}{2!} + \dfrac{g^2 T^3}{3!} + \cdots}$, and $g > ag + \beta$.

and the square bracket contains terms of the following signs:

$$[(+) + (-)(-)].$$

Hence the capital–output ratio must be rising. On the other hand, if $g < \beta/(1 - a)$, the square bracket contains terms of the following signs:

$$[(-)+(+)(-)]$$

and the capital–output ratio must be falling. Thus a rising capital output ratio, when we also observe rising shares of wages and investment, gives us case (1), in which there is absolute over-investment; and a falling capital–output ratio in the same circumstances gives us case (3), in which

$$\frac{\beta}{1 - a} > g > \frac{n + \alpha}{b}$$

and technical progress is too little labour-saving. The uncertainty over the interpretation of observations (ii) is resolved.

But unfortunately this is not the case with observations (iv) in Table I. Here $g < (n + \alpha)/b$ and so T is rising. If $g > \beta/(1 - a)$, the terms in the square bracket on the right-hand side of (18) run:

$$[(+) + (-)(+)]$$

and if $g < \beta/(1 - a)$, they run:

$$[(-) + (+)(+)].$$

The sign of the square bracket cannot be unequivocally determined, and the direction in which the capital–output ratio is changing cannot help decide whether the economy has absolute under-investment or technical change which is too little capital saving.

These extended results are summarized in Table II opposite.

The behaviour of the capital–output ratio gives us some additional discriminatory power, which may be felt to be enough to justify obtaining more accurate and meaningful observations of it by improving the capital stock statistics. This would involve, in particular, the collection of direct evidence on the age of capital assets in use, so that variations in T could be more accurately recorded. It is interesting that this is important for the interpretation of current trends in the economy of the U.K., which appear to show the rising shares of both wages and investment listed as (ii) of Table II. We cannot strictly reject the hypothesis that technical progress in the U.K. has a bias against labour saving, and accept the hypothesis that investment is growing faster than can be justified by either the capital-saving or the labour-saving element of technical progress, unless we are prepared to accept the observa-

TABLE II

Observations	Inferences

(i) $\dfrac{w(t)N(t)}{Y(t)}$ rising

$\dfrac{I(t)}{Y(t)}$ falling

Technical progress too little labour-saving; case (3).

(ii) $\dfrac{w(t)N(t)}{Y(t)}$ rising

$\dfrac{I(t)}{Y(t)}$ rising

If $K(t)/Y(t)$ is rising, absolute over-investment, as in case (1); if $K(t)/Y(t)$ is falling, technical progress too little labour-saving, as in case (3).

(iii) $\dfrac{w(t)N(t)}{Y(t)}$ falling

$\dfrac{I(t)}{Y(t)}$ rising

Technical progress too little capital-saving, case (2).

(iv) $\dfrac{w(t)N(t)}{Y(t)}$ falling

$\dfrac{I(t)}{Y(t)}$ falling

Either technical change too little capital-saving, as in case (2); or absolute under-investment as in case (4).

tions of the capital–output ratio that we now have as accurate enough.[10] On the other hand, I would be inclined to give priority over improving these observations to finding satisfactory methods of measuring or estimating α and β, the technical change parameters, together with a and b, the parameters reflecting returns to the scale of investment. The main reasons for this are two. First, the indirect inferences which we have been able to make about these parameters depend upon the unreal assumption that the economy has experienced a constant rate of growth of investment in the past. It would be a very lucky coincidence if the actual time-path of past investment were always capable of being represented in some mathematical form which enabled aggregate output, employment, and capital stock to be obtained by integration. With the assumption of a constant growth rate, the indirect inferences which can be drawn are really about an economy which satisfies this assumption, and can only be upheld with a certain amount of daring otherwise. And, secondly, the indirect inferences themselves may fail to emerge from a model less simplified than the one used here.

Nevertheless, the measurement and estimation of α and β, a and b, are beset with difficulties in the current state of information. In a vintage model, in which technical change is embodied in the capital installed in each period, the capital stock is like an iceberg. Its tip protrudes in the form of current investment, and at any time the topmost part of its shape can be descried in the

[10] In Sargent, 1963, I put my money on the first of these hypotheses (case (3)). In Sargent, 1968, I shifted it implicitly to the second (case (1)). I am now hedging both bets, although I would be prepared to stand on the second.

10—I.G.T.

recorded investment of the immediately preceding periods. But the full out-line of its shape is hidden well below the surface, because we lack direct knowledge of what capital installed some way back is still in use. We can hope that when retirement is being accelerated or postponed, it may show up in the current behaviour of the real wage, since this in theory determines how much it is rational to scrap and to retain in use. But rather than impose upon the model an undue burden of theory, it would be preferable to develop a statisti-cal asdic which could detect the shape of what lies below the surface. This means that, while the measurement and estimation of the parameters should be our aim, it is unlikely to be achieved without tackling the job of improving our knowledge of the capital stock which is currently in use, as we have im-proved our knowledge of the additions currently being made to it through gross investment. A periodic census of the capital stock, broken down by age, and supplemented by annual enquiries into current retirements, emerges as a priority requirement in the future development of our statistical knowledge. It is a formidable requirement. But the pay-off from meeting it would be, in the first place, to enable surer inferences to be drawn, from the observed be-haviour of the economy, about the nature of technical change and the scale of investment which it justifies—which would have immediate relevance to policies designed to influence these—and, in the second place, to help us to verify whether there are forces at work constraining both technical change and investment to the conjuncture which is required for maintainable growth.

ANNEX

This annex discusses some points raised by Professor Pyatt about the solutions of equations (6) and (7), which state the conditions of equilibrium in the pro-duct market and the labour market respectively.

Consider equation (6), which can be expressed as:

$$\frac{Y(0)}{y(0)} e^{(g(1-a)-\beta)t} = \frac{1 - e^{-(ag+\beta)T}}{ag + \beta}.$$

The right-hand side of this equation (given that $ag + \beta > 0$) is a bounded function of T which, as T approaches $+\infty$, approaches the value $1/(ag + \beta)$ (see Figure 1). The left-hand side is a function of t, which on the diagram rises or falls as a horizontal line according as

$$g > \frac{\beta}{1-a} \quad \text{or} \quad g < \frac{\beta}{1-a}.$$

At some arbitrary t (say $t = \bar{t}$), it may be in the position where it intersects the function of T at A and yields a solution $T = \bar{T}$. But if $g > \beta/(1-a)$ the horizontal function drifts upwards as t increases and after a while, when it exceeds $1/(ag + \beta)$, loses contact with the function of T, so that a solution for T no longer exists. In economic terms, if the growth of investment is large relatively to the rate of improvement of capital-productivity, the only way to keep equilibrium in the product market is to add to output by raising the age of scrapping. But the effect of this is progressively exhausted because as T rises the average productivity of capital falls. At some point keeping old capital in use for longer will simply not yield enough output to cope with the growth of investment without excess demand in the product market.

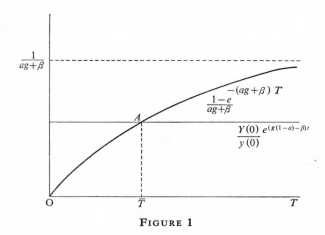

FIGURE 1

A similar possibility arises with equation (7), which can be expressed as:

$$\frac{N(0)}{n(0)} e^{(n - bg + \alpha)t} = \frac{1 - e^{-(bg - \alpha)T}}{bg - \alpha}.$$

If $bg - \alpha < 0$, the right-hand side is a monotonically increasing function of T, rising from zero for $T = 0$ towards $+\infty$ as T approaches $+\infty$; and in this case a solution for T always exists. But if $bg - \alpha > 0$, the function of T on the right-hand side has the same shape as in Figure 1; and if $n > bg - \alpha$ the system may drift, as t increases, out of the range in which a solution is possible. In this case, it is the relatively rapid rate of growth of the labour force which demands increasing T to provide full employment; but there comes a time when it can no longer provide it, because with $g > \alpha/b$ the relative size of the stock of the older machines available to provide employment is small.

The possibility that the system can develop into a state in which it has no equilibrium solution is interesting economically. But it raises the awkward methodological point: what if such a state existed in the past? The system could not then have started off. To derive from equations (6) and (7) the conditions under which equilibrium can be maintained in the product and labour markets is not possible without the assurance that equilibrium once existed, at least at the point from which we want to study the system's subsequent development.

Can we ensure the existence of an equilibrium at $t = 0$? This requires:

$$\frac{N(0)}{n(0)} = \frac{1 - e^{-(bg - \alpha)T(0)}}{bg - \alpha}$$

$$\frac{Y(0)}{y(0)} = \frac{1 - e^{-(ag + \beta)T(0)}}{ag + \beta}.$$

But the two expressions on the left-hand side are not independent of each other, since $n(0) = \lambda I(0)^b$, and $y(0) = \mu I(0)^a$. So we require to know whether the two equations:

$$\frac{N(0)}{\lambda I(0)^b} = \frac{1 - e^{-(bg - \alpha)T(0)}}{bg - \alpha}$$

$$\frac{Y(0)}{\mu I(0)^a} = \frac{1 - e^{-(ag + \beta)T(0)}}{ag + \beta}$$

have positive solutions for $T(0)$ and $I(0)$.

From equation (13) the equilibrium condition for scrapping, we have:

$$w(0) = \frac{\mu}{\lambda} I(0)^{a - b} e^{-(ag + \beta - bg + \alpha)T(0)}.$$

Combining this with the first equation above, we obtain:

$$N(0)w(0) = \mu I(0)^a e^{-(ag + \beta - bg + \alpha)T(0)} \frac{1 - e^{-(bg - \alpha)T(0)}}{bg - \alpha}.$$

The two equations can then be reformulated as:

$$\frac{I(0)^{-a}}{\mu} = \frac{1}{N(0)w(0)} e^{-(x - y)T(0)} \frac{1 - e^{-yT(0)}}{y} = f(T(0))$$

$$\frac{I(0)^{-a}}{\mu} = \frac{1}{Y(0)} \frac{1 - e^{-xT(0)}}{x} = \phi(T(0)).$$

where $x = ag + \beta$, $y = bg - \alpha$. (See Figure 2.)

Evidently, the ϕ function rises monotonically from 0 at $T(0) = 0$ towards $1/(xY(0))$ as $T(0)$ approaches $+\infty$. $\phi' > 0$ always, and

$$\phi'(0) = \frac{1}{Y(0)}.$$

The f function is zero at $T(0) = 0$ and returns to zero as $T(0)$ approaches $+\infty$. In between it can be shown that it reaches a maximum. For:

$$f'(T(0)) = \frac{1}{w(0)N(0)} \left(\frac{x e^{-xT(0)} - (x - y) e^{-(x - y)T(0)}}{y} \right)$$

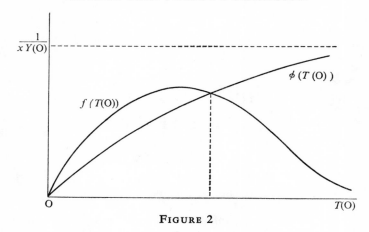

FIGURE 2

and

$$f''(T(0)) = \frac{1}{w(0)N(0)} \left(\frac{(x-y)^2\, e^{-(x-y)T(0)} - x^2\, e^{-xT(0)}}{y} \right).$$

But $f'(T(0)) = 0$ when $e^{yT(0)} = x/(x-y)$; and when this is the case:

$$f'' Y(0) = -\frac{1}{w(0)N(0)}\, x\, e^{-xT(0)} < 0.$$

It is possible, however, that the gradient of $f(T(0))$ is not steep enough to allow it to intersect $\phi(T(0))$. The intersection will occur only if:

$$f'(0) > \phi'(0)$$

that is if:

$$\frac{1}{w(0)N(0)} > \frac{1}{Y(0)}.$$

But this must be the case as long as $w(0)N(0)$, the wage bill, is less than $Y(0)$, the national income, at the outset. This is not an onerous condition for the existence of an initial solution.

REFERENCES

MATTHEWS, R. C. O., *Some Aspects of Post-war Growth in the British Economy in Relation to Historical Experience* (Manchester Statistical Society, 1964).
SARGENT, J. R., *Out of Stagnation* (Fabian Society, 1963).
——, 'Recent Growth Experience in the Economy of the United Kingdom', *Economic Journal*, March 1968.

10

ECONOMIC GROWTH AND THE PRICE LEVEL

TSUKUMO SHIONOYA

1. *Two Opinions on Price Inflation*

(1) FOR the past few years, inflation has been keenly discussed in Japan. Consumer prices have risen at 6 or 7 per cent p.a. since about 1960, when the Japanese economy turned from a labour surplus economy to an economy with labour scarcity, due to the high rate of economic growth during the preceding decade. Because of this inflation, consumers have been threatened with reductions in their standard of living. Furthermore, the discussion has become more heated owing to the failure of governments to stabilize prices in spite of their repeated declarations that they would do so.

In this discussion, it is noteworthy that there are two apparently contradictory opinions. One is that the rise in consumer prices is the inevitable result of economic growth, and that it is not necessary to worry about this provided that the rise in money incomes exceeds the rise of consumer prices; and that the objective of policy ought to be the stabilization of wholesale prices rather than consumer prices. The other is that the rise in consumer prices is the result of an excessively high rate of economic growth, and, in order to stabilize them, a more restrictive policy should be adopted to stabilize the rate of economic growth itself. The former opinion is represented by the school of growthmanship among academic economists and officials, and the latter by the monetary authorities, and consumers in general. Although these seem to be alternative opinions, they can be synthesized, and price policy can be based upon this synthesis.

(2) Where does this take us? It would, I think, take us to a dynamic point of view, in the sense that it would take up the problem in relation to economic growth. Looking back on the history of economics, I feel the problem of inflation has generally been dealt with from a static point of view, in spite of the fact that inflation is essentially dynamic. The quantity theory of money was a typical example of this. We should by now have escaped from that simple and naive traditional theory. Moreover, modern economics is now advancing, putting its emphasis on the theory of economic growth. However,

we cannot find in it a dynamic theory of prices useful enough for us to approach the present price problem of Japan, because, so far, the theory of economic growth has been developed in *real* terms, and the probem of changes in prices has retreated to the background. We must bring it back to the fore.

2. *Development of the Theory of Prices*

(1) The classical theory of prices is, as is well known, the Quantity Theory of Money. First of all, we must escape from it, together with Say's Law, because, although the economic system of the classics—whose main pillars were Say's Law and the Quantity Theory of Money—was struck down by Keynes, such classical ideas seem to be still alive.

Several years ago, when we were discussing the revision of the Bank of Japan Law in the government Committee on the Financial System, I maintained that the objectives of economic policy in general ought to be the maximization of output as well as the stabilization of prices, and that the task of monetary policy ought to be the pursuit of both of these objectives. I thought these ideas could be expressed by the following equation.

(1) $$M = L(p \cdot O, r),$$

where M stands for the supply of money, p for the price level, O for output as a whole, r for the rate of interest, and $p \cdot O = Y$, where Y is the money National Income. This equation indicates that the equalization of the demand for and the supply of money can be achieved through changes in p, O or r, and the point of my argument was that monetary policy should adjust so as to contribute to the situation of O_{max} and p_{const}. The reason why I argued such commonplace matters was that, in that Committee, the idea was dominant that monetary policy should aim *only* at the stabilization of the value of money, and that the adjustment of employment and output should be left to other policy variables. Such ideas seem to me to be nothing but the classical ones based on Say's Law and the Quantity Theory of Money. My argument, of course, was founded on Keynes's *General Theory*.

In the classical system, it is assumed that monetary factors are neutral to the volume of output, which is supposed to depend solely on productive capacity which is given. This assumption was supported by Say's Law and, therefore, maximum output was supposed to be realized automatically, and M was thought to determine only p. The argument that monetary policy should aim only at the stabilization of the value of money was the natural outcome of this theory. But, according to Keynes, output and employment depend on effective demand, which is determined, if the propensity to consume is given, by investment, which, in turn, is determined, if the marginal efficiency of capital is given, by the rate of interest, which, again, if the liquidity preference function is given, depends on the quantity of money.

It follows that control over the quantity of money allows the volume of output to be influenced in so far as the propensity to consume, the marginal efficiency of capital, and the liquidity preference function are given, and that output thus determined can, together with the wage level which is determined otherwise, determine the price level.

Then, in Keynes, the equation for the determination of prices is as follows.

$$(2) \qquad\qquad p = w \cdot \frac{dN}{dO}$$

where w stands for the money wage, N for employment, and dO/dN for the marginal productivity of labour. dO/dN will decrease as output increases in the short run when a production function can be assumed to be given. The real wage, on the other hand, is strongly inflexible downwards, but, as the demand for labour increases, it tends easily to rise. Then the supply of money can influence the price level through its influence on the demand for output and thus on dO/dN, and its influence over w which will partly depend on the demand for output.

These ideas were expressed more systematically in Keynes's 'generalized Quantity Theory of Money', which he wrote as follows:

$$(3) \qquad\qquad e = e_d[1 - e_e \cdot e_{o(n)}(1 - e_w)]$$

where e stands for $(dp/dM) \cdot (M/p)$, e_d for $(dD/dM) \cdot (M/D)$, where D is aggregate demand for output in terms of money, e_e for $(dN/dD_w) \cdot (D_w/N)$, where D_w is aggregate demand in terms of wage units, $e_{o(n)}$ for $(dO/dN) \cdot (N/O)$, and e_w for $(dW/dD) \cdot (D/W)$, where W is the money wage.[1] This equation indicates that when, for instance, the supply of money increases, the larger the values of e_e and $e_{o(n)}$ and the smaller the values of e_d and e_w, the lower the rate of inflation, and vice-versa. In other words, control over the supply of money can, through its effect on aggregate demand, influence not only the price level but also the volume of output.

It was this Keynesian theory which I was considering when I maintained, in the Committee I mentioned above, that the objectives of monetary policy must be both the stabilization of prices and the maximization of output.

(2) Although Keynes's generalized Quantity Theory of Money was a great contribution in that it replaced Say's Law connected with the classical Quantity Theory of Money by the Theory of Effective Demand, it is not

---

[1] The discrepancy between the equation, $e_p = 1 - e_o(1 - e_w)$ which appeared on p. 285 of the *General Theory*, and the equation $e_p = 1 - e_e \cdot e_o(1 - e_w)$ on p. 305 was recently discussed as Keynes's mathematical error (Naylor, 1968), but if we define e_o as $(dO/dN) \cdot (N/O)$ in the latter equation, and denote it as $e_{o(n)}$, we will find that $e_o = e_e \cdot e_{o(n)}$, because e_o in the former equation is $(dO/dD_w) \cdot (D_w/O)$, and $e_e \cdot e_{o(n)}$ in the latter is

$$\left(\frac{dN}{dD_w} \cdot \frac{D_w}{N}\right) \cdot \left(\frac{dO}{dN} \cdot \frac{N}{O}\right) = \frac{dO}{dD_w} \cdot \frac{D_w}{O}.$$

sufficient to offer us the clue with which our price problem can be approached. In order to do this, it is necessary to generalize his generalized Quantity Theory further. For this purpose, two things are important: first, to re-examine the concept of the general price level, and second, to regard the productivity of labour function as a variable. These points were already suggested by Keynes.

(3) As to the first point, in Keynes's generalized Quantity Theory it is clear that the price level is considered to be the reciprocal of the value of money. There is considerable difficulty with the concept of the general price level as the reciprocal of the value of money, in spite of its apparent simplicity. Keynes discussed this in great detail in his *Treatise on Money*, and what he especially emphasized there was that the general price level cannot be given uniquely. He says:

'Since the Purchasing Power of Money in a given context depends on the quantity of goods and services which a unit of money will purchase, it follows that it can be measured by the price of a *composite commodity*, made up of various individual goods and services in proportions corresponding to their importance as objects of expenditure. Moreover, there are many types and purposes of expenditure, in which we may be interested at one time or another, corresponding to each of which there is an appropriate composite commodity. The price of a composite commodity which is representative of some type of expenditure, we shall call a *Price-level*; and the series of numbers indicative of changes in a given price-level we shall call *Index-numbers*. It follows that the number of units of money which is "equivalent" in a given context to a unit of purchasing power, depends on the corresponding price-level and is given by the appropriate Index-number.' [2]

These words tell us in particular that the price-level and also the *price-index* which corresponds to it must be plural. Then, is there no price level which uniquely indicates the *general price-level* which is the reciprocal of the *value of money*? Or, could we think that various price-levels constitute one system, and that that system as a whole, or one particular price-level chosen arbitrarily, represents the value of money? Keynes thought that although there were various price levels corresponding to many types and objects of expenditure, there was one price-level which particularly expressed the purchasing power of money. This was the price level of the goods and services for consumers' expenditure. He wrote:

'Is there any one of these price-levels, and if so which, corresponding *par excellence* to what we mean by the Purchasing Power of Money? We need not hesitate over the answer to this question. We mean by the Purchasing Power of Money the power of money to buy the goods and services on the purchase of

[2] Keynes, 1930, Vol. I, pp. 53–4.

which for purposes of consumption a given community of individuals expend their money income.'[3]

Such an idea is not only Keynes's. We can find the same idea in Marshall's *Money, Credit and Commerce*. He says there, 'The term, "the general purchasing power of money" is usually and reasonably taken to mean the power which money has of purchasing commodities in a country (or other place) in those proportions in which they are in fact consumed there.'[4] And also Wicksell expressed the same idea as follows: 'It seems to me, therefore, that the ideally correct procedure for observing and measuring the general price level is to confine the calculation to objects of (direct) consumption, but over this range to make it as complete as possible, including not only commodities, but rents of houses, certain services, and the like.'[5]

The idea of measuring the purchasing power of money by the index-number of consumer prices is partly connected with the idea that all production has the ultimate purpose of satisfying consumers, and the prices of factors of production which include intermediate products as well as land and labour must affect consumer prices. So Keynes says that 'an index-number of the Purchasing Power of Money should include, directly or indirectly, once and once only, all the items which enter into final consumption (as distinct from an intermediate productive process) weighted in proportion to the amount of their money-income which the consuming public devote to them.'[6] But, the more important reason is the 'welfare', so to speak, point of view, which regards consumer prices as a vital determinant of the economic welfare of the public. Wicksell writes as follows.

'What one really wants to know is whether "living"—ordinary consumption—has become cheaper or dearer. It is true that this consumption comprises not only commodities in the strict sense of the term but also services and even the use of capital—but only if they enter *directly* into consumption as in the case of domestic service, houses, etc.'[7]

According to this line of thought, what economic policy ought to aim at is the stabilization of consumer prices. However, discussion must start from here, because even if it is desirable to stabilize consumer prices from the 'welfare' point of view, the question of how this is related to the other price-levels remains to be discussed. If we can think that when consumer prices are stabilized, the other price-levels will also be stabilized, sooner or later, the over-all problem will appear simpler. But this is not in fact the case. Keynes discussed and criticized the notion which widely permeated 'current economic theory' that the various price-levels measured by different standards 'whilst doubtless theoretically distinct, all come to much the same thing in

---

[3] Ibid., p. 54   [4] Marshall, 1924, p. 21.   [5] Wicksell, 1936, p. 16.
[6] Keynes, 1930, Vol. I, p. 57.   [7] Ibid., pp. 14–15.

practice'—the notion that 'in stable conditions different price-levels stand in defined relationships to each other, and that, if these relationships are temporarily disturbed, nevertheless, forces will be set up tending to restore the former relationships rapidly'. Keynes recognized, on the one hand, that there is an important element of truth in the notion that a change in any one price-level tends to be diffused, but, on the other hand, he thought that the failure of different price levels to move the same way is of the essence of economic fluctuations. According to him, the reasons for 'this failure' are 'a technical change in costs or processes of production by which something is produced at a changed real cost', 'a change in the direction of demand from a changed taste on the part of consumers', and the fact that 'there are many kinds of money contracts, money-customs and money-understandings fixed over periods of time', etc.[8]

These arguments of Keynes's are mainly concerned with the short-term fluctuations of price-levels. We shall find below that technical progress performs a most important role in causing different price-levels to move in different ways in a growing economy.

(4) We must also discuss the second point: the relation of changes in the productivity of labour to the various price-levels.

Although Keynes discussed the failure of different price-levels to move in the same way due to technical change, as we have just observed, he did not deal with the effects of technical progress on the various price levels systematically in either the *Treatise on Money* or the *General Theory*, because, like the neo-classics, he assumed that 'the state of technical knowledge' was given, and inventions were treated as a shock that bounced the economy from one equilibrium to another.[9]

This is represented by his 'Fundamental Equation' concerning the price-level of output as a whole in his *Treatise on Money*, which is as follows.

$$\Pi = \frac{E}{O} + \frac{I - S}{O}$$

(4)
$$= w \cdot \frac{N}{O} + \frac{Q}{O}$$

where Π stands for the price-level of output as a whole, E for money income =cost of production, I for investment, S for saving, and Q for windfall profit or loss. O/N stands for the average productivity of labour. This equation indicates that, assuming O/N and w are given, Π equals $w \cdot N/O$ in equilibrium where $I = S$, and its fluctuations about the equilibrium level depend on $I - S$. In his generalized Quantity Theory in the *General Theory*, the productivity of labour is again given, while the wage level is assumed to

[8] Keynes, 1930, Vol. I, pp. 89–93.   [9] Robinson, 1956, p. 101.

be variable. But, in the long period, both w and O/N must be liable to change, and therefore Keynes himself, after he discussed the long-term trend of the price level, wrote that 'the long-run stability or instability of prices will depend on the strength of the upward trend of the wage-unit (or, more precisely, of the cost-unit) compared with the rate of increase in the efficiency of the productive system'.[10] This is the clue to the problem of inflation in a growing economy.

3. *Technical Progress and the Price Level*

(1) The post-Keynesian theory of economic growth which was originally developed by Harrod (1939, 1948), Domar (1946), Samuelson (May 1939, December 1939), and others, was expected to contribute to the solution of problems posed by the old classical economists with the use of Keynesian methods.[11] In fact, it has made a great contribution towards changing the central theme of economics from short-term statics to long-term dynamics. Nevertheless, it did not offer a long-term dynamic theory of prices. But we can find some useful guides for it in the theories developed by Joan Robinson, Kaldor, and some others who are rather critical of the theories based mainly on the combination of the multiplier theory and the acceleration principle.

(2) The main points of criticism presented by Joan Robinson[12] and Kaldor[13] against the theories represented by Harrod and Hicks appears to be that they place too much emphasis on the acceleration principle, and that the growth of the labour force and its productivity are assumed to be independent variables. Adam Smith opened his *Wealth of Nations* by sketching the conditions where the wealth of nations will increase. According to him, the increase of wealth is determined by two circumstances; first, by the proportion of the population which is employed in useful labour, and, secondly, by 'the skill, dexterity and judgement' with which they apply their labour. The former, he maintained, is increased by the accumulation of capital, and the latter by the development of the division of labour, but the division of labour, in turn, will advance with the accumulation of capital. Such accumulation of capital must mean autonomous investment in Keynes's sense, and not induced investment due to the acceleration principle. The opinion of Joan Robinson and Kaldor seems to be in accordance with Smith, and I want to agree with them. In particular, Robinson's theory of technical progress seems to be useful.

(3) As mentioned above, it is the usual practice to assume a 'given state of technical knowledge'; it means that the production function which relates

---

[10] Keynes, 1936, p. 309.   [11] Robinson, 1949 (ii), p. 95.
[12] Robinson, 1949 (i) and (ii); 1956.   [13] Kaldor, 1954; 1960 (i) and (ii).

the productivity of a labour unit to capital per worker is given. But, in a growing economy, it will shift continuously. The causes which bring about that shift are various. Among them are the progress of scientific knowledge, and technological advance which are exogenous to the economic process, but much more important are the 'inventions' endogenous to the economic process which are induced by changes in the distribution of income between wages and profits, etc.

It was from this point of view that Joan Robinson developed her theory of technical progress. Roughly, it goes like this. If the rate of capital accumulation rises for some reason, and if it exceeds the rate of increase of the labour force, wage rates will rise. In this case, if the 'state of technical knowledge' is given, the rate of profit will fall, even if a 'more mechanized' technique of production is chosen. The way to prevent that fall in the rate of profit is to promote technical progress, namely, to make the production function shift upwards. The patterns of that shift are various, and according to the various differences, Joan Robinson divides the types of technical progress into capital-saving, labour saving, etc., but whichever direction technical progress takes, in so far as it brings about a rise in labour productivity which exceeds the rise in money wages, the price level being constant, it will raise the rate of profit and consequently favour the accumulation of capital and economic growth. Joan Robinson's apparently paradoxical conclusion is interesting, 'The rate of profit on capital will tend to be higher, and real wages lower; (1) the more plentiful are the technical opportunities for mechanizing production; (2) the slower is the rate of capital accumulation in relation to the growth of population; (3) the weaker is the force of competition (and the weaker is the bargaining power of workers, when competition is weak). Given the degree of competition and the rate of growth of population, the course of the rate of profit over the long run . . . depends on the interaction between technical progress and the rate of accumulation. Technical discoveries . . . are continuously tending to raise the rate of profit and accumulation is tending to depress it. Prosperous capitalist economies are those where the rate of profit is falling in spite of rapid technical progress, and miserable ones those where the rate of profit is high in spite of technical stagnation.'[14]

Robinson's theory is based on Wicksell's (1893) static theory of the choice of technique, or the degree of roundaboutness of production. But it also reminds me of Ricardo (1817), because it was thought by him that the falling rate of profit, and the trend towards the stationary state due to the use of less fertile land which must lead to lower output per worker in so far as technique is constant, would be checked by technical improvements brought about by entrepreneurs' active efforts to prevent the fall in the rate of profit.

It is very important for us to see that economic growth is, to a great extent,

[14] Robinson, 1953–4, p. 103.

the outcome of a struggle between rising wages and technical progress to prevent these higher wages from causing a fall in the rate of profit.

(4) I will approach the problem of inflation in a growing economy from such considerations. For this purpose, I want to recall Keynes's Fundamental Equation ((4) above), and to modify its terminology. Keynes's E includes 'normal profits', but here I exclude these from E and add them to Q. Therefore, in my terminology, E, i.e., $w \cdot N$, is the sum of factor costs represented by wages, and Q is the sum of realized profits.

The traditional theories of price have concentrated their attention on demand in relation to supply potential, but, since 1945, the vital problem has been the relation between wage increases and increases in the productivity of labour. This is because the demand for labour has been very strong, and money wages have risen continuously. In that case, if O/N and Π are constant, it is inevitable that Q/O will fall. The one way to prevent this is to raise Π, but, when competition between firms prevails, it is not always easy to raise prices, and the remaining way to prevent a fall in Q/O is to increase O/N through technical improvements. But in so far as it is absolutely necessary to maintain enough profit for the firm to survive, it is inevitable that prices will be raised if the productivity of labour fails to rise at least proportionately with the rise in wages.

Next, the problem of the plurality of price levels must be considered.

4. Stable Wholesale Prices and Rising Consumer Prices

(1) As I said at the outset, the characteristic of rising prices in Japan since about 1960 has been that, while wholesale prices have been almost stable, consumer prices have been rising continuously at 6 or 7 per cent p.a. This discrepancy between the two price levels was the consequence of the particular pattern of economic growth of Japan.

Immediately after the end of World War 2, the Japanese economy was said to be of 'dual-structure' in the sense that two distinct industrial sectors, which differ in labour productivity, the wage-level, and the rate of profit, co-exist; one of these, which I shall call the first sector, consists of large-scale secondary industries, and the other, the second sector, consists of the primary and tertiary industries as well as many small businesses. In the former sector, labour productivity, wages, and the rate of profit were all higher than in the latter, and the relative prices of its products were also higher.

We shall describe this dual structure by the following two equations.

(5)
$$p_1 = w_1\left(\frac{N}{O}\right)_1 + \left(\frac{Q}{O}\right)_1$$

(6)
$$p_2 = w_2\left(\frac{N}{O}\right)_2 + \left(\frac{Q}{O}\right)_2$$

where the suffixes 1 and 2 represent the first and the second sector respectively. The dual structure is characterized by $(O/N)_1 > (O/N)_2$, $w_1 > w_2$, $(Q/O)_1 > (Q/O)_2$, and the relation of p_1 to p_2 is favourable to the first sector.

This dual character of the Japanese economy was made possible by the redundant supply of labour in agriculture and small businesses.

The reconstruction of the Japanese economy after the war was associated with rapid changes in industrial structure; with heavy investment in the first sector, there was a continuous transfer of labour from the less productive second sector to the more productive first sector. This process was similar to the general description of industrialization by Lewis (1954) and Kaldor.[15] The substantial capital investment which was necessary was partly financed by the general 'forced saving' which was due to heavy post-war inflation, and partly from high profit margins which were due to the large reservoir of labour which kept wage rates low. But as time passed, the surplus of labour became less and less, and we reached the turning point where we began to feel labour scarcity. It was around 1960; 1959–61 was the period of super-rapid economic growth, the average annual rate of real growth reaching more than 15 per cent. Since then, wage differentials between the two sectors have become rapidly narrower, and at the same time, the general level of money wages has been rising.

In the first sector, rising money wages were sufficiently matched by rising labour productivity, with the result that there was no need for higher prices. This is the main reason why wholesale prices were stable. On the other hand, while w_2 rose pari-passu with w_1, $(O/N)_2$ did not increase equally with $(O/N)_1$, and in order for $(Q/O)_2$ to be maintained, p_2 needed to be raised. This is the fundamental reason for the continuous rise of consumer prices, for the prices of the products of the second sector have considerable weight in the consumers price-index.

(2) The stability of Japanese wholesale prices from about 1949, when the heavy post-war inflation ended, made a considerable contribution to Japan's high rate of economic growth. In many manufacturing industries, increases in productivity continuously exceeded rises in money wages, and the stability of the prices of their products contributed to the increase in the share of profits which stimulated investment in this sector. Moreover, the stability of wholesale prices, together with a wage level which was relatively low internationally, were favourable to our competitive power in international trade. Consequently, if we regard a high rate of economic growth as the primary objective of economic policy, price policy should perhaps aim at the stabilization of wholesale prices.

On the other hand, the continuous rise of consumer prices means a declining real wage to the extent that rising money wages lag behind the rise of

---

[15] Kaldor, 1966, pp. 26–7.

consumer prices, and therefore it is undesirable from a 'welfare' point of view.

Then, is the lag between the rise of $(O/N)_1$ and that of $(O/N)_2$ temporary or frictional, and will it disappear in due course? Historically, it may be so. But for Japan, economic maturity in the sense that the productivity gap between industries is eliminated, will not be reached in the near future. Consequently, which price level ought to be stabilized will remain a problem for economic policy. Of course, I think the stabilization of consumer prices is desirable and must be pursued as far as possible. But if we prefer the stabilization of p_2 in the strict sense of the term, in so far as there is the lag between the rise of $(O/N)_1$ and that of $(O/N)_2$, p_1 must be pulled down. This would not be easy. Then, I think, in Japan, it would be preferable to stabilize p_1, because we still have a labour reservoir in the second sector whose marginal productivity is relatively low, and therefore we still have a large potential for rapid economic growth, and in so far as the high rate of economic growth could be maintained, the standard of living would not be reduced in spite of the rise of p_2, because the rise of the general wage-level which depends on the rise of $(O/N)_1$ would be greater than the rise of p_2, which depends on the difference in the rate of rise of O/N in the two sectors. Japan's G.N.P. is the third highest in the world, next to the U.S.A. and Soviet Russia, but Japan's income per head is still in the twentieth rank. This means that increases in labour productivity must be promoted by more accumulation of capital. In Japan we have recently begun to discuss the adoption of an 'incomes policy', but I think it is preferable for us to promote increases in labour productivity rather than to adopt an incomes policy which would require us to keep rises in money wages in line with the average increase of productivity of labour as a whole.

REFERENCES

DOMAR, E. D., 'Capital Expansion, Rate of Growth, and Employment', *Econometrica*, April 1946.

HARROD, R. F., 'An Essay in Dynamic Theory', *Economic Journal*, March 1939.

——, *Towards a Dynamic Economics* (London, 1948).

HICKS, J. R., *A Contribution to the Theory of the Trade Cycle* (Oxford, 1950).

KALDOR, N., 'The Relation of Economic Growth and Cyclical Fluctuations', *Economic Journal*, March 1954.

——, *Essays on Economic Stability and Growth* (London, 1960) (i).

——, *Essays on Value and Distribution* (London, 1960) (ii).

——, *Causes of the Slow Rate of Economic Growth of the United Kingdom* (London, 1966).

KEYNES, J. M., *A Treatise on Money*, 2 vols. (London, 1930).

——, *The General Theory of Employment, Interest and Money* (London, 1936).

LEWIS, W. A., 'Development with Unlimited Supplies of Labour', *Manchester School*, May 1954.

MARSHALL, A., *Money, Credit and Commerce* (London, 1924).

NAYLOR, T. H., 'A Note on Keynesian Mathematics', *Economic Journal*, March 1968, pp. 172–3.

RICARDO, D., *Principles of Political Economy and Taxation* (London, 1817).

ROBINSON, JOAN, 'Mr. Harrod's Dynamics', *Economic Journal*, March 1949 (i).

——, *An Essay on Marxian Economics* (London, 1949) (ii).

——, 'The Production Function and the Theory of Capital', *Review of Economic Studies*, 1953–4, Vol. XXI (2).

——, *The Accumulation of Capital* (London, 1956).

——, *Economic Philosophy* (London, 1965).

SAMUELSON, P. A., 'Interrelation between the Multiplier Analysis and the Principle of Acceleration', *Review of Economic Statistics*, May 1939.

——, 'A Synthesis of the Principle of Acceleration and the Multiplier', *Journal of Political Economy*, December 1939.

SMITH, A., *An Inquiry into the Nature and Causes of the Wealth of Nations* (London 1776).

WICKSELL, K., *Über Wert, Kapital und Rente* (Jena, 1893).

——, *Interest and Prices*, translated by R. F. Kahn (London, 1936).

11

ECONOMETRICS IN THE WORLD OF TODAY

RAGNAR FRISCH

1. *Introduction*

WHEN I was invited to speak at the First World Congress of the Econometric Society, held in Rome in September 1965, it was inevitable that my memory should go back some thirty years to the First European Meeting of the Econometric Society, held in 1931 in Lausanne, the place where Walras[1] lived and taught. I had the good fortune to be present at that meeting and to speak about the nature of econometrics. If I remember correctly we were about twenty persons all counted. At the First World Congress in 1965 there were several hundred. But if it is possible to measure the absolute volume of enthusiasm I venture to say that the sum total of enthusiasm present at that first meeting was not very much below that which was present at the 1965 Congress. We, the Lausanne people, were indeed so enthusiastic all of us about the new venture, and so eager to give and take, that we had hardly time to eat when we sat together at lunch or at dinner with all our notes floating around on the table to the despair of the waiters.

When we take a look at the number of papers and the variety of subjects treated at the First World Congress and make a comparison with the list of papers given at the Lausanne meeting, we must be amazed at the development that has taken place in this single generation. This comparison could perhaps have tempted me, at the First World Congress, to indulge in a eulogy of econometricians and their work. However, I resisted this temptation. If there is one thing which our Society must *not* be, it is a society for self-admiration. My attitude had more a leaning towards the critical side than towards the eulogical, and so I was rather outspoken. So much so that some of the audience may perhaps have found it a bit embarrassing. However, at that juncture of econometric development, I believed I could render a better service to the econometric fraternity by being critical and outspoken than by sugar-coating the pill. I still hold that view today.

---

[1] As we learned from Walras's pupil and close friend Professor Bonninsegni, Walras himself and those who knew him pronounced Walras with the 's' sounded.

It is very much in line with the Editorial I wrote in the first Volume of *Econometrica*, published 1933, where I said *inter alia*: 'The policy of *Econometrica* will be as heartily to denounce futile playing with mathematical symbols in economics as to encourage their constructive use.'

The econometric army has now grown to such proportions that it cannot be beaten by the silly arguments that were used against us previously. This imposes on us a *social and scientific responsibility* of high order in the world of today.

To bring home forcefully what I mean by social and scientific responsibility in this connection, let me mention a signal development that has taken place in the economic life of Norway in recent years. During wage negotiations between trade unions and employers, with the government as a very active 'observer'—negotiations the outcome of which may mean the paralysis of active life in the Norwegian economy for months and years to come—it has now become customary to have at one's disposal a fairly advanced *econometric model* based on Norwegian data and coded on the electronic computer of the Central Bureau of Statistics, ready at any time *quickly* to produce estimates of answers to certain highly important questions that may come up in the course of the negotiations. Subsidies to agriculture and fishing are also worked into the model. Norway is probably a country where this kind of practical application of econometric models has been pushed the farthest. But year by year this and other kinds of practical applications of econometric models are penetrating deeper and deeper into economic decisions also at the *national* level. It is only in recent years that we begin to see the *real impact* of the econometric idea that began to take shape when the Econometric Society was founded in 1930.

Herein lies the great opportunity of the econometricians of today—but herein also lies the great social and scientific responsibility that is imposed on them.

2. *A simple Example illustrating the Mathematical Essence of the von Neumann Path*

There are many types of growth theories and growth models. There is in particular one which is relevant to my subject, namely, the type characterized by such concepts as the von Neumann path and turnpike theorems. Therefore let me begin at this end of the spectrum. I think it is possible to suggest the essence of the von Neumann path by an example which is so simple that it is really nothing more than a little exercise in elementary college algebra and function theory.

Let us consider a system of two homogeneous linear differential equations

$$(2.1) \quad \begin{aligned} \dot{x}_1 &= a_{11}x_1 + a_{12}x_2 \\ \dot{x}_2 &= a_{21}x_1 + a_{22}x_2 \end{aligned}$$

where the a_{ij} are given constants, x_1 and x_2 functions of time and $\dot{x}_1$ and $\dot{x}_2$ derivatives with respect to time. We may, if we like, look upon (2.1) as the definition of a *velocity vector* whose components $(\dot{x}_1, \dot{x}_2)$ are defined in any point (x_1, x_2) by (2.1).

A concrete interpretation of x_1 and x_2 might (apart from additive constants) be the physical outputs in two sectors in a dynamic growth model. In a realistic situation the number of variables in the model will, of course, have to be much greater, but for describing the principle involved two variables will suffice.

My little exercise on this example will not include the usual study of the time shapes of the solutions as a sum of two exponential functions whose exponents are the, possibly imaginary, roots of the characteristic equation, but it will be concerned with something that is even simpler than this.

Let us ask if there exists a beam—that is a straight line through the origin —which is such that in any point on this beam the velocity defined by (2.1) *is directed along the beam itself.*

Any beam through the origin is defined by the two equations

(2.2)
$$x_1 = d_1\omega$$
$$x_2 = d_2\omega$$

where d_1 and d_2 are two constant direction numbers defining the direction of the beam, and ω is a parameter whose variation from $-\infty$ to $+\infty$ generates the beam. The geometric properties of the beam are, of course, not changed if we multiply the two directing numbers d_1 and d_2 by a common non-zero factor. Therefore it is only the *ratio*

(2.3)
$$\lambda = \frac{d_2}{d_1}$$

between the direction numbers that counts. The ratio (2.3) assumes that $d_1 \neq 0$. In the case $d_1 = 0$ we simply consider the reciprocal of λ, or we may change the numbering of the variables. At least one of the two direction numbers must be different from zero if the beam is to have a meaning.

At any point on the beam (2.2) we have by (2.1)

(2.4)
$$\frac{\dot{x}_2}{\dot{x}_1} = \frac{a_{21}d_1 + a_{22}d_2}{a_{11}d_1 + a_{12}d_2} = \frac{a_{21} + a_{22}\lambda}{a_{11} + a_{12}\lambda}.$$

If this ratio is to be equal to λ, then λ must satisfy the equation

(2.5)
$$a_{12}\lambda^2 + (a_{11} - a_{22})\lambda = a_{21}$$

hence

(2.6)
$$\lambda = -\frac{(a_{11} - a_{22}) \pm \mid \sqrt{(a_{11} - a_{22})^2 + 4a_{12}a_{21}} \mid}{2a_{12}}.$$

This is a necessary condition on λ. On the other hand if λ has any of the values (2.6) it is easy to see that the properties we require from the beam are fulfilled. So the condition (2.5) is both necessary and sufficient. A beam whose λ value is determined by (2.6) will be called an *intrinsic beam* of the system.[2]

All the various cases that may occur can be classified as follows:

(2.6.1) $0 < a_{12}a_{21}$ (hence $a_{12} \neq 0$) gives one real finite positive root *and* one real finite negative root. No root $\lambda = 0$ and no complex roots.

(2.6.2) $a_{12}a_{21} = 0$. This case can be split into the following three subcases:

(A) $a_{12} \neq 0$, $a_{21} = 0$ gives one root $\lambda = 0$ *and* one root which has the opposite sign of $(a_{11} - a_{22})/a_{12}$ (zero if $a_{11} = a_{22}$).

(B) $a_{12} = 0$, $a_{21} \neq 0$ gives a single root which may be either positive or negative (infinite if $a_{11} = a_{22}$).

(C) $a_{12} = a_{21} = 0$ gives one root $\lambda = 0$ if $a_{11} \neq a_{22}$. If $a_{11} = a_{22}$ any finite value of λ will satisfy (2.5).

(2.6.3) $-\dfrac{(a_{11} - a_{22})^2}{4} < a_{12}a_{21} < 0$ (hence $a_{12} \neq 0$ and $a_{11} \neq a_{22}$) gives a case where *either* both roots are positive *or* both roots negative.

(2.6.4) $a_{12}a_{21} = -\dfrac{(a_{11} - a_{22})^2}{4} < 0$ (hence $a_{12} \neq 0$ and $a_{11} \neq a_{22}$) gives a double root which may be *either* positive *or* negative (but not zero).

(2.6.5) $a_{12}a_{21} < -\dfrac{(a_{11} - a_{22})^2}{4} < 0$ gives no λ root in the real domain.

It would not be difficult to study in more detail all these various cases, but this is of no interest for my purpose. I shall confine myself to the case (2.6.1), i.e. the case where the effect of x_1 on $\dot{x}_2$ is of *the same sort*—with regard to sign—as the effect of x_2 on $\dot{x}_1$. This case will give me all the examples I need.

If we confine ourselves to case (2.6.1) and we only consider points *in the first quadrant* i.e., where both x_1 and x_2 are positive, we are left with *one and only one* intrinsic beam, viz., the one characterized by the positive value of λ.

If we *happen* to be at a point on our intrinsic beam, the velocity vector defined by (2.1) is directed along the beam, and consequently *we will stay on this beam indefinitely.*

Along this beam x_1 and x_2 will be equal to the constant direction numbers

---

[2] The intrinsic beam has no direct connection with the characteristic roots and the characteristic vectors of the system (2.1).

d_1 and d_2 respectively, multiplied by a common function of time ω. The rate of change with respect to time of this common function is easily determined by noticing that along the beam we have $\dot{x}_1 = d_1\dot{\omega}$. Utilizing the first of the two equations in (2.2), we therefore get along the beam

$$(2.7) \qquad \frac{\dot{\omega}}{\omega} = a_{11} + a_{12}\,\lambda.$$

This rate of change is a constant *depending only on the coefficients of the given system of linear differential equations (2.1)*. Since the rate of change of ω is constant along the beam, x_1 and x_2 will by (2.2) also have the same rate of change along the beam. That is, we have[3]

$$(2.8) \qquad \frac{\dot{x}_1}{x_1} = \frac{\dot{x}_2}{x_2} = \frac{\dot{\omega}}{\omega} = a_{11} + a_{12}\lambda \qquad \text{(along the beam).}$$

This is as good a von Neumann path as you can ever hope to get. And you see how extremely simply it follows from the assumption of a linear and homogeneous system of differential equations. In the linear and homogeneous case it is really a next to obvious conclusion. The case would in its essence not be much different if we considered difference equations instead of differential equations or if we increased the number of variables in the system.

What will happen if we start at any initial point (x^0_1, x^0_2) and from there on let the movement be guided by the differential system (2.1)? This can best be exhibited by depicting (2.1) as a velocity field represented by a set of velocity vectors with components $(\dot{x}_1, \dot{x}_2)$, these vectors being distributed all over the first quadrant. Figures (2.9) and (2.10) are two numerical examples where the a_{ij} matrix of (2.1) is respectively

$$\begin{pmatrix} 1 & 1 \\ 2 & 0 \end{pmatrix} \quad \text{and} \quad \begin{pmatrix} -1 & 1.04 \\ 1.04 & -1 \end{pmatrix}.$$

If we start at an arbitrary point in the first quadrant, we will proceed along a trajectory defined by the velocity vector field and will end up by approaching the intrinsic beam of the system. And once we have gotten into the close vicinity of the intrinsic beam we will remain permanently in this vicinity.

The equations by which Figures (2.9) and (2.10) were computed are

$$(2.9) \qquad \begin{aligned} \dot{x}_1 &= x_1 + x_2 \\ \dot{x}_2 &= 2x_1 \end{aligned}$$

$$(2.10) \qquad \begin{aligned} \dot{x}_1 &= -x_1 + 1{\cdot}04x_2 \\ \dot{x}_2 &= 1{\cdot}04x_1 - x_2 \end{aligned}$$

---

[3] Instead of the right-hand expression in (2.8) we could have written $(a_{22} + a_{21} \cdot (1/\lambda))$. The two expressions are equal by virtue of (2.5).

For clarity the lengths of the vectors were reduced to one-fifth in (2.10). In (2.9) they have their original lengths.

In both cases the intrinsic path is a diagonal sloping upward at 45°. But otherwise there is a big difference. If in Figure (2.9) we start in the north-west or in the south-east, it would only be *very far out* and *after a very long time* that we would approach the vicinity of the diagonal. As we draw closer to the diagonal the movement in Figure (2.9) becomes, indeed, nearly parallel to the diagonal with only a next to imperceptible further approach to the

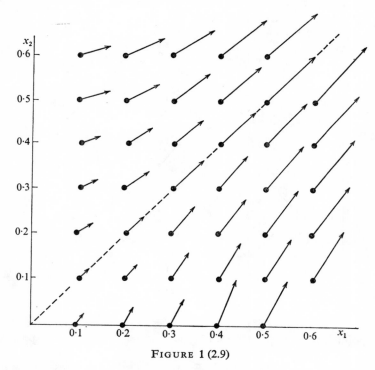

FIGURE 1 (2.9)

diagonal. On the contrary in Figure (2.10) the tendency towards approach to the intrinsic beam is very much *quicker*. Both figures can be taken to illustrate a *river bed*. In Figure (2.10) the banks of the river bed are much steeper than in Figure (2.9).

We note that if $a_{11} = a_{22}$ and if the units of measurement of x_1 and x_2 are conventionally chosen in such a way that the inclination of the intrinsic beam becomes $\lambda = 1$, and if the growth rate along the intrinsic beam is r, we have

(2.11)

$$a_{11} + a_{12} = r$$

$$a_{21} + a_{11} = r$$

the matrix of (2.1) becomes[4]

(2.12)
$$\begin{pmatrix} a_{11} & r - a_{11} \\ r - a_{11} & a_{11} \end{pmatrix}.$$

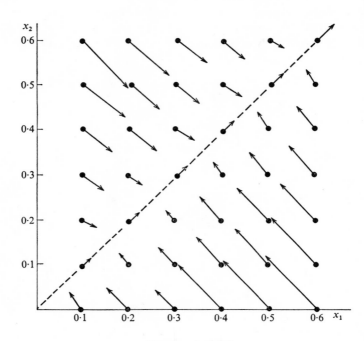

FIGURE 2 (2.10)

In the points ($x_1 = 1$, $x_2 = 2$) and ($x_1 = 2$, $x_2 = 1$) this gives respectively

(2.13)
$$\dot{x}_1 = - a_{11} + 2r$$
$$\dot{x}_2 = + a_{11} + r$$

and

(2.14)
$$\dot{x}_1 = + a_{11} + r$$
$$\dot{x}_2 = - a_{11} + r.$$

[4] As a check on (2.12) we note that in this case the positive root of (2.6) is 1, regardless of what r and a_{11} are. The matrix of Figure (2.10), being a special case of (2.12), must have $\lambda = 1$. The matrix of Figure (2.9) is not a special case of (2.12), but this example too has $\lambda = 1$, which is verified by inserting the matrix coefficients of (2.9) into (2.6).

This shows that if we choose a_{11} negative, say equal to -1, we can, by making r positive but small, produce an example with very steep banks, like the one illustrated in Figure (2.10).

In the case $\begin{pmatrix} 3 & 1 \\ 2 & 2 \end{pmatrix}$, the intrinsic beam will represent a *ridge* ('negative bank steepness') sloping downwards towards the north-west. In the case $\begin{pmatrix} -2 & 1 \\ 2 & 3 \end{pmatrix}$, growth will be negative. Putting $r = 0$ in (2.12) we get a stagnant case.

3. *The River-beddiness and the Bank Steepness of a General Field*

The case where there exists a single intrinsic path, which is even further specialized as being a beam—a straight line through the origin—is of course too simple to be realistic. We have to consider more general types of fields. In the case of two variables we get a good survey of the possibilities by thinking of the map of a hilly landscape and thinking of the trajectories which raindrops will follow when they fall on this country and seek their way to the ocean. Consider the projection of such trajectories on to the plane of the map. An extreme case would be one where the country contains a single river-bed with steep banks. We will then get a situation similar to Figure (2.10), perhaps with a river-bed that is curved instead of straight. In the case of a single river-bed with steep banks, any drop that falls will quickly find its way to the river and from there on it will follow the river to the ocean. In other cases there may be, say, two or three main river-beds, each with perhaps one or more tributaries and with banks that may be more steep or less steep. A look at the topographic maps of some region of the world will suggest the variety of cases that may exist.

In some cases the landscape may be more or less *diffuse* with no conspicuous river-beds so that nothing in particular can be said about the trajectories without specifying where precisely the *initial points* are, and the—more or less *random*—vicissitudes that may occur. For instance in the case of the Nile there is to begin with a fairly conspicuous river-bed. But later the waters of the Nile pass through a big diffuse swamp country at the end of which the river again gets back to a more conspicuous river-bed pattern, which is particularly sharply defined with steep banks in the cataracts immediately south of Aswan.

Economic life and technical possibility are—just as the pattern of river-beds and bank steepnesses we find in the concrete shape of a country—too diversified to be classified according to some rule derived from oversimplified assumptions.

4. *Technological and Preferential Features of the Field*

But for a moment let us nevertheless revert to the case (2.1) which led to the existence of a single, well-determined, intrinsic path in the form of a beam through the origin.

We note that there are many linear and homogeneous systems of the form (2.1) which will have the *same* intrinsic beams since the beam is defined by a single parameter λ while the system (2.1) contains no less than four constants.

Generalizing the set-up, we may drop the assumption that the system of differential equations is of the linear and homogeneous kind and consider a variety of forms, all of which may lead to a well-defined intrinsic beam, or possibly to an intrinsic curved line. We may even go further and drop the concept of a velocity vector that is deterministically *given* in each point, and instead proceed by the following general type of reasoning.

First, regarding the vector field (or more generally the transmission field). We postulate that if we are in any given point (x_1, x_2) the direction of move from (x_1, x_2) is subject to satisfying certain conditions expressed by *equations* and/or by *bounds*, i.e., inequalities that depend on the point (x_1, x_2). The equations and/or bounds may be deterministic or stochastic. This system of conditions we may call the *technology*, taking technology in a very broad sense. The technology is assumed to remain constant over the whole time period to be considered. All historical trajectories—or paths, if we like to call them so—will have to satisfy this constant technology. That is, they must be technologically *permissible*.

Second, we state a *supplementary convention*. This is an assumption about the vector field which makes it possible to define the concept of an *intrinsic* path. That is a path with the property that *if* we are on it (or close to it), this path is not only technologically permissible but such that we will stay on it (or close to it) for ever if we are guided by the vector field which has been specified through this supplementary convention.

Under a given set of supplementary conventions there may be *several* paths each with the property that we will stay on (or close to) it for ever, once we have gotten on (or close to) it.

If several intrinsic paths exist we may work towards the definition of *one specific* intrinsic path by *reinforcing* the supplementary convention in some way. There are several alternatives for doing this.

It may, for instance, be done by specifying that the bounds involved in the definition of the technology are everywhere to be replaced by strict equalities of such a particular sort that leads to a unique intrinsic path. We may specify in such a way that the uniquely defined intrinsic path derives its properties mainly from the *engineering* aspects of the technology. Or we might achieve the definition of the unique intrinsic path by assuming a specific *gaming rule* between the market and the engineering aspects of the technology, in which case the intrinsic path would to a large extent be influenced by our conception of some sort of behaviouristic pattern. At any rate the supplementary convention must be specified in sufficient detail to take away enough degrees of freedom so that we end up with a unique one-dimensional intrinsic path.

Third, regarding the preference function. There is a definite limit to the degree of reinforcement of the technological assumption that may be applied for the purpose of reaching the definition of a *unique* intrinsic path: the assumptions about the engineering aspects of the technology and about the gaming rules must not carry us too far away from the concrete situation studied. In most cases this limit will tend to lead us into a situation where we have to face, not a unique intrinsic path, but a *number of alternative intrinsic paths,* all of which are technologically permissible. In such cases it is necessary to introduce a *preference function* which will order all technologically permissible intrinsic paths in a preference order. This is the essence of a *purposeful* macroeconomic policy. That one of all technologically permissible paths which has the highest preference might be called the *optimal* path.

With such a theoretical set-up it might be possible to prove various types of turnpike theorems, i.e., theorems to the effect that under certain conditions the actual path will for a considerable part of the total time considered follow rather closely to the optimal path which has been defined through the three logical elements considered above: the vector field, the supplementary convention, and the preference function. To reach such theorems it is *necessary* to accept all the three logical elements discussed (or something equivalent to them). Whether it will or will not be possible to formulate a turnpike theorem will *depend essentially on how we specify the three logical elements in question.* Most turnpike analyses have escaped the problem of the preference function by—too often tacitly—making assumptions about the first and the second logical elements which will lead to a unique intrinsic path.

If we are resourceful enough we may invent a variety of supplementary conventions which may lead to a corresponding variety of kinds of intrinsic paths. And with an appropriate definition of the preference function we might be able to prove that the *optimal* path will for a time follow closely to one of the intrinsic paths we have introduced, and later, perhaps, switch to following closely to another of these intrinsic paths.

There is no end to the variety of turnpike theorems that could be invented in this way.

5. *The Economic Relevance of the Intrinsic Paths and Turnpike Type of Theorem*

What is the economic relevance of intrinsic paths and turnpike type of theorem of the kind I have mentioned?

To be quite frank I feel that the relevance of this type of theorem for active and realistic work on economic development, in industrialized or under-developed countries, is practically nil. The reason for this is that the conse-quences that are drawn in this type of theorem *depend so essentially on the nature of the assumptions made.* And these assumptions are frequently made more for the convenience of mathematical manipulation than for reasons of similarity to concrete reality.

In too many cases the procedure followed resembles too much the escapist procedure of the man who was facing the problem of multiplying 13 by 27. He was not very good at multiplication but very proficient in the art of adding figures, so he thought he would try to add these two figures. He did and got the answer 40, which mathematically speaking was the absolutely correct answer to the problem as he had formulated it. But how much does the figure 40 tell us about the size of the figure 351?

This example is not intended as a joke, but is meant to be a real character-ization of much of the activities that are *à la mode* today in growth theories. In particular it is characteristic of the very popular exercise of investigating what would happen under an infinite time horizon. Questions of convergence under an infinite time horizon will depend so much on epsilontic refinements in the system of assumptions—and on the infinite constancy of these refine-ments—that we are humanly speaking absolutely certain of getting infinite time horizon results which have no relevance to concrete reality. And in particular we are absolutely certain of getting irrelevant results if such epsilon-tic exercises are made under the assumption of a constant technology. 'In the long run we are all dead.' These words by Keynes ought to be engraved in marble and put on the desk of all epsilontologists in growth theory under an infinite horizon.

Turnpike theorems of the usual kind have no relevance to the problems faced by a politician in an underdeveloped country. He is not interested in an assumption about an unchanged technology. He is precisely interested in *changing* the technology. And he is not interested in knowing whether an actual development path in his country will come close to or be far away from some intrinsic path that has been defined by piling up queer assump-tions.

To avoid misunderstandings I must state explicitly three things to which I do not object in an absolute way, only in a relative way.

In the first place I have no objection in general to the application of rough approximation formulae. I use such formulae myself to a great extent. But there is a proviso. We must have a good reason to believe that the conclusions to be drawn—and to be taken seriously—are of such a kind that they depend primarily on the way in which the approximation *resembles* reality and not on the way in which the approximation incidentally *deviates from* reality.

For instance, if the purpose is to compare the speed of race-horses with that of ordinary horses, I might accept an analysis which assumes that all race-horses have the same speed. But if the purpose is to conjecture which one of the race-horses will win tomorrow, this approximation has, realistically speaking, no sense. But a sufficiently resourceful theorist might perhaps take this assumption as the starting point for proving a theory to the effect that no race-horse can ever win a race.

In the second place there is no topic under the sun, even the most abstract or the most seemingly useless one, which I would remove from the list of subjects which might occasionally be made the object of a respectable scientific research. I might even consider with respect a study of the pattern of keyholes in northern Iceland in the first half of the thirteenth century. But I would strongly object to a situation where too many of us too often used too much of our time and energy on the study of keyholes in northern Iceland in the first half of the thirteenth century. If we did, we would have failed in our social responsibilities as econometricians in the world of today.

In the case of the intrinsic paths and turnpike type of growth theory, I have a strong and uncomfortable feeling that too many of us too often use too much of our mental energy on problems similar to that of keyholes in northern Iceland, or on proving theories to the effect that no race-horse can ever win a race.

In the third place I have all my life insisted that factual observations alone —observations taken by themselves—do not have much sense. Observations get a meaning only if they are interpreted by an underlying *theory*. Therefore, theory, and sometimes very abstract theory, there must be. And no kind of mathematical analysis in economics should be rejected just because it might be difficult and refined mathematics. But at the same time I have insisted that econometrics must have relevance for concrete realities—otherwise it degenerates into something which is not worthy of the name econometrics, but ought rather to be called *playometrics*.

Once in every century there may come along a genius like John von Neumann who on some specific occasion, more or less on the spur of the moment, throws out an interesting thought on something that would happen under some very special assumptions. Such a thought thrown out by a genius is valuable and should be put on record. But we should leave it at that. We should not mobilize an army of people to produce queer assumptions so to speak on the conveyor band and deduce consequences from these assumptions. If we do, we are on the wrong track both socially and scientifically, and we are not living up to our responsibilities.

Such exercises may be an entertaining intellectual game. I admit that they *are* highly entertaining and I can understand the great number of students to whom this kind of exercise appeals. But it might be a dangerous game both socially and scientifically.

Let me give four examples of modern econometric analyses which illustrate what I would call econometric analyses of the *genuine* kind because they are built on a theoretical set-up, but at the same time are deeply rooted in realistic situations.

In 1964 I had the good fortune to be present at the Zürich meeting of the Econometric Society and T.I.M.S., the Institute of Management Science. At this meeting Professor H. Albach of Germany presented to us a paper on long-range production plans in the operation of coal pits, a very serious and important problem in Germany at this moment. He spent more than one-third of his time explaining to us what a coal pit is and what the profile of a coal pit is. We sort of felt that his paper was written with dirty fingers because he had just come back from digging in the coal pits. From this concrete pre-occupation he derived his theoretical concepts and formulated his program-ming problem which now appeared as a problem full of life and reality.

My second example is another paper presented at the Zürich meeting by W. K. Holstein of the United States and produced by him and his colleague S. Reiter. The paper was one on job scheduling and control in a special kind of shop. Holstein too used more than one-third of his time describing the particular shop in question, the various types of machine, the way the mach-ines were grouped together in stations, the way the incoming orders were recorded and passed on to the shop for execution, etc. On the basis of this concrete description he formulated the theoretical concepts and used the theory for a realistic programming set-up.

My third example is the paper presented at the Zürich meeting by J. Lesourne of France. He too used a good part of his time explaining the con-crete geographical and population facts of the problem.

As a fourth brilliant example let me mention a Rome 1965 presentation that was very abstract but still had no touch of playometrics in it, viz., Pro-fessor Jacob Marschak's Irving Fisher lecture on 'Economics of Organiza-tion'. Marschak's very abstract concepts were all based on realistic situations and did not distort reality by artificial assumptions. On the contrary he pointed out, for instance, that the usually accepted entropy concept in information theory was too simple because it did not take account of the *purpose* for which the information was to be used. This purpose was made explicit in Marschak's general formulae.

Such papers as these are of the kind which it is soothing to listen to in the middle of a cascade of papers of the playometric kind.

*

I am not the only person to have been seriously concerned about the development in econometrics. I vividly remember a reception in the Royal Palace in Oslo some thirty years ago, shortly after the founding of the Econometric Society. The reception was on the occasion of an international mathematical congress in Oslo. It was not by pure chance that Norbert

Wiener and I found ourselves deeply engaged in a conversation in one of the rooms of the Royal Palace, overlooking the main street of Oslo. Norbert Wiener was one of the founders of the Econometric Society, as you will see from the report of the organizing meeting of the Econometric Society held in Cleveland, Ohio, in December 1930. At the time of our conversation in the Royal Palace in Oslo, Norbert Wiener had begun to be quite alarmed by the happenings in econometrics and he appeared as a matter of fact to be rather sceptical about the whole thing. I was, as you can imagine, a bit disappointed by his attitude. But later developments have made me understand better the cause of his alarm, and have made me understand that basically his views and mine were genuinely the same. In his book *God and Golem, Inc. A Comment on Certain Points where Cybernetics Impinges on Religion*, written shortly before his death,[5] Norbert Wiener reverts to the misuses of econometrics. His attitude is just as critical against misuse as it was before, but now his pessimistic attitude is after all more positive than in our conversation in the Royal Palace in Oslo. On page 89 he says, 'The use of mathematical formulae had accompanied the development of the natural sciences and become the mode in the social sciences. Just as primitive people adopt the Western modes of denationalized clothing and of parliamentarism out of a vague feeling that these magic rites and vestments will at once put them abreast of modern culture and technique, so the economists have developed the habit of dressing up their rather imprecise ideas in the language of the infinitesimal calculus. . . . Difficult as it is to collect good physical data, it is far more difficult to collect long runs of economic or social data so that the whole of the run shall have a uniform significance. . . .'

These difficulties, of course, have been and are quite familiar to those working in econometrics. Therefore they try, whenever possible, to rely on *engineering data* instead of statistical time series. The difficulties are familiar to them in principle, but I am sorry to say that some econometricians have often been liable to forget these basic principles in practice and, therefore, have not been critical enough when they apply their techniques and mathematical analysis. This remark is particularly important when it is a question of drawing conclusions about *the economic policy to be followed in a concrete situation.*

Norbert Wiener concludes by saying, 'This does not mean, however, that the ideas of cybernetics are not applicable to sociology and economics. It means rather that these ideas should be tested in engineering and in biology before they are applied to so formless a field' (as economics).

I will subscribe to the essence of Wiener's critical remarks, and at the same time *emphasize the optimistic tone* at the end of what he says. And I would like to add that the time has now come when mathematics and statistics may

[5] Published by the Massachusetts Institute of Technology Press in 1964.

be and should be applied ever more intensively in economics, thus building up econometrics as a respectable science. But I must also, and must emphatically, add the proviso that we must work for genuine econometrics—not for playometrics.

12

ECONOMETRIC GROWTH MODELS FOR THE DEVELOPING ECONOMY

JERE BEHRMAN *and* L. R. KLEIN*

The Basic Model

THE Keynesian Revolution and the concomitant refinement of social accounting statistics formed the basis for what has become the standard short run model of the industrial economy. These models explain (1) the components of the GNP—consumption, capital formation, exports, imports, government expenditures; (2) the components of the national income—wages, profits, rentier income; (3) the reconciliation of these two social aggregates; (4) the production technology; (5) wage rate, price level, and interest rate determination. Many identities lace together these relationships and important institutional characteristics are displayed. The latter are the tax-transfer systems, the banking and monetary systems, the corporate form of organization, and various stabilization schemes such as agricultural price support.

The standard model appears to work well in explaining current short-run behaviour in many industrial countries. When model-building activities were extended to many countries, it is not surprising that the first attempts followed in the tradition of the standard model. In fact, with due allowance for changing points of emphasis to reflect institutional differences, the standard model has worked well.

Refinements, extensions, and improvements will occur in the short-run modelling of the industrial countries, but new developments now face the model builder. There is both a need and a desire to extend these activities to the analysis of the problems of the developing economy. The standard model must be reconsidered and developed in two directions for application to the non-industrial parts of the world. In the first place, we shall be more interested in long-term growth, and the short-run, business-cycle-type model must be

* This study is part of a larger project on model building for Brazil, Argentina, and Mexico undertaken in co-operation with the Development Department of E. I. du Pont de Nemours & Co. We acknowledge support and research stimulus from members of the du Pont staff. Our own research students, Denise de Souza Ford and Mahmoud Marzouk, provided invaluable assistance.

12—I.G.T.

modified to give a better picture of trend development. This is relevant for both the industrial and the developing economies. Secondly, we must re-examine the standard model to see whether it displays the characteristics and basic economic decisions of the developing countries, either for the short or the long run. There will undoubtedly be much to carry over from the standard model to the case of the developing economy, but we should not be surprised to see a very different system emerging. There is a basic question whether conditions exist that make the Keynesian analysis pertinent to the developing countries.[1]

If the now standard short-run model is to be called an extension of the Keynesian theory of effective demand, we may equally well call what is now emerging as the standard long-run model the Harrod theory of growth.[2] This theory is also being extended and amplified to apply to the real world, just as the Keynesian model evolved into the standard model of short-run macroeconometrics. Nevertheless, the underlying system is the Harrod model, which is based on the capital–output and savings–income relationships. There will have to be disaggregations, modifications for foreign trade, introduction of money, and other extensions. The starting point will be the Harrod model.

In the Harrod as in the Keynesian model, the savings–investment flow equilibrium is still of prime importance for output determination, but capital requirements replace labour requirements, and there is little emphasis on the level of unemployment and wage determination. Both models make artificial assumptions about technology. In general, there is substitution between labour and capital in either the short or long run, and a more satisfactory theory should be based on a production function that depends on both labour and capital inputs simultaneously. The long- and short-run models may eventually converge toward a common specification of the production function, but they will not have the same interest in wage rate determination. The short-run demand model must relate wage changes to the lack of balance between employment and labour supply, while the long-run model will not contain short-run labour market adjustments and corresponding wage movements. It should seek to explain the long-run tendency of wages to rise in accordance with productivity and price trends.

Investment in the short-run demand model must necessarily include inventory investment. Cyclical fluctuations in output are intimately associated with inventory accumulation and decumulation. These movements tend to be smoothed in a long-run model, and inventory investment is a simple trans-action function of output changes. Inventory investment may even be aggregated with fixed investment and not require separate treatment.

Some variables change imperceptibly in the short run. Income shares,

[1] See V. K. R. V. Rao, 1952.
[2] In recognition of Domar's independent development of this model, we might lengthen the term to be the Harrod–Domar theory of growth.

average age, average family size, and other demographic characteristics may not be relevant variables in a short-run demand model, yet they are likely to be of great importance in a long-run model. These variables are not explicitly included in the Harrod growth model; the extension of the model to allow for their inclusion is analogous to the extension of the simple Keynesian system to fit it to the real world.

Main structural characteristics of the developing economy that must be added to the Harrod–Domar model to render it appropriate for the econometric analysis of development are an explanation of (1) trade, with special emphasis on exports of primary commodities and the composition of imports between capital goods, consumer goods, and fuel; (2) sector composition of production and supply (primary, secondary, tertiary, e.g.); (3) income distribution; (4) prices and inflation; (5) politico–economic institutions. These considerations tend to be looked upon as refinements in model building for the industrial countries, but they are of primary importance for the developing economy.

A Tentative Model of Brazil

To illustrate some of the distinctions which are discussed in the previous section, a tentative macroeconometric model of Brazil is presented in this section, and decade simulations of the Brazilian economy on the basis of this model are presented in the subsequent section. In the present version of the Brazilian model, some of the concerns of the previous section are illustrated by the differences between this model and macroeconometric models of the more developed economies, but other such concerns clearly are not incorporated adequately. In the discussion of the individual relationships below, the extent to which distinctive features of the developing economy have been incorporated into the model will be noted. In ongoing work to improve the model, some of these features have been (or will be) better accounted for, but in other cases data inadequacies continue to present intractable obstacles.

The relationships in the tentative macroeconometric model of Brazil may be categorized conveniently into a tabular array which is a hybrid of those which are proposed for developed and developing economies in the introductory section:

> Production (value added)
> 1. primary industry
> 2. secondary industry
> 3. tertiary industry
>
> Consumer expenditures
> 1. private
> 2. government

Capital formation and depreciation
1. private fixed investment
2. government fixed investment
3. inventory investment
4. depreciation

National income and income distribution
1. wage income
2. non-wage, non-agricultural income

Government expenditures, receipts, and surplus
1. government expenditures
2. taxes
3. surplus

Price and money supply
1. implicit GNP price deflator
2. money supply

Foreign trade relations
1. exports of goods by major categories
2. imports of goods by major categories
3. balance of trade in goods
4. exchange rate determination

Domestic and national product relations
1. NDP and GDP in constant prices
2. GNP in current prices

As is suggested above, the hybrid character of these categories reflect considerable compromises between an ideal long-run model of an open developing economy proposed in the introduction and the available data. From an overall perspective, these compromises are most substantial with respect to the length of the period of estimation (1948–64), the lack of capital/capacity restraints in sectoral production, the accompanying lack of treatment of sectoral change in the allocation of factors and the distribution of income, and the inadequate incorporation of demographic and institutional factors. From the same overall perspective, on the other hand, the model does incorporate a number of the considerations of the introductory section: disaggregation of GDP by sectors, the imperfection or lack of capital markets, the importance of the government surplus in the determination of the money supply and the rate of inflation, relative emphasis on the foreign sector, and the role of primary exports in that sector. Further compromises and strong points of the model will be evident in the discussion of the individual relationships, which commences subsequent to the definition of the variables and the presentation of the model.

The Variables[3]

X_1	= value added in primary sector, in billions of 1953 cruzeiros.
$*POP_B$	= population in Brazil in millions of persons.
X_2	= value added in secondary sector, in billions of 1953 cruzeiros.
I	= total net investment expenditure on plant and equipment, in billions of 1953 cruzeiros.
C	= total consumption expenditure, in billions of 1953 cruzeiros.
X_3	= value added in the tertiary sector, in billions of 1953 cruzeiros.
I_G	= government net investment expenditure on plant and equipment, in billions of 1953 cruzeiros.
C_G	= government consumption expenditure, in billions of 1953 cruzeiros.
C_P	= private consumption expenditure, in billions of 1953 cruzeiros.
$*TXR_W$	= marginal real tax rate on non-agricultural wage income.
W	= total non-agricultural wage bill in billions of current cruzeiros.
P	= gross domestic product deflator with a value of 1·00 in 1953.
$*TXR_{NWNP}$	= marginal real tax rate on non-wage, non-primary income.
$*TXR_{X_1}$	= marginal real tax rate on agricultural value added.
$NWNP$	= non-wage, non-primary income in billions of current cruzeiros.
$*C_{GM}$	= government military consumption expenditure in billions of 1953 cruzeiros.
I_P	= private net investment expenditure on plant and equipment in billions of 1953 cruzeiros.
TXC_D	= direct-tax collections in billions of current cruzeiros.
INV	= total inventories in billions of 1953 cruzeiros.
TXC	= total tax collections in billions of current cruzeiros.
$*KTR$	= capital transfers to Brazil in billions of 1953 cruzeiros.
GNP	= gross national product in billions of current cruzeiros.
$BOTG$	= balance of trade of goods in billions of 1953 cruzeiros.
DPR	= depreciation charges in billions of 1953 cruzeiros.
DPR_G	= depreciation of government capital in billions of 1953 cruzeiros.
DPR_P	= depreciation of private capital in billions of 1953 cruzeiros.
$*SR$	= net service earnings from abroad in billions of 1953 cruzeiros.

[3] All variables are for annual time periods. Exogenous variables are marked with an asterisk. All variables refer to the tth time period unless otherwise indicated by subscripts. All cruzeiros are old cruzeiros.

$*F$	= net factor income from abroad in billions of 1953 cruzeiros.
K	= capital stock in billions of 1953 cruzeiros.
$NINC$	= national income in billions of current cruzeiros.
GDP	= gross domestic product in billions of 1953 cruzeiros.
$*SB_G$	= government subsidies less current surpluses of government enterprises in current cruzeiros.
TXC_I	= indirect tax collections in billions of current cruzeiros.
G	= government expenditures in billions of 1953 cruzeiros.
SUR_G	= government surplus in billions of current cruzeiros.
$*TR_G$	= government transfer payments in billions of current cruzeiros.
MS	= money supply in billions of current cruzeiros.
ECF_E	= value of exports of coffee to Europe in billions of 1953 cruzeiros.
$*PCF_B$	= price of Brazilian coffee in New York in current United States cents per pound.
$*PCF_A$	= price of African coffee in New York in current United States cents per pound.
$*POP_E$	= population in Europe in millions of persons.
ECF_{US}	= value of exports of coffee to the United States in billions of 1953 cruzeiros.
$*POP_{US}$	= population over fourteen years old in the United States in millions of persons.
$*PCF_C$	= price of Columbian coffee in New York in current United States cents per pound.
$ECOC$	= value of exports of cocoa in billions of 1953 cruzeiros.
$PCOC_{US}$	= price of cocoa in New York in current United States cents per pound.
$*PSUG_{US}$	= price of sugar in New York in current United States cents per pound.
$*\left(\dfrac{STCOC}{CCOC}\right)_W$	= current world stocks of cocoa relative to world consumption of cocoa.
$ECOT$	= value of exports of cotton in billions of 1953 cruzeiros.
$PCOT_B$	= price of Brazilian cotton in New York in current United States cents per pound.
$*PCOT_{E,US}$	= average of prices of Egyptian and United States cotton in New York in current United States cents per pound.
$*PCOT$	= average price of cotton in New York in current United States cents per pound.
$*PSYN$	= average price of synthetic fabrics in New York in current United States cents per pound.
$*TEXT$	= textile production in Brazilian export markets in tons.

$*\left(\dfrac{INVCOT_B}{CCOT_W}\right) =$ ratio of Brazilian inventories of cotton to current world consumption of cotton.

$EOTH$ = value of other exports in billions of 1953 cruzeiros.

$*PE_W$ = price index for world exports with a value of 1·00 in 1953.

$*PE_B$ = price index for Brazilian exports with a value of 1·00 in 1953.

E = value of exports in billions of 1953 cruzeiros.

MF = value of imports of fuels in billions of 1953 cruzeiros.

CM = capacity to import ($=PE_B \cdot E/PM_B$).

MI = value of imports of capital goods in billions of 1953 cruzeiros.

$R\$$ = exchange rate in cruzeiros per United States dollar.

MC = value of imports of consumption goods in billions of 1953 cruzeiros.

$*DUM$ = dummy variable with value of one in 1952 and zero for other years to represent large available foreign exchange reserves in that year due to Korean War boom in exports.

$MOTH$ = value of other imports in billions of 1953 cruzeiros.

$*PM_B$ = price index for Brazilian imports with a value of 1·00 in 1953.

M = value of imports in billions of 1953 cruzeiros.

NDP = net domestic product in billions of 1953 cruzeiros.

Model of the Brazilian Economy 1948–1964[4]

Production (value added)

(1) $\quad X_1 = -71·12 + 3·08POP_B \qquad\qquad (\bar{R}^2 = 0·93)$
$\qquad\qquad$ (5·25) (14·5)

(2) $\quad X_2 = -13·39 + 0·2586\ \ I\ \ + 0·2412\ \ C \qquad (\bar{R}^2 = 0·96)$
$\qquad\qquad$ (8·57) (1·19) (0·13) (6·79) (0·99)

(3) $\quad X_3 = \quad 77·76 + 1·538\ I_G\ \ + 1·343\ C_G \qquad (\bar{R}^2 = 0·94)$
$\qquad\qquad$ (8·30) (1·07) (0·12)   (3·79) (0·50)

Consumer Expenditure

(4) $\quad C_P = 30·98 + 1·377(1·0 - TXR_W)\dfrac{W}{P}\ \ + 0·4620(1·0 - TXR_{NWNP})\dfrac{NWNP}{P}$
$\qquad\qquad$ (0·95) (3·07) $\qquad\qquad\qquad$ (0·69) $\qquad$ (0·74) $\qquad\qquad\qquad\qquad\qquad$ (0·23)

$\qquad\qquad + 0·4390(1·0 - TXR_{X_1})\ X_1 \qquad\qquad (\bar{R}^2 = 0·97)$
$\qquad\qquad$ (0·74) $\qquad\qquad\qquad$ (0·23)

(5) $\quad C_G = 0·75(-90·71 + 2·655POP_B) + C_{GM} \qquad (\bar{R}^2 = 0·97)$
$\qquad\qquad$ (13·20) $\qquad\qquad$ (24·57)

---

[4] All simultaneous equations were estimated by a two-stage least squares procedure in which principal components of the predetermined variables were utilized in the first stage. Under each point estimate is the absolute value of the t-statistic. Under each right-hand side variable in the simultaneous equations is the elasticity of the dependent variable with respect to that variable at the point of sample means.

(6) $\quad C = C_G + C_P$

Capital Formation and Depreciation

(7) $\quad I_P = -17\cdot06 + 0\cdot2729 \dfrac{(NWNP + X_1 - TXC_D)}{P} - 0\cdot1740\,\Delta INV_{t-1}$
$\qquad\quad\ (2\cdot13)\quad (6\cdot86)\qquad\qquad\qquad\qquad\quad (0\cdot73)\quad (-0\cdot03)$
$\qquad\qquad\qquad\qquad\qquad\qquad (1\cdot47)$
$\qquad (\bar{R}^2 = 0\cdot79)$

(8) $\qquad I_G = 0\cdot044 + 0\cdot1418\dfrac{TXC}{P} + 0\cdot1036KTR \qquad (\bar{R}^2 = 0\cdot86)$
$\qquad\qquad (0\cdot02)\quad (7\cdot11)\qquad\quad (0\cdot88)$

(9) $\qquad\qquad\qquad\qquad I = I_P + I_G$

(10) $\qquad \Delta INV = \dfrac{GNP}{P} - C - I - BOTG - DPR - SR - F$

(11) $\qquad DPR = 1\cdot498 + 0\cdot02532\ K \qquad (\bar{R}^2 = 0\cdot97)$
$\qquad\qquad\quad (1\cdot23)\quad (21\cdot35)\quad (0\cdot94)$

(12) $\qquad\qquad\qquad DPR_P = \dfrac{\sum_{1948}^{t} I_{Pi}}{\sum_{1948}^{t} I_i}\,DPR$

(13) $\qquad\qquad\qquad DPR_G = DPR - DPR_P$

(14) $\qquad\qquad\qquad K = K_{t-1} + I$

National Income and Income Distribution

(15) $\qquad\qquad NINC = P(GDP + F - DPR) + SB - TXC_I$

(16) $\qquad\qquad W = 9\cdot386 + 0\cdot3666\ GNP \qquad (\bar{R}^2 = 0\cdot99)$
$\qquad\qquad\quad (0\cdot86)\quad (179\cdot73)\quad (0\cdot99)$

(17) $\qquad\qquad NWNP = NINC - W - P(X_1)$

Government Expenditure, Receipts and Surplus

(18) $\qquad\qquad\qquad G = C_G + I_G + DPR_G$

(19) $\qquad\qquad TXC_I = -6\cdot255 + 0\cdot7290\ TXC \qquad (\bar{R}^2 = 0\cdot99)$
$\qquad\qquad\qquad (-3\cdot18)\quad (456\cdot18)$

(20) $\quad TXC_D = -2\cdot405 + 0\cdot1323NWNP + 0\cdot1557(X_1)\ P \qquad (\bar{R}^2 = 0\cdot99)$
$\qquad\qquad (0\cdot69)\quad (1\cdot49)\qquad (0\cdot37)\quad (2\cdot06)\quad (0\cdot46)$

(21) $\qquad\qquad\qquad TXC = TXC_I + TXC_D$

(22) $\qquad\qquad SUR_G = TXC - P \cdot G - TR_G - SB_G$

Price and Money Supply

(23) $\qquad\qquad\qquad\qquad P = \dfrac{GNP}{GDP + F}$

(24) $\qquad\qquad \Delta MS = -48\cdot16 - 2\cdot314\ SUR_G \qquad (\bar{R}^2 = 0\cdot93)$
$\qquad\qquad\quad (1\cdot03)\quad (14\cdot44)\ (-0\cdot33)$

Foreign Trade Relations

(25) $\quad ECF_E = -20\cdot89 + 2\cdot599(PCF_B/PCF_A)_{t-2} + 0\cdot1530POP_E \quad (\bar{R}^2 = 0\cdot52)$
$\qquad\qquad (2\cdot83)\quad (1\cdot39)\qquad\qquad\qquad\qquad (2\cdot35)$

(26) $ECF_{US} = POP_{US}(0.3823 - 0.296(PCF_B/PCF_C) - 0.0643(PCF_B/PCF_A)$
$\phantom{ECF_{US} = POP_{US}(}(5.38)(5.20)$(3.24)

$\phantom{ECF_{US} = POP_{US}xxxx} + 0.6656(ECF_{US}/POP_{US})_{t-1}) \quad (\bar{R}^2 = 0.75)$
$\phantom{ECF_{US} = POP_{US}xxxx}$(5.20)

(27) $ECOC = 0.7933 + 0.2300(PCOC_{US}/PSUG_{US})_{t-2}$
(2.30)(3.77)

$ - 0.2264ECOC_{t-2} \quad (\bar{R}^2 = 0.46)$
(1.28)

(28) $PCOC_{US} = 48.66 - 43.12(STCOC/CCOC)_W \quad (\bar{R}^2 = 0.36)$
$\phantom{PCOC_{US} = }$(9.03)(3.18)

(29) $\log_{10}(ECOT) = 0.743 - 0.1102 \log_{10}(PCOT_B/PCOT_{E,US})_{t-1}$
$\phantom{\log_{10}(ECOT) = }(1.38)$(1.15)

$\phantom{\log_{10}(ECOT) = 0.743xx} - 0.3354 \log_{10}(PCOT/PSYN)_{t-1}$
$\phantom{\log_{10}(ECOT) = 0.743xx}$(1.88)

$\phantom{\log_{10}(ECOT) = 0.743xx} + 0.302 \log_{10}(ECOT)_{t-1}$
$\phantom{\log_{10}(ECOT) = 0.743xx}$(1.37)

$\phantom{\log_{10}(ECOT) = 0.743xx} + 0.10 \log_{10}(TEXT) \quad (\bar{R}^2 = 0.24)$
$\phantom{\log_{10}(ECOT) = 0.743xx}$(0.76)

(30) $PCOT_B = 2372.4 - 983.4 \dfrac{INVOCT_B}{CCOT_W}$
(2.09)(1.74)

$ + 0.6007PCOT_{B_{t-1}} \quad (\bar{R}^2 = 0.60)$
(3.12)

(31) $EOTH = -5.787 + 9.563(PE_W/PE_B)$
(1.34)(1.77)

$ + 0.5721EOTH_{t-1} \quad (\bar{R}^2 = 0.73)$
(2.61)

(32) $E = (ECF_E + ECF_{US} + ECOC + ECOT + EOTH)\dfrac{PE_B}{P}$

(33) $MF = -1.550 + 0.00265(X_2 + X_3) + 0.1547\,CM$
(1.59)(0.55)(0.13)(3.78)(0.83)

$ + 0.2856MF_{t-1} \quad (\bar{R}^2 = 0.89)$
(1.31)

(34) $MI = 13.853 - 0.1479\,\dfrac{R\$}{P} + 0.1511\,I \quad (\bar{R}^2 = 0.47)$
(3.69)(2.19)(3.42)(0.70)
(−0.94)

(35) $MC = 14.19 - 0.03568\,\dfrac{R\$}{P} - 0.00403\,C_{t-1}$
(6.39)(0.94)(1.16)(−0.17)
(−0.26)

$ + 5.514DUM \quad (\bar{R}^2 = 0.66)$
(5.32)

(36) $MOTH = 12.01 + 0.1940\,CM - 0.1461\,\dfrac{R\$}{P}$
(1.51)(1.25)(0.58)(1.58)
(−0.91)

$ 0.4299KTR_{t-1} \quad (\bar{R}^2 = 0.43)$
(2.27)(0.26)

(37)
$$M = (MF + MI + MC + MOTH)\frac{PM_B}{P}$$

(38)
$$BOTG = E - M$$

(39)
$$CM = \frac{PE_B \cdot E}{PM_B}$$

(40)
$$R\$ = -61 \cdot 88 + 15 \cdot 49P + 113 \cdot 7 \; P_{t-1} \qquad (\bar{R}^2 = 0 \cdot 99)$$
$$ (5 \cdot 06) \quad\; (2 \cdot 11) \qquad\; (7 \cdot 88)$$

Domestic and National Product Relations

(41)
$$NDP = X_1 + X_2 + X_3$$

(42)
$$GDP = NDP + DPR + (TXC_I - SB)/P$$

(43)
$$GNP = (MS + 9 \cdot 34 \; (P)) / 0 \cdot 3020 \qquad (\bar{R}^2 = 0 \cdot 95)$$
$$ (0 \cdot 60) \quad (1 \cdot 02)(0 \cdot 01)(17 \cdot 90)$$

Production of value added in each sector appears to be expressed in the form of demand relationships; the explanatory variables are elements of aggregate final demand, yet these equations can be interpreted as transformations of an input–output type of production process. Let us write

$$\begin{pmatrix} 1 - a_{11} & - a_{12} & - a_{13} \\ - a_{21} & 1 - a_{22} & - a_{23} \\ - a_{31} & - a_{32} & 1 - a_{33} \end{pmatrix} \begin{pmatrix} x_1{}^g \\ x_2{}^g \\ x_3{}^g \end{pmatrix} = \begin{pmatrix} f_1 \\ f_2 \\ f_3 \end{pmatrix}$$

as a 3×3 input–output model of current inter-industry flows and final demand (f_1, f_2, f_3). For the input–output formulation we use gross outputs $(x_1{}^g, x_2{}^g, x_3{}^g)$. We can invert this expression to obtain

$$\begin{pmatrix} x_1{}^g \\ x_2{}^g \\ x_3{}^g \end{pmatrix} = \begin{pmatrix} 1 - a_{11} & - a_{12} & - a_{13} \\ - a_{21} & 1 - a_{22} & - a_{23} \\ - a_{31} & - a_{32} & 1 - a_{33} \end{pmatrix}^{-1} \begin{pmatrix} f_1 \\ f_2 \\ f_3 \end{pmatrix}.$$

If we further assume that value added in each sector is proportional to gross output of the corresponding sector, we have

$$x_i = \lambda_i x_i{}^g,$$

and we can write

$$\begin{pmatrix} x_1 \\ x_2 \\ x_3 \end{pmatrix} = \begin{pmatrix} \lambda_1 & 0 & 0 \\ 0 & \lambda_2 & 0 \\ 0 & 0 & \lambda_3 \end{pmatrix} \begin{pmatrix} 1 - a_{11} & - a_{12} & - a_{13} \\ - a_{21} & 1 - a_{22} & - a_{23} \\ - a_{31} & - a_{32} & 1 - a_{33} \end{pmatrix}^{-1} \begin{pmatrix} f_1 \\ f_2 \\ f_3 \end{pmatrix};$$

therefore each sector's value added is a linear function of f_1, f_2, and f_3. We lack regular time series observations on f_1, f_2, and f_3. They are elements of

GNP (consumption, investment, exports, government expenditures) demanded by each sector. We approximate this linear relationship by replacing f_1, f_2, f_3, selectively, in each equation by GNP elements that are closely related to x_1, x_2, or x_3. The regression of sector values added on GNP components (or demand indexes of them) are our equations (1)–(3) interpreted as transformations of input–output relationships. From these considerations, we suggest that these are not purely demand relationships, but are based on production or supply processes. These equations do not go far enough in introducing supply factors into the model. A 3×3 input–output system reveals little about inter-industry flows in the production process. More sectors would be needed to show inter-industry production flows. Also capital and labour inputs, as well as current material inputs, restrict the supply of output. The production equations in the model need to be extended beyond a simple input–output formulation.

In the case of agricultural production there are special features that enable us to develop interesting supply relationships that are tied to structural characteristics of the sector. Equations have been estimated for Brazilian coffee supply and these are indicative of what can be done on detailing the supply side.[5] Equations like those presented below are currently being used in newer versions of the Brazil Model.

We explain acreage and yield separately for Brazilian coffee. The estimated equations are

$$A = -0.033 + 0.022\left(\frac{PCF_D}{P}\right)_{-2} + 0.925A_{-1} \qquad (\bar{R}^2 = 0.95)$$
$$\quad\;\; (0.15) \quad\;\; (3.20) \qquad\qquad\qquad (17.80)$$

$$Y = -0.246 + 0.0010(PCF_D)_{-1} + 0.00586(RN)_{-1} \qquad (\bar{R}^2 = 0.51)$$
$$\quad\;\; (1.29) \quad\;\; (3.24) \qquad\qquad (3.49)$$

where A is the area planted for coffee in thousands of hectares, PCF_D the domestic price of coffee in cruzeiros per kg, RN the average rainfall in coffee growing areas in millimetres, and Y the yield of coffee area in kg per hectare.

The acreage equation involves a substantial lag in the price variable. It is a distributed lag beginning two years prior to the decision to change acreages. This is reasonable in view of the fact that a tree crop such as coffee requires several years from the time of planting to bear output. The short run price elasticity is 0.10. Rainfall (in the coffee producing areas) is important for determining current yield. The yield equation has elasticity coefficients of 0.15 and 1.5 with respect to price and rainfall respectively. In some cases of estimated supply relationships of this sort, a price variable for substitute crops is used in the acreage equation. The product of the solutions for A and Y provides an estimate of total production. We can improve equation (1) by

[5] cf. Ady, 1968.

regressing $[X_1 - (PCF_D/P)AY]$ on Brazilian population, for the non-coffee part of Brazilian agricultural production should be more closely related to the population requirements for food.

Secondary production of value added in constant price is in response to the components of aggregate final demand in constant prices for the private and public sectors combined because large proportions of secondary output go to both the private and the public sector. Tertiary production of value added in constant prices, in contrast, is in response to the components of aggregate final demand in constant prices for the public sector alone because of the predominance of the Brazilian government in the provision of transportation, communication, and other similar services.[6] For both secondary and tertiary production, the t-values and the implied elasticities suggest that the larger response is to the relevant consumption component of final demand.

Consumer expenditures in constant prices are disaggregated into private consumer expenditures, government non-military consumer expenditures, and government military consumer expenditures. This split is useful for the purpose of policy simulation. Private consumer expenditures in constant prices are determined by the three major components of national income in constant prices—wages, primary sector income, and non-wage, non-primary sector income. This is an example of our use of income distribution variables in explaining consumption. The distribution is between wages and other income and also between farm and non-farm income. Because direct tax collections and transfers disaggregated by these components are not available, the right-hand side variables are expressed in gross terms for estimation, but the coefficients are adjusted by marginal direct tax rates (the determination of which are discussed below) for purposes of simulation. The estimated marginal propensity to consume out of wages, in fact, is greater than one (although not significantly so). For estimation, total government consumption expenditures are explained in terms of the provision of services to the growing population. Fragmentary evidence indicates that about one-quarter of this expenditure has historically been military. In order to facilitate the examination of possible changes (exogenous to the economic model) in the political power of the military and thus in the government military consumption expenditures, for purposes of simulations the government military consumption expenditures are assumed to be exogenous, and government non-military consumption expenditures are assumed to be three-quarters of the historically estimated total government consumption expenditures.

Net capital formation in constant prices is divided into private fixed investment, government fixed investment, and inventory additions. Private net

---

[6] Significant proportions of private consumer expenditures are for services, but if we include C_P as an additional variable in (3), we obtain a non-significant coefficient. This result may be due to multi-collinearity.

fixed investment in constant prices is determined by net non-wage income in constant prices and by lagged inventory changes in constant prices. The inclusion of the former variable (as well as the exclusion of any variables such as interest rates) reflects the predominant dependence on internal funds for private investment and the very limited role of capital markets. On the basis of some preliminary simulations, it was found that inventory depletion occurred regularly without any feedback into the rest of the model. We therefore revised the model and included lagged inventory change in constant prices in the investment equation to represent opportunities for capital formation as a result of aggregate demands exceeding production (and capacity). In some alternative specifications, the rate of inflation seems to be a direct positive inducement for private net fixed investment in constant prices, but the addition of this variable to equation (7) results in a coefficient estimate which is even substantially less significant than is the coefficient estimate for the lagged change in inventories in constant prices.[7] Government net fixed investment in constant prices is determined primarily by the availability of internal funds, as represented by total tax collections in constant prices, and secondarily by the availability of foreign funds in the form of foreign capital transfers to Brazil in constant prices.[8] Inventory additions in constant prices, finally, are determined as the discrepancy between gross national product in constant prices and the components of final demand (other than inventory additions) in constant prices.

Depreciation is related to a crude estimate of the total fixed capital stock in the economy, which is based on a 1947 estimate adjusted for subsequent total net investment. To obtain a measure of the total government surplus in constant prices for use in the determination of money supply in equation (24), gross government fixed investment (and, thus, depreciation) in constant prices is required. Total depreciation in constant prices, therefore, is subdivided in private and government depreciation in constant prices on the basis of the relative cumulative net fixed investment in constant prices in the two sectors since 1947. If depreciation rates of fixed capital are the same in the two sectors or if the real capital stocks have been maintained in approximately the same proportions, such a procedure should be reasonably satisfactory.

Income distribution is determined in three components. The wage bill in current prices is related to the level of gross national product in current prices. The coefficient estimate and the relatively small constant estimate imply

---

[7] In the present version the price level is positively correlated indirectly with subsequent private fixed investment in constant prices. See the discussion of the price determination equation below.

[8] Note that investment in human capital cannot be treated explicitly as an investment which improves the quality of the labour force, but is lumped together with other private and government consumption and investment because of the unavailability of disaggregated data.

marginal average shares of the wage bill in gross national product of 37 per cent. Because of the absence of employment and wage data, interesting alternative approaches to the wage bill determination (and, as mentioned above, to the distribution of labour between sectors) could not be pursued. Primary sector income in current prices is the value added in primary production in current prices. Non-wage, non-primary sector income in current prices is calculated as a residual from total national income in current prices and the previously mentioned two components thereof.

Government expenditure in constant prices is defined on the basis of previously discussed components of government aggregate demand and on the assumption that government inventories in constant prices remain constant. *Government tax collections* in current prices are subdivided into direct and indirect taxes. Indirect taxes in current prices are related to total tax collections in current prices as is indicated in equations (19) and (21). In some simulations, alternatively, average tax rates on the basis of fragmentary observations are used to calculate import tax receipts in current prices from each of the import categories, and indirect internal tax receipts in current prices from the current value of net domestic product. Direct tax collections in current prices are estimated to be a linear function of non-wage, non-primary sector income in current prices and of primary sector income in current prices. If the wage bill in current prices is added as a right-hand side variable in equation (20), the related coefficient estimate is negative and insignificant due to multi-collinearity. Since wage taxes are known to be significant and to be collected relatively efficiently through a withholding system, these results are unsatisfactory. The lack of disaggregated data on direct taxes, moreover, precludes the option of estimating the tax rates for the three components of national income separately. On the basis of somewhat limited information, therefore, in some simulations effective marginal tax rates of 5, 9, and 12·5 per cent are utilized, respectively, for wage, primary, and non-wage, non-primary income. Government transfers in current prices and government subsidies less current surpluses of government enterprises in current prices are assumed to be exogenously determined policy variables. Government surplus in current prices follows from its definition and previously discussed components thereof.

The implicit gross national product deflator is defined to be consistent with the monetary value of gross national product as determined by the monetary supply in current prices and the implicit gross national product deflator in equation (43), and with the real value of gross national product as determined by the sectoral value added production relations in constant prices and the exogenous net factor income from abroad in constant prices. In the present version of the model this indicator of the rate of inflation feeds back to the real magnitudes directly only through imports, but indirectly affects subsequent fixed private investment in constant prices (which has interactions throughout the simultaneous system) through the inventory variable in the investment function. If information were readily available, the determination of a number of price indices would be preferable in order to examine the uneven affects of inflation on allocation and growth for various parts of the economy.

The change in the money supply is determined by the size of the government surplus as a result of the printing of more money and through pressure which the government imposes on the banking system to make loans to finance government projects. This mechanism clearly differs substantially from that which prevails in an economy such as in the United States.

The foreign trade relations are examined in greatest relative detail in the model because of the importance of foreign trade in the open developing economy of Brazil. Exports are divided into three major products (coffee, cocoa, and cotton) and a residual category. Because of the tremendous importance of coffee as a foreign exchange earner and because of the institutional differences between European and United States demands due to different tastes and due to the European relationships with former African colonies, the demand for Brazilian coffee exports is further subdivided between these two areas. For the European demand for Brazilian coffee in constant prices, the price of Brazilian coffee relative to African coffee and the population are the determinants. The population variable, in addition to representing an expanding market due to there being more people, probably also represents secular changes in tastes in regard to alternative beverages. This is not yet a satisfactory export equation and requires further analysis. For the United States demand for Brazilian coffee in constant prices, the determinants are similar, but Colombian coffee is a more important alternative. For the Brazilian exports of cocoa in constant prices, equation (27) apparently represents a Brazilian supply response to the price of cocoa relative to the price of sugar, with a cyclical factor superimposed. For the demand for Brazilian exports of cotton in constant prices, price relative to those of natural and synthetic substitutes, and an index of overall textile production in Brazilian export markets are all determinants. For the residual category of exports in constant prices, demand is determined by the relative index of world export prices to Brazilian export prices. In this last relationship, as in some of the other trade functions, the lagged dependent variable apparently reflects a distributed lag adjustment mechanism.

The export relations which are presented in the tentative version of the model have some interesting aspects, especially in regard to the adjustment to relative prices. On the other hand, both the cocoa and the cotton export functions are relatively unsatisfactory and several alternatives should be examined. For one example, with the disaggregation of primary sector production mentioned above, the effects of supply considerations can be tied in more explicitly to the export functions. For another example, the effects of the international coffee agreement and other possible international institutional changes should be incorporated more explicitly.[9]

The cotton export equation is log–linear; therefore its coefficients are direct estimates of elasticities. In both cases, the relative price variables suggest that the reactions are inelastic: -0.1 and -0.3 respectively in the short run. The corresponding long-run values are -0.16 and -0.50. In the case of coffee exports to Europe there is no suitable estimate of the relative price effect; the point estimate is of the wrong sign and unreliable. In the case of exports to the U.S., however, the price coefficients are more firmly established and the substitutability between Colombian and Brazilian varieties appears to be large. The elasticity coefficient at the point of means is -2.5 in the short-run. For the Brazilian/African price ratio it is smaller, at -0.86. The corresponding long-run estimates are three times as large in each case.

In the cocoa export equation, the coefficient of the relative price term implies a short-run elasticity value of 0.85 at the point of means. The long-run reaction is smaller, being only 0.8 as large. Finally, residual exports have a short-run elasticity response of approximately 1.05. This response is 75 per cent larger in the long run.

Imports in constant prices are divided into four major categories: fuels, investment goods, consumption goods, and other imports. Fuels are treated separately because they have been a critical Brazilian import in recent years. Investment and consumption imports are separated because of government policies which attempt to discriminate in favour of the former (for example, through multiple exchange rates). Government policies which affect imports are represented by the capacity to import index, exchange rate variations (which differed for various product categories until the end of the sample period), and the dummy variable in equation (35). The capacity to import is an important determinant of the import value in constant prices of fuels and of the import value of other imports in constant prices. The ratio of the exchange rate to the implicit gross national product price deflator enters into the determination of all imports other than fuels with a negative sign to represent the trade off, from the point of view of demanders of imports, between the cost of foreign exchange for import goods and domestic substitutes. That this ratio is insignificant if included in the import relationship for fuels reflects the paucity of domestic substitutes for imported fuels. The dummy variable in equation (35) represents the unusually high value of consumption good imports in constant prices in the early 1950's which apparently occurred because Brazil possessed unusually large foreign exchange reserves as a result of the Korean War export boom. One additional variable is included in each of the four import functions. For the import value of fuels in

[9] Both of these alternatives currently are being explored in the on-going research on this model.

constant prices, non-primary production in constant prices enters with a positive (but insignificant) coefficient estimate. For the import value of investment goods in constant prices, the interaction between such imports and the value of total fixed investment in constant prices is represented by the positive coefficient estimate of the latter variable. For the import value of consumption goods in constant prices, a small negative feedback apparently occurs from the lagged value of total consumption in constant prices. For the value of other imports in constant prices, finally, the magnitude of lagged capital transfers to Brazil in constant prices is reflected in current government policies for such imports.

The exchange rate is determined by current and lagged values of the implicit deflator for gross national product. Apparently the larger coefficient of the lagged price reflects the lagged adjustment of the exchange rate to internal inflation, while the smaller coefficient of the current price reflects the simultaneous feedback of the exchange rate on the current rate of inflation. Neither this equation nor several alternatives predict exchange rates well in 1964–6, apparently because of the efforts of the revolutionary coup government to limit official depreciation. For this reason, in some simulations alternatives to equation (40) (including making the exchange rate exogenous) are explored. By early 1968, however, the actual exchange rates had been adjusted to be much more in line with the predictions of equation (40) and of other alternative estimated relationships.

The last relationship is the determination of gross national product in current prices by the monetary supply in current prices and by the implicit deflator for gross national product in equation (43).[10] The value of gross national product in current prices is seen to be positively related to the money supply and the price level.

A Simulation Study of Decade Growth Projections

The model presented in the previous section can be used simply as an empirical description of the structural characteristics discussed in the first section. It can also be used, during the construction phase, as a statistical testing device for alternative components of the system as a whole. We contemplate, however, a more active and positive use of such a model, namely to formulate or predict growth patterns. Given the initial values of 1964, the end of the sample span, we have projected the statistical model of Brazilian economic development forward to 1973. Including 1964, we have a decade projection.

To make the projection, it is necessary to substitute all lagged values of

[10] This equation originally was estimated with the money supply in current prices as the left-hand side variable, but is normalized as is indicated for the simulations.

13—I.G.T.

dependent (endogenous) variables for periods prior to 1964. As the simulation develops, *computed* values of these lagged variables are used as inputs after 1964. In addition, we need to assign a decade time path to exogenous variables. We must assume the numerical pattern of overseas variables, Brazilian population, tax rates, and all the other exogenous variables. These are listed separately in Table 1. The goodness or the applicability of our particular simulation to a problem depends on the validity of these assumptions. The reader can see that we have assumed either a steady level or a smooth pattern of development for the exogenous variables.

Given the lags and the exogenous variables, we have *solved* the estimated model as a system of finite difference equations. The solution method used is known as the Gauss–Seidel iteration technique, which has been used to solve a large number of such systems of finite difference equations for both industrial and developing country models.[11] There were difficulties in achieving convergence with a high degree of numerical accuracy because of a failure of the model to project money supply (equation (24)) well. For the simulation calculation, therefore, we replaced this equation by an alternative that specified a fixed (compound interest) rate of growth of money supply at the level of recent experience; otherwise, the model was solved in the form written in the previous section. It may have been possible to re-arrange the computational algorithm and achieve full convergence of the iterative process, but the solution with a realistic growth path imposed on the money supply is a highly suitable alternative, for the hypothesised behaviour in (24) is quite tentative and possibly incomplete.

In the course of constructing the Brazil model, we have made many such simulations—some to test different methods of parameter estimation, some to test the general coherence of the model as a complete system, and some to test the influence of particular equation specifications. In all these simulations, there is one 'robust' finding that persists even though some variables have changed from simulation to simulation. This stable finding is that the real growth rate (for aggregate GDP in constant prices) is modest. In nine years, GDP is projected to grow by 43 per cent, which comes to approximately 4 per cent p.a. This is not out of line with Brazilian history, and of course the model essentially continues a smooth interpretation of such history, but it is below the high aspirations of developing countries. The 4 per cent growth rate in aggregate real output is associated with an assumed growth of population of about 2·5 per cent; therefore the per capita improvement is quite modest. We have considered many alternative formulations of the basic model, yet the 4 per cent real growth rate is a persistent result in all the simulations we have made.

[11] For interpretation and analysis of the numerical methods of solution, see Klein, 1967, and Fromm and Klein, 1969.

With this general background result, let us turn to a more detailed consideration of the projected solution. First, to establish credibility of the result, we can compare the solution values for 1964 with the last sample values. Also, selected variables are known for 1965–6. The precision of the solution in Table 2 is not of the same order of magnitude that we customarily find in similar short-run model studies of industrial countries. Standards used in genuine forecast projections generally require errors to be less than 5 per cent and frequently as small as 1 per cent. Our main objective in the present study is to produce a solution in the neighbourhood of reality and proceed from there with extrapolations. A central variable like GDP comes out in the solution with an error no larger than 5 per cent. This is true of some of the other main activity variables. Although exports and imports are individually in error by more than 10 per cent, the trade balance comes very close to the observed value.

TABLE 2

Model Solutions and Actual Values, 1964

Variable	Solution	Actual	Variable	Solution	Actual
ECF_E	12·1	10·8	GDP	756·8	723·4
ECF_{US}	10·1	10·1	GNP	14,464·7	18,726·0
$ECOC$	1·15	1·05	$NINC$	11,667·8	15,112·0
$EOTH$	13·3	15·3	K	1,506·7	1,502·3
$PCOC_{US}$	20·6	23·3	I_G	24·9	22·5
$PCOT_B$	1,976·0	2,262·0	DPR_P	26·4	27·0
C_G	121·3	116·6	$R\$/p$	89·3	70·8
X_1	174·8	169·3	C	632·5	595·4
E_{COT}	1·39	1·43	G	159·4	134·1
X_2	157·7	162·5	SUR_G	−1,162·1	−563·2
X_3	278·9	247·5	$NWNP$	2,990·6	3,876·1
W	5,312·7	6,816·0	I	71·6	67·2
C_P	511·2	483·8	M	61·7	47·4
I_P	46·7	44·7	$BOTG$	−4·02	−4·33
M_S	4,188·0	5,191·0	P	19·2	26·1
TXC_I	2,444·2	3,204·3	MC	10·5	11·3
MI	11·5	8·7	CM	32·3	39·4
MF	6·9	7·4	$MOTH$	5·72	8·80
DPR	39·6	36·2	E	57·6	43·1
NDP	611·4	585·0	ΔINV	−14·4	15·7
TXC	3,361·3	4,389·3	TXC_D	917·1	1,885·0
			DPR_G	13·2	14·0

Among the known values of variables for 1965–6, net domestic product has been estimated at 638·1 (1965) and 643·0 (1966), while the model projects 640·3 and 667·8 respectively. There was less actual growth than the model suggested, but inflation was greater than computed. The model underestimated the general price deflator by 7 index points in 1964, by 10 in 1965, and by 13 in 1966. Export growth from 1964 to 1966 was stronger than predicted, 30 billion cr. (1953) as compared with 8 billion cr.; correspondingly, the net trade balance was slightly in surplus in 1966 while the model projected a slight deficit. The capacity to import was greater than projected in 1966, and aggregate investment was also larger, although the 1965 value for total investment was almost the same as the projection.

Turning now to the simulation path of the system until 1973, we see that the moderate growth trajectory is accompanied by continuing large inflation.[12] The price level rises by a factor in excess of 20 by 1973, even though we start the simulation with an underestimate of level and change. The exchange rate is expected to rise (cruzeiros/dollar) but a fairly steady ratio is preserved so that $R\$/p$ hardly changes over the whole period. There is good investment growth and moderate consumption growth. Both total exports and total imports grow, but the former by a smaller factor than the latter. The negative net foreign trade balance grows substantially. This is a net inflow of resources for Brazil's development. A good part of the import growth is projected to be in capital goods, with consumer imports steady.

A disturbing aspect of the solution is the slightly growing negative inventory change variable. This is a residual estimate and therefore lacks reliability, yet it is implausible to have decumulation of stocks for such a long period of time. Physically, this is not possible. It shows a need for resources, and these could also come from even-larger import surpluses. In previous solutions of the alternative versions of the model, we have noted a trade-off between stock depletion and an import surplus. If inventory change were to be positive, the identity (10) could hold if imports were correspondingly larger. The solution would work out this way since the GDP estimate is so robust. If we had a changed propensity to import or more investment in working capital, the model would produce a new solution with positive inventory change (or less negative inventory change), a larger import surplus and the same GDP. We simply feel that we are uncertain about the mixture between inventory change and the trade balance, but the rest of the solution appears to be reasonable.

One of the sources of Brazilian economic growth could be in exports. Export sales develop a capacity to import, and this enables the economy to acquire foreign capital goods, fuels, and materials. These are growth stimulating imports. Exports grow but not by unusual amounts. The leading exports—coffee, cocoa, and cotton—are not strong growth commodities. They are limited by world population trends, world need for food and clothing, and by competition from other countries or other commodites; therefore, a strong growth stimulus from expanding export markets is severely limited. This is clearly a part of our solution.

Our solution is passive. It is based on our best judgement as to evolution

[12] Early reports of 1967–8 price changes are quite optimistic on the side of controlling inflation, at a rate of no more than 25 per cent p.a.

of exogenous variables and the maintenance of our estimated structure. The model could be simulated in many directions in search of 'optimal' paths based on different economic policies. We have merely tried to present a useful tool and make some elementary tests of it. We have not tried to optimize the long-run growth path.

REFERENCES

ADY, P., 'Supply Functions in Tropical Agriculture', *Bulletin of the Oxford University Institute of Economics and Statistics*, Vol. 30, May 1968, pp. 157–88.

FROMM, G., and KLEIN, L. R., 'Solutions of the Complete System', in *The Brookings Model: Some Further Results*, J. Duesenberry *et al.*, eds. (Chicago, 1969).

KLEIN, L. R., 'Comment on Solving the Wharton Model', *Review of Economics and Statistics*, XLIX, November 1967, pp. 647–51.

RAO, V. K. R. V., 'Investment, Income and the Multiplier in an Underdeveloped Economy', *Indian Economic Review*, February 1952, reprinted in A. N. Agarawala and S. P. Singh, *The Economics of Underdevelopment* (Oxford, 1963), pp. 204–18.

13

A SIMPLE APPROACH TO THE ECONOMETRICS OF GROWTH

F. P. R. BRECHLING *and* J. N. WOLFE

MANY writers have attempted to utilize the reasonably uniform international statistics made available by the O.E.C.D. to investigate the causes of economic growth. Many of these studies have utilized cross-section methods, but have suffered because of the small number of observations available. The present study involves the bold step of combining time series and cross-sections (with all that this implies) and hence enables us to use somewhat more complex techniques than have been common hitherto.[1] No serious defence of this step is possible here; but some analysis of its empirical implications is attempted.

Let us attempt to deduce the determinants of the rate of growth from an analysis of the production function. Let us assume the Cobb-Douglas form of function:

$$(1) \qquad Q = AK^\alpha M^\beta.$$

Specifying this function, we may say that K is the total capital stock available at any time. M is the total labour force available. Then, by our definition, Q must be the value of production, using all the resources of capital and labour available at any moment.[2] This relationship will seldom be observed in the real world. In practice, we would expect to see only partial utilization of labour and capital. We may observe a relationship of the form

$$(1a) \qquad Y = A(K')^\alpha E^\beta,$$

where K' is the amount of capital actually employed, and E is the amount of labour actually employed. Y is actual output.

In order to move from (1) to (1a) we must find some relationship between

---

[1] The data used in this analysis are conveniently presented in Maddison, 1965.

[2] In some formulations an exponential term is added to take account of technical change. In the present formulation this would cause some difficulty in the interpretation of the intercept term. This term might, in a combined time series and cross-section, reflect either technical progress or the effect of replacement, or some combination of these two elements with statistical error.

K and K', between E and M. Let us define a variable C which is identically equal to E/M, the proportion of the labour force actually employed

(2) $$C \equiv E/M.$$

Our principal task is now to define the relationship between K, K' and C. We would not ordinarily expect this relationship to be linear. Let us assume that the relationship takes the form:

(3) $$K'/K = HC^\gamma.$$

Putting this in another way we have

(4) $$K' = KHC^\gamma.$$

We are now in a position to express the actual income Y in terms of the observable variables E, actual employment, and K, the total capital stock. This is shown by equation (5).

(5) $$Y = A(KHC^\gamma)^\alpha E^\beta.$$

Taking logarithms and differentiating with respect to time, we have the important relation (6)

(6) $$y = \alpha k + \alpha \gamma c + \beta e,$$

where y is the percentage rate of growth of income, k is the percentage rate of growth of the capital stock, e is the percentage growth of employment, and c is the percentage change in C, the capacity utilization variable.

The rate of growth is then seen to depend in a definite way upon the rate of growth of the capital stock, the rate of growth of employment and the rate of change of the degree of capacity utilization variable. The most striking point here is that it is not the degree of capacity utilization which seems to influence the rate of growth but rather the change in the degree of capacity utilization.

Now let us look more closely at k, the rate of growth of the capital stock. This is of course equal to $\dot{K}/K$, the absolute rate of change of capital over K, the capital stock.

(7) $$k = Z'/K.$$

We may replace $\dot{K}$ by Z', the level of net investment. In that case (6) becomes (6a):

(6a) $$y = \alpha(Z'/K) + \alpha \gamma c + \beta e,$$

where K is the total capital stock.

In practice we know only the level of gross investment, and must estimate the level of net investment. To do so we must assume that the level of replacement expenditure depends upon the size of the capital stock and on its age distribution. At any point of time new capital equipment will have varying life expectancy, and we would expect that replacement will, because of this, become necessary in a fairly random way, even though the capital equipment was installed in a cyclically bunched pattern. It follows that replacement expenditure will ordinarily increase with the trend-line of the capital stock, which is itself normally growing over time. Thus, if we include an expression for time, t, as an independent variable, we would expect its coefficient to indicate the allowance to be made for replacement. We would expect this coefficient to have a negative sign.[3]

We cannot, moreover, feel very happy about our estimate of the total capital stock K. In practice we will follow other writers in the assumption that the total capital stock is roughly proportional to output. As a result we will use two independent variables Z/Y and t as our proxies for the theoretically indicated variable $\dot{K}/K$.

This leads then to expression (8) which we call the generalized form of the Cobb-Douglas growth function:

$$(8) \qquad\qquad y = \alpha(Z/Y) + \alpha\gamma c + \beta e + \lambda t,$$

where Z is the level of gross investment, or writing I for Z/Y, we have

$$(8a) \qquad\qquad y = \alpha I + \alpha\gamma c + e + \lambda t.$$

There are two possible variations on this theme. Instead of I we may consider I', the ratio of gross investment in machinery to Gross Domestic Product; and I'', the ratio of gross investment in non-machinery items to Gross Domestic Product. This break-up becomes meaningful in terms of the discussion of the relative merits of investment in infra-structure as compared with investment in machinery.

Finally, some account must be taken of the gestation period of capital goods. Investment activity ordinarily enters into the national accounts at the time it is undertaken, but investment goods presumably have no effect upon output until the whole production complex is completed. To allow for this it is usual to assume that the relevant investment figure is some weighted average of present and past investments. In our models we have assumed that the relevant figure is the average of the investment of the three years up to and including the present. Thus I in our regressions is the average proportion of gross income invested over the three years up to and including the present.

$$(9) \qquad\qquad I_t = \frac{Z_t + Z_{t-1} + Z_{t-2}}{Y_t + Y_{t-1} + Y_{t-2}}.$$

[3] See Brechling, 1965. When t is included as an independent variable, the interpretation of the intercept term becomes particularly difficult. It is possible that technical progress may be distributed between t and the intercept. The negativeness of the coefficient of time depends partly on the neo-classical assumption that capital stock is growing more rapidly than income.

Let us now consider a variable U, the level of unemployment as a percentage of the labour force. There has been considerable controversy about the optimal level of unemployment in the context of the determination of the growth rate. Some have argued that at a low level of unemployment, the incentive to innovate and to become efficient diminishes. Others have said that at high levels of unemployment the incentive to invest in new machinery may diminish and that high unemployment wastes resources which might otherwise be used for growth (although this should be picked up by the investment variable).

Next we introduce p, the annual percentage change in the wholesale price index. It has been widely argued that inflation would by itself have a damaging effect upon the real rate of growth because of the distorting effects it would have upon resource allocation. It has also been argued of course that inflation would induce a high investment ratio. (On the other hand this should be picked up in a multiple regression by the coefficient of the investment variable.)

Next we consider the inclusion of the variable L which represents the lag of any particular country behind the leading country. More specifically it indicates the effect of the relationship of output per man-hour in the particular country being considered compared with output per man-hour in the United States in each particular year.

X indicates the ratio of exports to Gross Domestic Product and is included to test the hypothesis that countries with a large dependence upon foreign trade are *ipso facto* less likely to grow rapidly. On the other hand, x, which is the annual percentage change in X, is included so as to test the hypothesis that a 'leading' export sector is an influence in speeding growth. We take it that if the export proportion is growing in a country then this country can be said to have a 'leading' export sector.

The expression t measures the time trend.

The sample we study was drawn up on the basis of ten countries, Belgium, Denmark, France, Germany, Italy, the Netherlands, Sweden, the United Kingdom, Canada, and the United States. There are nine annual observations for all of these countries except Germany and Belgium. In the former there are six annual observations and in the latter seven.

Our procedure will be first of all to present the results of a number of regressions using alternative formulations of a growth hypothesis. These regressions can be compared to indicate the stability of result as well as to examine the size of the coefficient in various cases.

$$(A.1) \quad g = 0{\cdot}608 + 0{\cdot}213I + 0{\cdot}799c + 0{\cdot}291e - 0{\cdot}164t \quad (\bar{R}^2 = 0{\cdot}53)$$
$$\quad \quad \quad (1{\cdot}350) \quad (0{\cdot}075) \quad (0{\cdot}279) \quad (0{\cdot}145) \quad (0{\cdot}089)$$

The first case (A.1) which we consider measures the effect of the investment ratio, the change in capacity variable, the change in employment, and time, t.

It will be seen that all the coefficients are significant with the exception of t, which is barely significant but has the right sign. It will be noticed that the intercept term is positive rather than negative as has been suggested by earlier cross-section studies but is not significant. This positiveness reappears and seems to be very stable even when t is dropped as an independent variable.

In Regression (A.4) we consider the effect of splitting gross investment into machinery (I') and non-machinery (I'') components in a regression which is otherwise identical to Regression (A.1). It will be seen that the intercept term remains positive but insignificant; that the t term is not quite significant; that e is now not quite significant, but that both I' and I'' are just significant, and have very similar standard errors and coefficients. This suggests that there is little difference in the impact of machinery and non-machinery investment on growth.[4]

$$(A.4) \quad g = 0 \cdot 284 + 0 \cdot 214 I' + 0 \cdot 211 I'' + 1 \cdot 711 c + 0 \cdot 282 e - 0 \cdot 164 t$$
$$(1 \cdot 409) \quad (0 \cdot 102) \quad (0 \cdot 087) \quad (0 \cdot 285) \quad (0 \cdot 148) \quad (0 \cdot 088)$$
$$(\bar{R}^2 = 0 \cdot 53)$$

Now what is the impact of including some of the other variables we have mentioned as additions to our basic model? This is shown in the following regressions:

$$(A.21) \quad g = 1 \cdot 254 + 0 \cdot 197 I + 1 \cdot 780 c + 0 \cdot 391 e - 0 \cdot 147 U - 1 \cdot 543 t$$
$$(0 \cdot 147) \quad (0 \cdot 079) \quad (0 \cdot 279) \quad (0 \cdot 1714) \quad (0 \cdot 135) \quad (0 \cdot 894)$$
$$(\bar{R}^2 = 0 \cdot 53)$$

$$(A.25) \quad g = 0 \cdot 867 + 0 \cdot 196 I + 1 \cdot 785 c + 0 \cdot 296 e - 0 \cdot 090 p - 1 \cdot 43 t$$
$$(1 \cdot 306) \quad (0 \cdot 079) \quad (0 \cdot 279) \quad (0 \cdot 145) \quad (0 \cdot 077) \quad (0 \cdot 907)$$
$$(\bar{R}^2 = 0 \cdot 53)$$

$$(A.29) \quad g = 1 \cdot 106 + 0 \cdot 237 I + 1 \cdot 723 c + 0 \cdot 279 e - 1 \cdot 672 t - 0 \cdot 016 L$$
$$(1 \cdot 389) \quad (0 \cdot 079) \quad (0 \cdot 283) \quad (0 \cdot 145) \quad (0 \cdot 885) \quad (0 \cdot 011)$$
$$(\bar{R}^2 = 0 \cdot 53)$$

$$(A.33) \quad g = 0 \cdot 558 + 0 \cdot 211 I + 1 \cdot 786 c + 0 \cdot 298 e - 1 \cdot 630 t + 0 \cdot 003 X$$
$$(1 \cdot 384) \quad (0 \cdot 080) \quad (0 \cdot 288) \quad (0 \cdot 152) \quad (0 \cdot 898) \quad (0 \cdot 016)$$
$$(\bar{R}^2 = 0 \cdot 52)$$

$$(A.37) \quad g = 0 \cdot 643 + 0 \cdot 215 I + 1 \cdot 801 c + 0 \cdot 274 e - 1 \cdot 721 t + 0 \cdot 013 X$$
$$(1 \cdot 361) \quad (0 \cdot 079) \quad (0 \cdot 281) \quad (0 \cdot 154) \quad (0 \cdot 921) \quad (0 \cdot 037)$$
$$(\bar{R}^2 = 0 \cdot 54)$$

It will be seen from Regression (A.21) that unemployment does not by itself have a significant influence on growth and its influence—such as it is—is negative.

---

[4] It will be observed that an alternative model would make growth influence investment via the accelerator. It would not be very easy to discriminate between these hypotheses without knowing the lag structure of investment. For this point as well as for footnote [5], we are indebted to Messrs. Scott and Eltis.

Regression (A.25) shows that price change does not significantly affect growth. Regression (A.29) shows that the degree to which a country lags in income per head is not a significant influence. Regression (A.33) indicates that the role of exports in the economy is not a significant influence on growth. Regression (A.37) does not seem to support the 'leading export sector' hypothesis.

Now we must introduce a variable which is different in some respects from those we have been using. Our variable J is intended as a proxy for the volume of migration of workers from agriculture to industry. More exactly, it is the average percentage movement of labour from agriculture, country by country. In almost every case we can only obtain such a figure by using census data which appears at widely spread intervals. Thus we have not had several annual observations on J for each country. We incorporate J in Regression

(A.13) $g = 1.019 + 0.136I + 1.784c + 0.2693e - 0.135t + 0.160J$
         $\quad\ (1.353)\quad (0.089)\quad (0.276)\quad (0.143)\quad (0.089)\quad (0.091)$
$$(\bar{R}^2 = 0.54)$$

Comparing this with Regression (A.1), it will be seen that while J is not itself significant, its inclusion has caused the coefficient of I to become insignificant. We may go a step further by dividing the investment ratio into its two components. This is done in (A.16) below:

(A.16) $g = 0.355 + 0.182I' + 0.1353I'' + 1.710c + 0.258e - 0.143t + 0.173J$
         $\quad\ (0.383)\quad (0.102)\quad\ (0.094)\quad\ (0.279)\quad (0.147)\quad (0.088)\quad (0.086)$
$$(\bar{R}^2 = 0.55)$$

Comparing this with (A.4) we notice that the significance of non-machinery investment is more strikingly affected by the inclusion of J than is that of investment in machinery. This suggests that non-machinery investment is highly correlated with the movement from agriculture to industry. It may be that much of the apparent importance of overhead capital arises because this investment has accompanied a movement of labour out of agriculture, rather than because of its own effect on productivity.

We may, however, surmise that the relatively weak results we have obtained do not tell the whole story. For one thing it may be that we have neglected the effect of a country's growth experience upon its economic structure. Countries may behave differently after a period of rapid growth. To test this possibility we have divided our data into two sub-groups. We group together observations which show growth above the average rate experienced by each particular country. These above-average observations were subjected to a variety of regressions, labelled B. Below average growth periods were subjected to similar regressions, labelled C.

The rationale of this procedure is as follows. Suppose that, in each country, there is a 'normal' growth rate of capacity which is accomplished through the foundation of some new firms and the expansion of others. Assume further that as long as demand grows at a rate equal to the growth of capacity all firms operate at some fixed degree of excess capacity. If demand grows more quickly than this, firms will be forced up their short-run marginal cost curves, which rise rapidly after some point. Thereafter expansion can only take place through the building of new plant and equipment.

If, on the other hand, the growth of demand is less than the growth of capacity, all firms are assumed to operate at an increased degree of excess capacity. In that case output can readily be expanded without any new capital being installed. Indeed, the installation of new capital may have a very limited effect on total output, since any growth in output by newly equipped firms would largely be offset by the contraction of output from firms with older machinery.

We might expect, then, that investment would have a more important effect on output growth when demand is growing rapidly. While we have no independent measure of demand growth we may surmise that it is high when output growth is high, and this is the basis of our division of the data, into above average growth and below average growth groupings.[5]

$$(\text{A.1}) \quad g = 0 \cdot 608 + 0 \cdot 2135I + 1 \cdot 799c + 0 \cdot 291e - 0 \cdot 164t \quad (\bar{R}^2 = 0 \cdot 53)$$
$$\qquad\quad (1 \cdot 350) \quad (0 \cdot 078) \quad\; (0 \cdot 279) \quad (0 \cdot 145) \quad (0 \cdot 089)$$

$$(\text{A.4}) \quad g = 0 \cdot 287 + 0 \cdot 214I' + 0 \cdot 212I'' + 1 \cdot 711c + 0 \cdot 282e - 0 \cdot 165t$$
$$\qquad\quad (1 \cdot 410) \quad (0 \cdot 102) \quad\; (0 \cdot 087) \quad\; (0 \cdot 285) \quad (0 \cdot 149) \quad (0 \cdot 088)$$
$$\qquad\qquad\qquad\qquad\qquad\qquad\qquad\qquad\qquad\qquad (\bar{R}^2 = 0 \cdot 53)$$

$$(\text{B.1}) \quad g = -1 \cdot 221 + 0 \cdot 407I + 1 \cdot 082c + 0 \cdot 062e - 0 \cdot 165t \quad (\bar{R} = 0 \cdot 44)$$
$$\qquad\quad (1 \cdot 488) \quad (0 \cdot 084) \quad\; (0 \cdot 461) \quad (0 \cdot 146) \quad (0 \cdot 086)$$

$$(\text{B.4}) \quad g = -1 \cdot 145 + 0 \cdot 367I' + 0 \cdot 398I'' + 0 \cdot 957c + 0 \cdot 023e - 0 \cdot 194t$$
$$\qquad\quad (1 \cdot 545) \quad (0 \cdot 118) \quad\; (0 \cdot 091) \quad\; (0 \cdot 484) \quad (0 \cdot 155) \quad (0 \cdot 089)$$
$$\qquad\qquad\qquad\qquad\qquad\qquad\qquad\qquad\qquad\qquad (\bar{R}^2 = 0 \cdot 43)$$

$$(\text{C.1}) \quad g = -0 \cdot 182 + 0 \cdot 139I + 1 \cdot 064c + 0 \cdot 500e - 0 \cdot 066t \quad (\bar{R}^2 = 0 \cdot 52)$$
$$\qquad\quad (1 \cdot 549) \quad (0 \cdot 092) \quad\; (0 \cdot 277) \quad (0 \cdot 205) \quad (0 \cdot 117)$$

$$(\text{C.4}) \quad g = -1 \cdot 624 + 0 \cdot 245I' + 0 \cdot 155I'' + 0 \cdot 945c + 0 \cdot 486e - 0 \cdot 064t$$
$$\qquad\quad (1 \cdot 581) \quad (0 \cdot 104) \quad\; (0 \cdot 102) \quad\; (0 \cdot 268) \quad (0 \cdot 198) \quad (0 \cdot 107)$$
$$\qquad\qquad\qquad\qquad\qquad\qquad\qquad\qquad\qquad\qquad (\bar{R}^2 = 0 \cdot 56)$$

$$(\text{A.13}) \, g = 1 \cdot 019 + 0 \cdot 136I + 1 \cdot 783c + 0 \cdot 269e - 0 \cdot 135t + 0 \cdot 160J$$
$$\qquad\quad (1 \cdot 353) \quad (0 \cdot 089) \quad\; (0 \cdot 276) \quad (0 \cdot 144) \quad (0 \cdot 089) \quad\; (0 \cdot 091)$$
$$\qquad\qquad\qquad\qquad\qquad\qquad\qquad\qquad\qquad\qquad (\bar{R}^2 = 0 \cdot 54)$$

$$(\text{A.16}) \, g = 0 \cdot 355 + 0 \cdot 182I' + 0 \cdot 135I'' + 1 \cdot 710c + 0 \cdot 258e - 0 \cdot 143t + 0 \cdot 174J$$
$$\qquad\quad (1 \cdot 383) \quad (0 \cdot 102) \quad\; (0 \cdot 094) \quad\; (0 \cdot 280) \quad (0 \cdot 147) \quad (0 \cdot 088) \quad\; (0 \cdot 086)$$
$$\qquad\qquad\qquad\qquad\qquad\qquad\qquad\qquad\qquad\qquad (\bar{R}^2 = 0 \cdot 55)$$

[5] Alternatively growth may be slow because demand is slack. This illustrates again the well-known proposition that the interpretation of data in an econometric model depends in an essential way upon the theoretical structure assumed.

(B.13) $g = -0.710 + 0.303I + 1.148c + 0.030e - 0.125t + 0.214J$
$\quad\quad\quad (1.420)\quad (0.090)\quad\quad (0.436)\quad\quad (0.139)\quad\quad (0.083)\quad\quad (0.086)$
$$(\bar{R}^2 = 0.50)$$

(B.16) $g = -1.128 + 0.309I' + 0.230I'' + 1.049c - 0.13e - 0.150t + 0.243J$
$\quad\quad\quad (1.415)\quad (0.110)\quad\quad (0.090)\quad\quad (0.445)\quad\quad (0.142)\quad (0.083)\quad (0.081)$
$$(\bar{R}^2 = 0.52)$$

(C.13) $g = 0.024 + 0.092I + 1.037c + 0.468e - 0.049t + 0.108J$
$\quad\quad\quad (1.567)\quad (0.105)\quad\quad (0.278)\quad\quad (0.208)\quad\quad (0.119)\quad\quad (0.114)$
$$(\bar{R}^2 = 0.52)$$

(C.16) $g = -1.610 + 0.231I' + 0.108I'' + 0.927c + 0.449e - 0.060t + 0.111J$
$\quad\quad\quad (1.578)\quad (0.105)\quad\quad (0.111)\quad\quad (0.269)\quad\quad (0.201)\quad (0.107)\quad (0.104)$
$$(\bar{R}^2 = 0.56)$$

Comparing (A.1) with (B.1) it will be seen that there is a considerable increase in the significance of I in the latter, while e becomes insignificant. If we divide investment up and compare (A.4) with (B.4) we find that the increase in significance is almost equally shared by the two components of investment. Comparing (A.1) with (C.1), the slow-growth observations, we find that there is a sharp decline in the significance of I in the latter. Looking at (A.4) and (C.4) we see that the decline in significance is more marked in the case of non-machinery investments.

When we include variable J for movement from agriculture to industry as in (A.13), (B.13), (C.13), and (A.16), (B.16), and (C.16), we obtain even more striking results. When we consider the fast growth periods we see that investment becomes highly significant. In slow growth periods machinery investment is a significant variable, but non-machinery investment remains insignificant. This suggests that the correlation of migration from agriculture with overhead capital investment is largely confined to slow growth periods, and allows scope for the independent influence of non-machinery investment in fast growth periods.

To amalgamate time-series and cross-section data is implicitly to assume that all data involved are drawn from the same population. More exactly, it is assumed that all data are generated by the same statistical model. But even if the forces determining the cross-section observations are the same as those determining the time-series observations, the lag structure may be different in the two cases. Moreover, the strength of the forces operating on the time-series may be different from the strength of the forces operating on the cross-section.

The way to see whether the data are indeed drawn from the same population is to subject the data to an analysis of co-variance. We may do this in various ways. The simplest is to insert dummy variables standing for each of the countries in our cross-section. We could then run the regression once more, using as independent variables the dummies plus certain other variables. Those we have used are in fact the investment ratio, the change in capacity utilization variable and the change in employment variable. It should be noticed that when dummy variables are utilized for the different countries it is no longer possible to include as an independent variable J, the average movement of labour from agriculture. Results are given in (A.9), using all observations of both fast and slow growth.

In the first place the coefficient of the investment ratio becomes nearly significant, but now has the wrong sign. The change in employment variable is not quite significant. The only one of the original variables which remains significant and possesses the right sign is the change in capacity utilization variable, which is highly significant. The $\bar{R}^2$ for the regression as a whole is 0·59.

In the case of France, Germany, the Netherlands, Sweden, Canada, and the United States the country dummies show up as significant. This suggests that our analysis has not fully succeeded in explaining the differential growth rates experienced by different countries. It leaves open the possibility that the explanation of the varying experience of different countries is to be sought in non-economic forces.

The negativeness of the regression coefficient of the investment ratio suggests that when the differences between countries are allowed for by the dummy variables, an increase in the investment ratio actually lowers the rate of growth. One possible explanation for this observation is the possibility that, within countries, periods of high investment ratio are correlated with low growth because of a cyclical lag in the economy.

$$(A.9) \quad g = 12{\cdot}033 + 1{\cdot}541c + 0{\cdot}321e + 2{\cdot}021t - 0{\cdot}709I + 11{\cdot}179a_{21}$$
$$\quad\quad\quad (4{\cdot}158) \quad (0{\cdot}286) \quad (0{\cdot}192) \quad (1{\cdot}361) \quad (0{\cdot}384) \quad (9{\cdot}525)$$
$$\quad + 30{\cdot}136a_{22} + 72{\cdot}428a_{23} + 36{\cdot}99a_{24} + 67{\cdot}219a_{25} + 43{\cdot}901a_{26}$$
$$\quad\quad (10{\cdot}540) \quad (19{\cdot}599) \quad (19{\cdot}783) \quad (21{\cdot}353) \quad (16{\cdot}200)$$
$$\quad - 8{\cdot}519a_{27} + 72{\cdot}480a_{28} + 25{\cdot}502a_{29} \quad (\bar{R}^2 = 0{\cdot}59)$$
$$\quad\quad (10{\cdot}140) \quad (26{\cdot}223) \quad (12{\cdot}229)$$

where a_{21} is Denmark, a_{22} is France, a_{23} is Germany, a_{24} is Italy, a_{25} is The Netherlands, a_{26} is Sweden, a_{27} is the United Kingdom, a_{28} is Canada, and a_{29} is the United States.

REFERENCES

BRECHLING, F. P. R., 'The Relationship between Output and Employment', *Review of Economic Studies*, 1965.

MADDISON, A. *Economic Growth in the West. Comparative Experience in Europe and North America*ˌ(London, 1965).

14

THE LIFE CYCLE HYPOTHESIS OF SAVING AND INTERCOUNTRY DIFFERENCES IN THE SAVING RATIO*

FRANCO MODIGLIANI

1. *Introduction*

IN Chapter 2 of *Towards a Dynamic Economics*, Sir Roy Harrod made a pioneering contribution to the study of aggregate saving by analysing the implications of the basic assumption that current saving decisions of households reflect an endeavour to achieve the preferred allocation of lifetime resources to consumption (and bequests) over the life cycle. Since that time, this approach has been pursued by a number of authors, both at the theoretical level and for the analysis of empirical data.[1] In particular, in Goldsmith (1956) and Modigliani (1966) it was found that this hypothesis is quite effective in accounting for the behaviour of aggregate saving and wealth in the United States both in the short and in the long run. The purpose of the present paper is to show that this approach appears equally fruitful for an understanding of observed inter-country differences in the average saving ratio.

A number of implications of the hypothesis of life cycle planning have been derived in Modigliani (1966) by combining that hypothesis with the assumption that the preferred pattern of allocation of consumption over life and the rate of return on assets remain reasonably stable in time. The following are directly relevant to the tests presented here:

(1) If productivity (output per employed person) tends to grow at a

* The tests reported in this paper were first presented in a paper entitled 'The Life Cycle Hypothesis of Saving, The Demand for Wealth and the Supply of Capital' prepared for the First International Meeting of the Econometric Society, Rome, Italy, September 1965. Other parts of that paper have since been published in Modigliani (1966). I am greatly indebted to Dr. Antonio Fazio of the Bank of Italy for advice and help in the design and execution of the statistical tests. Research support from a Ford Foundation grant to the Sloan School of Management for research in Finance is gratefully acknowledged.

[1] A partial list of references is given in Modigliani (1966). Among the contributions that have appeared since publication of that paper Meade (1966) and Tobin (1967) are particularly noteworthy.

constant rate, say y, and population at the rate p, and if aggregate output fluctuates cyclically around the growth trend $\varrho = y + p$, then the saving income ratio will tend to fluctuate *cyclically* around a constant level, say s.

(2) The value of s is independent of real income (aggregate or per capita) and depends instead on y and p or, more precisely, on y and the age structure of population, which, however, is uniquely related to p if population is in balanced growth. Furthermore the 'long run' saving ratio will be zero if y and p are zero (stationary economy) and will tend to grow with both y and p, though less than in proportion.

Implication (1) has long been known to be at least broadly consistent with the American experience over the last century or so; the available estimates of income and saving suggest in fact (i) a reasonably stable overall growth trend of real income; (ii) a saving income ratio characterized by marked cyclical movements but no significant overall upward or downward trend, despite the enormous rise in both aggregate and per capita real income. Implication (2), on the other hand, cannot be readily tested from U.S. data for the very same reason that makes the U.S. experience relevant for a test of implication (1), namely the overall stability of the growth trend of income over the period covered by the available data. More generally, there seems to be little chance that a satisfactory test of this set of implications can be carried out at present from time series data for individual countries because income is unlikely to exhibit very different growth trends within the span of time for which the required information is typically available. In what follows we propose instead to test these propositions by an analysis of intercountry differences in the saving ratio, and to show that they seem to account for a substantial proportion of the observed variations.

The raw material for our test is provided by the extensive compilation of data assembled in the United Nations *Yearbook of National Accounts Statistics*. With the help of this source and a few auxiliary ones, it has been possible to assemble usable data for a sample of some 36 countries. These are listed in the Data Appendix together with the values of the variables which will be used in our tests. It is readily apparent from this table and from the last column of Table 3, which provides a number of summary statistics, that the variables relevant to our tests exhibit a very wide variation, even though each of these variables represents an average over a span of several years, mostly seven to nine years (see below). In particular, the saving ratio, which averages 11·2 per cent for the sample as a whole, ranges all the way from −2·1 to 21·0 per cent, while the rate of growth of real income, averaging 4·7 per cent per year, varies between 1·5 and 9·9 per cent. Equally striking is the variation in estimated real per capita income in U.S. dollars, which ranges from $65 to $1,700, compared with a mean value of $790.

In assembling, as well as in analysing, the data, we have relied heavily on the methodology proposed and followed by Houthakker in two recent papers (see list of References) dealing with the determinants of inter-country differences in saving behaviour. The second of these papers contains the first attempt of which we are aware at testing the specific implications of the life cycle hypothesis with which we are presently concerned. In the following section we briefly review Houthakker's methodology and some of his results, and in the remaining ones we rely on the same methodology to extend the tests in a variety of directions.

2. *Review of Houthakker Methodology and Results*

The method used by Houthakker in deriving the observations for each country is explained in the above references. The sample consists of all countries for which the required information is reported in the U.N. *Yearbook of National Accounts Statistics*. The saving and income variable for each country is an average of annual data for as many years as were available between 1952 and 1959, converted into real per capita U.S. dollars by means of population data, appropriate price indices and official exchange rates. The use of official exchange rates is, of course, a crude approximation, and probably subject to considerable error; fortunately, in most of our own tests we are able to rely on ratios which are unaffected by the choice of exchange rates. The most serious error is likely to occur in the estimates of per capita real income, though even here the spread between countries is so wide that we doubt that this source of error can affect the results to a significant extent.

Of the numerous results reported by Houthakker, the relevant ones for our purpose are those in which he has tested the effect of per capita income and of the rate of growth of income. These tests consist in fitting to the sample equations of the form

$$(1) \qquad (S_{\text{pers}})_i = b_0 + b_1(Y_{\text{pd}})_i + b_2(\Delta Y_{\text{pd}})_i$$

and

$$(2) \qquad \frac{(S_{\text{pers}})_i}{(Y_{\text{pd}})_i} = c_1 + c_2(\Delta^* Y_{\text{pd}})_i,$$

where $(S_{\text{pers}})_i$ and $(Y_{\text{pd}})_i$ denote, respectively, average annual *per capita* personal saving and disposable personal income for country i (measured in $/year), ΔY_{pd} is the average annual increment in Y_{pd} (with dimension $/(year)^2), and $\Delta^* Y_{\text{pd}}$ is the average annual rate of growth of *aggregate* personal income (with dimension 1/year).

Before we examine his empirical results we may stop to inquire whether the life cycle hypothesis can provide us with some notion as to the plausible range of values for the parameters of equations (1) and (2). To answer this question we must turn to a number of results established in Modigliani (1966).

It was shown there that, if income fluctuates cyclically around the growth trend $\varrho = y + p$, the behaviour of the saving income ratio implied by the life cycle model can be approximated by

$$(3) \qquad S_t/Y_t = \frac{\sigma\varrho}{\delta + \varrho} + \frac{\delta\varrho}{\sigma + \varrho} Q_t,$$

where S denotes private saving, Y private income net of taxes, σ and δ are constants and Q_t stands for the 'cyclical income index'

$$Q_t = \frac{Y_t - (1 + \varrho)^n \mathring{Y}_t}{Y_t},$$

$\mathring{Y}_t$ being the highest value reached by real income Y in any year preceding t and n the number of years from then to t. Since Q measures deviations from the growth trend, it must average out to zero over a sufficiently long span of years. Therefore, from equation (3), we can infer that, provided the number of years utilized in computing the average saving ratio for each country in our sample is sufficiently large to wash out roughly the cyclical effects, the life cycle hypothesis would imply

$$(4) \qquad S_i/Y_i = \frac{\sigma_i \varrho_i}{\delta_i + \varrho_i}.$$

The parameters σ and δ might differ from country to country, as implied by the subscript i, since, in principle, they depend on such forces as the overall rate of growth and its distribution between y and p, the rate of return on assets, and, of course, tastes. However, a number of results reported in Modigliani and Brumberg (unpublished) and Modigliani (1966, Table 1) suggest that these parameters may not be, in fact, very responsive to the above forces, within the relevant range of variation. Indeed, it is found that there are broad similarities in the relation between s and ϱ implied by alternative assumptions about the source of growth (i.e., y versus p) and the representative life profile of income and consumption.[2] Furthermore, this relation is also similar to that implied by equation (4) by assigning to σ and δ the values estimated for the U.S. in the post-war period, namely, around 0·35 for σ and 0·05 for δ.[3] Such results suggest that intercountry differences in

---

[2] See also footnote 15.

[3] These values are derived in Modigliani (1966) from estimates obtained in Ando and Modigliani (1963 and 1964), by fitting to the U.S. data the consumption function

$$C_t = \alpha L^e_t + \beta A_{t-1}$$

where L^e is expected labour income and A is private wealth. The parameters σ and δ are related to α and β by

$$\sigma = 1 - \alpha \qquad \delta = \beta - \alpha r$$

where r is the rate of return on assets. The relation between s and ϱ implied by (4) for the parameters σ and δ may be sufficiently small and unsystematic to be impounded in the error term without destroying the explanatory and predictive value of the model[4]. Under these assumptions, (4) can be rewritten as

$$(5) \qquad\qquad S_i/Y_i = \frac{\sigma \varrho_i}{\delta + \varrho_i} + e_i.$$

By further noting that the ratio of per capita saving to per capita income is the same as the ratio of aggregate saving to aggregate income, we can conclude that Houthakker's equation (2) is simply a linear approximation to (5) with ϱ_i approximated empirically by the rate of growth of personal income, $\Delta^* Y_{pd}$. A rough idea of the magnitude of the coefficient c_1 and c_2 implied by the model can then be obtained by expanding the right-hand side of (5) linearly around $\bar{\varrho}$, the mean value of ϱ in the sample, and relying on the estimates of σ and δ obtained for the United States, which is one of the countries included in the sample. Let

$$s(\varrho) \equiv \frac{\sigma \varrho}{\delta + \varrho}, \quad \text{and} \quad s'(\varrho) = \frac{ds}{d\varrho}.$$

Then

$$s(\varrho) \simeq s(\bar{\varrho}) + s'(\bar{\varrho})(\varrho - \bar{\varrho}) = [s(\bar{\varrho}) - \bar{\varrho}s'(\bar{\varrho})] + s'(\bar{\varrho})\varrho;$$

$$(6) \qquad\qquad s(\bar{\varrho}) = \frac{\sigma \bar{\varrho}}{\delta + \bar{\varrho}} \qquad s'(\bar{\varrho}) = \frac{\sigma \delta}{(\delta + \bar{\varrho})^2}.$$

Substituting the U.S. estimates, $\sigma \simeq 0.35$, $\delta \simeq 0.05$, and the value of $\bar{\varrho}$ for

$\sigma = 0.35$, $\delta = 0.05$, is shown below for selected values of ϱ

ϱ (%)	0	1	2	3	4	5	10
s (%)	0	6	10	13	16	18	23

It should be noted that the life profile of consumption assumed in deriving the relation between s and ϱ referred to in the text imply no bequests and hence the only source of saving is Harrod's 'hump-saving' [Harrod (1948), p. 49]. However, as shown in Modigliani and Brumberg (unpublished) and Modigliani (1966) the above consumption function, and hence equation (4), also hold if we allow for bequests, under appropriate assumptions.

   [4] Tobin (1967) also exhibits the relation between p and y and the saving ratio (derivable from his wealth income ratio) under rather different assumptions about income expectations and life consumption than those used in Modigliani (1966) and referred to above. His findings confirm that, generally, s tends to rise with both p and y and less than in proportion. However, they imply a far greater positive responsiveness of s to r than suggested by calculations carried out in Modigliani and Brumberg (unpublished). The difference seems to arise from the fact that contrary to what was assumed in the latter, he assumes (at least in part for computational convenience) that consumption is rather responsive to changes in r. As a result even for moderate values of r his values of s tend to be substantially above those shown in Table 1 of Modigliani (1966) and in footnote 3 above.

Houthakker's sample, 0·04, we find [5]

$$c_2 \simeq s'(\bar{\varrho}) = \frac{(0·35)(0·05)}{(0·05 + 0·04)^2} = 2·2,$$

(7)

$$c_1 \simeq s(\bar{\varrho}) - \bar{\varrho}s'(\bar{\varrho}) = \frac{(0·35)(0·04)}{0·05 + 0·04} - (0·04)(2·2) = 0·067.$$

These *a priori* estimates of c_1 and c_2 would be directly applicable if S and Y were measured in accordance with the definitions underlying our model and the parameter estimates for the United States. There are, in fact, a number of significant differences. The income measure in Houthakker's tests is 'disposable personal income', which differs from our 'private income net of taxes' primarily by the exclusion of corporate saving. Similarly, his 'personal saving' differs from our concept by the exclusion of corporate saving as well as of the net addition to the stock of consumers' durables. Some idea of the extent to which these differences may affect the values of c_1 and c_2 can be gathered from an examination of Table 1. The statistics in column (1) are

TABLE 1

Saving Ratios and Growth Rates for Different Concepts of Saving and Income—22 Countries

(a) *Mean Values*	Our Sample (1)	Houthakker Sample (2)
Ratio of corporate saving to private income (%)	4·2	
Ratio of private saving to private income (%)	11·7	
Ratio of personal saving to personal income (%)	7·8	7·3
Rate of growth of private income (% per year)	4·6	
Rate of growth of personal income (% per year)	4·5	4·0
(b) *Correlations*		
Rate of growth of private income with rate of growth of personal income	0·995	
Private saving ratio with personal saving ratio	0·92	

based on a 22-country subsample of the sample used in our own analysis for which it is possible to estimate both private and corporate saving, and hence also personal saving. This sample overlaps to a considerable extent with the 28-country sample used by Houthakker, for which the available information is reported in column (2). It is apparent that the substitution of personal income for private income is unlikely to affect the results materially, but the difference in the definition of saving is important; the personal saving ratio is on the average only about two-thirds as large as the private saving ratio, although the correlation between the two measures is fairly high.

[5] Note that the result for c_1 implies that the constant term of the linear approximation to (5) should be positive even though (5) implies zero saving for a zero rate of growth. It reflects the fact that, according to (5), s rises proportionally less than ϱ.

The omission of saving in the form of additions to the stock of durable goods is common both to Houthakker's personal saving and to the measure of private saving used in Table 1 and in the rest of our analysis. Estimates for the United States based on Goldsmith (1956 and 1962) as well as on the Flow of Funds series (1961, Table 2), suggest that this form of saving is far from negligible and has tended to account for some 15 to 20 per cent of private saving, although this figure may not be very typical for other countries. On the whole, however, we should not be very far off in concluding that Houthakker's saving ratio is likely to be, on the average, 40 to 50 per cent lower than if he had used the measure called for by the model.

In the light of the above considerations it is significant that the mean saving ratio of Houthakker's sample, 7·3 per cent, is just below one-half the value of $s(\bar{\varrho})$ implied by equation (6) with U.S. parameters, namely, $[(0·35)(0·04)]/[(0·05) + (0·04)] = 15·5$ per cent, considering also that $s(\bar{\varrho})$ will tend to overestimate the mean value of s implied by the model because of the negative curvature of $s(\varrho)$. These results also suggest that the coefficients of equation (2) should be on the order of 40 to 50 per cent lower than implied by (7), or around 1·1 to 1·3 for c_2, the coefficient of ϱ, and around 0·03 to 0·04 for the constant term c_1.[6] The result reported by Houthakker (1965, p. 218, equation (7)) is

$$(2a) \qquad \frac{S_{pers}}{Y_{pd}} = \underset{(0·012)}{0·020} + \underset{(0·28)}{1·36\Delta^* Y_{pd}}.$$

(The figure in parentheses underneath each coefficient is the standard error of the coefficient.) The coefficient of the rate of growth term is highly significant as indicated by a t-ratio of nearly 5, and what matters most, both this coefficient and the constant term agree rather well with the values implied by the hypothesis. The results reported by Houthakker for equation (1) are equally suggestive even though the variables used here are further removed from those called for by the model. A rough idea of the value of the coefficients of this equation implied by the model can be obtained by observing that the rate of growth of total income $\Delta^* Y_{pd}$, can be approximated as the sum of per capita income and population growth. Substituting this approximation in (2) and multiplying through by Y_{pd} we find

$$(S_{pers})_i = c_1(Y_{pd})_i + c_2\left[\frac{(\Delta Y_{pd})_i}{(Y_{pd})_i} + \left(\frac{\Delta P}{P}\right)_i\right](Y_{pd})_i$$

$$= c_1(Y_{pd})_i + c_2(\Delta Y_{pd})_i + c_2\left(\frac{\Delta P}{P}\right)_i(Y_{pd})_i.$$

This equation differs from equation (1) on account of the last term, which

[6] In the case of c_1 the estimate should presumably be reduced somewhat further because, as noted, $s(\bar{\varrho})$ is likely to overstate $\bar{s}$.

is omitted in Houthakker's test, and because of the absence of the constant term. We can conclude, therefore, that provided the omitted variable is not markedly correlated with the remaining two, our model would lead us to expect the following approximate relation between the parameters of (1) and (2)

$$b_1 \simeq c_1, \qquad b_2 \simeq c_2, \qquad b_0 \simeq 0.$$

The relation $b_0 \simeq 0$ deserves particular note for it expresses in operational form the independence of the saving *ratio* from the *level* of per capita income, implied by the model. According to the traditional view, instead the saving function should have a substantial negative intercept, i.e., $b_0 < 0$, implying that the saving ratio is an increasing function of per capita income.

A simple correlation of per capita income and per capita saving yields (Houthakker, 1965, p. 215, equation (1))

(1a)
$$S_{\text{pers}} = -1 \cdot 1 + 0 \cdot 081 \, Y_{\text{pd}}.$$
$$\phantom{S_{\text{pers}} = } (2 \cdot 3) \quad (0 \cdot 011)$$

It is apparent that the constant term is negligibly small and insignificant, as predicted by the hypothesis and contrary to prevailing views.[7]

Addition of the variable ΔY_{pd} leads to (Houthakker, 1965, p. 218, equation (5))

(1b)
$$S'_{\text{pers}} = -1 \cdot 0 + 0 \cdot 040 \, Y_{\text{pd}} + 1 \cdot 59 \, \Delta Y_{\text{pd}}.$$
$$\phantom{S'_{\text{pers}} = } (1 \cdot 6) \quad (0 \cdot 010) \qquad (0 \cdot 28)$$

Once more, the contribution of the rate of growth variable is highly significant and the values of the coefficients are rather close to those implied by the model.[8]

3. *Replication of the Basic Test for Private Saving*

The major shortcoming of Houthakker's tests for our purposes is that they are based on a definition of income and especially saving, which differs appreciably from that called for by our model. While it does not seem feasible at present to estimate saving in the form of net additions to durables for any significant number of countries, there is no serious difficulty in obtaining

---

[7] The independence of the saving ratio from per capita income is also confirmed by the logarithmic regression (*ibid.*, page 216, equation (3)),
$$\log C_{\text{pers}} = -0 \cdot 035 + 1 \cdot 004 \log Y_{\text{pd}},$$
$$\phantom{\log C_{\text{pers}} = } (0 \cdot 021) \quad (0 \cdot 0076)$$
where C_{pers} is per capita consumption, which shows that the elasticity of consumption with respect to income is remarkably close to unity.

[8] Houthakker's comment [1965, p. 218] that the 'large coefficient' of the growth term in (1b) and (2a) is 'disturbing' is very hard to understand and seems to be based on heuristic considerations which fail to take into account the dimension of the variable ΔY_{pd} namely, $/(\text{year})^2$ rather than $/\text{year}$, as his comment seems to imply.

estimates of private income and of private saving excluding durables. Indeed, relying on the U.N. *Yearbook* and on auxiliary data generously provided by Houthakker, we have found it possible to estimate these variables for 36 countries including all but three of the 28 countries in Houthakker's sample.[9] We have also included in our averages the year 1960, whenever available. In estimating the regression equations reported below, the observations for each country were weighted following the procedure recommended by Houthakker. Since in our tests the dependent variable is always the saving ratio, application of Houthakker's procedure leads to a weight equal to the product of average population times the number of years included in the country's average. This weight is shown in the Data Appendix (Column 4).

We may begin by testing whether the enlarged sample provides any support for the conventional view, rejected by our model, that the proportion of income saved tends to be an increasing function of, and can be largely explained by, per capita income. To this end we could replicate test (1a), and check whether the constant term is significantly negative. Since hereafter we intend to focus on the behaviour of the saving ratio, S/Y, or, more precisely, of the percentage of income saved, $s = 100(S/Y)$, it is convenient to rely on a simple variant of the above test obtained by dividing both sides of the equation by per capita income. We thus obtain the test equation

$$(8) \qquad s = 100(S/Y) = 100(S'/Y') = 100(b_0/Y' + b_1)$$
$$= b_0(100/Y') + (100b_1),$$

where primed symbols denote per capita values. The empirical result is

$$(8a) \qquad s = -2 \cdot 6 \frac{100}{\underset{(2 \cdot 4)}{Y'}} + 12 \cdot 1 \qquad (r = -0 \cdot 18).$$

It confirms that b_0, though negative, is negligible and that variations in per capita income account, at best, for a negligible proportion of the variation in the saving ratio.

Our next step is to add to the test equation (8a) the variable ϱ, i.e., to estimate the parameters of

$$(9) \qquad s = c_0 \left(\frac{100}{Y'} \right) + c_1 + c_2 \varrho,$$

---

[9] The three countries we lose are Ghana, Mauritius, and Sweden. The loss of Sweden is especially regrettable and results from the fact that the available data yield an estimate of gross but not net private saving.

For those countries for which both estimates of personal saving and of corporate saving are available, private saving was defined as the sum of these two flows, while private income was defined as Houthakker's personal income plus corporate saving. For the remaining countries private income was derived from national income by subtracting all personal and corporate income taxes and adding transfers. Private saving was then obtained by subtracting consumption expenditure from private income.

where ϱ is an estimate of the rate of growth of income (expressed as per cent per year). This estimate was computed from the formula

$$\varrho_i = \{[(Y_t)_i/(Y_0)_i]^{1/(n_i-1)} - 1\}\,100,$$

where $(Y_0)_i$ and $(Y_t)_i$ denote, respectively, real private income in the initial and terminal year, and n_i is the number of years available for country i.

According to our model in (9), c_0 should still be zero while rough *a priori* estimates of c_1 and c_2 can again be obtained from formula (6), but using for ϱ the value of 0·047, which is the mean for our sample. This yields for c_2 a value of 1·8 and for c_1 a value of $100 \times (0·085)$ or 8·5. Both values, however, should again be reduced by some 10 to 20 per cent to allow for the fact that saving does not include the addition to the stock of durables.

A least squares estimate of the parameters of (9) yields

$$\text{(9a)} \qquad s = -2 \cdot 6 \frac{100}{Y'} + 5 \cdot 4 + 1 \cdot 42\varrho \qquad (R = 0 \cdot 69;\ S_e = 3 \cdot 53).$$
$$\phantom{\text{(9a)} \qquad s = }\,(1 \cdot 7)\phantom{\frac{100}{Y'}\ } (1 \cdot 4)\ \ (0 \cdot 25)$$

Thus, (i) the coefficient c_0 remains very close to 0 (though it is statistically somewhat more significant than in (8a)), confirming the approximate independence of the saving ratio from per capita income; (ii) the variable ϱ is highly significant; (iii) the point estimate of c_2 and c_1 are quite close to the values suggested by the model. For later reference, dropping the barely significant income variable yields

$$\text{(9b)} \qquad s = 4 \cdot 5 + 1 \cdot 42\varrho \qquad (r = 0 \cdot 67;\ S_e = 3 \cdot 59).$$
$$\phantom{\text{(9b)} \qquad s = }\,(1 \cdot 3)\ \ (0 \cdot 25)$$

4. *The Identification Problem: The Interaction between Saving, Investment, and the Growth Rate*

While the above results seem to provide strong support for the life cycle model it must be acknowledged that they are open to an entirely different interpretation. Specifically, the rate of saving could be determined by some mechanism entirely different from the one we postulate and the strong association between the rate of saving and the rate of growth could result from the dependence of the rate of growth on the rate of investment $i = I/Y$ and the identity of saving and investment. Indeed, assuming a reasonably stable 'capital requirement', C_r (cf. Harrod, 1948, p. 82), ϱ is related to i by the well-known formula

$$\text{(10)} \qquad\qquad \varrho = \frac{i}{C_r}$$

which is commonly stated in the form $\varrho = s/C_r$ by relying on the identity of saving and investment. (A third possible interpretation for the association between s and ϱ provided by the Kaldorian model, according to which growth determines investment which determines saving through the share of profit, will be considered briefly in 6 (iii) below.)

It must be immediately acknowledged that the empirical evidence appears to provide rather good support for hypothesis (10). Estimates of the rate of investment I, which we may identify with domestic capital formation, are available for all 36 countries in our sample and from these we can readily compute the investment ratio i. Correlation of ϱ with i yields the regression equation

$$(10a) \qquad \varrho = 0\text{·}52 + 0\text{·}265i \qquad (r = 0\text{·}73).$$
$$ (0\text{·}72) \quad (0\text{·}042)$$

The implied capital requirement, just below 4, may be somewhat on the high side, but not unrealistically so. But the interpretation of this empirical result is open to the very same question that applies to (9b): it could be the indirect outcome of the relation between s and ϱ hypothesized by the life cycle model.

It is readily apparent that *if s* were the same as *i*, it would be impossible to answer the question: does ϱ cause s or does i cause ϱ, or, quite conceivably, are both mechanisms simultaneously at work? At least from the kind of data under consideration, the parameters of equations (9b) and (10) could not be 'identified'. Fortunately, the rate of domestic capital formation I is not identical with S. It differs by two major components, to wit, the net foreign deficit on current account, or net capital imports, and government surplus on current account, or excess of government capital formation over government borrowing. Denote the difference between I and S by N, and let $n = N/Y$, implying

$$(11) \qquad i = s + n.$$

It will be seen from the Data Appendix that the 'wedge' n between s and i is by no means negligible for our sample; its mean value, 4·5 per cent, is about 40 per cent as large as mean s, and, what is even more important, its variability is considerable, the standard deviation being about 70 per cent as large as that of s. This substantial discrepancy between s and i can be exploited to untangle the causal mechanism underlying the observed association between ϱ on the one hand and s and i on the other.

To this end, let us use (11) to eliminate i from (10) and rewrite that equation in the general form

$$(12) \qquad \varrho = g_1 + g_2(s + n) + v.$$

Taking also into account the relation postulated by the life cycle model

$$(13) \qquad s = c_1 + c_2\varrho + u$$

we have a system of two simultaneous equations in the two endogenous variables s and ϱ and the exogenous variable n.[10] Solving this system for s and ϱ in terms of n yields the 'reduced form' equations[11]

$$(14) \qquad s = \frac{c_1 + c_2 g_1}{\varDelta} + \frac{c_2 g_2}{\varDelta} n + \frac{u + c_2 v}{\varDelta}$$

$$(15) \qquad \varrho = \frac{g_1 + g_2 c_1}{\varDelta} + \frac{g_2}{\varDelta} n + \frac{v + g_2 u}{\varDelta}$$

$$\varDelta = 1 - c_2 g_2.$$

From these reduced forms one can obtain unbiased estimates of the 'structural' coefficients of equations (12) and (13), provided one is willing to assume that the variable n can be regarded as exogenous to the system in the sense of being uncorrelated with the error terms u and v. This is because the coefficients of the system (12), (13) turn out to be just identified, though these equations contain but one exogenous variable, n. Identification is ensured by the fact that n does not appear in (13) and that the coefficients of n and s must be the same in (12). Accordingly, a least squares estimate of (14) and (15) yields four coefficients from which we can estimate uniquely the four structural coefficients g_1, g_2, c_1, c_2.

The coefficients of the reduced forms are

$$s = 9\cdot2 + 0\cdot44n$$

$$\varrho = 3\cdot2 + 0\cdot33n,$$

which imply the following structural estimates of (12) and (13)

$$(13a) \qquad s = 4\cdot9 + 1\cdot35\varrho$$

$$(12a) \qquad \varrho = 1\cdot1 + 0\cdot23i.$$

Comparison with (9b) and (10a) shows that in the present instance the structural estimates do not differ appreciably from those obtained by direct least square. In particular, the estimate of c_2, $1\cdot35$, remains broadly consistent with the *a priori* estimate given in the last section.

It may be argued that because of the conceptual and statistical problems involved in obtaining a meaningful estimate of depreciation (D), equation (10) should be stated in terms of gross capital formation $I_g = I + D$. Under this formulation, i should be replaced everywhere by $i_g = (I + D)/Y = i + d$,

---

[10] We rely here on this system as a device to check for possible gross biases in least square estimates of coefficients such as those of equations (2a) and (9b). This does not mean, however, that we regard the assumption underlying (12) that the (marginal) capital coefficient is a given constant and roughly the same for all countries, as a valid one.

[11] In what follows, it will be taken for granted that $\varDelta$ is positive (which is also supported by the empirical estimates). A negative value of $\varDelta$ would imply that the solution to the system (12) to (13) for given n corresponds to a dynamically unstable equilibrium.

and n by $n_g = n + d$. It is apparent that with this substitution, the equations (12), (13) still form a system whose four parameters are just identified, if n_g is taken as exogenous, and can be estimated from reduced forms obtained by regressing s and ϱ respectively on n_g. The alternative structural estimates obtained in this way are[12]

(13b) $$s = 2{\cdot}5 + 1{\cdot}83\varrho$$

(12b) $$\varrho = 0{\cdot}33 + 0{\cdot}163i_g.$$

These results, on the whole, confirm and support our earlier ones. In particular, the two alternative structural estimates of c_2 (1·35 and 1·83) are seen to bracket narrowly the range of *a priori* estimates.

5. *Refinements of the Basic Hypothesis: Productivity Growth, Population Growth and Age Structure*

In our tests so far we have been focusing on the effects of the overall rate of growth of income, on the presumption that the two sources of income growth, productivity growth and growth in labour force, were likely to have a similar quantitative effect on the saving ratio. This conjecture, however, deserves explicit testing, especially since the mechanism through which the two sources of growth affect saving is really quite different.

A straightforward test consists of breaking up ϱ into its two components, growth in productivity or output per person employed, y, and growth in employment, p, and regressing s on p and y separately. If our conjecture is valid, the partial regression coefficient of the two variables should be roughly equal.

Unfortunately, there are serious difficulties in carrying out the test, since periodic estimates of employment are not available for a substantial proportion of the countries in our sample. The closest alternative might be to approximate p by the growth of population of working age and y by $\varrho - p$. Even this approximation presents problems, as it requires information on the age distribution of population for at least two years reasonably close to the beginning and end of the period covered by the national income estimates. This information could be secured only for 24 of the 36 countries, as shown in the Data Appendix. For these countries, p was measured as the growth of population aged 20 to 65, which we shall label hereafter as 'working age population', and y was computed as $\varrho - p$. The only information that could be secured for the entire sample was an estimate of growth in total population

---

[12] The direct least square estimate of equation (12b) is:
$$\varrho = -1{\cdot}0 + 0{\cdot}210i_g \qquad (r = 0{\cdot}68)$$
$$(1{\cdot}1) \quad (0{\cdot}038)$$

(United Nations *Demographic Yearbook*), denoted by p', and hence of growth in income per capita $y' = \varrho - p'$.

It might appear that p and p' ought to be close to each other and excellent proxies for the growth in the labour force. This would actually be the case if population were in 'balanced growth', by which we mean that the number of persons born in each successive age cohort grows at a constant rate and that age specific mortality is constant; indeed, in this situation p and p' would be identical and could not differ significantly from growth in the labour force, since labour force participation is unlikely to change appreciably in the span of a few years. In fact, this close association between alternative measures of growth cannot be counted upon for our sample in view of the sudden post war spurt in the birth rate in many countries and the simultaneous decline in other countries which were previously growing rapidly. As a matter of fact, for the 24 countries for which we were able to compute both p and p', the correlation between the two measures turns out to be only 0·47. Under these circumstances, the best that can be done is to regress s on y' and p' for the entire sample and check the results by using instead y and p for the subsample of 24 countries for which the information is available—denoted hereafter as 'sample p'.

The results obtained are set forth in Table 2, rows (a) to (e). It is apparent that they fail to provide any support for the hypothesis. Although the effect of per capita income growth on saving is confirmed, there is no evidence that population, whether measured by p or p', plays a similar role; indeed, its coefficient is consistently negative, though hardly significant.

There are, however, ample grounds for holding that this test does not do justice to the model. For, according to the model, the saving ratio does not depend on population growth *per se*, but rather on the relative frequency of active and retired households. The association between s and p was deduced from the fact that, under balanced growth, that relative frequency will be a well-defined function of p. But, as we have seen, for many countries in our sample population growth departed widely from a balanced pattern, and under these conditions p can no longer be supposed a good proxy for the relevant age composition. This point can be clarified with the help of a very simple model (cf. Modigliani and Audo, 1957), which will also prove useful in suggesting an alternative, more relevant test.

Denote by w and r, respectively, the expected number of working and retired years for a person at the beginning of his active span, and let ω denote the ratio r/w. Clearly, ω can be taken as a parameter reflecting prevailing practices affecting the customary working span and mortality experience. Similarly, denote c_w and c_r the planned (and realized) rate of average annual consumption during the working and retirement span, and let $\chi = c_r/c_w$. Finally, let e denote the average rate of earnings from labour during the working span. Since for present purposes, we can abstract from productivity

TABLE 2

Tests of the Effect of Different Sources of Income Growth on the Rate of Saving (s)[a]

		Coefficient of									
Equation Number	Sample	y'	y	p'	p	R/W	M/W	$\frac{100}{Y'}$	Constant Term	$\bar{R}$	S_e
(1)	(2)	(3)	(4)	(5)	(6)	(7)	(8)	(9)	(10)	(11)	(12)
(a)	A	1·34 (0·20)							7·0 (0·8)	0·73	3·31
(b)	A	1·24 (0·25)		−0·67 (0·87)					8·4 (2·0)	0·73	3·32
(c)	p		1·90 (0·26)						4·3 (1·2)	0·83	2·68
(d)	p	1·33 (0·23)		−0·98 (0·85)					8·4 (1·8)	0·83	2·65
(e)	p		1·98 (0·29)		−0·60 (0·81)				4·6 (1·3)	0·82	2·71
(f)	A	1·15 (0·19)				−45 (16)	−12·7 (3·6)		23·1 (4·9)	0·81	2·88
(g)	p	1·03 (0·23)				−78 (30)	−18·9 (5·8)		32·9 (9·0)	0·88	2·24
(h)	p		1·31 (0·28)			−88 (28)	−20·0 (5·4)		33·7 (8·5)	0·89	2·16
(i)	A	1·10 (0·17)				−101 (25)	−15·4 (3·4)	−8·0 (2·8)	35·4 (6·2)	0·84	2·68
(j)	p		1·51 (0·29)			−96 (27)	−16·3 (5·7)	−6·0 (3·9)	32·9 (8·2)	0·90	2·09
(k)	A TLS	(1·06) (0·22)				−102 (25)	−15·7 (3·5)	−8·1 (2·9)	35·9 (6·4)		2·70
(l)	p TLS		1·86 (0·80)			−78 (45)	−11·7 (11·3)	−8·2 (5·8)	26·0 (16·0)		2·22

[a] The dependent variable is s. For sample A, including 36 countries, s has a mean of 11·2 and standard deviation 4·87. For sample p, which includes 24 countries, the mean is 12·0 and the standard deviation 4·69.

growth, we can take c_w, c_r, and e as constant over time. We will also assume a zero rate of return, as this greatly simplifies the exposition while the implications would not be significantly affected if we allowed for a positive rate (as long as it were also constant in time).[13] Then, we is aggregate lifetime earning and, in the absence of bequests, the value of c_w can be inferred from the lifetime budget equation

$$we = wc_w + rc_r = c_w[w + r\chi],$$

which implies

(16) $$c_w = \frac{we}{w + r\chi} = \frac{e}{1 + \omega\chi}.$$

Now, let W and R denote, respectively, the number of persons of working and retired age present in a given year. Then (assuming that income and

[13] See footnote 14, below.

consumption are not significantly correlated linearly with age within the active and the retired span), aggregate consumption and income can be approximated by

$$C = Wc_w + Rc_r = c_w(W + \chi R)$$

$$Y = We.$$

These relations, together with (16) imply

$$\frac{C}{Y} = \frac{c_w}{e}\left(1 + \chi\,\frac{R}{W}\right) = \frac{1 + \chi\,(R/W)}{1 + \omega\chi},$$

or

(17) $$\frac{S}{Y} = 1 - \frac{C}{Y} = \frac{\omega\chi}{1 + \omega\chi} - \frac{\chi}{1 + \omega\chi}\left(\frac{R}{W}\right)$$

i.e., the saving ratio is a *linear* function of the ratio of retired to working age population with parameters depending on tastes (χ) and mortality experience and working span (ω).[14]

If population is in balanced growth, then there will be a one–one relation between R/W and the rate of population growth p, say $R/W = \Omega(p)$. Hence, the saving ratio s is itself a well-defined function of p,

(18) $$s = 100\left[\frac{\chi\omega}{1 + \chi\omega} - \frac{\chi}{1 + \chi\omega}\,\Omega(p)\right] = s(p),$$

with the properties: (i) $s(0) = 0$ (since $\Omega(0)$ is precisely ω, reflecting the fact that, with a stationary population, the ratio R/W is the same as the ratio of retired to active men years for any given age cohort); (ii) $s'(p) > 0$ (since clearly $\Omega'(p) < 0$).[15]

[14] As indicated earlier, a similar conclusion holds if we allow for a non-zero rate of return on assets, as long as this rate, say i, is itself constant in time. The constant term and the coefficient of R/W in (17) will be functions of i in addition to χ, r, and w.

[15] Equation (18) was used to compute the relation between s and p reported in Modigliani (1966, Table 1, column (2)). For that computation, χ was taken as unity and it was assumed that every person had a life span of exactly 50 years, 40 in the labour force and 10 after retirement. To check whether the resulting relation between s and p would be significantly changed by more realistic assumptions about mortality, we computed the value of R/W for different values of p (the annual rate of growth in the number born) by relying on the Italian mortality experience of the early fifties (*Annuario Statistico Italiano*, 1961) with W defined as population aged 20 to 65 and R as population over 65. Substituting these values of R/W in (17) (and still assuming $\chi = 1$) one obtains the values of s reported below. For later references we also show the value of M/W where M is defined as population below age 20.

Rate of growth, p %	R/W %	s %	M/W %
0·0	23·7	0·0	48·0
1·0	17·2	5·7	66·0
2·0	12·2	9·7	89·0
3·0	8·6	12·6	118·0
4·0	6·0	14·7	155·0

[*continued opposite.*

But if, as in the case of our sample, population growth is prevailingly far from balanced, equation (18) or a linear approximation thereof cannot be expected to hold, since when such is the case p need not bear any stable relation to the relevant variable R/W. Equation (17) suggests that under these conditions p should be replaced by R/W and that according to the life cycle model, s should be a decreasing linear function of this variable.

As already noted, explicit estimates of active and retired population are not available for most countries. Accordingly, we shall approximate the variable R with population aged over 65 and W with population aged 20 to 65. Ideally, for each country we would want the mean value of R/W for the years used in computing the other averages. Since information is generally not available on a yearly basis, we have used for the 24 countries in sample p the mean value of R/W in the two years used to compute p. For the remaining countries we have to rely on a single year, choosing the one closest to the middle of the period. Since the age structure can be expected to change but slowly, this approximation should be adequate.

Some rough notion of the order of magnitude of the coefficient of R/W implied by the model can be inferred from (17). For ω a reasonable guess might be between 1/4 and 1/5 (cf. footnote 15 above). The value of χ is much harder to guess, but a casual perusal of survey data would suggest that 0·5 and 1·0 constitute safe outside limits, at least for the United States. Substituting these values in the coefficients of (17) yields an estimate of the slope between 45 and 80, the corresponding values of the constant term being 10 and 20 (in the absence of *productivity* growth).

Before we proceed to an empirical test, we need to pay some attention to the possible role of the third component of the population, namely, the portion which has not yet reached working age (operationally defined as age 20). Since this group, denoted hereafter by M (for minors!), contributes to consumption without contributing to income, one would conjecture that the saving ratio might be negatively associated with the size of M in relation to W. This conjecture can be checked by a straightforward generalization of the approach used in establishing the effect of retired population. That is, denote by m the average number of 'minor' years attached to a household over its life cycle, and let $\mu = m/w$; similarly, let χ_m denote the average yearly rate of consumption expenditure per minor relative to the rate of expenditure per active adult. Then by a repetition of the reasoning leading

The value of ω in (17) was taken as 0·24, which is the value of R/W corresponding to a stationary population.

The relation between s and p exhibited above is again quite close to that obtained neglecting the force of mortality, though it moves closer to that reported in footnote 3, based on equation (5) and the U.S. estimates of σ and δ. One can also readily verify that varying the assumed value of χ within reasonable limits, say between one-half and unity, would still lead to results broadly similar to those reported above and in Table 1 of Modigliani (1966).

up to (17) we arrive at the following generalization of that equation

$$(19) \quad \frac{S}{Y} = \frac{\omega\chi + \mu\chi_m}{1 + \omega\chi + \mu\chi_m} - \frac{\chi_m}{1 + \omega\chi + \mu\chi_m}\frac{M}{W} - \frac{\chi}{1 + \omega\chi + \mu\chi_m}\frac{R}{W}.$$

Under balanced growth M/W will again be uniquely related to p, and therefore s remains a well-defined function of p. Of course, M/W in contrast to R/W should tend to rise with p (as is confirmed by figures reported in footnote 15 above) and this will tend to affect adversely the saving ratio. Still, (19) suggests that, for reasonable guesses about χ_m and χ, s will rise with p and at a decreasing rate.

In the absence of balanced growth (19) suggests that (i) p should be replaced by two measures of age structure, R/W and M/W; (ii) s should be a decreasing function of both variables; (iii) the coefficient of R/W should be somewhat smaller than what was inferred earlier from (17) because of the additional term χ_m in the denominator; and (iv) since χ_m is likely to be less than χ, one might expect the coefficient of M/W to be smaller (in absolute value) than that of R/W.[16]

The empirical results are summarized in rows (f), (g), and (h) of Table 2. It is seen that the variables R/W and M/W contribute substantially to the explanation of s; for the entire sample the correlation rises to 0·81 as compared with a value of 0·67 when using as a single explanatory variable the overall rate of growth, ϱ. Also, the estimated coefficients agree rather well with the implications of the model derived above.[17] Finally comparison of row g and h suggests that the theoretically more relevant measure of income growth, y, performs somewhat better than y' as its coefficient is more in line with *a priori* estimates and the correlation is a little higher, though not significantly. The only mildly surprising results in this battery are those reported in rows (i) and (j), in which we test once more the effect of per capita income. The reliability of this result will be taken up in the next section.

The estimates presented in rows (a) to (j), are based on direct least squares, a procedure that might yield biased estimates in view of the simultaneous presence of a second relation between the growth rate and saving by way of investment, noted in section 4. These estimates were therefore recomputed by an alternative two-stage procedure which takes account of this second relation. These results were found to agree sufficiently closely with those shown in the table, so that they are not worth reporting separately. Just for the sake of

[16] This conclusion is reinforced by the consideration that μ in contrast to ω cannot be taken as a constant but must instead be positively associated with M/W. Under these conditions, the coefficient of M/W obtained by least square will be smaller (and that of R/W larger) than might be inferred from (18) by assigning to μ the mean value for the sample.

[17] Note that the constant term cannot be directly identified with that of (19), since it includes effects of productivity growth assumed absent in deriving that equation.

illustration we exhibit in rows (k) and (l) the alternative estimates obtained for the most inclusive equations, (i) and (j).[18]

6. Some Further Tests

(i) The Role of Differences in Socio-Economic Structure and Possible Biases Resulting Therefrom

In the test described so far, we have used every country for which the required information could be obtained from the above-mentioned sources. While this procedure has the advantage of being objective and maximizing sample size, it has the drawback of lumping together countries differing radically in terms of socio-economic structure and stage of economic development. Now the life cycle model does not purport to represent a universal theory of individual and aggregate saving formation and wealth holding, but is instead basically designed to apply to private capitalistic economies in which at least the bulk of income, consumption, and accumulation transactions occur through markets. Furthermore, even for economies satisfying this requirement, significant differences in economic structure might be associated with differences in such factors as tastes, life cycle profiles of earnings, and family structure, which, in turn, affect the parameters of the long run saving function.

Even at a very superficial level of analysis the countries in our sample can be classified into at least four major groups, namely, (1) Western and/or industrialized (W), (2) Latin American (L), (3) Far Eastern (E) and (4) Colonial African (C). The group to which a given country has been classified is shown by the letter entered in column (3) of the Data Appendix. In the first group we have included the 19 countries of Western culture outside Central and South America, plus Japan and, with some questions, South Africa; this is the largest group numerically and accounts for almost four-fifths of the total weight under the weighting scheme discussed in section 3. The second group consists of ten Central and South American countries and accounts for some 11 per cent of the weight. The third includes China (Taiwan), Korea, and the Philippines, with $7\frac{1}{2}$ per cent of the weight. The remaining two countries, Congo and Rhodesia, with some 3 per cent of the weight, are combined in the last group.

It is apparent from the information summarized in Table 3 that the differences in cultural and socio-economic characteristics are accompanied by

[18] To derive the alternative estimates we started from the two simultaneous relations:
$$s = c_1 + c_2 y + c_3(100/Y') + c_4(R/W) + c_5(M/W) + u$$
$$y = g_1 + g_2(n_g + s) + g_3 p + v$$
in the jointly dependent variables s and y (for sample A, y and p were replaced by y' and p'). Accordingly, the instrumental variables used in the first stage were: R/W, M/W, $100/Y'$, $n_g = i_g - s$, p.

15—I.G.T.

TABLE 3

*Means and Standard Deviations of Selected Variables for
Four Groups of Countries*

Variable	Statistic	W	L	Group E	C	All
Saving Ratio	Mean (%)	12·5	7·1	3·3	13·2	11·2
(s)	std. dev.	4·1	4·3	*	*	4·9
Growth Rate	Mean (%)	5·1	3·2	4·8	2·5	4·7
(ϱ)	std. dev.	2·5	1·1	*	*	2·4
Productivity Growth Rate	Mean (%)	3·8	0·8	1·7	0·1	3·2
(y)	std. dev.	2·7	1·0	*	*	2·7
Population Growth Rate	Mean (%)	1·2	2·4	2·9	2·4	1·5
(p)	std. dev.	0·56	0·55	*	*	0·6
Ratio of Retired to Working	Mean (%)	15·6	6·1	4·7	4·0	13·4
Population	std. dev.	3·3	1·3	*	*	5·2
(R/W)						
Ratio of Minors to Working	Mean (%)	64	116	126	57	75
Population	std. dev.	10·7	7·8	*	*	24·2
(M/W)						
Per Capita Income	Mean (U.S. $)	970	156	108	83	790
(Y)	std. dev.	200	42	*	*	360
Number of Countries		21	10	3	2	36
Relative Weight		78·5	11·4	7·3	2·8	100·0

* Standard deviation was not computed when there were three or less observations.

equally wide differences in the mean values of most of the variables which are called for by our analysis.

These marked differences, together with the fact that, for most variables the within-group dispersion is distinctly smaller than the overall dispersion, imply that our observations tend to fall into more or less tight clusters, a situation which may give rise to spurious correlations and seriously biased parameter estimates. It is conceivable, for instance, that the low rate of saving and per capita income growth prevailing for L and E countries as compared with the W group might be the result of certain cultural and socio-economic characteristics and not be casually related to each other through the mechanisms envisaged by our model. In this case the regression coefficient of equation (a) in Table 2 would be measuring the slope of the line joining the two clusters of points in the (s, y) plane rather than measuring the true effect of income growth on the saving ratio, an effect which might be totally non-existent. Similar doubt must be entertained about the other parameter estimates presented in Table 2.

A simple and yet fairly effective way of testing for the possible effect of this type of spuriousness consists of introducing into the various regression equations we have estimated in the last section dummy variables, taking the value 1 if the country belongs to a given group and 0 otherwise. In view of the fact that the E group contains but three countries and the C group but two, we have felt it advisable to apply this method to the 31-country sub-sample consisting of 21 W countries and 10 L countries. In this case, one needs a single dummy variable, say D, taking the value 0 if the country belongs to the W group and the value 1 if it belongs to the L group. To illustrate the method, suppose we retest equation (a) of Table 2 by fitting

$$s = b_0 + b_1 y + b_2 D.$$

Then the regression coefficient b_1 will provide an estimate of the relation between s and y uncontaminated by possible clusters effect. It measures, in effect, the average relation existing *within* the two clusters, while the dummy variable takes care of any differences between the mean values of s in the two clusters, say $\bar{s}_1 - \bar{s}_2$, which cannot be explained by the within-clusters slope, i.e., by $b_1 (\bar{y}_1 - \bar{y}_2)$.

The salient results of this test are summarized in Table 4. From rows (a) and (b) we can infer that the relation between the rate of saving and the rate of growth is not significantly contaminated by cluster effects. However, a re-estimation of the most inclusive hypothesis represented by equations (i) and (j) of Table 2, produces some rather striking results. Row (c) shows that merely dropping the five countries of the E and C groups results in a coefficient of M/W which is a good deal smaller and hardly significant. When the dummy variable is added in row (d) its coefficient is fairly large and significant, and while the coefficients of y' and R/W are only affected to a minor extent and remain within, or close to, the range of *a priori* estimates, the coefficient of the income variable becomes small and insignificant and that of M/W even has the wrong sign. Furthermore, the effect of income remains rather insignificant, even if we drop the variable M/W (row (e)). These results suggest that the effects of M/W and per capita income are unimportant (or else appreciably different) within each cluster of countries.

In an attempt to shed further light on this result we report in the remaining rows of Table 4 some estimates obtained when the test is repeated separately for each of the two groups of countries. Of particular interest are the results for the 21 W countries where the sample is more sizeable, the data probably more reliable, and the life cycle hypothesis is more clearly relevant.[19] The simple correlation between s and per capita income is substantial but in the

---

[19] For this sample the measure of income growth used is y rather than y'. An estimate of y is directly available for all but three of the 21 W countries. For the three remaining ones y was estimated by interpolation from a regression of y on y' computed for the remaining 18 countries. As a check the tests reported in row (f) to (i) were repeated using y' but in no case were the results appreciably different from those reported.

wrong direction! (row (f)). By contrast, the two principal variables suggested by the life cycle model have coefficients broadly consistent with the model and explain 80 per cent of the variance (cf. row (g)). (The remaining population variable M/W is consistently quite insignificant and with the wrong sign,

TABLE 4

Tests of the Effect of Country Type[a]

Equa-tion Number	Sample	Coefficient of					Con-stant Term	$\bar{R}$	S_e
		y'[b]	R/W	M/W	$100/Y'$	Dummy (D)			
(a)	31 W and L Countries	1·32 (0·18)					7·4 (0·8)	0·79	2·75
(b)	,,	1·25 (0·19)				−1·7 (1·6)	7·8 (0·9)	0·79	2·74
(c)	,,	1·29 (0·24)	−66·7 (31·7)	−5·4 (7·4)	−8·3 (4·2)		23·0 (9·8)	0·82	2·57
(d)	,,	1·11 (0·25)	−52·1 (31·7)	1·0 (8·0)	−3·8 (4·9)	−5·7 (3·3)	16·5 (10·1)	0·84	2·46
(e)	,,	1·10 (0·23)	−55·1 (19·1)		−3·8 (4·8)	−5·5 (2·8)	17·7 (3·6)	0·84	2·43
(f)	21 W Countries[b]				18·3 (4·7)		9·2 (1·1)	0·61	3·24
(g)	,,	1·39 (0·22)	−44·6 (13·9)				13·9 (2·7)	0·88	1·93
(h)	,,	1·44 (0·27)	−49·0 (18·3)		−1·8 (4·8)		14·7 (3·5)	0·88	1·98
(i)	,, TLS	1·78 (0·65)	−50·0 (19·0)		−5·3 (7·6)		13·9 (3·7)		2·12
(j)	10 L Countries				0·37 (0·98)		4·6 (6·8)	0	4·27
(k)	,,	1·45 (0·22)	−329 (98)				26·0 (5·4)	0·71	3·01
(l)	,,	1·29 (1·26)	−354 (104)		−6·2 (7·1)		31·8 (8·7)	0·69	3·07

[a] The dependent variable is s. For the 31 countries' sample its mean is 11·9 and its standard deviation 4·5. For 21 W countries the mean is 12·5 and the standard deviation is 4·1. For the 10 L countries the mean is 7·1 with a standard deviation of 4·3.

[b] For the tests reported in rows (f) to (i) the rate of growth of income was measured by y rather than y'. See footnote 19.

and has therefore been omitted.) Row (h) suggests that, given these variables, the net contribution of per capita income is nil. These inferences are broadly supported if the coefficients are re-estimated by a two stage procedure (row (i)) except for a somewhat higher estimate of the effect of per capita income.[20]

[20] Concern with the possibility that the results for the W countries might be swayed by one extreme observation, that of Japan—which has by far the largest saving ratio (21%) and per capita rate of growth (7·8%), the lowest R/W ratio (0·10) and the second lowest per capita income (after Portugal) led us to repeat the tests of rows (g) and (h) omitting Japan. The results seem to us on the whole to be reassuring, though not unmistakably so,

[*continued opposite.*

Finally, rows (j) to (l) indicate that similar results are obtained also for the sample of 10 L countries, except that the simple correlation between s and per capita income is essentially zero. This supporting evidence, however, is of limited value in view of the small size of the sample and the very limited variation of the key variables (cf. Table 3).

In summary, all the evidence supports both qualitatively and quantitatively the role of the two principal variables suggested by the life cycle model, productivity growth of income, and the age structure of the adult population. Furthermore, these variables appear to account for two-thirds to four-fifths of the inter-country variance in the saving ratio. There remains, instead, considerable doubt about the role of the proportion of 'youngs', suggested by the model, and of per capita income, which cannot be accounted for by the model. There is some prima facie evidence from Table 2 that these variables have some effect on the observed differences in s, but the more probing tests of Table 4 suggest that this effect may be spurious or at any rate considerably over-estimated.

(ii) *Test of Saving Concepts: Private, Personal and Corporate Saving*

In our tests the measure of saving utilized has been private saving—the sum of personal saving (S_p) and corporate saving (S_c). The reasons for focusing on this total have been clearly stated by Harrod (1948, Chapter 2). In short, the life cycle model endeavours to account for aggregate saving by focusing on the forces that lead individual households to accumulate and decumulate wealth over the life cycle. Now '... while the motive for this kind [i.e., corporate and business] saving is different, the result is that individuals ... are provided with additional capital resources which may serve to meet their private needs as already classified. For this reason corporate saving may not be additional to personal saving, but part of it' (Harrod, 1948, p. 47). This implication of the life cycle model is in contrast with a widely held view that personal saving is unrelated to corporate

as is well illustrated by the following replication of the test of row (h)

$$s = 1\cdot07y - 30\,(R/W) - 2\cdot9\,(100/Y') \qquad (\bar{R} = 0\cdot56;\, S_e = 1\cdot93).$$
$$(0\cdot33) \quad (21) \qquad (4\cdot5)$$

The multiple correlation is a good deal lower and so are the t ratios for individual coefficients—but this result was to be expected in view of the appreciable reduction in the variance of both the dependent and the independent variables (*e.g.*, the variance of s is reduced from 16·8 to 5·4). On the other hand the point estimates of the coefficients are not drastically changed, the standard error of the residuals is very nearly the same, and, what is probably most significant, the above equation does help to explain the extremely high saving ratio of Japan. Indeed if we substitute the values of the independent variables for Japan in that equation we obtain a computed value of s of 17, which, though some two standard deviations below the actual value of 21, is still distinctly higher than for any other country in the sample. Furthermore the Life Cycle model may help to provide an explanation for the underestimate, as related to an abnormally depressed wealth-income ratio, as a consequence of the war experience (Cf. [Modigliani, 1961, p. 753]).

retention policies and therefore total private saving is the sum of two largely independent components. It seems, therefore, desirable, before concluding this investigation, to test which of these two rival views seems more nearly consistent with the empirical evidence, thereby also verifying the appropriateness of using the private saving ratio as the dependent variable throughout our analysis.

The most direct way of carrying out such a test is to examine whether, and to what extent, the private saving ratio $s = S_p/Y + S_c/Y$ is affected by variations in the corporate component, $S_c/Y = s_c$. If personal saving is unaffected by corporate retention, total private saving should tend to increase with corporate saving, and roughly by a dollar per dollar on the average. Thus the addition of s_c to the variables we have used so far should contribute significantly to the explanation of s and its regression coefficient should be close to unity.[21] On the other hand, if corporate saving is a close substitute for personal saving as implied by our model, the contribution of s_c should be insignificant and its coefficient should be close to zero.

Unfortunately, the above test cannot be carried out for our entire sample since estimates of corporate saving are available only for a sub-sample of 24 countries, basically Houthakker's original sample. This sub-sample consists of 14 of the 21 W countries (the seven countries lost including Germany and Italy and accounting for some one-fourth of the weight), eight of the ten L countries and the two C countries. In the interest of homogeneity, it seems advisable to discard the two C countries, which leaves a sample of 22 countries.

The results of our tests for this sub-sample are recorded in Table 5. A comparison of rows (a) and (b) shows that when s_c is added to the variables called for by the model, its coefficient is close to zero and totally insignificant. Equivalently the partial regression coefficient of corporate saving, s_c on the personal saving ratio is -0.8, almost three times its standard error of 0.3, and not significantly different from the value of -1 implied by the model. This is a rather striking result considering also that, for most countries, private saving is estimated as the sum of personal and corporate saving and hence errors of measurement in corporate saving will tend to bias the result against our model. However, a comparison of rows (c) and (d) reveals that the addition of per capita income to the list of explanatory variables, though adding little to the explanation, has the effect of increasing a good deal the point estimate of the coefficient of s_c. Accordingly, the test of row (d) turns out to be somewhat of a draw. The contribution of s_c is quite small as implied by the model, and its coefficient is clearly much smaller than implied by the rival hypothesis. At the same time, it is distinctly larger than zero, and

---

[21] Because increased corporate saving will reduce personal income, the level of private saving will be increased not by one but by one minus the marginal propensity to save out of personal income (about 0.1).

in view of some reasonable doubts about the role of per capita income (and M/W) and of the large standard error, no clear-cut conclusion can be reached from our data. However, some further evidence in support of our hypothesis is provided by the last four rows of Table 5, which replicate the test for the more nearly homogeneous, though very thin, sample represented by the 14 W countries. It might be added that this hypothesis also receives some confirmation from other empirical studies. Particularly noteworthy in this connection are the results reported by Denison (1958) working with time series data for the United States, which suggest that total (gross) private saving is 'not affected by changes in the proportion of corporate profits paid out as dividends' (p. 264).

TABLE 5

Tests of Alternative Saving Concepts[a]

| Equation Number | Coefficient of | | | | | | $\bar{R}$ | S_e |
	y	R/W	M/W	$100/Y'$	s_c	Constant Term		
(1)	(2)	(3)	(4)	(5)	(6)	(7)	(8)	(9)
			A—22 Countries					
(a)	1·05	−85	−18·1			34	0·87	2·09
	(0·22)	(33)	(7·5)			(11)		
(b)	1·02	−77	−16·7		0·20	31	0·86	2·13
	(0·23)	(36)	(7·9)		(0·32)	(12)		
(c)	1·17	−88	−14·0	−4·6		32	0·87	2·09
	(0·25)	(34)	(8·5)	(4·5)		(11)		
(d)	1·19	−71	−7·8	−8·0	0·48	24	0·87	2·04
	(0·25)	(35)	(9·5)	(5·1)	(0·35)	(12)		
			B—14 W Countries					
(e)	1·42					7·4	0·90	1·68
	(0·18)					(0·8)		
(f)	1·33				0·23	6·8	0·88	1·80
	(0·23)				(0·34)	(1·2)		
(g)	1·05	−37			0·25	13·5	0·92	1·50
	(0·24)	(18)			(0·30)	(3·4)		
(h)	1·60	−47		−13	0·30	15·0	0·92	1·47
	(0·52)	(19)		(11)	(0·29)	(3·6)		

[a] The dependent variable is s. In part A of the table its mean is 7·8 and the standard deviation is 4·20. In part B the mean is 8·6 and the standard deviation is 3·82.

(iii) Tests of the Effect of the Functional Distribution of Income

We will conclude by reporting briefly on a battery of tests, admittedly rather crude, of one alternative hypothesis which has recently received a good deal of attention, according to which the proportion of income saved is related to, and explained by, the distribution of income as between profits (P) and labour income (L). This model, which provides the foundations for the well-known Kaldorian theory of income distribution (see e.g., Kaldor, 1960 (i), esp. essay 10, and 1960 (ii), esp. essay 13), rests on the proposition that the long-run, average propensity s_P to save out of profits P is substantially higher than the propensity s_L to save out of labour income, L. Thus

$$(20) \qquad S = s_L L + s_P P, \qquad L + P = Y,$$

or, denoting by $\pi = P/Y$ the share of income going to profits,

$$(21) \qquad S/Y = s_L + (s_P - s_L)\pi \qquad (s_P - s_L \gg 0),$$

i.e., the saving ratio is an increasing function of the share of profits.

This hypothesis is not necessarily unreconcilable with the life cycle model, unless it purports to be the sole or major explanation of saving behaviour. It is quite conceivable that, given income growth and age structure, the saving ratio might be somewhat affected by the distribution of income. This might occur in particular because persons engaged in entrepreneurial capacity might tend to have a more delayed pattern of life consumption (implying a life pattern of wealth holding relative to income higher than for other income receivers through all or most of the life cycle) and/or a higher propensity to leave bequests at any given level of income.[22] In other words, inter-country differences in the saving ratio could reflect in part differences in both s_L *and* s_P accounted for by the life cycle hypothesis, and, in part, differences in the distribution of income affecting savings, through differences *between* s_L and s_P.

There are, unfortunately, a number of serious problems in testing (21), among which is the fact that profits plus labour income do not exhaust income, unless profits is understood to embrace all property income, including interest and rents. Even if P be so interpreted, the only approximation to π that we can readily derive from our source of data is the ratio $Y_{nw}/(Y_w + Y_{nw})$ where Y_w denotes compensation of employees and Y_{nw} all other private income. This ratio differs from P/Y in two major respects: (1) Y_w and Y_{nw} are before taxes and transfers, as there is no way of allocating these between the two components; (2) Y_{nw} includes, in addition to all types of property income, the total earnings of the self-employed, a good portion of which cannot be considered as property income in the usual economic sense.

The discrepancy under (1) is hopefully not too serious since $Y_{nw}/(Y_w + Y_{nw})$ is likely to be, on the whole, a reasonably good proxy for the corresponding net of tax ratio. The difference under (2), however, could be a serious shortcoming *if* the hypothesis is interpreted literally to mean that income recipients save a larger fraction of income arising from property

---

[22] Evidence that persons engaged in entrepreneurial activity tend to save more at given levels of income has been reported in many studies, though much of the evidence is open to question since it may simply reflect the greater short run variability of measured income typically associated with entrepreneurship. However, these results have recently received some support from analysis relying on instrumental variable techniques such as Modigliani and Ando (1960).

than of income arising from labour services. For, if the proportion of labour income included in Y_{nw} varies appreciably between countries, then $Y_{nw}/(Y_w + Y_{nw})$ could be a poor proxy for P/Y. One might suppose, however, that differences in the propensity to save would be associated with whether the income recipient was engaged in an entrepreneurial activity (including risk bearing) rather than with whether the income received could be traced to the ownership of property or to the performance of labour services.[23] Under this interpretation the variable $Y_{nw}/(Y_w + Y_{nw})$ might well be a somewhat more relevant measure of the distribution of income than P/Y.

A breakdown of national income (less government income from property and entrepreneurship) between Y_w and Y_{nw} could be estimated for all but two countries of the W group (Portugal and South Africa) and one of the L group (Chile), leaving us with a sizeable sample of 33 countries. The results obtained for this sample are summarized in part A of Table 6. The constant term in column (2) can be interpreted as an estimate of $100s_L$, the propensity to save—expressed as a percentage—out of Y_w, the earnings of employees, while the coefficient of $Y_{nw}/(Y_w + Y_{nw})$, in column (3) is an estimate of $100(s_P - s_L)$, the differential propensity to save out of other income. According to the Kaldorian hypothesis this coefficient should be significantly positive. It is apparent that our data provide absolutely no support for the hypothesis

TABLE 6

Test of the Effect of the Functional Distribution of Income[a]

Equation Number	Constant Term	Coefficient of $\frac{Y_{nw}}{Y_w + Y_{nw}}$	y	ϱ	R/W	M/W	$100/Y'$	$\bar{R}$	S_e
(1)	(2)	(3)	(4)		(5)	(6)	(7)	(8)	(9)
				A—33 Countries					
(a)	12·1	−1·8						0·0	4·70
	(3·3)	(7·8)							
(b)	9·8	−7·0	1·37					0·77	3·00
	(2·1)	(5·0)	(0·20)						
(c)	28·5	−10·7	1·25		−60	−11·7		0·84	2·54
	(5·3)	(7·5)	(0·19)		(17)	(3·4)			
(d)	35·7	1·1	1·06		−101	−16·1	−7·8	0·87	2·35
	(5·8)	(8·5)	(0·23)		(23)	(3·7)	(3·2)		
				B—19 W Countries					
(e)	−0·4	35·2						0·67	3·00
	(3·2)	(8·4)							
(f)	4·2	4·2		1·35				0·88	1·91
	(2·2)	(8·1)		(0·26)					
(g)	14·7	−1·0	1·10		−38			0·91	1·77
	(4·0)	(8·0)	(0·25)		(15)				
(h)	15·0	1·3	1·21		−43		−4·3	0·91	1·76
	(4·1)	(9·3)	(0·32)		(18)		(8·0)		

[a] The dependent variable is s. In Part A, its mean value is 11·1 and the standard deviation 4·72. In Part B, the mean is 12·6, the standard deviation 4·05.

[23] Cf. footnote 22.

of systematic differences between the average propensity to save out of wage income and out of property and self-employment income. The simple correlation between s and our measure of π reported in row (a) is actually negative, though entirely negligible and rows (b) to (d) show that this coefficient remains equally negative and/or insignificant when we take into account the variables called for by our model.

We must, however, again face the possibility that this unfavourable outcome might be the spurious result of clusters, especially since the less developed countries of the L, E, and C groups which, as we know from Table 3, tend to have a lower saving ratio, also tend to have a large share of self-employed—partly reflecting the importance of the agricultural sector. Accordingly, in Part B of Table 6 we report results for the more nearly homogeneous sub-sample of the 19 W countries. It appears from row (e) that for this sub-sample the simple correlation of s with the non-wage share is positive, and in fact quite substantial (though the estimated coefficients do not make much sense!). However, as can be verified from rows (f) and (g), once we take into account the main variables suggested by our model— income growth, or per capita income growth and population age structure— the coefficient of π drops close to zero and becomes totally insignificant. This result holds whether or not we include per capita income, the other main variable suggested by the traditional view (cf. row (h)). There is, in short, no evidence that inter-country differences in the distribution of income between wage and non-wage income contribute to the explanation of differences in the saving ratio or, equivalently, no evidence of systematic differences in the average propensity to save out of these two sources of income.

Summing up, the outcome of this last battery of tests confirms our earlier results, whereas it provides no support for the hypothesis that the saving ratio is controlled or even significantly affected by the functional distribution of income. This negative verdict must, no doubt, be qualified first in recognition of the considerable margin or error to which our data are subject and because the measure of income distribution we have been forced to use may not be the most suitable one.[24]

[24] With all due regard to the above qualifications, the tests presented in Table 6 do serve as useful complements to the other tests reported in this paper because they help to come to grips with an identification problem analogous to that discussed in Section 4. It could be argued in fact that the strong association between the rate of saving and the rate of growth of income revealed by our tests is equally consistent with the Kaldorian model and hence is not an effective way of discriminating between that model and the life cycle model. However, the tests of Table 6 do help to make this discrimination. For the full sample of Part A the Kaldorian model is inconsistent with the simple correlation of row (a). But even in Part B, where the simple correlation is substantial, that model is not consistent with the results of rows (f) to (h). For in the Kaldorian model the rate of growth is supposed to affect the rate of saving *through the link of the profit share*. Thus, while s should be correlated both with π and ϱ, in a multiple regression of s on π and ϱ, as in row (f), the partial regression coefficient of π should be the same as the simple

[continued opposite.

It is conceivable that better data and/or a different measure of income shares would have led to different results. However, the presently available evidence does suggest that such variables are unlikely to supplant or even add significantly to the mechanism suggested by the life cycle model.

REFERENCES

ANDO, A. and MODIGLIANI, F., 'The Life Cycle Hypothesis of Saving: Aggregate Implications and Tests', *American Economic Review*, Vol. 53, May 1963, pp. 55–84, and Vol. 54, Part I, March 1964, pp. 111–13.

DENISON, E. F., 'A Note on Private Saving', *The Review of Economics and Statistics*, Vol. 50, No. 3, August 1958, pp. 261–7.

Flow of Funds/Savings Accounts, 1946–1960, Supplement 5, Board of Governors of the Federal Reserve System (Washington, 1961).

GOLDSMITH, R. W., *A Study of Saving in the United States* (Princeton University Press, Princeton, 1956).

——, *The National Wealth of the United States in the Postwar Period*, National Bureau of Economic Research (Princeton University Press, Princeton, 1962).

HARROD, R. F., *Towards a Dynamic Economics* (London, Macmillan, 1948).

HOUTHAKKER, H. S., 'An International Comparison of Personal Saving', *Bulletin of the International Statistical Institute*, Vol. 38, pp. 56–9.

——, 'On Some Determinants of Saving in Developed and Underdeveloped Countries', in *Problems in Economic Development*, edited by E. A. G. Robinson (London, Macmillan, 1965), Chapter 10, pp. 212–24.

INSTITUTO CENTRALE DI STATISTICA, *Annuario Statistico Italiano*, 1961.

KALDOR, N., *Essays in Value and Distribution* (London, 1960) (i).

——, *Essays on Economic Stability and Growth* (London, 1960) (ii).

MEADE, J. E., 'Life Cycle Saving, Inheritance and Economic Growth', *Review of Economic Studies*, Vol. 33 (1966), pp. 61–78.

MODIGLIANI, F. and ANDO, A., 'Tests of the Life Cycle Hypothesis of Saving', *Bulletin of the Oxford University Institute of Statistics*, Vol. 19, May 1957, pp. 99–124.

——, 'The Permanent Income and the Life Cycle Hypothesis of Saving Behavior: Comparisons and Tests', in *Proceedings of the Conference on Consumption and Saving*, Vol. 2, Philadelphia, 1960.

MODIGLIANI, F. and BRUMBERG, R., 'Utility Analysis and Aggregate Consumption Functions: An Attempt at Integration', unpublished.

MODIGLIANI, F., 'Long Run Implications of Alternative Fiscal Policies and the Burden of the National Debt', *The Economic Journal*, Vol. 71, December 1961, pp. 730–65.

——, 'The Life Cycle Hypothesis of Saving, the Demand for Wealth and the Supply of Capital', *Social Research*, Vol. 33, No. 2, Summer 1966, pp. 160–217.

TOBIN, J., 'Life Cycle Saving and Balanced Growth', in *Ten Economic Essays in the Tradition of Irving Fisher* (Wiley, New York, 1967), Chapter 9.

United Nations Department of Economic and Social Affairs, Statistical Office, *United Nations' Yearbook of National Accounts Statistics*, United Nations, New York.

——, *United Nations' Demographic Yearbook*, United Nations, New York.

regression coefficient of row (e), while the partial regression coefficient of ϱ should vanish. The result found in row (f) is just about the reverse. (This test could break down if ϱ and π were colinear, which however is not the case for our sample, as indicated by the result of row (f).) The tests of rows (g) and (h) are even more telling in this respect, for here ϱ is replaced by per capita growth and population structure, variables whose effect on s, as far as we can see, cannot be accounted for by the Kaldorian model.

15

A DIDACTICAL NOTE ON THE TWO-GAP THEORY

J. TINBERGEN

1. IN development planning as well as in development theory the so-called *two-gap theory* has quickly won popularity. Its main contents are that we can distinguish between (i) a savings gap, equal to $I - S$, where I are investments and S are national savings, and (ii) a trade gap, equal to $M - E$, where M are imports and E exports (in the broadest sense, including services as well as goods); that an equation can be formulated for each of the four variables I, S, M, and E and that these equations do not necessarily imply that the two gaps are equal, as they must be '*ex post*'. One of the two gaps (*ex ante*, at least) may therefore surpass the other or, in other words, 'be *dominant*'. The theory then suggests that a possible dominance is indicative of where to put the main emphasis in policy recommendations. Finally, this mental product of planning estimates has been transferred to development theory (by which I mean the explanation of past development) and it has been suggested that there are a few different *phases of development*, during which first the savings gap and afterwards the trade gap is dominant.[1]

2. Some of the simplest equations assumed for the 'explanation' and hence *ex ante* estimation of the four variables mentioned are:

$$(2.1) \qquad I_t = \varkappa(Y_{t+1} - Y_t)$$

$$(2.2) \qquad S_t = \sigma(Y_t - Y_0) + S_0$$

$$(2.3) \qquad M_t = \mu_1 Y_t + \mu_2 I_t$$

$$(2.4) \qquad E_t = E_0(1 + \varepsilon)^t.$$

These express that:

(1) investments depend on the planned rate of increase in national income, $Y_{t+1} - Y_t$, with as co-factor the capital–output ratio $\varkappa$;

(2) savings depend on national income, through a marginal savings rate σ;

---

[1] McKinnon, 1964.

(3) imports depend on national income and investments, with import ratios μ_1 and μ_2, respectively;

(4) exports show an autonomous rate of growth ε, which may depend on the development of incomes in developed countries.

Clearly these equations need not be compatible with the identity

$$(2.5) \qquad\qquad I_t - S_t = M_t - E_t$$

which follows from the definition of national income:

$$(2.6) \qquad\qquad Y_t = C_t + S_t = C_t + I_t + E_t - M_t.$$

They may be compatible if at least one of the variables or coefficients are assumed to be dependent on the others; for instance, Y_{t+1}. In the planning process we do consider Y_{t+1} as given beforehand, and the coefficients as given, too, however. This implies that at least one of the equations (2.1) through (2.4) and possibly more are not correct or, rather, not complete. From them one or more '*adjustment variables*' must have been left out, that is, variables which adjust the equations (2.1) through (2.4) to equation (2.5). Several authors dealing with the two-gap theory mention examples of such adjusting variables or adjustors. Thus, Chenery and McEwan (1966) and Tims (1965), in models for Pakistan, introduce additional import substitution as an adjustor; Mosak (1967), mentions the price level, taxes supposed to influence savings in particular, the productivity of capital (the inverse of $\varkappa$), trade restrictions or export stimulation and monetary policies (possibly the discount rate) as examples, and Vanek (1967), adds control of non-essential imports as a possible adjustor.

3. The way the two-gap theory is presented is apt to create *misunderstandings* which it is the intention of this note to specify and to eliminate with the aid of a somewhat more precise terminology and some additional concepts to be used. It should not be forgotten that *ex post*, that is, *in reality, there is only one gap*, which is simultaneously the savings gap, the trade gap, and the foreign inflow of capital F. It follows that in reality no gap is actually dominant; they are equal. In reality we cannot therefore have a succession of phases in which first the savings gap and then the trade gap is dominant.

Before making suggestions for the improvement of our terminology it may be useful to remind the reader of the *origins* of the two-gap approach. There are two which differ in presentation rather than in essence.

One may be called the *estimation* origin, characteristic for econometric model building. Using this method we cannot avoid limiting ourselves to the inclusion, in equations such as (2.1) through (2.4), of the most important and the measurable variables which influence the variable 'to be explained' and placed at the left-hand side of our equations (2.1) through (2.4). Adjustors may have been omitted because they were not important in the past or because we have no figures for them. This again stresses the incompleteness of our equations; in precise econometric notation an error term u might have been added to represent the omitted terms. But this error term need not necessarily behave as a random variable.

Another way of characterizing the origin of the two-gap theory is to think of *linear programming* models as its basis. In a linear programming model we have restrictions which under some conditions are active and under other circumstances are inactive. In this latter situation we introduce 'slack variables' and these are another way of completing the relationship considered.

4. Thus the *incompleteness* of some relations is the crucial feature of the system of equations used, with (2.1) through (2.4) as an example. As a consequence these equations do not yield the actual values to be taken *ex post* by the variables at the left-hand side, but only provisional estimates. Such *ex-ante* variables are in fact *imaginary* only, comparable to expectations or intended values, and should be recognizable immediately by a special notation, for instance by adding a prime, or by writing them in another script: fat, or gothic, etc. Let us take the prime simply and hence distinguish between I'_t and I_t, S'_t and S_t, etc.

Next, as much as possible, we should *specify the omitted terms*. In the simplest form of linear equations such terms will consist of two factors: the adjusting variable (or adjustor) and a coefficient indicating the intensity of its influence on the variable to be explained. Suppose we follow Chenery and McEwan and Tims in their Pakistani models and consider additional import replacement R as the adjustor, then we have, instead of (2.3):

$$(2.3')\qquad M_t = M'_t - R_t = \mu_1 Y_t + \mu_2 I_t - R_t.$$

By chance the coefficient is 1 here.

If, as another example, we add a term to equation (2.2) representing the influence on savings of a change in some tax rate T we may obtain:

$$(2.2')\qquad S_t = S'_t + \sigma_1 T_t = \sigma(Y_t - Y_0) + S_0 + \sigma_1 T_t.$$

Here an as yet unknown coefficient σ_1 must be introduced, representing the influence exerted by a unit change in the tax rate T_t on savings S_t.

A third contribution to the clarification of the two-gap theory consists of *categorizing the adjusting variables*. This can best be done by simultaneously *categorizing* the types of adjustment *processes* or *problems* we want to distinguish. In this field some useful contributions have already been made by Vanek (1967), who makes a distinction between an *autonomous* and a *policy-induced* adjustment process. An autonomous adjustment works through, let us say, market forces, whereas a policy-induced one works through the deliberate change in one or more instruments of policy. Accordingly the adjusting variables may be (as in the latter case) policy instruments or (as in the former case) other variables. If we want to use the categorization of variables used in the theory of economic policy,[2] the other variables will not as a rule be data (or exogenous variables) or target variables, but mostly what I called 'irrelevant' variables.

Moreover, we may want to subdivide the problems into problems without or with degrees of freedom. No degrees of freedom will exist if we introduce only one additional term to one of the equations, since we have to satisfy only one additional equation, namely (2.5). This is no longer true, however, if some restriction exists on the value which the adjustor can assume. Thus, there may be a limit to import substitution. We may then have to introduce one more adjustor, whether a policy instrument or not.

A practical difficulty of adding the omitted terms to our equation system is, of course, that we do not know the values of the coefficients, such as σ_1 in our example (2.2'). Supplementary research may be needed in order to estimate such coefficients. Similarly we may not know in advance any restrictions applying to an adjusting variable such as import substitution.

5. If in reality there cannot be a dominant gap, the *phase theory* of development, for instance as presented by McKinnon (1964), must be *reformulated* in another terminology. The actual savings gap cannot be dominant. The phases must be characterized by different values of some coefficients, representing differences in sensitivity to some adjustors, whether instruments of policy or not. Such a reformulation has the additional advantage that it suggests a less sudden transition from one phase to the next. The essence of the change from what is loosely called a dominant savings gap to a dominant trade gap is that at a very low level of income very little can be saved and even the marginal savings rate is low. The pressure of any adjustment (whether autonomous or consciously political) will then be felt in the realm of savings: considerable tax rates will be needed. With increasing income the level and the slope of the savings function $S_t(Y_t)$ will become higher and less pressure will be needed in that field. But exports of traditional products may reach a saturation point whereas the demand for imports rises increasingly with income. Now measures to further exports, maybe nontraditional ones, or to restrict non-essential imports will become more pressing, that is, require bigger policy changes.

6. An eminently practical question of development planning for the coming decade will be *what will happen to the* (savings and trade) *gap if we push up the rate of development* we aim at for the developing countries. We will illustrate the problem with the aid of two very simple numerical examples, using as the adjustor, first, only import replacement and, next, also tax measures to raise savings (problems A and B, respectively).

[2] Tinbergen, 1956.

Problem A: Import Replacement R being the Adjustor

In each problem we compare two rates of growth of national income, $\omega_I = 4$ per cent p.a. and $\omega_{II} = 6$ per cent p.a. We start from an income $Y_1 = 100$, savings *ex-ante* S' of 10 per cent, exports $E_1 = 10$ rising to $E_{10} = 13$ and a capital–output ratio $\varkappa$ of 3. We assume imports *ex-ante* M'_t to be composed of 9 per cent of Y_t plus 50 per cent of I_t. This gives rise to the figures in Table 1.

TABLE 1

Key figures for Development over 10 years

Case I: $\omega_I = 4$ per cent p.a.; Case II: $\omega_{II} = 6$ per cent p.a.

I		II	
$Y_1 = 100$	$Y_{10} = 142 \cdot 4$	$Y_1 = 100$	$Y_{10} = 169$
$S'_1 = 10$	$S'_{10} = 14 \cdot 2$	$S'_1 = 10$	$S'_{10} = 16 \cdot 9$
$I_1 = 12$	$I_{10} = 16 \cdot 8$	$I_1 = 18$	$I_{10} = 30 \cdot 6$
$M'_1 = 9 + 6 = 15$	$M'_{10} = 12 \cdot 8 + 8 \cdot 4 = 21 \cdot 2$	$M'_1 = 9 + 9 = 18$	$M'_{10} = 15 \cdot 2 + 15 \cdot 3 = 30 \cdot 5$
$E_1 = 10$	$E_{10} = 13$	$E_1 = 10$	$E_{10} = 13$
$I_1 - S'_1 = 2$	$I_{10} - S'_{10} = 2 \cdot 6$	$I_1 - S'_1 = 8$	$I_{10} - S'_{10} = 13 \cdot 7$
$M'_1 - E_1 = 5$	$M'_{10} - E_{10} = 8 \cdot 2$	$M'_1 - E_1 = 8$	$M'_{10} - E_{10} = 17 \cdot 5$

From the table we see that the *ex-ante* trade gap is dominant during all 10 years of case I, but no longer in year 1 for case II, where the *ex-ante* savings gap is equal to the *ex-ante* trade gap. In year 10, however, the *ex-ante* trade gap is dominant again.

If the adjustor is import replacement R, the values for it and for the *ex post* gap G are as in Table 2.

TABLE 2

Values of Import Replacement R and the Ex-post Gap G in Cases I and II for years 1 and 10

	Case I		Case II	
Year	1	10	1	10
R	3	5·6	0	3·9
G	2	2·6	8	13·7

Problem B. Import Replacement R used to the same Extent in Case I and Case II: Additional Adjustor: More Savings

Since it may seem somewhat unsatisfactory that the developing country considered makes a smaller contribution in import replacement in Case II than in Case I, we may assume that what is possible in this respect in Case I is also possible in Case II; so we get the picture shown in Table 3.

For evident reasons both *ex-ante* gaps are now equal in Case I, whereas in Case II the *ex-ante* savings gap now becomes dominant in both years. If

TABLE 3
Values of Ex-ante Gaps assuming the Same Values of
Import Replacement R in Case I and Case II

	Case I		Case II	
Year	1	10	1	10
$I - S'$	2	2·6	8	13·7
$M' - E$	2	2·6	$8 - 3 = 5$	$17·5 - 5·6 = 11·9$

now we want to introduce additional savings in order to adjust the gaps we are faced with a complication. A change in savings affects consumption and it is natural to assume that this affects imports and hence the *ex-ante* trade gap. For year 1 we get the following computation:

Let the additional savings be s_1 and let the component of imports represented by the first member in (2.3) be proportional to consumption. With the numerical coefficient 0.09 we chose for μ_1 this means that it actually stands for $0·1(Y_t - S_t)$ and that an increase in savings by s_t will cause a decrease in imports by $0·1s_t$. This yields, for year 1, a formula for M'_t running:

$$(6.1) \qquad M'_t = 0·09\,Y_t - 0·1s_t + 0·5I_t.$$

Taking into account R also we will have

$$(6.2) \qquad M_t = 0·09\,Y_t - 0·1s_t + 0·5I_t - R_t.$$

With its help we get

$$M_1 = 9 - 0·1s_1 + 9 - 3 = 15 - 0·1s_1.$$

Equality of the trade gap and the savings gap then requires

$$(6.3) \qquad 15 - 0·1s_1 - 10 = 8 - s_1 \quad \text{or} \quad s_1 = 3·3.$$

This leads to a gap

$$(6.4) \qquad G_1 = 4·7.$$

For year 10 we have:

$$(6.5) \qquad M_{10} = 30·5 - 0·1s_{10} - R_{10} = 24·9 - 0·1s_{10}$$

$$(6.6) \qquad 11·9 - 0·1s_{10} = 13·7 - s_{10}$$

or

$$(6.7) \qquad s_{10} = 2·0 \quad \text{and} \quad G_{10} = 11·7.$$

This means that the additional savings effort needed in case II diminishes from 3·3 to 1·6 between year 1 and year 10.

7. Of course we have given an example only. This can show no more than that a higher rate of growth aimed at may imply that in the beginning the

dominance of the *ex-ante* trade gap disappears and that later on it reappears. We leave it to the reader to generalize the set-up, to discuss under what conditions these phenomena appear and what other situations are possible.

For international development planning purposes another important question comes up. We may say that our example illustrates the well-known necessity that both developing and developed countries make a contribution if a quicker development of the former is desired. These contributions consist of, in our example:

(i) import replacement and additional savings by the developing countries and

(ii) a higher capital inflow from developed into developing countries.

Quantitatively these are, for year 1: an effort $R_1 = 3$, $s_1 = 3\cdot3$, and an increase in gap of $2\cdot7$; for year 10: $R_{10} = 5\cdot6$; $s_{10} = 2\cdot0$, and an increase in gap of $9\cdot1$ (between Case II and Case I). The question which arises is whether these contributions to quicker development, being an interest of the world as a whole, are equitably distributed among the developing and the developed countries. An objective measure of the sacrifices made on both sides has not yet been developed. An answer to the question requires the solution of two problems at least. One is, to bring import replacement efforts and savings efforts on a common denominator. Since import replacement requires an effort of macro-economically speaking, the same nations as increased savings, the common denominator can be found by asking these nations—that is, their rulers—what relative value they attach to a unit of effort in each. In the special case chosen here, where the efforts required from the developed countries are supposed to take the form of additional savings, it seems natural also to express the effort of the developing countries in terms of savings.

The other problem to be solved is to compare a unit effort in savings by the developing countries with a unit effort in savings by the developed countries. Although many economists maintain that such a comparison cannot be made, any political decision implies one. The simplest, though debatable, answer an economist can suggest is that the comparison should be based on the marginal utilities at different levels of income, taking it for granted that all peoples 'are equal'. If we can establish a ratio of marginal utilities at the average income level of, say $1000 per annum (representing the developed countries) and of, say, $100 per annum, we may use that same ratio as a means to compare the significance of a unit savings effort by these two groups of countries. Suppose the marginal utilities at these two levels show a ratio of 1 to 10 (implying an elasticity of one for marginal utility as a function of income), then an effort of 10 units per person by the developed countries would be equivalent to an effort of 1 unit per person by the developing countries. If the elasticity were found to be higher, the ratio of equal efforts of rich and poor countries would also be higher. What little evidence we have is due to Frisch (1959), and to those who applied similar methods.[3] The elasticity they find, under the assumption of 'almost additive utility' is 2 rather than 1, meaning that the marginal utilities corresponding to incomes of \$1000 and \$100 respectively show a ratio of 1 to 100. The implication is that an equitable distribution of efforts requires an effort per head 100 times as large in the developed than in the developing countries. Such a figure may at least be used as a start of a political discussion in order to arrive at a choice.

REFERENCES

BARTEN, A. P., 'Consumer Demand Functions under Conditions of Almost Additive Preferences', *Econometrica* 32 (1964), p. 1.

CHENERY, H. B. and McEWAN, A., 'Optimal Patterns of Growth and Aid: The Case of Pakistan', in I. Adelman and E. Thorbecke, eds., *The Theory and Design of Economic Development* (Baltimore, 1966).

FRISCH, R., 'A Complete Scheme for Computing All Direct and Cross Demand Elasticities in a Model with Many Sectors', *Econometrica* 27 (1959), p. 177.

JOHANSEN, L., *A Multi-Sector Study of Economic Growth* (Amsterdam, 1960).

McKINNON, R. I., 'Foreign Exchange Constraints in Economic Development and Efficient Aid Allocation', *The Economic Journal*, LXXIV (1964), p. 388.

MOSAK, J. L., 'A Methodological Note on Some Gap Projections for Developing Countries', Doc E/AC 54/L 21, Econ. and Social Council, United Nations, 1967.

TIMS, W., *Growth Model for the Pakistan Economy*: *Macro-economic Projections for Pakistan's Third Plan* (Karachi, 1965).

TINBERGEN, J., *Economic Policy: Principles and Design* (Amsterdam, 1956).

VANEK, J., *Estimating Foreign Resource Needs for Economic Development* (New York, 1967).

[3] Barten, 1964; Johansen, 1960.

16

EXPORT-LED GROWTH:
THE POST-WAR INDUSTRIAL SETTING*

RICHARD E. CAVES

THE comparative rates of growth achieved by the industrial countries since World War II have provided a rich supply of surprises and paradoxes, and a corresponding stimulus to research. Hypotheses have been advanced to explain differing growth rates of productivity or total output, stressing such strategic factors as the level or stability of aggregate demand, international price competitiveness, the rate of capital formation, elasticity of the labour supply, and degree of competition in national product markets. Quantitative research has tested the explanatory power of some of these hypotheses with varying thoroughness. Schools of thought can be detected emphasizing 'demand' and 'supply' factors respectively as the principal governors of growth performance; as Cornwall (1968) recently noted, the impeccably Marshallian conclusion seems to be emerging that both demand and supply factors are important.

Several students of recent growth experience, notably Beckerman (1962, 1966, 1965) and Lamfalussy (1963; December, 1963) have picked the rapid growth of exports as a necessary and perhaps sufficient condition for bringing about rapid growth of income, or at least a necessary factor for facilitating it. The obvious tendency for fast growing industrial countries to enjoy favourable balances of payments during the period from the early 1950's to the mid-1960's, although Keynesian income theory predicts the contrary, has offered the challenge of explaining why a favourable balance of payments should encourage sustained rapid growth, or at least how it could co-exist with rapid growth. Keynesian theory of course explains how rising exports can increase employment without inducing an equally large increase in imports, but it offers little enlightenment as to why export growth, the growth of full-employment output or productivity, and favourable payments positions, should all tend to coincide.

This paper does not attempt any full-blown test of the family of hypotheses associating the rapid growth of exports and real income. I seek only to comment on some theoretical properties of export-led growth models and on

* Research underlying an earlier version of this paper was supported by a Social Science Research Council Faculty Research Fellowship.

the empirical evidence available (or needed) for assessing the plausibility of their principal functional relationships.

1. *General Structure of the Models*

It is convenient first to sketch the model of export-led growth in 'literary' form, in order to display the alternative strategies for assembling it, without worrying immediately about all the details involved in specifying its individual functions. In order to keep 'supply' influences on growth in the background, however, I shall suppose that the goal is to explain differing margins by which national growth rates exceed what could be attributed to common rates of population growth and the growth of disembodied technical knowledge that is freely mobile across national boundaries. We noted above that a distinction might be drawn between export-led and export-assisted growth; as will become clear, the two possibilities need not be considered as separate and parallel, for the latter drops out as a subset of the functional relations needed to describe the former. I shall refer to them collectively as 'the export-led growth model'.

The disturbing force that initiates rapid growth is some competitive advantage in international trade that causes the nation's share of world exports to rise (and possibly also the share of imports in domestic consumption and investment to fall). Without excluding other possibilities, this advantage might be due to a rate of new product development exceeding that in other countries, or to an initial level of money costs which, at the existing (fixed) exchange rate, renders profitable the expansion of a significant number of lines of exportable or import-competing production. In either case, the consequence is to present the nation's entrepreneurs with opportunities for the profitable expansion of the production of tradable goods at rates not constrained by the average growth rate of either the domestic or the foreign market. Note that a disequilibrium situation is implied at the start, with the rate of growth of exports (or improvement in the trade balance) not continuously subject to conditions of long-run equilibrium in individual product markets.

This opportunity for the profitable expansion of traded-goods production next affects the rate of capital formation, the productivity of new investment (measured by the marginal capital–output ratio), or both. Either way, a higher growth rate of real income and labour productivity results. Finally, this higher real growth rate is supposed either to affect the trade balance favourably, or to entail an unfavourable effect so small that on balance no need arises to restrict domestic demand to protect the balance of payments. The higher growth rate is thus alleged to be self-sustaining to a degree, and able to persist so long as the conditions favourable to export growth are sustained. This last requirement brings into parallel the propositions that fast growth may be led by exports and that fast growth will be facilitated by the current-account flows. To tell a plausible story of either type requires some explanation of why fast growth (from whatever source) will not bring about its own downfall through a deterioration of the balance of payments, forcing the adoption of policies to restrain the rate of capital formation or the growth of aggregate demand.

Let us consider these connections running through the domestic economy in somewhat more detail, since they can be and have been formulated in rather different ways by Beckerman and Lamfalussy. First, in order to relate export growth to the growth of real income, one requires some causal linkage between export growth and either the rate of capital formation or the rate of productivity growth. Beckerman (1965, Chapter 2) emphasizes the dependence of a high rate of capital formation on entrepreneurs' expectations that a rapid and steady growth of aggregate demand will continue over some unspecified future period. These animal spirits require not only the current and recent experience of unencumbered fast growth but also a rising trend in exports to provide assurance that this market growth will not be stunted by demand–management policies seeking to protect the nation's balance-of-payments position. It is not clear to what extent this argument makes a virtue of open inflation. On the one hand, the model seems to demand not so much a very high growth rate for aggregate demand as reasonably fast growth coupled with guaranteed freedom from restrictive policies which would impose a short-term bite on profit margins. On the other hand, Beckerman suggests that a high rate of capital formation may also result when businessmen believe that the authorities are unable to restrain aggregate demand.

Beckerman next links the high rate of capital formation to a continued favourable state of the balance of payments through the alleged favourable effects of high capital formation and fast growth of output on the rate of productivity growth. Productivity gains stem from high rates of capital formation because much technological change must be embodied in new plant and equipment. They flow from the fast growth of output because of the ubiquitous availability of scale economies. Thus, either the widening or the deepening of the capital stock furthers the growth of productivity, and no great need arises to differentiate between their effects. Rapid productivity growth in turn deters the upward movement of the price level, on the presumption that while money wages respond positively to the rate of productivity growth, the net relation between the growth rates of productivity and unit labour costs remains negative. In turn this assures a negative relation between productivity growth and the increase of the general price level. Finally, because a lower rate of price inflation will have favourable effects on the trade balance, given the rate of real income growth, the chances are improved that faster growth will not have to be choked off to protect the balance of payments.

Lamfalussy's account of the network of relations between growing exports and the domestic growth rate contains some different elements. The effect of export growth on the desired rate of capital formation is described in roughly the same fashion as by Beckerman, with the addition of the concept of defensive investment as an explanation of how a higher rate of capital formation may encourage a higher rate of growth or productivity. The concept turns on the dependence of the net productivity of any particular piece of capital equipment on the bundle of capital goods with which it collaborates in the plant; 'modern' machinery incorporated in an old plant layout, as is likely when the rate of capital formation is low, raises total output less than when the same machine is added to a newer plant layout in the context of a high rate of capital formation. Lamfalussy also stresses the response of saving to a sudden quickening of the rate of growth of income, especially in the corporate sector through the retention of a large share of the short-run increase in profits and in the government sector with a rise in tax revenues not immediately matched by increased expenditures or offset by reduced tax rates.

Lamfalussy uses this non-linear relation of both saving and investment to the level of income, occasioned by export-led growth, to explain why induced increases in imports fail to spoil the game. In the absence of international capital movements, the excess of exports over imports must be equal (*ex post*) to the excess of domestic saving over investment. Export growth is asserted to raise both saving and investment. If the growth of saving matches that of investment, then the initial trade balance is preserved.

These models proposed by Lamfalussy and Beckerman are aptly identified as describing a 'virtuous circle' of growth. Growth engendered by export expansion will preserve the initially favourable trade balance position. An even stronger proposition of virtue holds that fast growth generated by domestic forces or policy measures will improve the trade balance, or leave it no worse off than otherwise.[1] In Professor Kindleberger's phrase, 'nothing exceeds like excess'.

2. *Theoretical Properties*

The models that have been briefly sketched here raise a number of theoretical issues. Do their functional relations add up to equilibrium growth paths? Do these paths necessarily yield positive rates of income change, and are they stable? Do they support the 'virtuous circle' in either its strong or its weak form? These issues can be treated usefully in the framework of short-term income growth models of Keynesian origin, developed by Harrod

---

[1] The formal difference between these weak and strong propositions of virtue lies in whether or not one assumes an exogenous component of growth in export demand at least equal to the initial growth rate of domestic real income.

(1948) and others. Indeed, they refer precisely to the properties of the warranted rate of growth and its relation to the natural rate.

It is useful to consider two simple models of this type. The first, a simplification of one proposed by Lamfalussy,[2] seems to capture the main features of 'export-assisted' growth. It can be altered into one containing an exogenous growth rate for exports. The essential equations are four: one relating investment to income (or vice versa); one relating saving to income; one relating income to the balance of trade; and one imposing an equilibrium constraint on the system.

The investment–income relation can be treated in several ways. Following Domar, the increment of output can simply be equated to the level of investment multiplied by the marginal output–capital ratio. Alternatively, following Harrod (1948), the level of investment can be considered to be what business will desire to sustain the increment of demand occurring at a given time. (The difference between these definitions, if any, lies in the stress placed on capacity utilization.) A useful general form for the relation of investment (I) to income (Y) is equation (1),

(1) $$I = a\,\Delta Y + \alpha Y,$$

which includes both a marginal capital–output relation and a term allowing for investment induced by the attained level of income (for example, replacement). If $\alpha = 0$, we have the Harrod–Domar relation. If equation (1) is divided through by Y, we have Lamfalussy's relation that declares I/Y to have a stable element, and a variable element that is sensitive to the rate of growth of demand (at least when the growth stems from exports).

The saving function can be written in identical form, to comprehend the conventional Keynesian relation of saving to income as well as the possibility that export-based growth of demand may bestir an increase in the proportion of income saved.

(2) $$S = b\,\Delta Y + \beta Y$$

The balance of trade can be related both to the level of income and separately to the level of investment, in order to capture the effect of the level of investment on the rate of growth of productivity, and that in turn on the trade balance. In equation (3), one would expect that $\pi > 0$ and $\mu > 0$.

(3) $$X - M = \pi I - \mu Y,$$

Lamfalussy employs essentially the same relation, but divided through by Y, so that μ stands alone to indicate the favourable influence of productivity growth (not embodied through capital formation)

---

[2] See Lamfalussy, December 1963. A convenient summary is provided by Stern, 1967, pp. 56–62.

or exogenous growth in external demand on the nation's exports.[3] This reinterpretation, like similar operations on equations (1) and (2), has no effect on the system's equilibrium growth rate, but does change the sign of μ.

The system is closed by the conventional requirement that the sum of injections into the income stream equal the sum of the leakages.

(4) $$S = I + (X - M).$$

Solving it by substituting (1), (2), and (3) into (4) gives

(5) $$g_1 \equiv \frac{\Delta Y}{Y} = \frac{\alpha(1 + \pi) - \mu - \beta}{b - a(1 + \pi)}.$$

For a closed economy (so that $\pi = \mu = 0$), with $\alpha = b = 0$, this reduces to β/a, equivalent to Harrod's s/C_r or Domar's $\alpha\sigma$. Despite its apparent familiarity, the expression for g_1 possesses some rather odd properties. If nothing is specified about the values of the parameters except their positive signs, the sign of neither numerator nor denominator can be predicted *a priori*; hence there is no assurance that a growth rate which satisfies these conditions will be positive. In general a positive denominator is necessary for the existence of a warranted growth path, but the significance of a negative numerator is not so clear. Nor does it help much to place further restrictions upon the signs of the coefficients. The assertion that the desired level of investment and supply of saving both respond positively to an increase in the growth rate of income implies that $a > \alpha$ and $b > \beta$, but this restriction still leaves the signs of both numerator and denominator indeterminate. Nor does anything clear up if we add the reasonable restriction that the propensity to invest in relation to the initial level of income is less than the propensity to save: $\alpha < \beta$. Finally, even if values of the coefficients are assumed that give rise to a positive growth rate g_1, no assurance can be drawn about another question central to the export-led models: whether or not the balance of payments on current account will remain favourable in the face of higher income growth. If the ratio of the trade balance to income is related to the determinants of the income growth rate, using equations (4) and (5), its sign is not predictable and depends sensitively (as one would expect) on the value of μ.

This version of the export-led model allots to trade expansion the passive role of favourable response to productivity growth, in order to render the deterioration of the trade balance in response to income growth less than

---

[3] Actually, equation (3) condenses two relations presented by Lamfalussy, one relating the trade balance to the growth rate of output per man, the other relating output per man to the share of income invested. Nothing is lost in the condensation because the relation determining the growth of output per man does not interact with those determining the growth of aggregate output, and so its role is only to determine (implicitly) the rate of growth of employment.

inevitable. It thus depicts what I have called export-assisted growth. A similar model will serve to describe export-led growth. A rate of export expansion exceeding those of other components of national expenditure is asserted to raise the desired rate of investment, the productivity of investment, or both. Its influence on the rate of investment might take the form of (1a), linking the growth of investment and exports through the proportions they claim of national expenditure.

(1a) $$I/Y = vX/Y + \alpha.$$

Multiplying (1a) through by Y, it is clear that the only essential change from equation (1) is the substitution of X for ΔY. Unless the system of relations is expanded, the substitution of (1a) requires some change in equation (3) to avoid overdetermination. The simplest tactic is to set $\pi = 0$, but we shall seize the opportunity to add a marginal effect of growth on the import share, like those employed for investment and saving in (1) and (2).

(3a) $$M/Y = m(\Delta Y/Y) - \mu.$$

Employing equilibrium condition (4) again, we get equation (5a).

(5a) $$g_2 \equiv \frac{\Delta Y}{Y} = \frac{\alpha - \mu - \beta}{b + m} + \frac{v + 1}{b + m} \cdot \frac{X}{Y}.$$

The relations determining g_2 are simple to interpret in light of the discussion of g_1. The partial relation of $\Delta Y/Y$ to X/Y is positive, but whether or not g_2 is positive overall depends on the peculiarities of the saving and investment functions noted above. As before, the overall relation of the trade balance to the growth rate of income is not of predictable sign, although its partial relation to exports is of course positive. A growth path satisfying the equilibrium conditions need not be positive, and if positive need not involve an improving trade balance.[4]

We know from the research of Harrod and others that the stability properties of such models as these may be rather unusual. Although further specification of these models is required to demonstrate these properties in detail, the growth paths are unstable if we assume the same sort of output adjustment process that has been shown to lead to instability for Harrod's warranted growth rate, namely, that producers increase the growth rate of output when inventory decumulation takes place, and cut it back when inventories increase. This instability may be relevant to two major questions about the working of export-led growth: whether a payments deficit can be continuously

---

[4] This result of course agrees with traditional Keynesian theory of the foreign-trade multiplier, which concludes that an exogenous increase in exports will exceed the increase of imports that it induces, so long as some net leakage into domestic saving takes place.

avoided; and what role must be given to the unemployment rate as an influence on unit labour costs.

We saw that warranted growth paths may permit continuous trade surpluses for either export-led or -assisted growth, but need not do so. If the growth process represents not movement at a warranted rate but displacement upward from a warranted rate, an additional reason arises for concern over the possible instability effects of rapid export growth which apparently produces a sustained favourable balance of payments. The disequilibrium which implies aggregate excess demand or inventory decumulation in a closed economy could, presumably, spill over to absorb a larger quantity of imports than the structural coefficients of the system would themselves indicate. The 'excess' imports would offset inventory decumulation to some degree, and thus change the functional relation governing the rate at which producers seek to expand output; the degree of explosiveness of the departure from the warranted rate would presumably be reduced. Even without extra imports filling the excess-demand gap, a deficit in the trade balance would probably be inevitable for any such divergent growth path. Duesenberry has developed a simple two-country model in which export-led growth for country I (an exogenous exponential rate) can cause II's income either to rise or fall. The sign of II's income change depends on the net change in I's trade balance (exogenous export growth minus induced import growth). He shows that an explosive multiplier-accelerator mechanism in country I is a sufficient condition to worsen I's balance of payments and raise II's income, but not a necessary condition for this.[5]

A warranted growth rate implies a certain rate of absorption of labour into the work force,[6] and this rate may either exceed or fall short of the natural growth rate of the labour force; the Harrod-type short-run models include no mechanism for bringing them into harmony, though it is obvious how this might occur in a neoclassical growth framework. If the employment growth rate exceeds the labour-force growth rate, sooner or later the onset of full employment presumably exerts an upward pressure on the wage rate and unit labour costs, thereby undermining the payments position and threatening termination of the growth process. A debate between Beckerman and Balassa turned on this question, phrased by them in terms of the 'convergence' of growth rates of different countries, some currently blessed with and others deprived of export-led growth.[7]

Beckerman originally proposed an export-led model similar to that set forth above, but containing no equilibrium condition and merely relating the growth rate of exports to the level of export prices relative to competitor's prices, the growth rate of productivity to the growth rate of exports, that of

---

[5] Duesenberry, 1950, pp. 99–102.   [6] See note 3 above.
[7] See Beckerman, 1962, 1963, 1964; Balassa, 1963, March 1964, September 1964.

wages to productivity, and finally equating the growth rate of domestic prices to the excess of wage increases over productivity. Because the determinants of crucial constant terms in these relations are omitted, little can be concluded about the model's properties, e.g., whether or not it refers to a warranted growth path. The model's original purpose, however, was to explain divergent growth rates among countries by the incidence of export-led growth, and, to accomplish this, unit labour costs (and thus prices) clearly must not rise, or at least not rise faster than prices in other countries. Balassa's comments urged the importance of the unemployment rate instead of productivity growth as a determinant of the rate of wage increase. That it ultimately becomes important is clear from the preceding discussion of growth paths, warranted and otherwise, but he did not develop the endogenous nature of the unemployment rate in the model, since it remains constant only in the special case of a coincidence of the warranted and natural growth rates.[8] Beckerman defended the role of productivity as a primary determinant of wages and attacked the role of unemployment variations on factual grounds. The empirical question is considered below. It is somewhat curious, though, that in arguing for productivity or unemployment as the primary determinant of wage increases neither participant saw the importance of the wages–productivity relation lying not in its *existence* but in its *size*. A relation involving a response of wages no more than proportional to the increase in productivity would allow unit labour costs to fall, and would presumably serve as a counterpart to Lamfalussy's non-linear saving function, itself justified in part on the basis of a likely redistribution from wage to profit income. A more than proportional increase would, of course, itself spike the export-led growth process without any necessary influence of the level of unemployment. In any case, the Beckerman–Balassa approach to export-led growth serves better to raise questions than to answer them.

The agnostic conclusions reached here about export-led growth contrast with the more certain and cheerful ones drawn from the 'literary' accounts on which they are based. Perhaps the problem is simply the inaptness of Harrod-type models of short-run income growth, against possible alternatives giving rise to growth that is stable without being relentlessly neo-classical. Another logical possibility, however, is that the inductive development of the export-led models from post-war European experience has omitted some crucial element. I would suggest that this is in fact the case, the missing element being long-term capital imports that are functionally related to the rate of growth of domestic income or exports.[9] Massell (1964) has shown in

[8] Gordon, 1965, presents a model that corrects this deficiency and also inserts the rate of change of domestic prices explicitly as a determinant of the growth rate of exports.
[9] Induced capital inflows were included in models of short-run export-led growth which preceded the recent discussion; cf. Caves and Holton, 1959, chap. 3, and references cited therein.

a model similar to those presented above that capital imports functionally related to income will raise the growth of gross national product[10] if the productivity of capital exceeds the interest rate that must be paid to foreign lenders; and will also raise the growth of gross domestic product if the level of foreign borrowing exceeds the amount of domestic saving foregone because of interest payments to foreigners on outstanding debt. These conclusions depend on the trade balance adapting itself passively to effect the current rate of financial capital transfer in real terms. If one assumes that the transfer is automatically effected without impairing the rate of export growth, and that foreign saving automatically fills any gap between *ex ante* investment and domestic saving, the character of the growth process will clearly be altered, apart from the increase in the warranted rate.

Nearly all of the European countries enjoyed great increases in the outflow of direct investment from the United States from the late 1950's, and it would probably be hard to develop satisfactory proof that this outflow to individual nations fluctuated in succeeding years to reflect variations in their domestic or export growth rates. None the less, I suspect that a strong case could be made that the *division* of the new flow among recipients during the last decade has been affected by their relative growth rates.

3. *Empirical Evidence*

On this note I turn to some issues concerned with the empirical validity of the relations contained in the models of export-led growth. It has clearly been difficult to develop any general tests of the influence of export growth, either against the null hypothesis or against competing substantive hypotheses enthroning some other 'strategic factor' governing growth patterns. The whole discussion pertains, at most, to the O.E.C.D. countries since the early 1950's. Almost any proposition about growth determinants can be supported by comparing the experience of some pair of these nations—and refuted by contrasting some other pair. Applying the usual techniques of statistical inference is difficult for lack of degrees of freedom. The number of countries to which these ideas seem appropriate will support no elaborate cross-country regression analyses. The same problem arises in the number of years available for time-series analysis of the development of individual countries, especially because of the need to employ lagged relationships and because cutting one's time periods more finely (e.g., quarterly data) yields less than a proportionate gain in true degrees of freedom when the relations concerned operate with long and irregular lags. Stern's (1967) analysis of the Italian experience is not

---

[10] Actually, this conclusion follows directly from Harrod's own discussion of the foreign balance, although he does not call attention to the role of capital imports nor deal with the associated interest payments (1948, pp. 101–6).

encouraging in terms of the statistical results produced, although his treatment of the problem of specifying the functional relations can be criticized as mechanical. In any case, the following comments will be confined to the empirical content of the individual functions making up the model of export-led growth rather than directly with problems of testing the statistical performance of the model as a whole.

What is special about the growth of exports, as compared to the growth of any other aggregate-demand segment of equal size? This is a crucial point if choices among policies to encourage growth must involve betting on one or another component of aggregate demand. Three possible answers suggest themselves. First, selling a given increment of a nation's exportables on the world market should require less of a relative price reduction—if any at all—than selling them on the home market. Although not a necessary proposition, this seems reasonable as a probabilistic proposition. Note that it has more in its favour than the usual view that the 'world' demand elasticity for a nation's exportables exceeds that for the same goods in the home market because of foreign substitutes; the greater size of the external market is also relevant. Exports are, in Keynes's simile, more like pyramids than like railways from London to York. The rate of return on their production and sale diminishes less rapidly at the margin. This means that, if exporting is profitable at the margin, its profitability is (*cet. par.*) not likely to be much impaired by the fast expansion of exports. The operative constraints on output growth are likely to stem from sources other than 'balanced growth' and the limited size of the market. This feature alone does not make export growth unique, however; compare government expenditures on national defence, a true economic equivalent of Keynes's pyramids.

Second, the unusual growth of a nation's exports, if due to a shift in world demand or gains in productivity (but *not* if due to devaluation), is likely to be confined to a relatively limited number of industries. This concentration proves important if one accepts the importance of 'defensive investment'—the difference between the productivity of capital formation taking the form of small increases in capacity to expand (or duplicate) existing facilities and investments in new plants built entirely afresh. How far this property distinguishes export expansion from the growth of other aggregate-demand sectors is debatable, and this feature of export expansion might be counted as a mere corollary of the preceding argument based on differing demand elasticities. None the less, some element of difference seems apparent.

Third, Beckerman stresses businessmen's fears that demand growth may not continue smoothly because of a need to screw down aggregate demand in order to protect the balance of payments. Their concern over this outcome would rationally remain (indeed, be intensified) if domestic expenditure patterns produced demand pressures which took the economy towards full employment. Export growth would then be needed to assure freedom from balance-of-payments restrictions on demand, even if the expansion otherwise provided no special spur to growth. This last feature goes further towards attributing uniquely favourable effects to demand expansion due to export growth than other arguments, but it does attribute to business enterprises an aversion to demand fluctuations induced by public authorities that defies easy credibility. This is especially the case since the one broad statistical study of the effects of trade instability among underdeveloped countries has reported negative results.[11]

The next link in the model of export-led growth runs from the expansion of (export) markets to faster growth through a higher rate of capital formation, greater productivity gains from a given level of capital formation, or both. The amount of theorizing and testing that could be undertaken with this bundle of relations is immense, and I wish only to comment on some evidence that has been put forward. The hypothesised relation between income or market growth and productivity growth can be tested in several different forms or settings. For a national economy or manufacturing sector as a whole, it has taken the form of predicting that faster growth will be associated with a lower marginal capital–output ratio. For economies as a whole, or for individual industries, the prediction can be made that faster growth of total output leads to faster productivity growth. Let us examine each of these in turn.

Output growth and marginal capital–output ratios. Some O.E.C.D. countries grew significantly faster than others during the 1950's and early 1960's and also suffered relatively fewer balance-of-payments problems. If these favoured economies also enjoyed relatively high real rates of return on investment, one would feel confident of being on the right track in exploring the relations between trade performance and capital formation. The quest for this evidence leads immediately to the incremental gross capital–output ratio (I.C.O.R.) as the only readily available indicator of the productivity of new investment. But this measure *definitionally* equals the share of income invested divided by the rate of growth of income, a fact which immediately identifies the problems of detecting causal relations among these variables. Furthermore, the appropriate measure of this type to demonstrate aggregate levels of investment productivity is the net and not the gross capital–output ratio; yet it is well-known that the faster a nation's (steady state) growth rate, *ceteris paribus*, the smaller is the share of gross investment serving as replacement. This fact supplies a second, independent reason why relations between national rates of income growth and I.C.O.R.'s cannot be compared to test the productivity of net investment in fast growing economies.

[11] MacBean, 1966, chap. 4, reports no relation in cross-section over a sample of less-developed countries between an index of export instability and the rate of growth of investment, the rate of growth of gross domestic product, or the marginal capital–output ratio. Including developed countries in the sample left the result unchanged (p. 127).

Faced with these problems, both Lamfalussy and Beckerman have resorted to strong assumptions about the net–gross relation in manipulating the available data. Lamfalussy, assigning to capital goods a constant productivity over their assumed lifespans, finds that fast growing Germany enjoyed a lower I.C.O.R. in the aggregate than did slow growing Britain, from 1953 to 1960, both for the total economy and for industry alone, but not for manufacturing industry taken by itself. Furthermore, the computation for the aggregate economy assumes a lifespan of 40 years for capital goods (25 for industry), and halving this would eliminate the difference (Lamfalussy, 1963, Chapters, 6, 7). Beckerman (1965, Chapter 1) calculates capital–output relations from gross capital stocks net of estimated retirements; this procedure also embodies the assumption that the productivity of capital goods remains intact until they are scrapped, but estimates scrapping from accounting depreciation rather than assumed lifespans.

The more quickly capital goods wear out, the less is the leverage of faster growth on the apparent productivity of gross investment through an increasing ratio of net to gross. Shorter economic lifespans result either from shorter intervals between the installation and scrapping of capital equipment or from the extraction of greater productivity from capital goods earlier in their lives rather than evenly throughout. Little evidence exists, of course, to test Lamfalussy's assumed lifespans of 25 to 40 years, though I doubt whether they could be attacked as being too short.[12] In an unpublished paper, Stauffer, (1968), has shown the effects of allowing for exponential decline in the productivity of capital goods over their life-spans. Using Beckerman's data for the period 1956–62, he finds that assuming an exponential decay rate of 2 per cent for all investment goods, truncated after 30 years, the observed relation between income growth and gross I.C.O.R.'s is consistent with investment productivities for the countries studied by Lamfalussy that are not systematically related to income growth rates. No decisive evidence seems available to establish estimates of 'true' investment productivities at the margin for fast and slow growing countries. On the other hand, it seems fair to say that the null hypothesis of no correlation between growth rates and investment productivity levels survives handily.[13] No support emerges for

[12] Crum, 1953, studying the age distribution of United States corporate assets at the end of World War II, found that the mean elapsed time since incorporation was 33 years. This is by age of the corporation owning the assets, not the age of the assets themselves; the latter would surely be much less. The years 1945 and 1946 in the United States hardly succeeded a sustained period of fast growth of corporate assets.

[13] One might guess that the durability of capital goods used in a given industry varies little among the developed countries, but that significant variations occur among industries or sectors. If that is true, nations with a comparative advantage in industries with long-lived capital goods would devote relatively large portions of their capital stock to these industries, and thus incur longer-than-average lifespans for their typical capital goods. They would require relatively high investment ratios (investment as percentage of G.N.P.) to sustain a given growth rate. Casual observation suggests that Canada and

a relation, *ex post*, between high investment productivity and fast growth, let alone a causal relation running from the latter to the former.

Output growth and productivity growth. The second form in which a link between aggregate growth and productivity might appear is a direct connection between the rate of growth of total output (for a nation or industry) and productivity, usually measured as productivity per worker. This link, often called Verdoorn's law, has been cited by Beckerman and Kaldor in support of models or policies that assume a causal connection running from output growth to productivity growth. Evidence of the raw correlation between the two variables is widespread, but the direction of causation is anything but clear.[14] A simple supply-and-demand diagram (Figure 1) brings out the essentials of the problem.

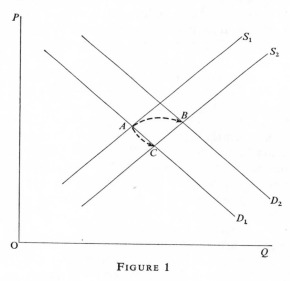

FIGURE 1

The Beckerman–Kaldor interpretation suggests that a shift of demand (between time periods 1 and 2) from D_1 to D_2 will induce productivity gains shifting the supply curve downward from S_1 to S_2.[15] The greater the increase

Norway might specialize in industries with long-lived capital, Italy and France the opposite. Stauffer's and most other calculations confirm this pattern, after adjustment is made for the mechanics of growth, and thus support the relevance of the comparisons discussed in the text.

[14] See Beckerman, 1965, pp. 221–9; Kaldor, 1966, p. 25. Katz, 1968, has shown that statistical estimates of the Verdoorn relation are typically biased upward, because of the influence of variables influencing the productivity of labour that are typically omitted from the calculations.

[15] This paragraph expands somewhat on an argument developed in Caves, 1968, pp. 297–8.

17—I.G.T.

in demand, the greater the increase in productivity. But suppose that the exogenous factor is the gain in productivity, rather than the growth of demand. Given some elasticity to the demand curve, the greater the growth in productivity, the greater the growth of sales (observed demand). The two sets of assumptions about causation are cleanly opposed, yet they yield identical qualitative predictions. The diagram, however, immediately suggests a possible way to discriminate between the two causal sequences on the basis of the behaviour of price. A disturbance originating in a demand shift involves a movement from equilibrium point A to B. Obviously no definite prediction emerges about the associated price change, which depends on the slopes of the two schedules and the size of the productivity response to demand growth. If the response is small, price change and output growth would tend to be positively related. Any lag in the response of productivity to output would also make the observed price–quantity relation in transition from A to B (the dashed line) likely to show a positive relation. On the other hand, causation running from productivity to sales implies a shift from observed point A to C, and an unambiguous negative relation between price and output changes except in the extreme case of a perfectly elastic demand curve.

The more tractable unit of observation for testing this argument—though not necessarily the more appropriate—is the industry, rather than the country (because of the extra complications of varying national financial policies, differing mixes of industries, varying factor prices, etc.). A significant negative correlation across industries between the relative increase of output and change in price would tend to support the predominant causal channel running from productivity change to market growth. A positive or uncorrelated relation tends to support the opposite causation. The cross-industry evidence that I have seen for the United Kingdom uniformly discloses the positive correlations between output growth and productivity growth predicted by both causal arguments, but also presents high negative correlations between either output–growth variable and price. Nicholson and Gupta find this across 138 British industries for 1948–54 and Salter for 28 industries 1924–50.[16] Again, the evidence fails to produce a convincing causal link running from the growth of output to the growth of productivity.

If this review of the evidence takes a somewhat negative view of the effect of output growth on the growth of productivity, several compelling lines of argument remain to support the proposition that fast growth of output (either exports or total output) encourages both an increased rate of capital formation and increased efficiency of capital formation. Even if we conclude,

---

[16] See Nicholson and Gupta, 1960, pp. 443–4, and Salter, 1960, p. 110. The argument that demand growth raises productivity is relatively more persuasive when addressed to the short run, and indeed its proponents have credited it with sufficient swiftness to serve in formulating policy for the balance of payments. Hence, Salter's test may cover too long a period for relevance.

ex post, that the productivity of incremental capital cannot be proved to be higher in the fast growing than the slow growing countries, this leaves unscathed the proposition that faster growth will create the expectation of higher short-run rates of return and thus induce a higher level of capital formation. Recent research using United States data shows rather rapid responses in the capital formation rates of individual industries to variations in their profit rates or sales levels.[17] In the aggregate, with various supply constraints (labour, capital goods, etc.) permitting, output or export growth could encourage an augmented rate of capital formation without revealing its motivation statistically, either through sustained high rates of return on capital or an improved marginal capital–output ratio.

Finally, a negative finding on cross-industry data does not necessarily upset the operation of Verdoorn's law for a country as a whole, and indeed Kaldor has argued that the two questions are quite separate.[18] 'Demand' factors could conceivably set the national rate of productivity advance, 'supply' factors the dispersion of industry rates of productivity growth around the national weighted average. If the rough data available exhibit no national productivity gain associated with the more rapid capital formation induced by fast output growth, we should hardly leap to total pessimism about the reality of this gain. The qualitative argument presented by Lamfalussy and Scitovsky, predicting such a gain because businessmen bedazzled by market growth may build new plants rather than refurbish old ones, or build plants of efficient rather than suboptimal scale,[19] is quite compelling and consistent with a good deal of empirical evidence. On the other hand, the productivity gain that could result through improved output scale in response to any rise in market growth rates that we are likely to observe is quite small. The sensitivity of productivity measures to the level of capacity utilization and the level of aggregation at which the relevant data reach us make it no surprise that hard evidence of its existence is lacking.

The group of functional relations needed to close the export-led model can be constructed in varying ways. It may relate the change in wages or prices to the growth rate of productivity or capital stock, on the presumption that a negative partial relation here will favour the trade balance and allow the 'virtuous circle' to be sustained. Or it may relate the trade balance directly to domestic saving, investment, and productivity growth. The preceding discussion of the theoretical structures of export-led models showed that the appropriate specification and interpretation of these relations depends on the rest of the model, so that not much can be accomplished by examining the empirical evidence on different specific possibilities. One issue that calls for comment, however, is the use of time-series evidence for individual

[17] See Stigler, 1965, chap. 2, and Hall and Weiss, 1967, pp. 327–8.
[18] Kaldor, 1967, pp. 12–15.
[19] Lamfalussy, 1963, pp. 105–9; Scitovsky, 1958, chap. 3.

countries versus cross-country data for testing these relations. Time-series data tend to reveal short-term relationships, cross-country data long-run ones. The export-led models have been advanced to explain differences in the growth experience of industrial countries since World War II, and clearly have something to offer for this purpose. Nonetheless, the functions included in the model clearly address themselves to short-term interactions. An appropriate and successful test would show that its functional relations are consistent with the experience *over time* both of countries with fast and countries with slow growing trade and productivity. Direct cross-country fitting of the functions tends strongly to mis-specification. Reflection on the policy implications of the model should remove any doubt on this score: if a country hoping for export-led growth devalues, thereby raising the level of aggregate-demand pressure, should it anticipate no higher growth rate for money wages because, across countries, productivity growth explains wage increases better than unemployment levels?[20]

A final problem with the empirical content of export-led growth cuts across the various functional relations and deals with the conventions of null-hypothesis testing. It is very difficult, especially after data limitations have taken their toll, to avoid testing these relations by regressions that contain identical components in both the dependent and independent variables. For instance, when productivity growth is related to export growth, the growth of exports (as a component of total output) is present on both sides. The dice become loaded in favour of accepting the hypothesis that a relation exists. Procedures exist for getting around this problem, of course, but its existence calls to mind the broader question of the performance of the export-led model against other hypotheses that purport to identify some critical growth factor holding the key to the growth of the economy as a whole. Why is the growth of exports better than, say, the growth of manufactured output, or the growth of the output of capital goods? Whatever the theoretical case that can be erected in favour of these or other 'strategic factors', it is a reasonable bet that a good econometrician could propel each of them individually past the sandtrap of the null hypothesis onto the green of statistical significance. This has been done for export leadership in a broad (fifty-country) cross-country sample, using average annual growth of exports and real G.N.P. per capita over the period 1953–63. The relation holds for the sample as a whole, and holds more strongly (higher correlation *and* regression coefficients) for the industrialized countries in the sample taken separately.[21] But tests of other hypotheses about the strategic factors determining productivity levels or growth rates have also turned out positively.

---

[20] Cf. Beckerman, 1963, p. 786.
[21] See Emery, 1967, and Syron and Walsh, 1968. In the same discussion, Severn, 1968, calls attention to the problem of time series *versus* cross-sectional inference that was discussed above.

What shall the policy maker conclude who must bet on one strategic factor or another?

Largely in a spirit of pump-priming, I undertook a very simple test of the main prediction of the export-led model by comparing the correlation across fifteen industrialized countries[22] of the growth rate of real gross domestic product with the growth rate of real exports of goods and services leading by 2 years, coinciding, and lagging by 2 years. All growth rates were calculated over 5-year periods (to wash out short-run fluctuations), so that (e.g.) the growth rate of G.D.P. for 1957–61 was correlated with the growth rate of exports for 1955–9, 1957–61, and 1959–63. The rationale for the lagging relation would be that export growth might primarily depend on availability and supply influences, and thus lag slightly behind the growth of G.D.P. (see Kaldor, 1967, pp. 43–4). Table 1 shows the rather uninspiring results, which give neatly opposed patterns for income growth in the 1957–61 and 1959–63 periods. A courageous soul might conclude that rates of export growth in the late 1950's determined subsequent income growth rates, with the influence of 'capacity' or supply factors on export growth being felt only in the 1960's; a timid soul would not.

TABLE 1

Correlation Coefficients between Five-year Growth Rates of Gross Domestic Product and Leading, Coinciding, and Lagging Five-year Growth Rates of Exports of Goods and Services, Fifteen Countries, 1955–65

Average Rate of Income Growth	Average Rate of Export Growth		
	Leading 2 years	Coinciding	Lagging 2 years
1955–59	—	0·553	0·389
1957–61	0·717	0·741	0·484
1959–63	0·495	0·550	0·785
1961–65	0·430	0·734	—

Source: Calculated from United Nations, Department of Economic and Social Affairs, *Yearbook of National Accounts Statistics, 1966* (New York: United Nations, 1967).

4. Policy Implications

Suppose that further quantitative research shows export-led growth to be an attainable reality for most industrial countries, in terms of the fillip for

[22] Australia, Austria, Belgium, Canada, Denmark, France, Germany, Italy, Japan, Netherlands, Norway, Sweden, Switzerland, United Kingdom, United States.

the growth of output per capita attainable from faster export growth. What conclusions would follow for the management of national economic policy and its co-ordination among countries?

Export-led growth may, of course, simply happen to a nation, especially in the aftermath of the disturbances of wartime and reconstruction. The only way it might be brought about, however, is through devaluation (or equivalent export subsidies). Contrary to the prediction of foreign trade-multiplier theory, an equal improvement in the trade balance through the restriction of imports will not do the trick.[23] Once set in motion, export-led growth must be protected from a shortage of saving or (what may be the same thing) rising product and factor-price levels. Flexible access to capital imports or, barring that, an effective incomes policy, becomes important for sustained growth as well as for the conventional goals of full employment and price stability. If balance of payments difficulties arise, however, most writers on the subject agree that the game is up. This is obviously so if aggregate demand or investment must be restricted directly. The restriction of imports poses the threat of retaliation cutting the growth of exports; devaluation improves investors' confidence only if undertaken seldom.

The alarming implication of export-led growth for economic policy is conflict of interest among countries. If the process requires an *ex post* current-account surplus to keep going, then success for some countries condemns others to failure. In a world that generally succeeds in maintaining full employment, devaluation becomes not a beggar-thy-neighbour but a shrink-thy-neighbour policy. One can imagine an export-led growth process in which the level of imports catches up with, but does not outpace, the level of exports; this would dissolve the conflict of national interests, but is clearly a special case. If capital flows can be pulled toward countries enjoying export-led growth, the conflict of interest over current-account balances is removed. The underlying disharmony of interest remains, however, because the expansion of a nation's exports through long-term capital outflows must coincide with a reduction of domestic capital formation, an increase in saving that is channelled abroad, or some combination of the two.

Taking note of the 'confidence' aspect of investment, as its quantity and quality are affected by the growth of exports, perhaps the one policy tool that could be employed in international harmony is the formation of customs unions. Even in this case, those investors enjoying suddenly improved export prospects would require some immunity to the distress calls of sectors facing increased import competition.

---

[23] This mechanical deduction from the export-led model does, of course, raise the question of its relation to prescriptions for growth through import substitution frequently offered to the less-developed countries.

REFERENCES

BALASSA, B., 'Some Observations on Mr. Beckerman's "Export-Propelled" Growth Model', *Economic Journal*, LXXIII (December, 1963), 781–5.

——, 'Some Observations on Mr. Beckerman's Export-Propelled Growth Model: A Rejoinder', *Economic Journal*, LXXIV (March, 1964), 240–2.

——, 'Some Observations on Mr. Beckerman's Export-Propelled Growth Model: A Further Note', *Economic Journal*, LXXIV (September, 1964), 740–2.

BECKERMAN, W., 'Projecting Europe's Growth', *Economic Journal*, LXXII (December, 1962), 912–25.

——, 'Some Observations on Mr. Beckerman's "Export-Propelled" Growth Model: A Reply', *Economic Journal*, LXXIII (December, 1963), 785–7.

——, 'Professor Balassa's Comments on My "Export-Propelled" Growth Model: A Rebuttal', *Economic Journal*, LXXIV (September, 1964), 738–40.

——, 'The Determinants of Economic Growth', *Economic Growth in Britain*, ed. P. D. Henderson (London, Weidenfeld & Nicolson, 1966), pp. 55–83.

——, and ASSOCIATES, *The British Economy in 1975*. National Institute of Economic and Social Research, Economic and Social Studies, XXIII (Cambridge, Cambridge University Press, 1965).

CAVES, R. E. and HOLTON, R. H., *The Canadian Economy: Prospect and Retrospect*. Harvard Economic Studies, No. 112 (Cambridge, Mass., Harvard University Press, 1959).

——, *et al.*, *Britain's Economic Prospects* (Washington and London, Brookings Institution and George Allen & Unwin, 1968).

CORNWALL, J., 'Postwar Growth in Western Europe: A Re-evaluation', *Review of Economics and Statistics*, L (August, 1968), 361–8.

CRUM, W. L., *The Age Structure of the Corporate System* (Berkeley and Los Angeles, University of California Press, 1953).

DUESENBERRY, J. S., 'Some Aspects of the Theory of Economic Development', *Explorations in Entrepreneurial History*, III (December, 1950), 63–102.

EMERY, R. F., 'The Relation of Exports and Economic Growth', *Kyklos*, XX (No. 2, 1967), 470–86.

GORDON, R. J., 'Unemployment, the Balance of Payments, and the Growth Goal', unpublished paper, Massachusetts Institute of Technology, 1965.

HALL, M. and WEISS, L., 'Firm Size and Profitability', *Review of Economics and Statistics*, XLIX (August, 1967), 319–31.

HARROD, R. F., *Towards a Dynamic Economics* (London, Macmillan, 1948).

KALDOR, N., *Causes of the Slow Rate of Economic Growth of the United Kingdom* (Cambridge, Cambridge University Press, 1966).

——, *Strategic Factors in Economic Development* (Ithaca, New York, New York State School of Industrial and Labour Relations, Cornell University, 1967).

KATZ, J. M., '"Verdoorn Effects", Returns to Scale, and the Elasticity of Factor Substitution', *Oxford Economic Papers*, XX (November, 1968), 342–52.

LAMFALUSSY, A. *The United Kingdom and the Six: An Essay on Economic Growth in Western Europe* (Homewood, Ill., Richard D. Irwin, 1963).

——, 'Contribution à une théorie de la croissance en économie ouverte', *Recherches Économiques de Louvain*, XXIX (December, 1963), 715–34.

MACBEAN, A. I., *Export Instability and Economic Development* (London, George Allen & Unwin, 1966).

MASSELL, B. F., 'Exports, Capital Imports and Economic Growth', *Kyklos*, XVII (No. 4, 1964), 627–34.

NICHOLSON, R. J. and GUPTA, S., 'Output and Productivity Changes in British Manufacturing Industry, 1948–1954: A Study from Census of Production Data', *Journal of the Royal Statistical Society, Series A (General)*, CXXIII (Part 4, 1960), 427–59.

SALTER, W. E. G., *Productivity and Technical Change*. University of Cambridge, Department of Applied Economics, Monograph No. 6 (Cambridge, Cambridge University Press, 1960).

SCITOVSKY, T., *Economic Theory and Western European Integration* (London, George Allen & Unwin, 1958).

SEVERN, A. K., 'Exports and Economic Growth: Comment', *Kyklos*, XXI (No. 3, 1968), 546–8.

STAUFFER, T. E., 'Growth-Induced Bias in the Computation of Incremental Capital-Output Ratios', unpublished paper, Harvard University, 1968.

STERN, R. M., *Foreign Trade and Economic Growth in Italy* (New York, Praeger, 1967).

STIGLER, G. J., *Capital and Rates of Return in Manufacturing Industries*. National Bureau of Economic Research, No. 78, General Series (Princeton, N.J., Princeton University Press, 1963).

SYRON, R. M. and WALSH, B. M., 'The Relation of Exports and Economic Growth', *Kyklos*, XXI (No. 3, 1968), 541–5.

17

INTERNATIONAL PRICE STRUCTURES AND ECONOMIC PROGRESS

A SECULAR VIEW

LÉON H. DUPRIEZ

A LAYMAN may wonder why certain economic problems attract widespread attention and are put in the centre of theoretical formulations, while others, no less important, are hardly mentioned, and receive only casual attention. Obviously, there are fashions in this respect, but some most important factors which affect international relationships have not yet been seriously analysed.

It is my purpose to analyse one of these less observed problems of our economic system, to relate certain well-known facts to the relevant economic theory, and to grope toward an enlarged economic theory capable of covering the new field of research. More new problems than precise new conclusions will emerge from this analysis.

My excuse for such an attempt is that it rests on several years of research work pursued under my responsibility at the University of Louvain. The present contribution is a preliminary assessment of the results, which is being published in detail.[1]

The problem to be analysed is the very obvious fact that price levels and relative price structures vary very widely from country to country. We all know that differences in price levels and relative structures are associated with states of technique and technological advance, and that factors like natural resources and political organization also play a part in their determination. Furthermore, we know that these relationships have an immense inertia and can therefore be taken as given in any short period analysis. For this latter reason they have often been left outside the range of theoretical analysis.

In fact, within the framework of national income analysis, price levels—but not relative price structures—have been considered in framing economic policy; directly for determining barter terms of trade, indirectly through comparisons of wages or of incomes per head. The emphasis in analysis has been on average price levels.

[1] Dupriez, 1966–8.

Such averages give an over-simplified view of the situation and leave us uneasy. We do feel that in the 'quality of life' and its perspectives the differences between countries may be much greater than the averages suggest, but this is unquantifiable. On the other hand, at a strictly economic level, it is quite obvious that no man can subsist for any length of time in New York at $50 per annum, which is the common estimate of the subsistence level in scarcely monetized regions of the world, nor even at $500, which can give a man rank and distinction in these parts of the world. Averages are therefore tricky: they describe but they do not explain. We cannot explain the existing relations, except by an analysis of relative price structures, which will reveal certain important interrelationships of the economic system.

An explanation of relative structures is obviously important in the perspective of present efforts to redress price relations which are detrimental to the underdeveloped countries, for these can only be changed by a proper appraisal of relative prices and productivities, in national and international terms. What are the functional relations which cannot be disregarded?

Economic theory requires that we should interpret the facts in the light of comparative advantages. How are the relative structures of countries with different levels of technique and organization related? How are price levels and structures brought together when a country catches up with the technique of another? How are they reft asunder when these levels move apart?

Before answering these questions empirically, let us state that Ricardo led economists astray when he chose his examples of comparative advantage. The comparative advantage of Portugal in making Port wine is certainly as natural as it is absolute, and as to the British advantage in making woollen cloth, it was obviously also based on the 'natural' proficiency of the English workers, and this too did not require explanation.

At a later stage, the high prices and wages of the United States were also invariably attributed to its wealth in natural resources. But why did other favoured regions of the world not follow suit? Why do relative advantages remain today with the U.S.A. and Europe, where raw materials dwindle?[2]

It must be that 'natural advantages', though important at some stage of history, are not permanently important; acquired advantages, foremost among which are the qualities of the population, play a more decisive and a more lasting role. As we move towards higher techniques, requiring less raw materials and more working up of those materials per unit of product, acquired advantages assume increasing importance. This means that comparative advantages enter the realm of economic rather than natural and geographical interpretation.

As relative price structures have immense inertia, we needed to study long-term, secular, changes in relative price systems, where changes in

[2] cf. Paley Report, 1952.

technique and organization can exert pressure. Short-term market analysis is irrelevant.

We therefore proceeded to analyse cases of historical change in relative price levels and associated price structures. Three monographs of a widely different character were chosen to establish certain basic relationships. Others are under way in order to define the general historical pattern of change under the impact of the industrial revolution.

A first monograph bears on a change in relative price structures which has been completed. At the end of the Napoleonic wars, the German states were still in the pre-industrial era, with a low general price level, based on low agricultural prices and wages. By 1913 Germany had largely caught up with Great Britain in industrial techniques, and her wage and price system moved up asymptotically toward the British. To give an example based on prices divergent at the outset, corn prices rose two and a half times in Prussia from 1820–1913, while there was no upward trend in Britain. This was the perfect historical case, with a strong movement towards adaptation favoured by economic integration.

A second monograph bears on more recent developments, which still have enormous implications for economic policy. Since the turn of the century, the degree to which United States techniques were more advanced than European techniques has at times increased, at other times decreased. Periods of war have invariably been associated with widening discrepancies; periods of peace have generally been periods with a consequent reduction in the technical gap due to adaptation in Europe. These show, and actually did show, in relative prices.

An analysis of British, Belgian, and German relative prices, *vis-à-vis* the U.S.A., shows adaptation towards United States relative prices during each of the three peacetime periods, with Belgian and German prices moving faster towards United States prices. This is attributable to some 'catching up' with the British price system in 1899–1913 and 1920–39 and even the development of a pricing system appropriate to a higher stage of development than the British after 1945. But the upward move in the twentieth century was not nearly as great as the German change in the nineteenth century, and disruption by wars twice widened the differences between European relative prices and those in the United States.

The politically interesting fact brought out by this analysis is the rate of the adaptation of European relative prices to United States relative prices since 1945. Moreover, the movement was faster in Belgium and Germany than in Great Britain from 1958 to 1968. Here the analogy with nineteenth century Germany is clear: the industrial structure in the Common Market started to adapt as soon as the dismantling of frontiers went beyond the point of no return. Zollerein in the nineteenth century and the Common Market in the twentieth have had the same kind of influence.

Of course, Europe is still at a distance from United States standards. Take the case of industrial wages; they are now about 60–65 per cent of American wages, while they were 45–50 per cent in the decade after 1945. The present discrepancy is due to differences in physical productivity in many of the most important industries, i.e., it is due to acquired advantages in the processes of production. As experience in the latter decade, 1958–68, suggests, any move upward in relative productivity should push the whole European price system towards the United States system.

The third case to be analysed is of a very different character. Prices in the Congo were compared with Belgian prices from 1910 to 1960, i.e., right through the colonial period. Here convergence is in a double direction: at the start, prices of products produced in the Congo were exceedingly low, prices of products of European origin very high; the same applied to local wages versus wages and salaries of Europeans. In the course of time and with the development of transport and commerce, such differences were substantially reduced, even though they were still very important. Gradual integration of the local price system into the international price system prevailed. Internal unification between regions was also important.

In this respect, Katanga prices proved more flexible than Lower Congo prices, and rightly so. The latter were already linked to European prices in 1910 through railway communications; the former only had a very tenuous link with the world, through the Cape. In 1960 the local market had many points of contact with the outside world.

These three cases furnish typical examples of the problem of relative price structures, and enable us to put a number of theoretical questions, which should guide us in further studies. But they leave many questions unanswered. Among other things, the relative position of any country in the process of industrial development can be assessed by comparing its relative price system with that of the leaders in the industrial revolution. A further analysis of the relative importance of natural and of acquired advantages in furthering a price system, associated with high productivities, should also be of great interest and even of political importance. This can be illustrated by two cases relating to mining problems.

Until 1939 Belgium suffered from a wage level which was some 25–30 per cent below that of its neighbours, and from a correspondingly backward price structure. Yet by 1946 the country had been able to push its whole pricing system above that of its neighbours and to adapt its industrial structure rapidly to this new set of price relationships. Detailed analysis shows that the country's wage level was restricted to what its most important industry, coal mining, could pay; and this was restricted by the relatively poor mining conditions, in relation to those of England and of Germany. This limitation disappeared when the mines had to resort to foreign labour for underground work. It has no longer any significance, with dwindling coal mining activity.

On the basis of acquired advantages of skill and organization, no negative difference with neighbouring regions should subsist.

Since the war, South Africa has been encountering a similar problem. The wage and salary level, especially for the white population, has been limited by what gold mining could pay—of course at advanced levels of technique and with exploitation restricted to the best seams. The effect of a fixed gold price has not been to restrict wages in gold mining only, but to put pressure on the whole nominal wage system of the country; this, in turn, bringing about a generally lower price structure. Diversification of industrial activity is an answer to this situation, but cannot bear fruit in the short run.

It is now time to establish how relative price structures are associated with relative price levels in theory, so that the observed relations can be logically interpreted. This involves the relations between price equalization forces ruling on the international market and price parities which tend to prevail between national markets. The first imply direct market contacts, the latter indirect relationships through factor prices and cost relationships.

The link between the differing price systems of two related countries obviously lies in the prices ruling on the international market, i.e., in mutual trade, or even through multilateral trade involving both countries. At the limit, in a perfect market ruling out transport costs, the price of a commodity should be the same at all ports of import before payment of national duties. Discrepancies between prices of the same goods in different countries will arrive in practice, either through duties, or through monopolistic market practices, or through the action of different factor costs and different techniques of production in different countries.

Let us examine first the validity of the hypothesis of a unique international market.

The hypothesis of a unified, if not unique, market for international commodities can be considered to be approximately true for relations between European countries, viz., for the Germany–Great Britain case. There cannot be great price differentials between Hamburg and London, either in reciprocal trade or for import or export trade with other nations. Differences in relative prices therefore do not rest on any appreciable differences in international prices.

The case of Europe versus the U.S.A. is a little more complicated. Prices of raw materials and food from other continents should not be very different in New York, London, or Antwerp. But reciprocal trade is affected by transport costs, which are diminishing with the passage of time. There should arise some price differentials according to whether commodities move East or West; but they would be of little importance in explaining existing disparities.

The international market itself assumes a greater responsibility in framing price relations between the centres of the highly industrialized world and distant underdeveloped regions. For a long time these were only the maritime regions; even today links between inland sites, without good communications, and the international market sometimes remain very slender.

In these cases price formation in international commerce itself plays an important role in establishing disparities. We can represent the situation as follows. In London, taken as the central commercial market of the world, merchandise normally flows in from every part of the world through well-organized channels of transport. For every commodity, the London price is therefore relatively low, except in relation to the price in the producing country. The London average price for imports of primary products is therefore the lowest, as one expects price to be lowest in theory at the meeting point of commercial relations. For exports of manufactures, the position is more complex, but industrialized Europe, considered as a unit, benefits from the same condition of minimization of prices of manufactures in relation to the prices underdeveloped countries have to pay.

An inland region in the centre of Africa or South America finds itself in exactly the opposite position. It has very low local prices for its exports because expensive transport costs must be deducted from the international London price. On the other hand, it suffers from very high prices for all external goods as transport costs have to be added to prices fixed f.o.b. Europe or the U.S.A.

Barter terms of trade are obviously different according to the place where they are measured. The differences should be small as between European ports and not very different as between Europe and the U.S.A. They have been great between the seaports of the world and European ports, but have dwindled considerably. They do remain serious for underdeveloped inland regions.

As prices of internationally traded goods are given from outside, factor prices inside the country have to be adapted to them. With highly developed techniques in export industries, wages should be high in developed economies —all the more so as interest and profit rates in developed countries are relatively low. The lower prices in the less developed countries imply lower wage rates. The same rule applies for internal goods competing with external products. The crux of price structure differentials nevertheless remains in the internal market relations of the countries concerned in any comparison.

Purely internal relations, on each side, govern thereafter the price formation of local goods, of services, of commercial margins, etc. The cost of labour is largely unified by forces acting on the labour market; but there is a serious factor holding down wages in small-scale activities in underdeveloped countries. While elaborate services in developed economies may fetch higher wages than work in standard industries, Malthusian conditions tend to keep wages down in service industries in underdeveloped countries with structural unemployment.

Local price systems are built up to conform to cost systems which take account of these wage differentials. Indeed, they actually increase these differentials, as the pressure for progress is considerably less in traditional activities than in mining, manufactures, and large-scale agriculture.

The result of such factors is that the whole system of internal prices may be high where average import prices are low, while internal prices may remain very low when import prices are high. Higher wages in the former case may be associated with a high degree of monetized services, while lower wages in the latter may be associated with a high degree of self-subsistence.

In the case of an underdeveloped country with high import prices, a high percentage of the community, working in agriculture with traditional inefficient methods, produces much of its food itself. For the rest of the community, food is generally sold without processing. Commerce bears on a limited assortment of articles. Roundabout processes of production cannot be organized, partly because of a lack of liquid funds.

In a developed economy with low import prices everything is sold at the highest level of processing; production processes enter the costing process up to the very point of immediate consumption. When prepared sandwiches or cornflakes are commonly sold, basic food prices do not have the same meaning as they had in pre-industrialized Europe, when city people bought flour, or in underdeveloped countries, where rice or manioc are standard goods.

This summary explanation is meant to show how and why internal price structures keep widely apart, without any reference to balance of payments problems. Relative states of technique and organization, with all their pervasive effects, are paramount, while the form of the international market itself increases the discrepancies where the distances involved in trade and communication are large. Any change in the relative development of techniques between countries must therefore show in prices.

This type of adjustment must be shown through a double set of price ratios:

(1) Ratios between prices of traded goods in the less developed countries to prices of the same goods in more developed countries; here tendencies toward unification should be observed.
(2) Ratios between internal prices and wages within each of the countries considered, especially between prices at successive stages of production; here prices should move in relation to the degree of progress achieved at every point.

This latter influence does, in many cases, increase the margin between the higher prices of the developed countries and the lower prices of the less developed. Corn and bread are an interesting case in this respect. Corn prices have been subject to unification (even with present protective measures, which bring about similar results by different methods), but bread prices are increasingly different. The reason is that there is less technical advance in making and commercializing bread than in the production of corn or in production techniques generally. General progress therefore increases the relative price of bread! Obviously, this argument is still clearer for those types of pure services which cannot be rationalized. Baby-sitting costs more in the United States than a housemaid in nineteenth-century Europe or in twentieth-century Asia.

It is not our purpose to define here the precise equilibrium of international relations under whose influence relative price systems are established and tend to move together or asunder. For the world at large, they should move toward each other as larger and larger areas are brought under the influence of the industrial revolution. Our sole aim is to show the kind of way in which this vast economic and political problem can be integrated into general economic theory.

Here we must face a fundamental fact: we are concerned with parities between internal price systems and not with the price equalization of the international market, which constitutes the link between countries which has largely been explained. These parities imply indirect relations whose equilibria and disequilibria can only be defined by bringing in an elaborate set of relations, external and internal, none of which can be permanently disregarded without serious error. But, due to their roundaboutness, these relations will normally act very slowly.

At the root of the discrepancies, one finds the fact that factor prices, and primarily the price of labour, must differ with physical productivities in the countries that are compared—let us not call it precisely average productivities —and with market conditions for labour, capital, and land. The price of capital is very much under international influence. The price of labour, on the contrary, appears as the most representative element of the inner economic conditions of the country.

It would, therefore, be significant to pursue the study of changes in secular price relationships in relation to factorial terms of trade. Factorial terms of trade have a profound significance for the social nature of relations between countries, and relative economic progress must have a beneficial impact on them. No such clear and simple relation exists for barter terms of trade; short-run movements are, of course, a sign of better or worsened market relations and imply corresponding changes in technique. In the long run, 'worsened' terms of trade can very well be the sign of rapid economic progress entailing lower export prices with higher wages and profits.

Political attention has none the less been concentrated on barter terms of trade and factorial terms have been discussed at a rather more formal level. Factual content and numerous interesting applications could result from the study of relative price structures which we have begun. The whole theory of the terms of trade would be based on more profound relationships than current reasoning on barter terms.

When relative price structures move toward each other, in the very long period, the equilibria involved in the process are subject to change under the impact of changing levels of technique, they react as consequences of fundamental changes in economic organization. Owing to the length of such processes, adaptation is intermittent but there seems to be no reason why a durable discrepancy need occur; changes in parities between internal price systems and factorial terms of trade are provoked by general economic equilibrium relations; they are not autonomous disequilibria which require the economy to adapt itself. Moving purchasing power parities appear as the *result* of changing economic structures. In this context, their relation to double factorial terms of trade is clear.

Early analyses of purchasing power parities were, nevertheless, made in relation to a quite different kind of problem. Cassel (1922) first, Triffin (1937), and others were concerned, between 1919 and 1940, with sudden discrepancies arising between national price systems owing to important and rapid changes in the exchange rates of their currencies: widely fluctuating exchange rates, as in 1919–20, were the case examined by Cassel, sudden devaluations the case examined by Triffin in 1936. Cassel already insisted that internal prices, less rapid to adapt, had to be considered, and not the instantaneous prices of international commerce; but his statistical apparatus was faulty, as wholesale price indexes alone were at his disposal; these were an undefined mixture of international and local prices.

Triffin based his analysis systematically on retail prices and on wages, i.e., on reciprocal *internal* conditions. He showed how disparities due to shifts in exchange rates reacted on the economy: export and import prices were under constraint to adapt themselves rapidly to international conditions, and the root of the difficulties was therefore not in the barter terms of trade. But internal costing systems were not in balance with external prices, provoking either unduly harsh or unduly lax conditions of production. Internal productive conditions were thus put under duress or abnormally stimulated. It is unnecessary to enter into details here.

In this context, where disparities are of monetary origin, the practical problems involved are quite different from those which we have been examining. The foremost object of statistical analysis was evidently to measure existing disparities in order to determine a range of approximate parity, within which political action on exchange rates might re-establish the national economy in correct relation to international markets. A subsidiary, more sophisticated, view might be to devise policies based on the maintenance of a limited degree of over or under-valuation of the currency in order to obtain some specific results. Even in these cases, the statistical problem of measuring the position of parity is complex.

18—I.G.T.

Now, this statistical problem has always been approached by measuring differences between a 'present' position of relative prices and wages and the position at some past time considered as 'normal'. In such cases, normality meant that mutual commercial relations were carried on without strain in any of the countries involved. If no such ideal conditions could be found, any past disparity existing at the statistical base period had to be allowed for. This is, in fact, what statisticians did when analysing in 1935 the position of continental currencies against sterling on the basis of 1928 comparisons; the pound presented a disparity of some 15 per cent overvaluation in 1928.

This method of reasoning based on the measurement of change was used over periods of time of a few years at most. And rightly so: it was acceptable only in so far as relative conditions of organization and technique had not been modified. Figures of disparity always had to be accepted by discounting any conditions which had been modified in the meantime.

Such a statistical procedure and the ensuing economic interpretation could be developed much better for small than for big nations. Politically, a small economic unit was faced with the obvious necessity of correcting any calculated disparity, either by changing its exchange rate or by internal adaptation; it had no possibility of shifting the load of adaptation onto the 'rest of the world'. Large economic units, as 1931–6 showed, were able to create disastrous disparities and to shift the load of adaptation onto 'the rest of the world'.

Furthermore, it is clear that, when a disparity develops, a small economic unit suffers rapidly and harshly internally; processes of adaptation are set going immediately, or political necessity imposes rapid moves in exchange rates. Large economic units, on the other hand, can develop more considerable disparities and struggle along with them for a considerable time, with a more limited impact on internal conditions.

This difference between smaller and bigger economic units probably explains to a large extent why economic theory currently looks askance at the purchasing power parity doctrine, and why the U.S.A. and Great Britain, with the hopeful exception of 1967, have given purchasing power parities only slight consideration in fixing the extent of a devaluation. For the smaller economic units of the world the relation between the exchange rate and purchasing power parity has been paramount.

This discussion of purchasing power disparities of monetary origin and of the implications of a search for parity through monetary reform may seem out of the way in a discussion of international price structures and economic progress. But it is not for several reasons.

First, at the practical level, it is clear that international trading arrangements and their effect on the domestic economy play a large part in creating conditions for economic progress. It is a moot point in any given circumstances whether a position of parity or of slight over or under-valuation should be chosen, but such a choice has an impact on the type of economic progress which is furthered. It would, moreover, be agreed that large disparities either way are detrimental.

Second, it is arguable that a systematic historical analysis of events since 1919 may be very revealing of the forces at work, especially if a proper distinction is made between the larger and smaller economic units. Here, very extensive factual material is at our disposal.

Third, the concept of parity between internal conditions—and the price structures appertaining to them—is not a 'monetary' concept, to be opposed to the 'real' concept of barter terms. Purchasing power parities were first studied in a monetary context because serious disparities after 1919 had a monetary origin. However, our present studies on secular changes in price structures rest on parities which move quasi-adiabatically and remain largely outside the monetary sphere.

The explanation of a very fundamental problem of the economic structure of the world thus obliges us to broaden the theory of international economics. Neither economic conditions in the short period, nor economic progress in the long period, can be entirely understood without proper consideration of purchasing power parities or disparities. These must be integrated in the general theory of economic equilibrium. This should be made easier if it is admitted that parities and disparities are not monetary by nature, as our secular monographs have shown, but that practical problems of parity can have either a monetary or a 'real' origin. Purchasing power parity is thus a concept of general economic theory.

REFERENCES

CASSEL, G., *Money and Foreign Exchange after 1914* (London, 1922).

DUPRIEZ, L. H., BARDOS-FELTORONYI, N., SZAPARY, G., and PEEMANS, J. P., *Diffusion du progrès et convergences des prix—études internationales*, 2 vols. (Louvain and Paris, 1966–70).

PALEY REPORT: *Resources for Freedom*, A report to the President by the President's Materials Policy Commission, 5 vols. (Washington, 1952).

TRIFFIN, R., 'La Théorie de la surévaluation monétaire et la dévaluation belge', *Bulletin de l'Institut de Recherches Économiques*, t. IX, I (Louvain, 1937), pp. 19–52.

18

ROY HARROD ON THE PRICE OF GOLD

HARRY G. JOHNSON

ONE of the most endearing and enlivening—though occasionally exasperating—characteristics of Roy Harrod's distinguished public career as a running commentator on current issues of economic policy has been his Oxonian capacity cheerfully to espouse causes which his professional colleagues have been virtually unanimous in regarding as hopelessly lost, if not downright hopeless. One such cause has been his advocacy, throughout the period since the end of the second world war and the establishment of the International Monetary Fund, of an increase in the monetary price of gold as a contribution to the solution of the problems of the international monetary system.[1] In espousing this remedy, Roy Harrod has been fully aware that his position both conflicted with that of the overwhelming majority of international monetary experts, who prefer the logicality of replacing commodity by credit money internationally as nationally, and courted the risk of giving aid and comfort to the vested interests in gold mining and to those who hanker after the automaticity of the gold standard, as well as challenging deeply emotional attitudes about the dollar held by public opinion in the United States, a country for which he has always felt both admiration and concern. It says much, therefore, for his sense of professional responsibility that he has not allowed the expression of his views on this subject to be inhibited by the knowledge that they were unpopular, and likely to be ridiculed or misinterpreted.[2] It says more for his unique powers of intuitive insight into complex problems of political economy in the broad sense that the evolution of the international monetary system in recent years, culminating in the gold crisis of March 1968 and the establishment of the necessarily transitory 'two-tier' gold price system, has brought the problem of the monetary price of gold into the forefront of discussion, and created a strengthening likelihood that an increase in the monetary price of gold will be necessary to the restoration of international monetary order.

[1] An intriguing subject for speculation is why academic advocacy of an increase in the price of gold in the United Kingdom has been confined to a few economists in Oxford University, the traditional home of lost causes: Roy Harrod, Donald MacDougall around 1949–50, and recently Peter Oppenheimer.

[2] Harrod's sense of professional responsibility is movingly explicit in the chapter on 'Gold' in his *Reforming The World's Money*, 1966.

In view of Roy Harrod's long-sustained advocacy of an increase in the monetary price of gold, and the relevance of his arguments on that subject to the contemporary international monetary crisis, it seems appropriate to contribute to a volume in his honour an essay on the problem of the gold price and his contributions to our understanding of the issues involved. The essay begins with a theoretical analysis of the gold and gold exchange standards, designed to show why the gold-based international monetary system tends inevitably to evolve towards a crisis involving a choice between raising the monetary price of gold and demonetizing gold by replacing it with some form of credit money.[3] The current international monetary situation is then briefly discussed within this framework. Finally, Roy Harrod's major contributions on the price of gold are critically reviewed and evaluated.

1. *A Theoretical Analysis of the Gold Standard*

The pure gold standard is a commodity money standard, and the gold exchange standard uses a mixture of commodity money and credit money based on a commodity money reserve. From the point of view of abstract monetary theory, the use of a commodity as money is both unnecessary and inefficient: unnecessary because what gives money its monetary attributes is its general acceptability in exchange and the settlement of debts, and not the intrinsic value of the monetary substance; and inefficient because it involves locking up in the monetary substance real resources that could otherwise be employed directly or indirectly in the satisfaction of human wants. Consequently, theory would predict that a commodity money system will be subject to continuing erosion deriving from the economic incentives to substitute for commodity money alternative assets with monetary attributes of equal acceptability, or of lesser acceptability compensated for by a monetary or service yield, thus freeing the monetary substance for more productive use. The pace of the erosion process will be determined by the strength of the incentives to release real resources locked up in the monetary substance, the ingenuity applied to devising acceptable credit substitutes for commodity money, and the speed of public habituation to the use of these substitutes. Eventually, a point will be reached in the substitution process at which either the commodity money naturally falls out of use for practical purposes, or its use can be suppressed by governmental action without great public protest or disturbance.

In the national monetary systems of the advanced industrial countries,

---

[3] This analysis draws on the published writings and unpublished comments of academic colleagues in the so-called 'Bellagio group', especially Robert Triffin, Peter B. Kenen, R. A. Mundell, and Fritz Machlup. Acknowledgements are also due to the writings of Milton Gilbert and Peter Oppenheimer. A preliminary version of the analysis is contained in Johnson, 1969.

the evolution from a commodity money system, via a commodity money exchange system, into a pure credit money system was completed in the first third of this century. It is relevant to the international monetary problem, however, to note that the final stage of the process—the removal of gold from private circulation—was effected by legislation prompted by international monetary disorders and did not simply happen naturally; and also that the commodity money exchange standard stage was marked by frequent confidence crises requiring the development of the techniques of central banking.

The same economic pressures as produced the transition at the national money level from commodity to commodity exchange to pure credit money have been operating on the international monetary system, to convert it from a gold standard into a gold exchange standard. But the way these pressures operate, in a world divided into sovereign national states, is to produce an increasingly unstable situation of a non-sustainable sort, which must culminate in a crisis. The reason is that the process of substitution of credit money for commodity money, which depends on confidence in the convertibility of the former into the latter, helps to create a growing relative shortage of the commodity money which undermines the confidence on which the continuation of the process depends. The problem is aggravated by political rivalries and uncertainties which enhance the desire for the commodity money and inhibit the willingness to develop more efficient credit substitutes for it. Hence, instead of the relatively smooth evolution from pure commodity to pure credit money that has characterized the history of national monies, the international system arrives at a crisis in which the ultimate choice is between an increase in the price of the commodity base money of the system and a leap forward into international co-operation in the provision of a superior substitute for it. Logically, and in accordance with the history of domestic monetary arrangements, the latter solution commends itself to the academic expert; but political economy suggests that the former may be the only practicable alternative.

To elaborate the analysis, it is convenient to begin with the traditional theory of the gold standard as an international monetary system. According to that theory, the gold standard has the virtue of a commodity money standard, in that money derives its value from the intrinsic worth of the monetary substance. Actually this is the reverse of the truth, in either a static or a dynamic context: in a static equilibrium system, the real value of the monetary substance will be higher, as a result of the monetary demand for it, than it would be if the value were determined solely by non-monetary demand; and in a growing world economy, additional supplies of monetary gold to support the growth of the system will require the real price of gold to be high enough to generate an excess of new production over the private demand for it. In either case, the private value adjusts to the monetary value rather than determines it. The doctrine of intrinsic worth is a fiction, but a useful one since if everyone believes it gold will be acceptable without question in international settlements—one aspect of the alleged virtue of 'anonymity' of gold.

A more important and relevant aspect of the theory of the gold standard is the proposition that the standard provides an automatic mechanism for monetary stabilization through the dependence of the profitability of gold production on the level of wages and other prices relative to the fixed monetary price of gold. According to the theory inflation will be limited by its effects in choking off, and deflation by its effect in stimulating, new gold production. Critics of the gold standard have emphasized the deficiencies of a price stabilization mechanism that links the money supply to a depleting mineral resource, whose supply depends on new discoveries and developments in extractive technologies, whose current production is small relative to total stocks and whose price-inducible variations in current production are smaller still. A more fundamental criticism is that the theory assumes that the use of gold as international money is immutable, and neglects the economic incentives for substitution of credit money for gold. It is the resort to these substitutes that permits continuing inflation to occur under the gold standard, and substitution and inflation that lead ultimately to crisis.

Assume a situation in which, due say to the unavoidable inflationary effects of a major war, the monetary price of gold has been fixed so low that the net flow of new gold production into monetary stocks is inadequate to provide a rate of growth of international reserves in the form of gold appropriate to the growing demands for reserves of a growing world economy. Under a pure gold standard, the deficiency would have to be overcome by deflation, or else the growth of world trade and payments would have to be restricted to what the growth of monetary gold stocks would support. But the deficiency could alternatively be made good by resorting to the use of credit substitutes. Such substitutes could be provided by international invention, as was the intention of the designers of the International Monetary Fund. But, the market mechanism would itself provide attractive substitutes, given the fact that gold holdings are barren, in the form of interest-bearing holdings of a national currency or currencies whose convertibility into gold on demand was beyond doubt. Resort to such a reserve currency or currencies would permit total international reserves to grow at the rate required by world economic expansion, and would also permit national policies of full employment and growth that generated an inflationary upward pressure on prices. Moreover, so long as the reserve currency country was content to see its monetary liabilities to other countries increase and allow its gold reserves to fall, the growing overall substitution of credit money for gold would be consistent with the other reserve-holding countries expanding both their gold-holdings and their holdings of the reserve currency in some desired portfolio-balance relationship, by drawing on the gold reserves of the reserve-currency countries to supplement new gold production for monetary use.

This process of providing for growth of international reserves is, however, bound to end in a crisis, for two reasons.

First, the gradual inflation of prices will tend in the long run to reduce gold production by reducing its profitability. More important, the associated reduction in the real cost of gold to private users will add to the effects of rising world real income on private demand for gold for industrial and artistic purposes a substitution effect in favour of gold as against alternative metals, and will also have a 'real balance effect' on the demand for gold for long-range hoarding, since it will take increasing physical quantities of gold to provide the same store of purchasing power over goods and services. Further the rise in private demand relative to supply will generate speculation as to the ability of the monetary authorities to continue to maintain the monetary price of gold, and will add to the other private demands a short-run speculative demand that, by further reducing the net flow of monetary gold, will tend to appear self-justifying or at least induce speculators to hold onto their acquisitions of gold in hopes of a delayed profit. Eventually, the net inflow of new gold to monetary uses will be converted into a net outflow to private holdings, the monetary authorities will be converted from price-supporters of gold to price-suppressors, and the problem of what they will do in these circumstances will constitute the makings of a crisis.

Second, the reserve currency country cannot continue to have its monetary reserve liabilities increasing and its gold reserves decreasing, without the confidence of other countries in its capacity to maintain the value of its currency in terms of gold being undermined. At the same time, the dwindling of the supply of new monetary gold will require it to have both larger balance-of-payments deficits and larger gold losses if the reserve asset preferences of the other countries are to be satisfied, and will also make the other countries increasingly reluctant to accumulate holdings of its currency, and anxious to hold gold instead. This anxiety will be aggravated by increasing resentment of the reserve currency country's ability to run a continuing deficit. In these circumstances, private speculators will anticipate a devaluation of the reserve currency in terms of gold, for which it is an increasingly unsatisfactory substitute, and will be prompted to move their funds out of that and other currencies into gold.

While one of these reasons for crisis concerns the demand–supply situation for monetary gold, and the other the situation of the reserve currency country, they are interlinked through the implications of a growing shortage of new supplies of monetary gold for the willingness of other countries to accumulate holdings of the reserve currency in place of gold. That interlinking in turn implies a synchronization of the drying up of new monetary gold supplies with sharply increased reluctance on the part of other countries to accumulate more of the reserve currency, and the appearance of crisis in the form of a speculative raid on the monetary gold stocks of the system by private individuals anticipating a rise in the price of gold in terms of all currencies or of the reserve currency country.

The fundamental problem posed for the world's monetary authorities by the crisis is a choice between going forward and going back along the path of transition from a commodity to a credit international reserve money. Going back means raising the price of gold in order to restore a position in which the real price of gold is high enough to ensure an adequate net supply of new monetary gold to satisfy the portfolio-balance preferences of national central banks for growing holdings of monetary gold. It does not necessarily mean a return to 'automaticity' of the international monetary system, but rather a return to a higher degree of 'anonymity' and national discretion in international monetary affairs. Going forward means a decision to accept the need to demonetize gold deliberately, to cut the link between international money and the commodity base provided by the gold standard; and this means to accept the need to devise an international reserve asset, subject to international control, that will replace both gold and national currencies held as substitutes for gold in the reserve assets of central banks. The logic of monetary theory strongly suggests the desirability of going forward, towards some sort of equivalent of a world central bank, but political economy raises the question whether the participants in the international monetary system are capable of taking this step, and, if not, whether it might not be desirable to 'reculer pour mieux sauter'. This is the question on which Roy Harrod's work on the price of gold has consistently focused.

2. *The Gold Crisis of 1968*

The analysis of the preceding section is not so much a theory of the gold exchange standard as an explanation in terms of theoretical principles of the developments that led up to the gold crisis of March 1968. The world economy entered the post-war II period with a price of gold arrived at after the breakdown of the gold exchange standard in the 1930's and a general price level roughly double that of the latter 1930's. As a result of the war, the United States was the world's greatest trading nation and prime supplier of capital for foreign investment, and as a result of the 'golden avalanche' of the 1930's its gold reserves were inordinately and indeed embarrassingly large. It was therefore natural and easy for the United States to assume the role of reserve currency country for the rest of the world. In fact that role was assumed unconsciously and without recognition of its long-term implications: the resulting redistribution of U.S. gold reserves to the rest of the world was considered desirable, and the growth of New York's international banking operations regarded as a gratifying reflection of superior efficiency.

The inevitable tensions began to appear after 1958, when the level of the U.S. deficit rose sharply from the previous $1 billion average to the $2–3 billion dollar range. Explanations of the magnitude and persistence of the deficit have abounded. Initial explanations were *ad hoc* in the extreme, concentrating on transitory events in particular export markets and developing into a generalized assertion of decreased American 'competitiveness' in foreign markets. A more theoretical version of this explanation, which has substantial expert support, is that the dollar is overvalued. Official U.S. balance-of-payments policy has increasingly been based on the view that the source of the trouble is excessive private capital exports, associated with the superior efficiency of American capital markets over European and the dynamic expansionist drive of the giant American corporations. Some commentators, especially official European critics, attribute the deficit to excessive monetary expansion, or more generally to inflationary policies, in the United States.

All of these strands of explanation can be fitted into the framework of the absorption approach; where their proponents differ is in the policy recommendations they emphasize. All of them assume that the U.S. deficit is 'supply-determined',[4] that is, that it is due to factors in the U.S. economy susceptible of correction by U.S. policy action. More recently, the view has been gaining ground that the deficit is 'demand-determined', in the sense that it is necessary to enable other countries to achieve desired growth of international reserves through balance-of-payments surpluses, and particularly that other countries would retaliate against any action the United States might take, and specifically against a devaluation of the dollar, in order to preserve these surpluses. This view is consistent with the theoretical analysis of the preceding section, though one should always be cautious about placing excessive emphasis on one blade of Marshall's scissors.

The growth of the use of the dollar as an international reserve was accompanied by the theoretically expected dwindling of new supplies of monetary gold, ending in the appearance of a net outflow from monetary gold stocks after 1965. On the demand side, private absorption of gold rose rapidly, in a series of irregular steps corresponding to political events likely to prompt speculation on the price of gold or against currencies. The Korean war was accompanied by a rise in total annual private gold absorption from $375 million to $550 million in the early fifties, whereafter it declined to the $350 million per year mark. The Suez crisis was accompanied by a rise to a $600 million annual rate; with the speculative rise in the free market price of gold in the autumn of 1960, which led to the re-linking of the monetary and private gold markets through the formation of the gold pool, annual

---

[4] The useful distinction between 'supply-determined' and 'demand-determined' theories of deficit was coined by R. Z. Aliber.

private absorption rose to $1000 million; with the Cuban crisis of 1962 the level rose to $1100 million annually, and with France's 1965 declaration of unwillingness to continue accumulating dollars, the level rose to $1500 million (average 1965–6). The figures suggest that, prior to the gold crisis period of 1967–8, private purchases of gold prompted by the expectation of an immediate increase in its price were fairly rapidly converted, in the minds of the holders or through the market, into longer-range hoards. On the supply side, gold production from pre-existing mines fell slowly but steadily through the 1950's; the rise in private demand was satisfied, consistently with net increments to monetary stocks of $600 million on average from 1953 to 1964, by the growth of output from new South African mines on the one hand, and growing gold sales by Russia on the other. Production from the new mines had eventually to reach a peak, and Russian gold sales are known to be uneconomic, since Russian costs are estimated to be about double the world price. In 1966 Russian sales stopped; total new gold production peaked out; and the net acquisition of gold by monetary authorities turned negative. The conversion of the members of the gold pool from price-supporters to price-suppressors set the stage for the gold crisis that soon resulted.

Meanwhile, as the theoretical analysis indicated, dissatisfaction with the dependence of the system on the large-scale accumulation of dollars as international reserves was mounting. This was expressed, first, in the decision taken in 1963 to explore the creation of a new international reserve asset to supplement gold and to replace the dollar and sterling in future reserve expansion. The negotiations, which eventually produced the contingency plan for Special Drawing Rights agreed on at the 1967 Rio meetings of the International Monetary Fund, were impeded by a basic disagreement between the Americans and the British, who wanted to press ahead with the creation of the new asset, and the Europeans, who wanted the new asset introduced only after the U.S. deficit had been eliminated. This difference of opinion still lurks beneath the surface. The 'demand-determined' explanation of the U.S. deficit implies that the European view is a contradiction in terms. Second, growing reluctance to hold dollars was expressed in the declaration of France in February 1965, mentioned previously, that she would henceforth accumulate her surpluses in gold, a policy which was followed to varying extents by other European countries. Robert Triffin has recently called attention[5] to this aspect of the contemporary monetary crisis, the demise of the reserve currency role of the dollar (and, even more striking, though less crucially important, of sterling). Triffin distinguishes between 'traditional' (voluntarily held) foreign exchange reserves and 'negotiated' reserves (I.M.F. claims, 'swaps', 'Roosa bonds' and similar special instruments, and sterling accumulated in rescue operations for the pound), and calculates that for the

---

[5] Triffin, 1969, especially pp. 5–7 and appendix.

North Atlantic area from the beginning of 1964 to June 1968, 'negotiated' reserves have more than tripled, increasing by $8·8 billion, while 'traditional' reserves have declined by $3·5 billion.

The reserve currency role of sterling is of course now in process of being formally liquidated under the terms of the sterling area agreements announced in Basle in September 1968.

The gold crisis of 1967–8 was touched off by the devaluation of sterling in November 1967. Taken by itself, this devaluation was an excellent demonstration of how the International Monetary Fund exchange rate system was intended to work, in permitting agreed exchange rate changes of an appropriate magnitude in cases of 'fundamental disequilibrium'. But the devaluation prompted expectations that the dollar would be the next currency to fall, expectations reinforced by a sharp deterioration in the U.S. balance of payments in the latter part of 1967. Since a devaluation of the dollar meant a rise in the dollar price of gold these expectations merged with expectations (correct as matters turned out) that the gold pool countries would have to discontinue stabilization sales of gold, and led to massive waves of private purchases of gold which finally provoked a crisis decision to terminate the gold pool and break the link between the monetary and non-monetary gold markets.

The Washington agreement of March 1968 involved a commitment of the participating central banks neither to sell gold to nor to buy gold from the private gold market.The American intention behind the agreement was clearly to contrive a situation in which the private market gold price would be forced down to or below the official price by the liquidation of the 'speculative overhang' of gold acquired in the expectation of a quick profit from a rise in its price and by the pressure of sales of newly produced gold, which according to all calculations still substantially exceeds normal commercial and artistic demand. This intention has so far (February 1969) been frustrated by continued international monetary uncertainty, especially with respect to whether the European central banks would in fact be willing to allow the free gold price to fall below the monetary price, and by the ability of South Africa to hold new supplies off the market while manœuvring for a guaranteed floor at the monetary gold price. It has become increasingly certain that the central banks will provide this guarantee.

The persistence of a free market gold price substantially above the official price reflects uncertainty stemming from the ambiguity or self-contradictiveness of the Washington agreement itself. A refusal to sell gold at the official price implies that gold is more valuable in monetary use than the official price implies; a refusal to buy gold implies that the national and international monetary authorities will be able to devise international credit money arrangements that will permit them to dispense with additional gold supplies in providing for the growth of international reserves—in other words, gradually to liquidate gold as the ultimate reserve base of the system. These two conflicting implications reflect an unresolved difference of fundamental opinions over the future of gold between the United States on the one hand and certain European central banks on the other; perhaps it would be more accurate to describe them as reflecting a tension between the logic of progression in the substitution of credit for commodity money at the international level, and national sentiment in favour of gold as a safeguard of at least some national autonomy in international economic affairs.

The present two-tier gold price system is necessarily a transitory arrangement, since this issue must be somehow resolved. There are three possible lines of development.

The first is the economically logical one of proceeding towards the demonetization of gold by the development of a new international credit reserve money. This line is the one on which the official negotiations that produced the Special Drawing Rights scheme have been working. But it is generally agreed among the academic experts that the S.D.R. scheme is inadequate, both because of uncertainties about the timing and scale of its activation and because its gold guarantee provision preserves the primacy of gold. Hence these experts have propounded various schemes for funding existing assets in the form of gold, dollars, and sterling into a new international reserve asset or account.

The second would involve recognizing the division of opinion on the question of gold by establishing two currency blocs in the system, a U.S.-centred one based on the dollar and a European one based on gold, with a floating exchange rate between them. This change could be effected unilaterally by the United States, through the imposition of an embargo on U.S. sales of monetary gold to other central banks, a step which would force other countries to choose between pegging onto the dollar and letting their currencies fluctuate in terms of the dollar, with the European countries likely to keep the rates among their currencies fixed. This step has frequently been proposed by Americans disgruntled with the balance-of-payments interventions that the United States has been forced by the pressure of European opinion to adopt in order to protect its gold reserves. The obvious danger would be that it might provoke a wave of restrictions on international trade and payments, similar to that which followed the suspension of convertibility of sterling into gold in the 1930's.[6] And, as occurred in the 1930's, the end result would probably be a return to the gold standard at a higher monetary price of gold.

---

[6] Fears that international monetary disorder of this kind would give rise to a world depression on the scale of the 1930's, however, seem almost certainly unjustified, since full employment is now a major policy objective and governments have learned the use of the policy instruments required to achieve it. Moreover, given full employment, the welfare costs of trade and payments restrictions are unlikely to be intolerably great.

The third possibility is a rise in the monetary price of gold, as allowed by the Articles of Agreement of the International Monetary Fund. While various writers (including Roy Harrod) have dwelt on the difficulties of negotiating this solution, both in the I.M.F. and with the U.S. Congress, it could in practice be effected by a personal decision of the President of the United States, which Congress would have to ratify and with which the other nations would in all probability hasten to conform. This solution would raise certain technical difficulties, notably with regard to the handling of the revaluation profits and the possibly large reflux of gold from private into official hands, and is subject to a variety of objections, some not well founded. On the other hand it would have certain advantages over the other two alternatives just mentioned.

The following section is devoted to Roy Harrod's contributions on this subject.

3. *Roy Harrod on the Gold Question*

Roy Harrod has always been a prolific writer on economic policy questions, and the adjective applies equally to his writings on the gold question. It would be an arduous task to trace all of his more popular pronouncements on the subject, and a major scholarly undertaking to analyse them with proper care for changes in emphasis and argument over the years. The present section undertakes the less ambitious task of critical summary of his major scholarly contributions to the learned journals and in book form, though it also includes references to two influential articles published in *Optima*.[7]

For this purpose, Roy Harrod's writings can be grouped according to historical period: the study of imbalance of international payments commissioned by the International Monetary Fund (1953); several contributions on the price of gold in 1958; two in 1961, of which the major one was concerned with the dollar and gold; a short article on international liquidity in *Optima* (1964); and two contributions on international monetary reform in 1966 along with which may be considered an essay published in 1968 but completed before the devaluation of sterling.

(a) *The Gold Problem Circa 1953*

The report on 'Imbalance of International Payments', commissioned by the International Monetary Fund, was projected as an inquiry into the causes of existing imbalances, but took final form as a quantitative analysis of changes in the pattern of international payments between 1936–8 and 1950–mid-1952. The change in presentation was presumably not unconnected with the un-

---

[7] *Optima* is published by the Anglo-American Corporation of South Africa, DeBeers Consolidated Mines and Chartered Consolidated Groups of Companies and circulated to shareholders in all the companies mentioned, various universities and subscribers.

expectedly heavy emphasis the author placed on the change in the real value of gold and of new monetary gold supplies:

'The author of this report came to his work with no preconception on this matter. Indeed, it was only halfway through his work that the full significance of the changed position of gold was borne in on him; from this point forward there was no choice but to place emphasis on gold, since there was no other way of describing the larger changes of pattern that have taken place' (p. 1).

The bulk of the report was concerned with the nature of the contemporary dollar problem, and with the methods and prospects of adjustment to equilibrium. The details are not of present interest; they reflect a strong tinge of the 'elasticity pessimism' of the period. The main finding was that 'if new gold supplies had borne their pre-war relation to the value of world trade, the rest of the world would have been able to pay for its deficit of 1950–2 without aid' (p. 11), and that, taking account of the outflow from the United States of private long-term capital, 'the rest of the world could, as well as paying its deficit with the United States out of its own resources, have added to its gold reserves and/or reduced restrictions on dollar imports' (p. 11). The problem of adjusting imbalances therefore was one of changing trade patterns so that, instead of the rest of the world paying for a deficit with the United States with gold, trade with the United States was balanced; and this involved a particularly difficult problem for Europe, which in the 1930's had been financing its deficit with the United States by gold earned in trade with other countries.

The analysis of the contemporary imbalance was preceded by a short but highly prophetic section on gold. Harrod described the theoretical mechanism by which the real value of gold would be adjusted upwards by deflation and downwards by inflation to enable gold to provide sufficient international reserves in the aggregate; the emergence of fears of deflation necessitated by gold shortage in the 1920's; the fortunate by-product of the international monetary collapse of the 1930's, in raising the real value of existing and new gold supplies, and the neutralization of this effect by the flow of capital to the United States; and the contemporary paucity of gold outside the United States and the slow rate of new additions to monetary gold stocks. He stated three causes for this situation, of which the first was mentioned as one cause of the other two: reduction of the goods value of gold to about four-ninths of its 1936–8 value; a fall of gold production outside the U.S.A. and U.S.S.R. in face of a rise in the volume of world trade by a third[8]; and private hoarding of more than half of the new gold produced between 1946 and 1951. He then remarked that the traditional remedy of price deflation was out of the

---

[8] Subsequently, new monetary gold supplies rose quite sharply, due to production from new South African sources, and Russian gold sales.

question: not only had opinion moved strongly against deflation, but deflation would be of value only if adopted by the United States, since its goods dominated world trade, and the requisite reduction of U.S. wages would be not only quite impracticable, but also undesirable. Nor could import restrictions solve the problem of inadequate reserves: 'in this connection it is entirely beggar-my-neighbour' (p. 4).

There follows the prophetic pronouncement:

'The dollar imbalance is such a prominent evil, and attracts so much attention, that this more fundamental cause of trouble is likely to be overlooked. Many restrictions are due to the dollar shortage, but by no means all. It may safely be said that when the dollar imbalance is remedied, the other evil will remain, unless a specific cure is found, and will continue to give rise to restrictionism' (pp. 4–5).

The section concludes with a discussion of suggestions for supplementing an insufficient supply of gold by some gold substitute: bancor, the gold exchange standard ('the dollar would be a thoroughly acceptable currency for this purpose, but in present conditions it is as hard to obtain as the gold in Fort Knox' (p. 5)), sterling, and E.P.U. units of account. Significantly for the time and the sponsor, but surprisingly in the light of hindsight, no mention is made of the possibility of expanding I.M.F. quotas; instead, Harrod concluded 'while these *ad hoc* expedients may serve a useful purpose for the time being, there is no doubt that in due course it will be desirable to devise a radical cure for the gold standard' (p. 5).

(b) *The Gold Problem Circa 1958*

Though Harrod's report for the International Monetary Fund was presented as a quantitative analysis of changes in international payments patterns since the pre-war II period, it clearly implied recommendation of a rise in the price of gold as a solution to the problem of international imbalance. As such it encountered considerable hostility, on grounds that Harrod summarized in his next important contribution to the subject, a statement of the case for restoring the goods value of gold by raising the dollar price of gold proportionally to the rise in the dollar price of goods, presented in a lecture in Johannesburg in January 1958 and subsequently published in the *South African Journal of Economics*. He referred to the 'moral animus' apparent in these criticisms, which centred on the irrationality of paying more 'to people who dig out of the ground a substance destined only to be locked up in a safe' (p. 4)—the waste of resources argument— and on the American view that an increase in the gold price would merely be another 'hand-out' and that selective handouts would be preferable. Harrod rightly noted that this second argument assumed that the Americans had all the gold they needed, and opined that this situation might not long continue.

Harrod began his case with the proposition that adequate reserves are essential if the development of world trade is not to be impeded by import restrictions or excessively deflationary policies. In rebuttal of the contention that this might encourage inflationary policies, he argued that though this might occur in a few relatively backward countries, the argument greatly underrated the sense of responsibility of modern governments; and he made the clinching (but somewhat inconsistent) point that inadequacy of reserves had not prevented the postwar inflation.

He then turned to the argument that '*homo sapiens* has now reached a level of civilization in which it should be beneath his dignity to rely upon a physical substance, such as gold, for his ultimate medium of settlement' (p. 7) and could instead print paper in the right quantity.

He dismissed a World Bank of Issue as requiring so much centralized disciplinary power as to be Utopian at present. While he welcomed partial substitutes for gold as helping to preserve the role of gold, he argued that the holding of other countries' currencies as reserves has proved less useful than expected by the Geneva Conference, because the countries whose currencies are so held look at their net position and will try to cover their monetary liabilities with additional gold reserves. The United States had not attempted this yet, but the position of the United States was precarious, since it depended on externally held dollars being small in relation to gold reserves, and if the net figure fell there would be trouble. While I.M.F. Drawing Rights contributed to liquidity, they were less useful than gold owing to the fixed repayment terms.

Returning to the role of gold, Harrod rejected the argument that inflation, and not the gold position, should be blamed for the failure of the value of monetary gold to match the value of trade, on the argument that the inflation was the inevitable consequence of war and could not be reversed. He pointed out that the increase in gold and foreign exchange reserves outside the United States, which had ameliorated the situation, was attributable to two temporary factors unlikely to be repeated: the great pile-up of sterling balances consequent on British methods of war finance, and a gold surplus in United States reserves which allowed her to see a great pile-up of external liabilities with equanimity. The shortage of gold was due not only to past inflation but to insufficient current output, and makeshift resort to gold substitutes could not continue. A rise in the price of gold would both increase the value of world stocks and stimulate new output and discourage private hoarding.

In Harrod's view,

'It is simply a question now of breaking down certain prejudices' (p. 10).

'Thus the collective wisdom of mankind has assigned a certain role to gold. No one can claim that any complete substitute has been devised or is in prospect of being devised. So that is where we stand. It may not be a perfect device, but on the whole it is a remarkably good one. What could be more stupid than to have achieved this and to spoil the whole thing by refusing to assign a sufficient value to this medium, with the consequence that it can only play its part in a limping manner?' (p. 11).

The prejudices that had to be overcome were of course American. Harrod finished his lecture by pointing out that if the American deficit continued, a rise in the gold price would involve the Americans in no unselective hand-outs at all, and commented:

'It is an odd thing that the Americans should be so keen on multilateralism, and yet be unwilling to take the one step—raising the dollar price of gold—which could make the multilateral system permanently viable (p. 11).

'It is odd also that a nation should have the power to double the commodity value of her own reserve by a mere stroke of the pen, to the applause of the whole world, and yet be unwilling to do so' (p. 12).

If, on the other hand, the United States again developed a surplus, it could claim to be giving unselective hand-outs in gold purchased at a higher price; but, Harrod argued, it would in reality be postponing the necessity for other nations to discriminate against its trade. He concluded by referring to the ideological resistance: 'It is a conflict between plain common-sense and the vague and obscure' (p. 12) which must be brought into the open.

The lecture evoked a series of critical comments from Mr. L. Katzen, and an extensive rejoinder from Harrod.[9] The details of the interchange, which centred on the selection of a proper base-date for measuring gold reserve adequacy and on the interpretation of numerous facts of experience, are not worth recording. But Harrod was led to comment on the proposed increase in I.M.F. quotas at that time as follows:

'It is not feasible to increase international liquidity through the I.M.F. at the rate that it would increase in a perfectly ordinary way if the value of gold were readjusted. To offset the shrinking value of gold in relation to world trade, one would probably require an increase of quotas in the I.M.F. by about 50 per cent every year; and that clearly is not feasible' (p. 22).

Roy Harrod was led to further remarks on the gold price question in a review article of Robert Triffin's *Europe and the Money Muddle*. He took umbrage at Triffin's dismissal of the proposal to increase the dollar price of gold in a sentence ridiculing the process of disinterring gold only to re-inter it in 'gold graves':

'This is unadulterated prejudice and obscurantism. The main benefit of raising the price of gold would lie in the revaluation of existing stocks, the second in reducing the "disappearance" of gold into private hoards; higher production comes third. If liquidity is important, why should the devotion of a minute proportion of human labour to providing it be "barren"? Is all the work of all the clerks who ply their pens in banks also barren?' (p. 538).

[9] Katzen, 1959, and Harrod, 1959.

It may be observed that the prejudice and obscurantism is not all on one side: the effect of raising the price on the value of existing stocks is economically the same as if new international credit money were created; gold production *is* a waste of resources, justifiable only if there is no feasible alternative via the creation of credit money; and the gold standard requires no fewer clerks in banks, but additional staff in the form of guards and metal handlers, quite apart from those engaged in gold mining. Harrod was correct, however, in pointing out that the Triffin proposal for nations to place deposits at the I.M.F. would not increase net liquidity, and might be insufficient to offset the loss of liquidity due to the diminished real value of monetary gold stocks.

Harrod's final contribution on the question of gold in this period, an article in *Optima* entitled (it is to be hoped by the editor rather than himself), 'Why the Dollar Price of Gold Must Rise', is rather disappointing in quality by comparison with his previous and subsequent work on the subject. He began by arguing that a comparison with 1937 was likely to underestimate the contemporary shortage of gold, and then produced calculations to show that if the dollar price of gold had been raised so as to offset the deterioration of the goods value of the dollar, most but not all of the world liquidity shortage would have been solved; and that if (a) ex-Soviet gold production had remained at the 1937–40 level, (b) the private sector had absorbed only normal industrial usage plus a small amount of hoarding, (c) countries had been willing to carry the same ratio of foreign exchange reserves to a larger gold reserve that they actually carried, the international liquidity position would have been fractionally better in 1957 than in 1937. The figures are then recast to show a shortfall of $76,550 million in gold reserves, offset by a contribution of only $5,000 million from an above-trend increase in foreign exchange holdings; and these magnitudes are asserted to show that new international institutions could not conceivably solve the problem, quite apart from the fact that new reserves so credited would not be net additional reserves. Harrod next argues that, recent experience apparently to the contrary, a doubling of the gold price would probably result in the value of new annual accretions to the monetary gold stock matching the demand, though he would prefer 'an increase in the dollar price of gold by two-and-a-half times, or even a rise to the convenient figure of $100 an ounce' (p. 126).

The remainder of the article tackled the question of what the pressures on the United States would be in future, to induce the American authorities to raise the gold price, this question being set in the context of an expectation of continued world recession. If the recession continued and improved the U.S. balance of payments, there might be proposals for new international agencies to channel capital outwards; but Harrod argued that the United States would be more likely to channel capital inwards in this case, to domestic relief, and that in any case the quantitative effect would be small by comparison with that of a rise in the gold price. If either expansion came, or recession worsened the U.S. balance of payments, the U.S. net reserve would sink towards zero and the gold price would have to be increased. In that case, speculation against the dollar might accelerate the revaluation (Harrod did not distinguish between private and official speculation here). In conclusion, Harrod returned to the question of ideological prejudice, with specific reference to prospective Russian gains. 'To deny so great a benefit to the rest of the world, in order to avoid giving gain to the Russians, is surely rather curmudgeonly in peace time' (p. 127). In case of a war long enough to matter, a rise in the price of gold would benefit more the Americans or the Russians according to which were trading with the major part of the neutral world. Harrod argued, however, against the at least superficially wisest policy of waiting until war actually occurred to raise the price of gold, that this 'would savour of sharp practice and might not be acceptable to neutrals' (p. 127).

The article concludes:

'In his funny, tortuous way man is a rational being. What is so eminently rational as an increase in the dollar price of gold must surely come in due course' (p. 127).

Such an appeal to the inevitability of the rational solution constitutes a rather weak case for the prediction of a change as radical as a doubling or more of the price of gold, especially when the rational solution has been arrived at by excluding other solutions equally rational in their own frames of reference on the grounds of infeasibility. The commentator on economic policy has a hard course to steer between recommendation of the most rational policy within a defined set of policy constraints, and prediction that his recommendation will have to be accepted by the policy makers. In this case, Roy Harrod (or his editor), confused the issue by blurring the distinction between analysis of a situation and prediction of its outcome.

(c) *The Gold Problem Circa 1961*

Roy Harrod's contributions to the analysis of the gold problem in this period comprise some brief but percipient remarks in the course of a review article on Robert Triffin's *Gold and the Dollar Crisis*, and a contribution to the volume edited by Seymour Harris on *The Dollar in Crisis*.

The review of Triffin's book is primarily devoted to a perceptive critique of the Triffin plan for liquidating sterling and dollar reserves by depositing them in an I.M.F. converted effectively into a world central bank, the critique focusing on the consequent reduction of net reserves 'under the fist' of the national central banks. In relation to gold, its theme is that the plan could not solve the existing deficiency of international liquidity, and should be considered as a corollary of a rise in the dollar price of gold, designed to provide for adequate subsequent growth of reserves. In this connection,

Harrod produced some effective counter-arguments to Triffin's rejection of a rise in the price of gold: the price increase would not have to be repeated, because a higher price would increase the value of annual production at least proportionally; a temporary excess of reserves would be absorbed by the increase in trade (and, though Harrod did not say so here, should be sterilizable); the initial benefits would indeed be distributed haphazardly, but so have been loans and would be I.M.F. investments, and in any case the important point is the effect of greater liquidity in increasing world trade and investment. His most important point concerned the notion that a rise in the price of gold would give a present to the U.S.S.R. and South Africa:

'It is very obscure why an operation, which gives the U.S.S.R. a certain present but simultaneously gives the free world a much larger one, is said to benefit the U.S.S.R.

'As for South Africa, the benefit would go, in the first instance, to the gold mining companies. If it is desired to mitigate racial discrimination there, the more power that these companies, which on the whole have very enlightened leadership, have in South Africa the better. The benefit would go in the second instance to the Bantus, who work in mines; the gold companies are enlightened employers and would certainly pay more if they could afford to. . . . These Bantu mineworkers save most of their earnings, and when they return home with their money, they take a more commercial view of agriculture. . . . Nothing could do so much to improve the racial relations in South Africa as rendering the underprivileged more economically viable and therefore better able to stand up for themselves' (pp. 201–2).

The theory of wage determination in South Africa assumed in the last paragraph is a paternalistic one in conflict with general economic theory; but either competition or monopsony in the labour market would produce the same result of better conditions for the Bantu—if, of course, the gains were not counteracted by government policy, an eventuality for which there is some evidence from recent South African policy.[10] That eventuality apart, the remarks quoted penetrate to the heart of a proper economic analysis, which would indicate that side-payments may be well worth while if they increase one's own benefit from the game, and that if one believes in economic discrimination as an implement of policy it is important to determine who bears the burden of discrimination.

Harrod's contribution to the Seymour Harris volume, on 'The Dollar Problem and Gold Question,' begins with an extensive argument to the effect that the contemporary problems of the U.S. and U.K. deficits and the German surplus all exemplify a problem of overall reserve shortage, which obliges countries to adopt remedial measures of various kinds before they have had time to consider them properly. The chapter then proceeds to

[10] Hirsch, 1968.

discuss 'the case for a rise in the dollar value of gold'. Harrod describes this, somewhat misleadingly, as a 'devaluation'. The argument draws heavily on the writings previously discussed, in respect of the *prima facie* case constituted by the fall in the goods value of gold, the unlikelihood of foreign exchange continuing to supplement gold, the need for reserves adequate enough not to force countries into policy changes not required by their internal situations, the necessity of viewing schemes such as Triffin's as posterior to a rise in the price of gold and consequent restoration of adequacy of existing reserves, the benefits to the United States of greater world liquidity, and the question of the present to Russia involved. In this last context, the desirability of having 'a reserve under one's fist' in the event of war is stressed. The case for solving the racial problem in South Africa by raising the gold price rather than by futile protests against discrimination is more heavily stressed. The counter-argument against the contention that the benefits of gold appreciation would be randomly distributed, namely that the benefits of a Triffin scheme would not go to the most needy, but would instead go to those with 'absorptive capacity' or developed capital markets, is stated more emphatically than in the review article. The doubt about the quantitative scale of the increase in liquidity possible by expansion of the I.M.F. is restated.

A novel point is, however, introduced which builds on a brief paragraph in the Johannesburg lecture (p. 7) on the implications for freedom and discipline of owned as against borrowed reserves:

'Any scheme of the Triffin sort would involve repeated applications to some international committee, on a rising scale year by year. I am a liberal, and still adhere to the ancient British liberal creed that bureaucratic committees are apt to be foolish and tiresome. In the modern world we have to impose far wider responsibilities on governmental agencies than the mere maintenance of laws and justice. . . . But I would not increase the power of bureaucracy where the result can be achieved without it. On such difficult questions as monetary policy and liquidity, the sublime voice of the demos is not likely to make itself effective. Thus the bureaucracy becomes an autocracy.

'From a liberal point of view I therefore regard it as a far better thing that liquidity should be increased by giving to each country more reserve in the form of more gold (or reliable foreign exchange) under its own fist, than by giving it an opportunity of constantly having to renegotiate loans, on an ever larger scale, with an international committee. Gold—"that anonymous asset", as Sir Ralph Hawtrey once called it!! is the greatest sheet anchor of liberty in the economic world. If you have gold under your fist, you are a free man. If you have to argue with an international committee, you are not. . . .

'This has been a plea on the side of liberty. But on the other side, too, on the side of discipline, there is much to be said for gold in the long run. If a nation has its own gold (or foreign exchange) reserve, it will be pleased to have it, and in due course will learn how to observe such self-discipline as may be required to retain it. But if a nation's so-called liquid asset is derived from a loan, to be renegotiated each year, it may be much more likely to allow itself to slip into a position of doubtful solvency, so that international authority is more or less forced to extend, or even increase, the loan. Self-discipline is much more effective than attempts by an international committee to impose discipline' (pp. 61–62).

(d) *The Gold Problem in 1964*

In 1963, the United States reversed its stand on the need for additional international liquidity, and the 'Roosa Committee' was set up at the Tokyo meeting of the International Monetary Fund to work on the problem of devising arrangements to provide it. Roy Harrod's article in *Optima*, published in September 1964, entitled 'New Thinking Needed in International Liquidity' was his response to the problem, and in many respects his most statesmanlike pronouncement on the subject.

The article begins by commenting on the oddity of the fact that the decision to study such a fundamental problem was evoked by a reversal of the U.S. position occasioned by the deterioration of the U.S. balance of payments in the second quarter of 1963, which deterioration was corrected by new policy measures in the third quarter. Harrod attributed this to the difficulty that the official mind encounters in recognizing a new problem. It had never before been anyone's responsibility 'to determine the sum total of world reserves required for the smooth financing of international trade and investment' (p. 177). Under the gold standard liquidity was automatically adjusted to requirements by price level movements; this mechanism pre-supposed tolerance of unemployment, and downward price flexibility, and was facilitated by the relatively greater importance of primary products (flexibly priced) as compared with industrial products (administratively priced). 'This passing away of the old self-regulatory system has thrown to the surface a new problem and a new responsibility' (p. 177).

The arguments for the existence of a shortage of international liquidity were, first, that the ratio of the total of gold, sterling, dollars, and I.M.F. gold tranches to the dollar value of world trade were under 50 per cent of the corresponding ratio before the Second World War—the objective of providing more liquidity than then existed, through the I.M.F., 'has been totally frustrated owing to the diminishing value of an ounce of gold' (p. 178). Second, more rather than less reserves were now desirable, because governments had assumed responsibility for full employment and abjured import restrictions in favour of freer trade; hence imbalances would be corrected more slowly, and since balance-of-payments swings were unlikely to be smaller in the future than in the past, more reserves in proportion to trade turnover would be necessary.

Harrod then refers to the reasons for his 15-year advocacy of a rise in the price of gold. One reason is its simplicity: 'all other remedies require complicated and largely untried arrangements' (p. 178). Another is that changing the gold price permits a large increase, whereas:

'with the other arrangements, the obstacles to a large increase are much greater than the obstacles to a small increase. I have never recommended a change in the price of gold as the *sole* reform that is needed: I regard it as a necessary base for other improvements: to get the *whole* increase in liquidity that is required by means of those other improvements would be to place an intolerable strain upon them' (p. 178).

A further consideration is 'a point of fairness': the fixing of the monetary gold price is 'an extreme form of monopoly'; in no other case would 'a monopolistic group of employers in a particular industry hold wages fixed, when wages in all other industries have more than doubled' (p. 178). Harrod does not put much weight on this argument, however, by comparison with the wider issues. This is as well, since the argument is specious, both in drawing a comparison with wages, rather than profits, or rents (since the fixity of the gold price affects the profitability of mining, or the value of gold-yielding property, rather than the wages of potential mine-workers), and in ignoring the fact that at that time the central banks had historically been supporting the price of gold above the equilibrium private market price.

Harrod then digresses briefly on the solitariness of his position, which he distinguishes sharply from that on the one hand of those who, like Rueff and Heilperin, want to return to a semi-automatic gold standard system (an objective which he regards as both unrealistic and retrograde); and on the other hand of those who regard a rise in the gold price as irrational and would prefer to provide increased liquidity by 'printing bits of paper' (p. 179).

'The case for raising the price of gold should rest on two propositions. (1) More liquidity is probably needed now, and certainly will be needed in the near future, if we are to be saved from the evils of world-wide deflation, on the one hand, or growing trade restrictions, on the other. (2) Raising the price of gold is the simplest and most manageable method of getting the increase of liquidity. There is no reason to deny that in a certain sense it would be more "rational" to get what one wants by printing pieces of paper. But one then has to face up to the difficulties of who authorizes the printing of the paper and how is it to be distributed among the nations of the world? It is only when one tries to answer those two questions in detail that one appreciates how enormous the difficulties are.

'Nevertheless, I think that it is wrong to take an entirely negative attitude to plans for printing pieces of paper. Even if it were decided to raise the price of gold, such plans might be desirable as supplementary measures. Raising the price of gold should be a once-over job, a re-adjustment required by the inflation of the dollar (and of other currencies) during and after the Second World War. We do not want to contemplate a recurrent raising of the price of gold, since such a prospect would undermine confidence in currencies in an unfortunate way' (p. 179).

The two remedies should not be regarded as rivals: 'the important thing is to get people thinking in terms of the need for more liquidity' (p. 179). In this spirit, Harrod set himself the task of 'working out plans for printing pieces of paper'. He rejected the alternative of developing existing techniques of central bank co-operation, in terms which reflect the practical and liberal emphasis of his support for raising the price of gold. The great virtue of these techniques was that they had been *ad hoc*, relatively secret, and based on mutual confidence. Would public opinion accept their consolidation into formal legislated arrangements for central bank extension of large lines of credit to all other central banks? Would not the lines of credit be confined to the Group of Ten, constituting one law for the rich and another for the poor? Would other countries' deficits be financed by holders of their currencies as readily as the deficits of the United States?

'If we are to have a *system*, it must apply mutually, whether among all industrial countries or the whole world: it would not do to have a system which merely propped the dollar at such times as it was in difficulties, providing no corresponding props for the other currencies' (p. 180).

'For this reason I believe that thinking must move to the view that the main job will have to be done by the International Monetary Fund itself' (p. 181).

Harrod then proposed that drawing rights should be made unconditionally available as of right, that Fund holdings of currencies should be terminated (thereby eliminating some serious technical problems in Fund operations, as well as making quotas a genuine addition to international liquidity), that there should be an immediate large increase in the quotas, and that thereafter there should be annual increases in quotas, agreed on in advance, to keep pace with the growth of world trade. He rejects Triffin's plan for depositing dollar and sterling balances in the Fund, but argues for the Fund giving some marginal support to these currencies to give these countries greater freedom of domestic policy.

(e) *The Gold Problem in 1965–7*

The chapter on 'Gold' in Roy Harrod's book *Reforming the World's Money*[11] is his most extensive contribution on the subject. However, as many of the points made are presented in virtually the same form in his earlier publications, this summary will be brief, concentrating on novel points made.

As in earlier contributions, Harrod is aware that he confronts manifold and strong prejudices on the subject, and begins by attempting to dispel them. Raising the price of gold is presented as neither a panacea nor as indispensable to world monetary reform, but as a helpful first step. True, providing

---

[11] Harrod, Chapter 3, pp. 58–85.

international money by mining gold is irrational, but if it is the only way to do so it must be considered productive. The intention is not to revert to a semi-automatic gold standard. On the prejudice against giving a 'present' to the U.S.S.R., he argues that since the non-Communist world holds and produces more gold than Russia, the former would get the larger present and the net advantage, also that peaceful co-existence makes this objection less relevant. (This argument is less persuasive than some of his previous ones, since a present to one's rivals is different from a present to one's friends; the better argument is that the former present is trivial by comparison with the gains from an improved monetary system.) On the prejudice against a present to South Africa, he brings in the new point that a rise in the gold price would act contrarily to South Africa's objective of economic diversification, and summarizes his previous arguments as follows:

'In the long run, self-help is likely to do much more for improving the status of under-privileged peoples than outside agitation on their behalf. If you give them more wages, they will find means of bettering themselves on the social, as well as the economic, plane' (p. 62).

The most serious mental block Harrod sees is the attitude of the Americans, which involves a point of prestige and a point of honour.

On the humiliation of devaluation, Harrod points out that a rise in the price of gold is not a devaluation in relation to other currencies, that the real humiliation, if such, occurred when the dollar lost value in terms of goods, a blameless consequence of war in a great cause, and that a rise in the dollar price of gold would be merely an official recognition of facts. On the point of honour—the repeated assurances by the U.S. Administration that the price of gold would not be changed—Harrod argues that such assurances have to be made without a time limit to quell speculation, but that Americans have no moral right to bind the rest of the world in a matter of common concern, and that the assurances therefore should not be regarded as binding or as obliging the United States to compensate foreign dollar holders for a change in the gold price. The gentlemen's agreements by which foreign central banks hold more dollars than they would otherwise choose might imply an obligation to compensate their losses on the excess, but it is arguable that no compensation is morally required because the goods value of dollars would not be impaired.

To avoid speculation on further revaluations, Harrod recommends that the revaluation should be presented as a once-over job, a delayed tidying-up operation, with strong assurances that no further revaluation would be undertaken except in the event of a major world economic upheaval; and that all future reserve increases should be effected by the other methods outlined in his book.

Harrod then takes up the question of uneven distribution of benefits: 'it is surely better to have unevenly distributed benefits than no benefits at all' (p. 72), and no one will actually lose. The initial benefit is anyway not the main benefit, which would consist in permitting a more forceful growth policy in the United States (Harrod's writings on gold are typically flawed by excessive attention to the immediate conjuncture). And the benefits could be fairly distributed by giving the less developed countries a small percentage of the revaluation profits.

Harrod next discusses the preference of central banks and officials for conditional credit facilities instead of a higher gold price, motivated not by sympathy for the gold miners but by the desire for more extensive 'surveillance'. Harrod points out that this

'raises very wide questions about the correct borderline between world government of some sort and national independence. Is there not a proper place for each? What I would suggest is that the separate countries should have a certain quantum of means of settlement completely under their own control, which would give them liberty of action entirely at their own discretion within reasonable limits. Then, beyond this, further accommodation should be available through international agencies to meet cases of special difficulty from time to time. In regard to the latter, the international agency would be entirely justified in requiring some surveillance, and even in imposing conditions. Thus a line could be fairly drawn between autonomy and world government' (p. 75).

Instead, Harrod argues, the central bankers have confused the needs for owned reserves and for additional international accommodation in special cases:

'To put the matter in an unkind way, one might say that congenital interferers are taking this opportunity to muscle in. . . . They want to apply surveillance, and possibly control, . . . to deficits which in times past nations have been able to deal with according to their own ideas out of owned reserves. This is definitely a plan for encroachment and not simply one for the provision of supplementary facilities' (p. 76).

Harrod is averse to having international agencies take over control of domestic monetary policies, because the agencies would be dominated by central bankers, who would subordinate growth policies to monetary policy, and would also tend to work by general principles, whereas national growth problems differ widely. Price stability should be subordinate to growth, but central bankers do not think that way; and it is unlikely either that they will learn, or that other policy-makers will be given a large share in surveillance.

Harrod then enquires whether unconditional drawing rights could take the place of gold as a bulwark of national autonomy; his answer is no, because association with an international agency must imply some conditions. Hence his recommended compromise of reasonable owned reserves and conditional further accommodation. ('I regard gold as a sheet anchor of liberty' (p. 80).) In any case, it may be difficult to get a sufficient increase in 'paper money', because if such assets are increased too rapidly, countries would be unwilling to accept them as being as good as gold.

In the concluding pages of the chapter, Harrod discusses the counter-argument that people will not accept a change in the price of gold, and argues that the situation might change, in either of two ways. First, the Group of Ten might become convinced of the need for a change; in that case, the pre-sumed veto of the U.S. Congress would be outflanked by a vast speculative run on gold, refusal of the American authorities to pay out gold, a rise in the free market price, and eventual stabilization at a fixed higher price. Second, without such conviction of the need for change, rumours of dissension among the Group of Ten on the issue might produce the same sequence of a specula-tive run on gold, suspension of gold payments by the Americans, a rise in the gold price, and eventual official acquiescence in 'a *status quo* produced by world market forces' (p. 84). Harrod concludes his analysis by stating: 'I believe that, in the long run, the market forces will in fact win' (p. 75).

Harrod's second sequence, except for the last stage of it, occurred within two years of his analysis, sooner than his readers might have expected from his rather tentative discussion. A major reason for this was a factor never recognized in his analysis, owing to his consistent practice of comparing the contemporary with the pre-war situation: the gradual dwindling to zero of new supplies of monetary gold and the emergence of excess private demand for gold, in consequence of world growth and price inflation. But the final stage—official acceptance of an increased monetary price of gold—may or may not turn out as he assumed. The outcome will depend on whether the control bankers and officials can create a paper money substitute for gold on a large yet credible scale—an issue on which Harrod has always expressed scepticism.

Roy Harrod touched briefly on the question of gold and its price in two other recent publications that should be mentioned in this review of his contributions. In the first annual Scottish Economic Society Lecture (Glasgow, November 1965) on 'International Liquidity', a lecture mainly devoted to disputing the desirability and feasibility of prompt international adjustment, advocating an incomes policy as the best adjustment policy, and discussing alternative proposals for providing increased international liquidity, he re-marked:

'For many years I have advocated raising the price of gold, at least to give reconstruction a good start. To me it seems to be a mere matter of common sense. The gold values of currencies should be adjusted to their loss of commodity value since 1939.

'My interest in gold is partly due to a rather profound scepticism about whether we shall get an adequate increase in liquidity in any other way. In my book I proposed changes in non-gold reserve media which are far more moderate and closer to existing reality than those embodied in the other schemes that have been most discussed. Nonetheless I have been told by a learned and very kindly reviewer . . . that I am "out of touch with the scope of possible improvement". I believe that to be so. Hence I pin my faith to a rise in the price of gold which could occur in the market without any "by your leave" from the all-powerful authorities' (p. 199).

In his pamphlet *Dollar–Sterling Collaboration*, discussing the relative decline in the use of gold in international settlements, he disputed the view of some experts that this betokens a diminution of the role of gold premonitory of its eventually ceasing to play any important part:

'The matter can, however, be interpreted somewhat differently. It may be an indication that some countries continue to prefer gold to other instruments of reserve. This would be an illustration of Gresham's Law that "bad money drives out good". . . . To the extent that this is a correct interpretation . . . it means that the international authorities have still got work to do, to prevent other instruments for international settlement being regarded as less eligible than gold' (p. 8).

4. *Concluding Observations*

Roy Harrod's contributions on the gold question speak for themselves, and after the preceding lengthy review there is little point in attempting a summary. Certain summary evaluative comments seem however to be worth making.

First, Harrod obviously deserves great credit for calling attention, as long ago as 1953, to the fundamental role of the diminished real value of gold as a cause of international monetary difficulties, and for keeping it in the forefront of his analysis. On the other hand, his habit of always arguing on the basis of a comparison of the contemporary with the pre-war II situation led him to overlook the dynamic implications of world growth and inflation in attenuating new monetary gold supplies to the vanishing point. Nor is there any development in his work of the recently popular view that, in the absence of additional gold or other acceptable reserves, a continuing United States deficit may be necessary to provide the world with the additional liquidity it needs for steady growth. Further, the essentially monetary nature of his case for a rise in the price of gold has been occasionally obnubilated by forms of argument implying an appeal to the principle of parity prices for gold producers. Perhaps this was an aberration induced by consciousness of the particular audiences he was addressing; certainly his more recent analyses address themselves to the central monetary issues.

Second, Harrod commands admiration for his courage in being willing to state and re-state his case for an increase in the dollar price of gold, in the full knowledge that he would encounter strongly emotional hostile reactions both from Americans devoted to the $35 per ounce price and from international monetary experts convinced of the irrationality of the gold standard, and that at the same time he courted the risk of being identified with proponents of monetary automatism with whom he disagreed violently on other questions of economic policy. In addition, he has used economic theory and logic expertly (though occasionally with minor slips) to dispose of opposition prejudices. This is especially true of opposition based on aversion to giving 'presents' to the Russians and the South African Government.

Finally, in his most recent writings on the subject, he has concentrated on the central issue involved in the choice between raising the price of gold once-for-all and replacing gold by international credit money. This issue concerns the determination of the proper and acceptable line between national autonomy and world institutions. Harrod, as a liberal, argues for the presence of abundant gold as a guarantor of national autonomy, and for the confinement of conditional credit availability to special cases. Others—central banks and officials, and some academic experts with official experience—prefer the route of collaboration and surveillance. The issue raises questions at two levels: what kind of an international economic community of nations is desirable in principle?; and, what kind of a community are nations in fact likely to be able to establish? While each is eager enough to exercise surveillance over the others, none appears really willing to yield to an international agency the degree of sovereignty that a world central bank solution to the problem of international liquidity would require. On that fundamental uncertainty hinges the question of whether Roy Harrod's long-sustained advocacy of a rise in the price of gold will turn out to have been a far-sighted prediction or a short-sighted though well-reasoned hankering after a return to a historical golden age of liberalism combined with national independence, such as may be held to have obtained in the period before the First World War and to have been re-established, albeit precariously, in the nineteen-twenties.

REFERENCES

HARROD, R. F., 'Imbalance of International Payments', *International Monetary Fund Staff Papers*, Vol. 3, No. 1, April 1953, pp. 1–46.

——, 'The Role of Gold Today', *South African Journal of Economics*, Vol. 26, No. 1, March 1958, pp. 3–13.

——, 'Europe and the Money Muddle', *Economic Journal*, Vol. 68, No. 271, September 1958, pp. 534–8.

——, 'Why the Dollar Price of Gold Must Rise', *Optima*, Vol. 8, No. 3, September 1958, pp. 120–7.

——, 'Rejoinder to Mr. Katzen', *South African Journal of Economics*, Vol. 27, No. 1, March 1959, pp. 16–22.

——, 'A Plan for Increasing Liquidity: A Critique', *Economica*, Vol. 28, No. 110, May 1961, pp. 195–202.

——, 'The Dollar Problem and the Gold Question', pp. 46–62 in S. E. Harris (ed.) *The Dollar in Crisis* (New York and Burlingame, 1963).

——, 'New Thinking Needed on International Liquidity', *Optima*, Vol. 14, No. 3, September 1964, pp. 176–82.

——, *Reforming the World's Money* (London and New York, 1966).

——, 'International Liquidity', *Scottish Journal of Political Economy*, Vol. 13, No. 2, June 1966, pp. 189–204.

——, *Dollar–Sterling Collaboration: Basis for Initiative* (London, 1968).

HIRSCH, F., 'Influence on Gold Production', *International Monetary Fund Staff Papers*, Vol. 15, No. 2, November 1968, pp. 405–90.

JOHNSON, H. G., 'The Gold Rush of 1968 in Retrospect and Prospect', presented at the 1968 meetings of the American Economic Association and published in the May 1969 issue of the *American Economic Review*.

KATZEN, L., 'The Role of Gold Today—A Comment', *South African Journal of Economics*, Vol. 27, No. 1, March 1959, pp. 9–15.

TRIFFIN, R., 'International Monetary Co-operation in Asia and the Far East', paper for Second Pacific Trade and Development Conference, East-West Center, Honolulu, 8–11 January 1969.

19

FOREIGN TRADE AND INVESTMENT CRITERIA*

VIJAY JOSHI

1. *Introduction*

THERE is by now a large body of literature on criteria for project evaluation in the presence of 'distortions' which lead to a divergence between market prices and social benefits and costs. Early writings in this field concentrated fairly exclusively on allowing for distortions in the markets for labour and capital in the context of a closed economy.[1] More recently, the disenchantment with indiscriminate import-substitution in L.D.C.s has generated an interest in the effects of non-optimal foreign trade policies on resource allocation. Some attempts have therefore been made to devise methods which take proper account of the international trading opportunities of an economy in the optimal selection of industries and projects. In what follows, I propose to give a brief critical account of these methods, pointing out their relationships to each other and to economic theory.

It must be emphasized at the outset that project evaluation criteria have to strike a balance between theoretical sophistication on the one hand and practical relevance and usability on the other. It is nevertheless useful to begin the discussion at the level of abstract, general theorizing. The reason for this is that, in the absence of much practical experience in using these criteria, the distinction between a purely theoretical consideration and a consideration of real relevance is largely a matter of judgement. A preliminary theoretical discussion helps one to see clearly the simplifying assumptions involved in using these criteria. Whether and to what extent these assumptions are likely to lead to misleading results is an open question. I must emphasize that my discussion of the various methods is brief and simplified and does not in some cases do justice to the subtlety of thought of their exponents. I intend only to make some essential points and to indicate the areas where much further work remains to be done.

* I am grateful to Sudhir Anand, Max Corden, Ian Little, and Maurice Scott for useful conversations. They are not responsible for errors which remain.

[1] As late as 1967, the otherwise excellent book by Marglin devotes no more than a cursory page to the shadow price of foreign exchange (Marglin, 1967).

2. A Simple Model

The technique of project analysis consists of valuing inputs and outputs at 'shadow prices' which are accurate indicators of social benefits and costs. The idea is that this will allow only those projects to be undertaken which are socially profitable. To understand the meaning of shadow prices in an open economy consider a very simple case which nevertheless makes a surprising number of important points. Imagine an economy which satisfies the assumptions of the standard two-good two-factor model with the usual convexity properties. To simplify even further assume that this economy is a perfect competitor in international trade. Assume that any divergences between private and social benefits and costs can be eliminated by appropriate tax/subsidy measures. Given this information, the entire optimal configuration of production, consumption, exports and imports is determined. Going further, in this simple model the optimal pattern of production is determined *independently* of the pattern of demand. Once the terms of trade are given, the 'production point' is given though the 'consumption point' can of course vary. Furthermore, the entire optimal structure of relative prices is determined. Relative commodity prices are of course the same as the given terms of trade; relative factor prices are determined as soon as the 'production point' is known. If we now choose any one of these prices as the *numéraire*, all the other prices can be expressed in terms of it. These prices are of course the 'shadow prices' which tell us the marginal social value of each resource in the optimum situation measured in terms of the *numéraire*. If such an economy happened to be in a non-optimal situation, the task of the planning authorities would consist of persuading profit-maximizing producers (or Lange–Lerner bureaucrats) to use these derived shadow prices in their profitability calculations. This could be done either by tax/subsidy measures or by direct instruction. Social utility could then be maximized *in a separate step* by trading at the given terms of trade. The simplicity of this model is preserved even if we introduce intermediate goods so long as they are all traded; this is intuitively obvious but can be rigorously proved.[2] Nor is the admission of time damaging to the model. In principle, the optimal time-path of production is independent of the intertemporal utility function though one would of course expect shadow prices to be changing over time.[3]

3. The Shadow Exchange Rate

The important thing about shadow prices is that they represent the correct *relative* valuations associated with the optimum solution which is determined

[2] This is obvious from Samuelson's classic proof of 'The Gains from International Trade' (Samuelson, 1939).

[3] For a neat demonstration of this in the simple case of a finite time-horizon model with different desired terminal stocks see Bent Hansen, 1966.

20—I.G.T.

solely by 'real' considerations. This is of course a perfectly general point which is not restricted to the simple model above. The money values of the shadow prices can be derived given any single price fixed in money terms.

It would be useful to illustrate all this with respect to the foreign exchange rate in view of the suggestion frequently made that the proper way to allow for foreign trade in social investment decisions is to use a 'shadow price of foreign exchange'. The foreign exchange rate is of course stated in money terms: it is the price of foreign money in terms of domestic money.[4] It converts the value of foreign goods (stated in foreign money) into their domestic money equivalent. The *shadow* exchange rate converts the value of foreign goods (stated in foreign money) into their shadow domestic money values. But as we have already seen the optimal relative valuations between *all* goods and factors are determined by 'real' considerations. Thus the shadow exchange rate is determined as soon as a single domestic price and a single foreign price are fixed in money terms. As an example, take our two-good two-factor model above. Suppose that world prices are fixed in dollars and that some domestic factor price is given in domestic currency (say rupees). Then since we know the optimal factor price ratio, the rupee price of the other factor is determined. Given the optimal employments of the factors and the outputs of the two goods, rupee prices of the goods are determined. Since the dollar prices of the goods are given, the shadow exchange rate between the rupee and the dollar is determined.

It is clear that the money value of the shadow exchange rate depends on the domestic price level. In fact, there is an infinity of combinations of domestic money prices and exchange rates which will sustain the same 'real' situation. The preceding discussion should make it clear that the effort to find the 'shadow price of foreign exchange' for project evaluation is really directed to finding the optimal relative price between foreign and domestic resources. In fact, the foreign exchange rate as a *money* price could be abolished altogether by taking dollars as our *numéraire* and expressing *all* prices in foreign exchange. This, as we shall see, is done in the Little–Mirrlees method of project selection. The change of *numéraire* must not mislead us; there still remains a *relative* price between foreign and domestic resources which is what matters for resource allocation. Note, however, that the assumptions of the simple model above imply a *single* conversion factor between domestic and foreign resources (or shadow exchange rate) in the optimum situation. We shall see that if some of these assumptions are dropped, this convenient result is destroyed and we get a *set* of optimal conversion factors (or *multiple* shadow exchange rates).

---

[4] Note that whenever I talk about the foreign exchange rate, I mean the effective foreign exchange rate, i.e., the exchange rate *inclusive* of tariffs, subsidies, premia, etc. The effective exchange rate may of course be unified or multiple.

The preceding discussion is enough to dispel a few of the confusions which exist on this subject:

(a) It is sometimes suggested that the shadow exchange rate is that rate which would exist if all trade restrictions were swept away. This would be true only if in the free trade situation there were no divergences between private and social values. If the distortions causing such divergences persist, optimality cannot be attributed to the free trade exchange rate.

(b) Balassa and Schydlowsky attack the notion of an 'equilibrium' exchange rate in the context of project evaluation[5] on the ground that its value depends on trade, fiscal, and monetary policies. They claim, firstly, that 'a given degree of protection can be provided by different combinations of tariffs, subsidies and exchange rate'. This is a confusion. While it is true that different combinations of the *official* exchange rate and trade policies can give the same degree of protection, this does not mean that the shadow exchange rate is different in each case; for the shadow exchange rate refers to the *effective* exchange rate inclusive of tariffs, subsidies, etc. Balassa and Schydlowsky argue further that 'there are an infinite number of "equilibrium" exchange rates, each corresponding to a different configuration of trade, monetary and fiscal policies'. It is of course true that different specifications of the optimum problem (incorporating different restrictions on government policy) will imply different shadow prices (including the shadow exchange rate or rates).[6] But this does not mean that any given optimum problem has a multiplicity of solutions. The effort to find shadow prices (including the shadow exchange rate) is directed to finding the relative prices associated with the solution to the *given* optimum problem which faces the economic planners. In an open economy, the shadow exchange rate, far from being useless or irrelevant, is a crucial relative price.[7]

4. *Introducing Complications*

We now proceed to relax some of the assumptions of our simple model. At least in theory, this has very damaging effects on its simplicity. Recall that there are three assumptions implicit in the model:

(a) that there are no 'non-traded' goods;
(b) that the economy is a perfect competitor in world trade;
(c) that there are no restrictions on government tax/subsidy policies.

[5] The context makes it clear that they are talking about the shadow exchange rate (Balassa and Schydlowsky, 1968).

[6] I shall consider this question in greater detail below (Section 4).

[7] Of course particular values of the equilibrium exchange rate can be criticized as being based on an incomplete or unrealistic model. But this does not mean that the concept of the equilibrium exchange rate must be jettisoned. I agree with Balassa that the Nurkse and Meade definitions of equilibrium exchange rates involved an element of arbitrariness.

Consider each of these assumptions in turn.

(a) By definition, demand for non-traded goods can be satisfied only by domestic production. The optimum prices of traded goods are equal to their given world prices; these prices can be used for production decisions whatever the pattern of domestic preferences. But the optimum prices of non-traded goods cannot be determined independently of demand (or at least not without making some further assumptions). Clearly, this also means that the shadow prices of the domestic factors are not given independently of domestic consumption preferences as they were in the simple model (i.e., the shadow exchange rate is no longer independent of the pattern of demand).

(b) Dropping the assumption of perfect competition in world trade, however, means that production and consumption decisions cannot be separated even for *traded* goods; as a corollary it also means that the shadow prices of traded goods are *not* equal to their world prices. The reason is straightforward. Since the terms of trade are now variable, the 'production point' and the 'consumption point' have to be determined simultaneously. The latter is given by the tangency of a community indifference curve with the 'Baldwin envelope'. At this point the world relative prices, given by the *average* terms of trade, are different from the optimal domestic prices which are given by the *marginal* terms of trade. This is simply the familiar optimum tariff argument for trade intervention. Another way of saying this is that we no longer have a *single* shadow rate of exchange; we need a *dual* shadow rate of exchange. With many goods with different elasticities of demand and supply, we would clearly need a multiple shadow rate structure.[8]

(c) Relaxing the third assumption releases a Pandora's box of complications. The third assumption effectively means that the Planning Commission has at its disposal all the policy instruments which are required to achieve the first-best optimum. If we retain assumption (b) it can then be shown that the shadow prices of traded goods are their world prices; any domestic divergences between private and social profitability are optimally eliminated by the use of domestic subsidies.[9] But suppose some of these measures are not feasible. Then trade intervention may lead to the second best (or third best, or nth best) optimum. A problem with a realistic flavour has been examined in Ramaswami and Srinivasan (1968): suppose revenue has to be raised through trade taxes; this, they have shown, may justify a multiple exchange rate. World prices are *not* indicators of social value in such a case.

Presumably project evaluation *is* conducted in situations of a second-best kind. For one thing the government may control only part of the economy;

[8] Note that this is a first-best argument for a multiple rate. With sufficient ingenuity a few other first-best arguments for trade intervention (and therefore multiple rates) can be constructed. For a brilliant survey of recent work in this field see Bhagwati, 1968.

[9] This proposition is proved in Bhagwati and Ramaswami, 1963. It was really implicit in Meade, 1955, though he did not state it so succinctly.

the logic of shadow prices says that they have to be applied everywhere if they have to have significance. This inevitably leads us into problems of the second-best type. Indeed, the whole exercise of project evaluation would be redundant if the government had complete control over the economy! There is a further point. The project evaluator may have to take as a constraint not simply certain *infeasible* policies but also certain *irrational* policies. It may well be, to take an example, that a government wishes to maintain some irrational trade controls. It cannot then be assumed that the shadow prices associated with the first-best optimum are still relevant in this case.[10]

In summary, the more we complicate our simple model, the more we approach an *n*th best general equilibrium problem in which there are no simple rules for deriving shadow prices.[11] Of course this will not do. Decisions have to be taken and one cannot afford to be too fussy. A project evaluation method is good enough if it gives us shadow prices which are simply derived, approximately right and which will lead the economy in the right direction. And for this practical reason, a number of drastic assumptions may be justified.

5. *Programming Criteria*

The great attraction of programming models lies in the fact that they explicitly seek to solve a general equilibrium, inter-industry allocation problem.[12] In principle, one could maximize a non-linear objective function subject to technological constraints which provide an accurate inventory of all resources and an accurate description of all actual and potential productive processes in the economy. Conceptually, there is again no reason why one could not impose restrictions of the second-best type, which imply that some particular efficiency conditions cannot be satisfied. The solution of the problem would simultaneously throw up the efficient outputs and shadow prices. Foreign trade could be brought into the system by incorporating 'activities' which allow the possibility of importing (at a c.i.f. price) and exporting (at an f.o.b. price) for every traded good. If these import and export prices are stated in terms of foreign currency and if the *numéraire* is a unit of domestic currency we would get a shadow price(s) of foreign exchange. If a new project is to be evaluated, either the entire programming problem could be redone or the previously calculated shadow prices could be used, provided the project is marginal.

---

[10] M. FG. Scott, in an unpublished paper, has shown that the shadow exchange rate can have widely different values depending on the assumptions one makes about government policy for maintaining external balance.

[11] Note that I have throughout ignored the implications of relaxing the assumptions about 'appropriate' curvature properties. As is well known, this can have disastrous implications for the existence, uniqueness and administrative practicability of general equilibrium shadow prices.

[12] Chenery, among others, has championed their use (Chenery, 1961).

The actual practice of programming is, however, a far cry from the above idealized description. Firstly, for computational and other reasons, a programming problem has, on the whole, to be formulated in *linear* terms. This is a severe restriction. The assumption of linearity can lead to manifestly absurd results because the normal built-in constraint of diminishing returns is absent.[13] In order to counteract this, restrictions have to be imposed which rule out such results. But the combination of the linearity assumptions and the arbitrary restrictions make the results of such models somewhat suspect. These considerations are particularly relevant in their treatment of foreign trade. On the export side they generally operate with the assumption of an exogenously fixed export revenue (not only in total but sector by sector). This rules out any choice between consuming and exporting. With regard to imports, certain 'non-competitive imports' are postulated in each sector. As is obvious, this is an extremely artificial way of introducing the notion of comparative advantage into the model.

The second objection to the application of linear programming for project selection is that in practice it is impossible to disaggregate sufficiently and to allow for all the alternative techniques. If the initial programme is incomplete then the solution may not be optimal and this may lead to incorrect results in the evaluation of a *new* marginal project. Suppose as an example that the initial programme did not include possibilities of importing a certain product X and assumed that it would be produced domestically. It might well be that producing it domestically is the less efficient alternative. Now this mistake is likely to be compounded. Suppose a new project comes up for evaluation which uses X as an input. The inefficiency with regard to X (and therefore its 'incorrect' shadow price) may well penalize the new project. It may look socially unprofitable when in fact it is socially profitable.[14]

Bruno (1965) has suggested the use of the programming criterion for import-substituting and export-promoting projects. He recognizes that in practice it may be too cumbersome to calculate the shadow prices. He recommends that in practice the inputs into a project should be broken down into the key resources and that their prices—mainly the shadow wage of labour and the shadow price of foreign exchange—should be guessed. This is certainly vulnerable to the criticism made above about allowing previous production decisions to bias the choice of new projects. One possible point in defence of the criterion is that, in the real world, the project evaluator may have to take the existing production pattern as given: he is hardly likely to be allowed

---

[13] Linear programmers refer to this as the 'flip-flop' or 'bang-bang' tendency of a linear model.

[14] This point has also been made by Balassa and Schydlowsky (1968) with regard to Bruno's linear programming criterion (Bruno, 1965). They do not, however, point out that it is not a defect of linear programming in principle but only of its possible application.

to start from a clean slate. In other words, this is a way of taking account of a second-best type of problem. However, the idea that the entire production structure should be taken as given is equally extreme in the context of long-run planning.[15]

In summary, shadow prices derived from a linear programming model can be used for project evaluation and can take account of foreign trade opportunities; but the results are likely to be untrustworthy, because non-linearities and second-best type problems have to be forced into the linear framework, and because the practical application of linear programming is likely to lack the comprehensiveness which alone can give it validity.

6. The Little–Mirrlees Criterion
(Little and Mirrlees, 1968)

This criterion[16] can be seen as an attempt to introduce the notion of comparative advantage explicitly into micro-planning without getting into the difficulties of formulating a programming model. The criterion consists simply of valuing all inputs and outputs of a project in terms of foreign exchange. This change would not in itself make a great deal of difference. The substantive further step is to value all traded goods at world prices without any further adjustment.[17] Domestic factors are valued by guessing their optimal marginal value products in terms of foreign exchange.[18] This takes us back to our simple model and, as we have seen, it would hold full sway if the drastic assumptions we listed were made, viz., the absence of non-traded goods, perfect competition in world trade, and no restrictions on government policies in eliminating market distortions. Effectively this means that optimally the economy should pursue free trade. The real question is whether the simplicity of the method is preserved if we admit non-traded goods and

[15] The above remarks also apply to other *ad hoc* methods of project selection which proceed by guessing one or two important shadow prices (including the shadow exchange rate) in costing a project. Sometimes they apply a shadow exchange rate for valuing only direct foreign exchange costs and leave the prices of domestically bought inputs unadjusted. Sometimes they are slightly more detailed and estimate both the direct and the indirect foreign exchange costs. But even the latter alternative, as argued above, is not going far enough.

[16] This criterion is a more sophisticated version of the suggestion originally made by Little in 1965 in a paper which is as yet unpublished. A similar criterion has also been independently suggested by Tinbergen.

[17] There are some minor qualifications to this considered below.

[18] Explicit attention is paid only to labour and capital though land can be treated in the same way. Note that the 'shadow wage of labour' in the Little–Mirrlees method fulfils the same function as the 'shadow price of foreign exchange' in models which use domestic currency as the unit of account, viz., of making foreign and domestic resources comparable. Since Little and Mirrlees use foreign exchange as the unit of account one should not be surprised that the shadow price of foreign exchange is unnecessary in their scheme. Guessing the optimal marginal product of labour may sound very difficult. In fact it is not as difficult as all that in a 'labour surplus' economy. Little and Mirrlees discuss exhaustively how to estimate it in practice.

monopoly power in world trade and if we take as given certain constraints on government policy. Consider these questions one by one.

(a) The existence of non-traded goods does not by itself disturb the validity of valuing traded goods at world prices. But it does raise the question of how to price the non-traded goods themselves. In the general equilibrium optimal solution their prices would be determined simultaneously by demand/supply considerations. But how should they be valued when the economy is in a non-optimum situation? The Little–Mirrlees Manual deals with this by assuming that the extra demand for a non-traded input (such as electricity) is met by an increase in the total supply of electricity and recommends that electricity should be priced at the marginal social *cost* of producing it broken down into traded goods and labour.[19] There are two difficulties with this: first of all, in a non-optimal situation, the marginal social *value* of electricity may differ from its marginal social cost. Extra demand for electricity may not in fact be met by an increase in the production of electricity but by a reduction in its consumption elsewhere. If this were the case as a result of market distortions or government irrationality the correct shadow price of electricity is its marginal social value, whose foreign exchange equivalent would have to be assessed. Secondly, even if we assume that the government would in fact follow rational policies and eliminate the divergence between value and cost by changing the production of electricity, the marginal social cost of electricity in the optimum situation is equal to the prevailing marginal cost only on the assumption of constant costs.

(b) If we drop the assumption that the country is a perfect competitor in world trade then world prices do not, as we have already seen, give the correct shadow prices for traded goods, even in the first-best optimum situation. The Little–Mirrlees solution in this case is to use the marginal cost of importing or the marginal revenue from exporting as the appropriate shadow price of an input or output. Strictly speaking, this may not be correct in a non-optimal situation; it is the *optimal* marginal terms of trade that have to be used, not the prevailing ones.[20] But this may not be a very important problem in practice. L.D.C.s are monopolists only in a few export commodities and perhaps the optimum tariff on them could be plausibly guessed.

(c) If we impose constraints on domestic policies, the problem becomes very complicated as we have already seen. Consider first the shadow prices of the traded goods. These will be equal to their world prices only on the assumption that increases in the demand for and supply of traded goods as a result

---

[19] Theoretically, there is also a problem here about the valuation of the services of the inherited stock of capital goods. This has to be dealt with by approximate methods.

[20] A formal proof in the two-good case would be as follows: Suppose the economy happens *ex hypothesi* to be at the optimum *production* point but assume that it is not optimizing in *consumption*. Then using the prevailing marginal terms of trade for project evaluation would clearly lead the economy away from the optimum production point.

of the project will affect world trade; and that 'external balance' will be preserved without disturbing 'internal balance'. Perhaps the latter assumption, though unrealistic in the short-run, is justified in the context of long-run planning. But is it realistic to assume that changes in the demand for and supply of traded goods will necessarily and fully affect trade? An example of why they may not do so is the presence of import quotas (unless the quotas are operated like constant tariffs). The import price of a domestically bought input cannot be considered its shadow price if there is a permanent import control on it. Or consider a project to produce a final good on which there is a permanent import quota. Its shadow price may then be above its import price.[21] Of course if the shadow prices of traded goods are not equal to their world prices then the rules for finding the shadow prices of non-traded goods would also become more complicated.[22]

A possible answer to these objections is that a rational government would over the long run pursue a policy of internal and external balance and free trade. But apart from the question of whether rationality is necessarily to be expected, there is also the point that free trade may not be the best policy if the government cannot pursue optimum tax/subsidy policies.[23] These second-best type problems present themselves typically through the lack of control of the government over part of the economy. The use of the free-trade criterion in the 'operative' sector may then improve the allocation of resources within the sector but also result in undesirable movement of resources between the operative and non-operative sector.

The great merit of the Little–Mirrlees criterion is its simplicity. The price to be paid for this is that the criterion is strictly speaking correct only with first-best assumptions.[24] A great deal more work needs to be done on whether

[21] Another way of putting this point is simply that in order to benefit from a free-trade policy an economy must allow itself to make up the difference between production and consumption through trade. Note that if trade is restricted by tariffs, the criterion will move the economy in the right direction.

[22] It should be noted that the distinction between 'traded' and 'non-traded' goods is itself not easy to draw. Take as an example increased grain production by a subsistence farmer in the middle of India. This may have no effect on trade though grain is a 'traded' good. In such a case the increased grain production of the farmer must be valued as if it was a 'non-traded' good (unless we make some over-simple assumption about internal transport costs).

[23] Little and Mirrlees do allow for one significant distortion: a non-optimal saving rate in the economy. They deal with this as part of the valuation of labour. The idea is that the employment of additional disguisedly unemployed labour by a project increases aggregate consumption above what it would otherwise have been and that, in a situation of non-optimal saving, consumption and saving are not equally valuable. Thus the shadow wage of labour, the social discount rate, and the shadow price of saving are all connected with each other. There is a vast literature on this problem which we ignore here. Suffice it to say that Little and Mirrlees tackle this problem in a very sophisticated way while at the same time making it tractable for estimation purposes. Note that it does not affect the validity of their free-trade criterion.

[24] An exception is the 'saving distortion' which can be taken care of through the shadow wage of labour; it does not invalidate their treatment of traded goods.

and to what extent its use can be misleading in second-best situations and how it can be flexibly modified to deal with them.[25]

7. Conclusion

In an open economy comparative advantage considerations must obviously play an important part in the choice of projects. In theory this can only be done as part of a complex general equilibrium programming exercise which throws up the shadow prices of all goods and factors. In practice, simpler methods are necessary which will give approximately correct answers. The Little–Mirrlees method, whose theoretical foundations I have examined, is an important step in this direction. Much work remains to be done in adapting it to deal with second-best problems. But it has at least the merit of directing the attention of project planners to foreign trade in a detailed way. Other project criteria have generally included foreign trade only as an after-thought.

REFERENCES

BALASSA, B. and SCHYDLOWSKY, D., 'Effective Tariffs, Domestic Cost of Foreign Exchange and the Equilibrium Exchange Rate', *Journal of Political Economy*, 1968.

BHAGWATI, J., *The Theory and Practice of Commercial Policy: Departures from Unified Exchange Rates* (Princeton, 1968).

BHAGWATI, J. and RAMASWAMI, V. K., 'Domestic Distortions, Tariffs, and the Theory of Optimum Subsidy', *Journal of Political Economy*, 1963.

BRUNO, M., 'The Optimal Selection of Export-Promoting and Import-Substituting Projects' (1965), in *Planning the External Sector: Techniques, Problems and Policies* (U.N. 1967).

CHENERY, H. B., 'Comparative Advantage and Development Policy', *American Economic Review*, 1961.

HANSEN, B., *Long and Short-Term Planning in Underdeveloped Countries*, De Vries Lectures (Amsterdam, 1967).

LITTLE, I. M. D. and MIRRLEES, J. A., *Manual of Industrial Project Analysis in Developing Countries*, Vol. II, O.E.C.D. (Paris, 1968).

MARGLIN, S. A., *Public Investment Criteria* (London, 1967).

MEADE, J. E., *Trade and Welfare* (London, 1955).

RAMASWAMI, V. K. and SRINIVASAN, T. M., 'Optimal Subsidies and Taxes when some Factors are traded', *Journal of Political Economy*, 1968.

SAMUELSON, P. A., 'The Gains from International Trade', *Canadian Journal of Economics and Political Science*, 1939.

---

[25] Note that the effective protection criterion for selecting projects which has been recommended in Balassa and Schydlowsky, 1968, is a very rudimentary form of the Little–Mirrlees criterion. Effective protection given to an activity is defined as the increase in domestic value-added per unit of output compared with value-added per unit of output in a free-trade situation, and projects could be ranked in order of the effective protection they would require. However, this does not eliminate the necessity of estimating a shadow exchange rate, despite what the authors say. Those familiar with the literature on effective protection will also realise how badly the crude fixed input–output measure of effective protection may approximate to the true effective protection in a general equilibrium sense.

20

TOWARDS A THEORY OF AGREED
SPECIALIZATION: THE ECONOMICS OF
INTEGRATION

KIYOSHI KOJIMA

Introduction

AT the end of the Seminar on Asian Trade held by the Institute of Development Economics, Karachi, in 1961, Sir Roy Harrod concluded that 'it would be worth placing strong emphasis on the general idea of agreed specialization. This might be put forward, to those concerned, as a proposal urgently requiring study.'[1] Earlier he had suggested that the basic idea of agreed specialization was that 'the advantages of a larger market should be secured, not *ex post* by some tariff manipulation, but *ex ante* by some previous agreement about the directions into which investment should be channelled in each separate country. Thus, the danger of over-lapping and of the production of surpluses in the field of manufactures (for example, textiles) might be averted. A larger market might be secured for each industry by a more rational direction of investment resources in the first instance. The nations might authorize each other to specialize, by developing in some particular directions, and thus give each the advantage of the large market afforded by the region as a whole.'[2]

This paper is dedicated to Sir Roy Harrod and its purpose is to explore his idea of 'regional agreed specialization' as one of the most important fac-

---

[1] Harrod, 1962, p. 16.

[2] *Ibid.*, p. 14. So far as I am aware, Gunnar Myrdal was the first to express a similar idea. He argued the need for 'second-grade international specialization' among less developed countries. 'It would require co-operative planning and not only co-operative discrimination. On the basis of such planning, one country would allow preferential terms for imports of a particular product from another country in exchange for a similar treatment on the part of that country in regard to another product; and this agreement would then have to be followed up by a planned increase of the investments for production of the two products in the respective countries'. Myrdal, 1956, pp. 259 and 261. In 1966, he suggested that a common market among less developed countries 'must be completed by formal agreements, reached after negotiation, concerning what industries should be located in what countries. When thought through with all its consequences, this implies the need for a joint common planning', quoted by Lary, 1968, p. 12 fn.

tors which should motivate not only developing countries but also developed countries towards economic integration.

World trade in post-war years has been characterized by a decline in the importance of *vertical trade*, the exchange of foodstuffs and raw materials for manufactured goods, and growth in the importance of *horizontal trade*, the exchange of manufactured goods amongst advanced industrial countries. These trends have been accompanied by successful moves towards regional integration among advanced industrial countries at a similar stage of economic development within the E.E.C. and E.F.T.A. By most criteria, the economies which have participated in European integration might have been thought highly competitive. Following the success of these moves, less developed countries have become interested or actively involved in similar moves towards regional integration among neighbouring countries at a roughly similar stage of economic development. What are the reasons for these trends in world trade and what is the rationale of moves towards economic integration? How might realization of the gains from regional integration be facilitated by agreed specialization?

World Trade and Economic Integration

The shift away from vertical trade, which was the predominant pattern in the nineteenth century, towards horizontal trade, which has been fast becoming the predominant pattern since the second world war, can be explained in terms of shifts in the underlying determinants of comparative advantage.[3]

Suppose that goods are produced by the combined input of three factors of production: labour (L), which can be conceived of in the narrow sense of human time availability; natural resources (N), including land, fertility, climate, and other geographic factors; and capital (C), which can be conceived of in the broad sense as comprising social capital, human skills, and technological and organizational knowledge, as well as material capital equipment. The theory of factor proportions (the Heckscher–Ohlin theorem) cannot be applied easily or usefully to the three factor case, but if one of these three factors can be taken to have no significant influence in determining comparative advantage, some useful generalizations can be made.[4] Three

[3] Excellent surveys of the underlying causes of these changes in international specialization are provided by Bhagwati, 1964, pp. 1–84, and Johnson, 1968 (i).

[4] Broadly speaking, developments in the theory of international trade from Ricardo to recent theory, which emphasizes the R and D factor in trade specialization, can be seen in terms of explicit stress on a couple of dominant factors of production (or perhaps only one factor). The stress depends on the type of countries and the stages in their development which are being analysed. This way of thinking is seen typically in Hirsch, 1967, Appendix to Chapter II, pp. 34–41.

patterns of trade specialization are then possible, namely, an $N-L$ pattern, a $C-L$ pattern, or an $N-C$ pattern.

Briefly, it can be said that growth in world trade was determined mainly by the $N-L$ pattern of specialization during the nineteenth century and by the $C-L$ pattern of specialization after the second world war. In the nineteenth century, the structure of world trade was determined by the existence of abundant labour with limited natural resources in Britain and huge unutilized natural resources with scarce labour in newly settled regions. The third factor, capital, moved freely and was of no great importance in determining differences in comparative advantage. Natural resources were, of course, fixed in location, so that this $L-N$ pattern of complementary specialization was stable and brought about the transmission of economic growth through trade expansion.

In the twentieth century, particularly since the second world war, trade in manufactured goods amongst industrial countries has grown much more rapidly than trade in primary commodities. Because of the rapid and widespread progress of industrial technology, capital has displaced natural resources as the significant factor in trade growth.[5] Since primary inputs for manufacturing are available at almost the same price for different industrial countries,[6] the N factor can be regarded as making no substantial difference to comparative costs among industrial countries, so that the $C-L$ pattern has become the main determinant of world trade growth.

The shift in world trade expansion from the $N-L$ pattern to the $C-L$ pattern brought difficulties both for primary producing countries and for industrial countries. First, because of the proportionate decline in world demand for foodstuffs and raw materials, the growth of advanced economies no longer transmits itself strongly to peripheral economies. Not only has the transmission of growth through trade expansion almost ceased, but also less developed countries suffer from so called 'backwash effects',[7] the effect of 'immiserizing growth',[8] unstable terms of trade, and declining terms of trade, all of which reduce the attractiveness of development through specialization in the world economy. In consequence, less developed countries have turned towards policies to foster their own industrialization. Under these circumstances, there appears a strong case for promoting regional industrialization among countries which stand on a roughly equal footing, in order to realize economies of scale in manufacturing activity.

Second, the $C-L$ pattern of trade also brought difficulties for advanced

---

[5] See Nurkse, 1959, pp. 13–19 for an excellent analysis of these developments. See also G.A.T.T., 1960, Part I, and United Nations, 1959, Part I, Chapter 1.

[6] Lary, 1968, p. 48.

[7] As described by Myrdal, 1957, pp. 27–33.

[8] For an ingenious formal presentation of the theory of immiserizing growth, see Bhagwati, June 1958, and December 1958.

industrial countries. Since the C and L factors are variable in the long run, C/L ratios are intrinsically unstable and successive changes in international specialization between industrial and industrializing countries are inevitable. The closer the C/L ratio between countries, the smaller will be the difference in comparative costs. Competitive economies producing similar commodities without substantial cost differences can easily separate their markets through tariff and other protective measures. Hence, economic integration within the E.E.C. and E.F.T.A. was aimed at eliminating protective barriers, stabilizing trade in manufactures, and the achievement of economies of scale within a larger market.

The theory of customs union and the associated theory of the large markets set out to explain the gains from economic integration. The question arises, are there additional factors which experience suggests are necessary to realization of the gains from regional integration?

The theory of customs union focuses on analysis of the static gains from economic integration. Following Viner, if *trade creation* exceeds *trade diversion*, customs union, or the extension of tariff preferences, will be beneficial.[9] On the production side, *trade creation* requires incomplete specialization prior to integration and the contraction of import competing industries within the union. *Trade diversion* is consistent with complete specialization prior to union and involves the re-direction of union imports away from lower-cost outside sources of supply towards higher-cost union sources of supply. Thus, the gains from union appear greatest for protection-ridden economies with similar structures of industrial production. As Lipsey suggests 'the customs union is more likely to bring gain, the greater the degree of overlapping between the class of commodities produced under tariff protection in the two countries'.[10]

There are also potential gains from customs union on the consumption side. If there is substitutability in consumption, customs union may even result in welfare gains where there is Vinerian *trade diversion* on the production side, through the possibility of increased consumption of preferred imports from the partner country.[11] Or there may be welfare losses through a switch away from preferred outside imports to less preferred partner country substitutes.

Arguments for economic integration which rest upon the existence of favourable *trade creating* production or consumption effects are as much arguments for general tariff reductions as they are for preferential tariff

[9] Viner, 1950, p. 43.

[10] Lipsey, 1956, p. 499. Lipsey's article provides an excellent review of the main issues. My own thoughts about the issue of integration were originally published in *Hitotsubashi Ronso*, September 1962, in Japanese. Recent contributions by C. A. Cooper and B. F. Massell, and Harry G. Johnson lead to conclusions similar to those in my Japanese paper.

[11] *Ibid.*, p. 501.

reductions. Cooper and Massell, for example, rightly point out that the effect of customs union is the sum of two components: '(1) a non-preferential tariff reduction, and (2) a move from this position to a customs union with the initial tariff. This analytical distinction shows clearly that any rise in consumer welfare as a consequence of forming a union, whether the result of trade creation or a favourable consumption effect, is due entirely to the tariff reduction component of the move.'[12] Viner was also quite explicit that *trade creation* is good and *trade diversion* is bad from a free trade point of view.

What, among other things, traditional customs union theory fails to explain satisfactorily is why a country might be prepared to reduce tariffs preferentially and sacrifice inefficient import-competing industries yet not be prepared to reduce tariffs generally in order to achieve the same objective. This failure derives in part from the one-sector, partial equilibrium, nature of much of the analysis of customs union. But it also reflects inattention to the importance and nature of the bargaining process involved in tariff re-arrangements. Importantly, partners to customs unions are prepared to reduce tariffs preferentially, and cut back less efficient import competing production, on the strength of assured gains for efficient export industries in partner country markets. It appears, then, that some new theory about the way in which these gains can be realized is essential to a more complete analysis of the process of economic integration.

Agreed trade-liberalization is a prerequisite to realization of the mutual gains from preferential tariff reduction. Commonly, agreement will be premised on assurances from partners to the tariff reduction of reciprocal and approximately equal gains from trade expansion. Such agreement can be seen to constitute the first important element in any concept of agreed specialization.

Agreed specialization is a means, then, whereby a group of like-minded countries with similar structures of production can realize static gains from freer trade. Elsewhere, Johnson has suggested another reason for agreed specialization.[13] He developed a model in which it is assumed that countries have a preference for industrial production. In this model '. . . it is lower-cost satisfaction of the demand for collective consumption of industrial production that is involved, and this can only be achieved through the co-operation (via bargaining) of the other country. . . . Each country therefore stands to gain, in terms of real income, by exchanging a reduction of its industrial production through its own tariff reduction for an equal expansion of its industrial production through the other country's tariff reduction.'[14] Countries desirous of agreed industrial specialization have a clear interest in preferential trade-liberalization. They will commonly be weaker industrial economies—stronger industrial economies would have little to fear from multilateral trade liberalization since their industrial exports are likely to

[12] Cooper and Massell, 1965, p. 745.   [13] Johnson, 1965, pp. 256–83.
[14] *Ibid.*, p. 270.

expand more than their industrial imports with general tariff reductions. Preferential trade liberalization will enable weaker industrial countries to prevent market penetration from the strong industrial countries; to enjoy a more efficient allocation of regional resources, increased production, static trade gains; and to improve their competitiveness through various dynamic effects such as the securing of economies of scale.

Finally, a large market is said to ensure 'the full employment of machines, mass production, specialization, exploitation of the latest technical discoveries, a revival of competition—all these factors tend to reduce production costs and selling prices. In addition there is the possibility of a net reduction of one element of the price through the abolition of customs duties. The result should be an increase of purchasing power and a rise in the real standard of living. The increased number of consumers of a particular product should thus permit an increase in consumption and hence a greater increase in investment.'[15] Economic expansion begins to cumulate.

An enlargement of markets through economic integration undoubtedly increases the scope for large scale production. And the securing of economies of scale is certainly a primary objective in establishing large markets. But how exactly can the benefits of large scale production be achieved?

Most economists rely on the effects of increased competition within larger markets to ensure that benefits from economies of scale are secured.[16] Increased competition has two important effects. First, it stimulates the reallocation of resources that yields static gains from economic integration, as marginal producers contract production and shift into more efficient lines of production. Second, increased competition is likely to induce the employment of mass-production methods and the best industrial practices. Scitovsky, for example, argued that economic integration as such may not increase trade among member countries substantially.[17] Increased competition is likely to have its main effect through the adoption of mass production techniques to supply national markets in effective competition with lower cost suppliers within the union. This second, dynamic, effect, therefore, results from an increase 'merely in competition'.[18]

Of course, greater economies of scale would be obtainable if the larger integrated markets, not national markets, were the target of mass production. But agreement in specialization would be necessary between partner countries if these were to be achieved. Without agreement location theory suggests that increased competition is most likely to result in the agglomeration of industries in particular areas.[19]

---

[15] Deniau, 1960, p. 16.   [16] *Ibid.*, p. 15.
[17] Scitovsky, 1958, p. 31; see also Humphrey, 1961, pp. 283–4.
[18] Scitovsky, 1958, p. 31.
[19] Isard, 1956, Chapter VIII. Balassa refers to location theory as one of the important ingredients of the theory of economic integration. Balassa, 1961, pp. 6–8.

Moreover, the stimulation of increased competition is attainable through non-discriminatory trade liberalization at least equally as well as it is through discriminatory trade liberalization.[20] The case for regional integration rests on the logic, therefore, that economies of scale can be achieved within a larger integrated market and competitive power improved through union *but that* it is also beneficial to resist the pressure from more competitive producers outside the integrated market. A plausible theory of economic integration must spell this logic out in some detail.

A Model of Agreed Specialization

What should be the principle of the international division of labour within a large integrated market? Is some special theory necessary to explain the gains from market integration?

Many economists would argue that re-allocation of resources within the member countries of an economic union should follow the usual principles of comparative advantage and that no special theory is required to analyse the changes consequent upon union.[21] This is correct once integration has been set in motion and in so far as the static re-allocation of resources is the only important effect of integration, although some agreement will be necessary even to effect tariff reductions and ensure a fair share of the static gains from specialization among participating countries. Already Johnson has explored this question, so it is not the main concern here. But a new theory of agreed specialization does appear crucial to an understanding of how the dynamic gains from regional specialization can be achieved.

The benefits of specialization through the achievement of economies of scale in different lines of production will require agreement among the participants in economic union.

Assume that long-run decreasing costs characterize industrial production. The production function can be written:

$$(1) \qquad P = T \cdot f(C, L)$$

where P stands for output, C for capital, L for labour, and T for the level of technology.

The level of technology chosen can be supposed to depend upon the size of the market:

$$(2) \qquad T = \phi(M)$$

[20] See Robinson, 1960, p. xviii, who concludes that 'most of the major industrial economies of scale could be achieved by a relatively high-income nation of 50 million, that nations of 10–15 million were probably too small to get all the technical economies available; that the industrial economies of scale beyond a size of 50 million were mainly those that derive from a change in the character of competition and of specialization'. See also Johnson, 1960, p. 33.

[21] Scitovsky, 1958, pp. 41 and 48.

21—I.G.T.

where M represents the size of the market; ϕ is an increasing function, or $dT/dM > 0$, and has a limit at the maximum level of technology T^*. Note that the size of the market is dependent upon the nature of competition within the industry as well as the volume of national output, since the degree of monopoly or extent of oligopoly clearly affects the size of the market for each producer. Note also that the function relating the level of technology and market size is likely to be a stepped non-continuous function since indivisibilities of plant and equipment are likely to be prevalent.

Assume a two country model in which country 1 and country 2 initially produce two commodities x and y. Production functions are of the type described above, and the same as between countries, but different as between industries. Productive factors are identical but immobile internationally and technology is known in both countries. Prior to economic integration assume that there was no trade, or negligible trade, between the countries because of the existence of tariff or other protective barriers. Each country adopted the most profitable level of technology in relation to its domestic market size and the prevailing degree of competition. Country 1 employed technology T_x^i and T_y^i appropriate to the size of the market for each commodity M_{ix} and M_{iy}. Country 2 employed technologies T_x^j and T_y^j appropriate to the size of its markets M_{jx} and M_{jy}.

Suppose there is economic union between two such countries through which tariff and other trade barriers are removed and commodity prices equalized in both national markets, transport costs being assumed insignificant. The integrated market for each commodity will be larger than each separate national market, since

$$M_{tx} = M_{ix} + M_{jx}$$

and

$$M_{ty} = M_{iy} + M_{jy}.$$

Hence, it will be feasible for a superior level of technology, T_x^t and T_y^t, to be adopted within each of the integrated markets, M_{tx} and M_{ty}, if the two countries can agree to specialize in the production of one or the other of the two commodities. If, for example, country 1 agreed to concentrate on the production of x and country 2 on the production of y, the two countries would be able to achieve economies of scale, increased output, and higher economic welfare. Thus, agreed specialization primarily aims at securing improved production methods in both countries and dynamic gains from trade specialization. These dynamic gains from trade specialization are different in kind from the static gains from specialization which merely involve the re-allocation of resources with a given level of technology.[22]

[22] Interestingly Ohlin, 1967, pp. 38–41, recognized increasing returns to scale as a potent cause of trade specialization. See also Johnson, 1967, p. 205, fn. 9.

Figure 1 describes the foregoing argument diagrammatically. $T^I, T^{II}\dots T^*$ are short-run supply curves corresponding to various levels of technology related to market size. The long-run supply curve, S, is an envelope of these short-run curves.[23] Prior to economic integration, both countries of similar market size employed technology T^I and produced x and y at cost levels represented by the unbroken lines. After integration, agreement on complete specialization is reached between the two countries, whereby country 1 produces a larger volume of x for the combined market in countries 1 and 2

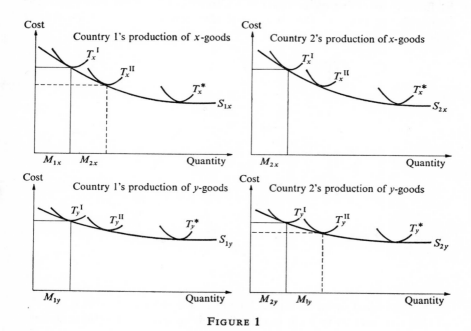

FIGURE 1

at a lower cost, shown by the broken line, through shifting from technology level T_x^I to T_x^{II}. Similarly, country 2 specializes in the production of a larger output of commodity y at a lower cost by shifting from technology T_y^I to T_y^{II}. Here, the gains from agreed specialization are shown by the reduced costs, in terms of costs per unit of commodity and total resources required to meet the pre-union level of demand in both countries taken together.

The logic of agreed specialization appears simple. But some further explanation is in order. First of all, why is agreed specialization a prerequisite to the realization of these gains? Significantly, agreed specialization is neces-

[23] This kind of envelope curve was developed by Harrod, 1930, pp. 232–41, and 1931, pp. 566–76. See also Viner, 1931–2, pp. 23–46. (Reprinted in Stigler and Boulding, 1952, pp. 198–232.)

sary because of the nature of the market for industries subject to decreasing costs of production.[24] It is widely held that 'if economies of scale are internal to the unit of production, monopoly will establish itself and . . . one country will exploit the other monopolistically or else there will be bilateral monopoly and indeterminancy', and therefore that 'analysis in terms of competition is applicable only if we suppose the diminishing costs to be due to external economies'.[25] Let us assume following Meade, however, that 'the economic system behaves as if there were perfect competition', an assumption justified by further 'assuming *either* that the economies of scale are external to the individual firms and that there is a system of taxes and subsidies which equates

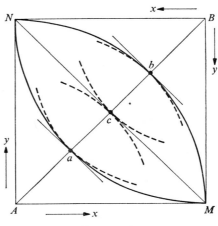

FIGURE 2

price to marginal social cost in each competitive industry, *or* that economies of scale are internal to large monopolistic firms and that the State controls each industry in such a way that it produces up to the point at which the price is equal to the marginal social cost of production.'[26]

To begin with, assume a model in which the two integrating countries are identical, possessing the same factor endowments, production functions, market size, and tastes. If there are economies of scale in industries x and y, the transformation curve will be convex to the origin as shown in Figure 2. Let A represent the origin for country 1 and B the origin for country 2, then the transformation curves MaN for country 1 and MbN for country 2 are identical. Further, assume identical production functions in each industry so

[24] For an excellent survey of this subject and areas worth further investigation, see Ohlin, 1967, Chapter 9.

[25] Matthews, 1949–50, p. 152.

[26] Meade, 1952, p. 33.

that the lengths of the vertical and horizontal axes are the same and the transformation box $AMBN$ is a square.

On the demand side, make some additional simplifying assumptions as a reference point. Social preferences are depicted by homothetic indifference curves which will be symmetric with respect to the 45 degree line. This implies not only that the income elasticity of demand for each good is unitary but also that the propensity to consume each good is the same and equal to one half. That is, both goods will be consumed equally with unitary relative prices at all levels of income. The nature of homothetic indifference curves also implies that the 'contract line' will be the diagonal AB.

Now it follows that one of the indifference curves in each map will be tangential to country 1's transformation curve at such a point as a and country 2's transformation curve at such a point as b, both on the 'contract curve' AB. These are the pre-integration equilibrium positions for each country and they are stable equilibria since the convexity of the indifference curve is greater than the convexity of the transformation curve. The pre-integration relative price lines, which are tangential to both the transformation and consumption curves at a for country 1 and b for country 2, will be parallel to each other and intersect the 'contract curve' at right angles. Neither of these completely identical countries has any comparative advantage in producing one or the other commodity and there is no price incentive to specialize and trade. This conclusion is quite independent of the existence of trade barriers between the two countries.

It is usually argued that with decreasing costs, whatever the terms of trade, each country should specialize completely. For it is clear that if the terms of trade are more favourable to commodity x (or y) than the slope of the line connecting the extremities of the production frontier, consumption possibilities are highest if all resources are devoted to the production of x (or y).[27] This is applicable to both countries. As can be seen from Figure 2, either the two countries specialize completely at M, where country 1 produces AM of commodity x and country 2 produces BM of y, or they specialize completely at N, where country 1 produces $AN (=BM)$ of y, and country 2 produces $BN (=AM)$ of x. In either case, international equilibrium is attained at c, where the consumption indifference curves of the two countries are tangential to each other on the 'contract curve', and the equilibrium terms of trade line, McN, is parallel to the initial domestic price relatives for both countries and at right angles to the 'contract curve'. Thus, complete specialization either at M or at N will bring about large and equal gains for both countries in this reference model.

It has been shown that, although there is initially no price incentive for the two countries to specialize and engage in trade, the realization of economies

[27] Matthews, 1949–50, p. 152.

of scale through specialization would clearly be beneficial to both countries.[28] It is, indeed, the specialization itself which creates comparative advantage. How can two such countries achieve these advantages from specialization? There is no price incentive so that the price mechanism will not be effective in encouraging the benefits from specialization. An agreement to specialize in order to realize these dynamic trade gains *would* be effective.

It emerges that trade liberalization *per se* might be a relatively insignificant element in agreed specialization since the existence of two such identical economies in which there are opportunities for gains from integration does not depend on the prevalence of tariff protectionism. Free trade is necessary to the achievement of gains once agreement has been reached, specialization begun, and comparative advantages revealed. On the other hand, it is also clear that, without agreement, development through regional integration would result in the agglomeration of industrial activity.[29]

Where partners are completely identical, as shown in Figure 2, it is of no consequence which partner specializes in the production of which commodity. In either case, complete specialization would yield equal gains for both countries and leave the terms of trade the same as they were before integration. Under these circumstances, there is no basis for conflict in reaching agreement on specialization. In most circumstances, however, the gains from trade are likely to be unequally distributed and the more unequally they are distributed, the more difficult it will be to reach agreement on specialization.

(i) Some of the assumptions of our reference model can now be relaxed in order to explore these possibilities. First, assume that all other assump-

---

[28] 'The traditional comparative cost analysis thus is not a reliable predictor of the pattern of national specialization under conditions of decreasing cost'. Grubel, 1967, p. 385. See also the diagrammatic presentation in Minabe, 1968, pp. 150–56.

[29] Some alternative paths towards specialization through the realization of economies of scale have been suggested. First, Ohlin suggests that increasing returns to scale will be a powerful cause of trade specialization, arguing that when 'a number of regions are isolated from each other, and . . . their factor endowments and their demand are so balanced that the relative prices of factors and commodities are everywhere the same, . . . no trade is then possible. As a matter of fact, in so far as the market for some articles within each region is not large enough to permit the most efficient scale of production, division of labour and trade will be profitable. Each region will specialize on some of these articles and exchange them for the rest. The character of this trade will be entirely *a matter of chance* if factor equipment is everywhere the same, for it doesn't matter whether a certain region specializes in one commodity or another' (my italics) (1967, p. 38). Second, Meade concludes that 'in the case of important increasing returns to scale in both countries *a structural jolt* might be able to shift the world economy from one position of stable equilibrium (in which one country specialized wholly on one line of product) to a second position of stable equilibrium (in which that country specialized wholly on the other line of product), and that such a change might be better for both countries, worse for both, or better for one and worse for the other' (my italics) (1952, pp. 42–3). Finally, Janssen, in a model similar to mine, stresses that: '*Where, however, for political reasons, both countries specialize in the same product, considerable wastage results. Mutual agreements, or perhaps even a supranational form of control, will then be necessary to obtain an optimum result*' (Author's italics) (1961, p. 29).

tions remain unchanged but that the propensity to consume one of the two commodities is higher, say two-thirds for x and one-third for y.[30] Inspection shows that in this case, the equilibrium terms of trade will be more favourable to x than the slope of the line, MN, in Figure 2, connecting the extremities of the production frontier so long as demand is elastic with respect to price. Although the total output of both countries together is the same whether they specialize at either extremity of the production frontier, total demand in both countries increases more for commodity x than for y under unitary relative prices. Hence, both countries would prefer to specialize in the production of commodity x. That is not to say that specialization at extremity M or N would not benefit both countries. But there would be divergent gains from trade. For example, at M country 1 would specialize completely in the production of commodity x and obtain greater gains from trade than country 2. Agreed specialization would be more difficult to arrange. The inequality of gains would have to be compensated for within a more comprehensive type of agreement. In practice, of course, as the number of pairs of commodities being traded increases, the inequality of gains resulting from agreed specialization in one pair of commodities is able to be offset by reverse inequalities for other commodities, and agreement will be thereby facilitated.

(ii) Now, let all other assumptions remain unchanged, but assume more rapidly decreasing costs in one industry, x say, than in the other. In this case, the horizontal axis in Figure 2 becomes longer than the vertical axis. The equilibrium terms of trade will be less favourable to commodity x than the slope of the line connecting the extremities of the production frontier for both countries, since although total demand for the two commodities in the two countries taken together increases proportionately in value, because of the assumption of an equal propensity to consume each commodity, combined output of x will be larger than that of y. In this case, as in case (i), there will also be divergent gains from specialization, arising on the supply side.

Various cases which incorporate different consumption and production conditions for each commodity can be explored in this way. It may be that on rare occasions, for example, bias on the consumption side will offset bias on the production side so that each country would be indifferent as to the activity in which it specialized completely, as in the identical economies case. But more commonly some divergence in the gains from specialization could be expected.

Two useful generalizations emerge from the above analysis. Firstly, it is advantageous for countries to specialize completely in decreasing cost industries for which the terms of trade are likely to become more favourable

---

[30] The homothetic indifference curves would then be symmetric to a line from A or B less steep than the diagonal of the transformation box. The tangencies of the two indifference maps would yield terms of trade more favourable to x, or steeper than the diagonal MN.

than the slope of the line connecting the extremities of the production frontier. Secondly, the more similar the propensity to consume the two commodities and the more similar the nature of scale economies in their production, the more likely it is that they can be traded with equal gain through agreed specialization.

(iii) Finally, let all other assumptions remain unchanged, but assume that country 1 is a large country and country 2 is small. The size of a country is revealed in the size of its factor endowment, although the assumption of identical C/L ratios or factor proportions is retained. Again, inspection reveals that it is of no consequence to either country whether it specializes at one or the other extremity, M or N in Figure 2. The result is the same as in the identical economies case. But the equilibrium terms of trade would become less favourable than the slope of the line connecting the extremities of the production frontier for the industry in which the large country happens to specialize production. This makes sense. Although total demand for the two commodities in both countries taken together increases proportionately in value, because of the assumption of equal propensities to consume each commodity, combined output would be larger for the commodity produced in the larger country. Thus, the gains from trade would be larger for the small country and smaller for the large country relative to their respective national incomes. Note that the terms of trade for the commodity in the production of which the large country specializes could, under certain circumstances, become so unfavourable as to induce the large country back into the production of both commodities. There would then be no gains accruing to the large country. These conclusions are quite compatible with the classical treatment of large country–small country trade.

The rationale of agreed specialization and the conditions for its success can now be summarized. Agreed specialization is necessary to realize economies of scale in decreasing cost industrial activities. Countries aiming at agreement should be at the same stage of development, as measured by similarity in their factor proportions, and also be of similar size, as measured by the size of their factor endowment and the size and structure of their national markets. The more similar their productive and consumptive structures the better the prospect for agreed specialization.

Finally, what is likely to prompt countries to integrate their markets through agreed specialization? Importantly, they will be most willing to come to some agreement on specialization if they face competition from third countries with superior competitive power.

Introduce a third country into the model. Country 3 has a higher C/L ratio than countries 1 and 2 and larger factor endowments than either country separately, or even both of them put together. Introduce, too, a third commodity, z, the production of which requires lower capital intensity than both x and y at any factor price ratio. Treat countries 1 and 2 as one integrated country in relation to country 3 and commodities x and y as variants of the same commodity group (say machinery) in relation to commodity z (say textiles).

If the C/L ratio is substantially lower in countries 1 and 2 than in country 3, the Heckscher–Ohlin theorem suggests that the former countries should specialize completely in the production of z and give up the production of commodities x and y. Even if the difference in the C/L ratio is not large, though they will produce all three commodities, countries 1 and 2 should remain importers of x and y and exporters of z.

In addition, assume that while commodities x and y are subject to long-run decreasing costs, z is subject to increasing costs in the long-run. Then, the direction of comparative advantage already specified is even more pronounced and there will be a tendency towards complete specialization as country 3 develops economies of scale in industries x and y where output is expanding.[31]

Countries 1 and 2 might well opt for a policy of import substitution against competition from country 3. Perhaps they attempt import substitution because of balance of payments difficulties, a faster rate of technological progress in industries x and y, a more rapid increase in demand for x and y, or because more significant external economies are expected to be created by the import-competing industries. Or perhaps, following Johnson, there is simply some 'preference for heavy industrialization'.[32] Small market size and the low level of technology appropriate to the small market will prevent effective import-competition by countries 1 and 2 separately. The only effective means of meeting country 3's superior competitive power is through agreed specialization and regional integration. Agreed specialization will increase industrial efficiency within the integrated markets of countries 1 and 2 and improve the position of these smaller producers against their larger competitor. It will reduce, if not eliminate, the need for inefficient protectionism.

Agreed Specialization in Practice

It has been argued that agreed specialization is an essential component in regional integration which aims at the achievement of economies of scale in industrial production; that agreement will be easiest to effect between countries the greater the similarity in their structures of production and demand; and that the prime motive force towards agreed specialization will be the superior competitive power of outside producers.

In practice, agreed specialization might be effected through a variety of

[31] Graham justified protection on grounds similar to these: 1923, pp. 199–227.
[32] Johnson, 1967, pp. 256–83.

agencies: supra-national planning; the re-organization of market conditions; or rationalization within multi-national business firms.

(i) The Central American Common Market's principal objective is agreed specialization through supra-national planning among a group of small, less developed countries at a similar stage of industrialization. 'Planned complementarity' is formally incorporated into the articles of agreement among member countries. There is provision for the joint planning and development of 'integrated industries', those industries considered to require access to the whole common market for efficient operation at minimum capacity. Moreover, there is provision that one such industry must be established in each participating country before a second is developed in any one member country, so that the gains from specialization will be shared as evenly as possible. These 'integrated industries' represent agreed specialization of the kind Sir Roy Harrod recommended to Asian developing countries.[33]

Supra-national agreed specialization seems the most appropriate course for developing countries undertaking 'a policy of regionally co-ordinated import substitution'.[34] The United Nations Conference on Trade and Development has recommended regional integration and the exchange of trade preferences among developing countries at a similar stage of industrial development in order to ensure complementarity and balance in regional development and avoid the wasteful duplication of small-scale manufacturing operations.[35] These recommendations appear to have sound justification in theory.

Supra-national agreed specialization also seems an appropriate course for centrally planned economies, which have some characteristics and industrialization objectives in common with developing countries.[36] Centrally planned economies are apparently committed to planned industrial specialization 'on the basis of mutual co-ordination of their long-term plans, of purposeful specialization and co-operation',[37] within the framework of the Council for Economic Mutual Assistance. But the adequacy of this particular planning is difficult for us to assess.[38]

Supra-national agreed specialization will even be appropriate within the European Economic Community as it becomes necessary to foster the development of giant industrial companies against outside competition.

(ii) Changing the institutional framework within which industrial competition takes place also provides a means towards agreed specialization. Competitive market structures sometimes prevent the attainment of economies of scale. The development of large-scale enterprise within a unified market will often be desirable. Only mergers and specialization agreements can foster

---

[33] See Dell, 1966; Wionczek, 1966.
[34] E.C.A.F.E., 1963, p. 95. Cf. Balassa, 1965, Chapter 3. Lloyd, 1968, Chapter 7.
[35] Prebisch, 1964 and 1968.   [36] Johnson, 1968 (ii), p. 395.
[37] Kavásznai and Kozma, 1966, p. 144.
[38] See, for example, Góra and Hokowski, 1966; Sergeyev, 1963, pp. 277–96.

the competitive power of industries within a newly integrated market such as the E.E.C. against outside competition from larger producers, say in the United States. It is for this reason that, subject to certain limitations, the European Economic Community favours the removal of legal and psychological barriers to mergers across national frontiers, the conclusion of specialization, rationalization, joint purchasing, and joint research agreements.[39] Fostering market re-organization of this kind constitutes an important means to agreed specialization.[40]

(iii) Rationalization of production within multi-national firms represents a final means whereby agreed specialization may be effected. As has already been shown, the scope for agreed specialization is greatest among producers of similar types of industrial commodities which are subject to the same production and demand conditions. Thus, agreed specialization would commonly involve intra-industry specialization rather than inter-industry specialization. This has certainly been the effect of European integration.[41] Significantly, intra-industry specialization may be made effective through the rationalization of resources within multi-national firms.[42]

The theory of agreed specialization outlined above does not pretend to be a comprehensive theory of economic integration. But it may be thought of as one small step towards a more comprehensive and dynamic theory of international specialization.

It is commonly held that international trade results in unequal gains unless trading partners stand on an equal footing. Yet once countries do stand on an equal footing, traditional theory also suggests that the incentives to trade disappear. Here it has been argued that there can be significant gains from trade among similar countries through the realization of economies of scale and dynamic comparative advantage.

In the post-Kennedy Round world, trade policies need fresh direction. The European Economic Community is still in the process of development, and free trade schemes such as the North Atlantic Free Trade Area[43] and the Pacific Free Trade Area[44] are now being advocated. Regional integration

---

[39] See McLachlan and Swann, 1967, Chapters 5 (esp. pp. 72–3) and 8.

[40] The reorganization of market and industrial structures in Canada is one of the reasons why a U.S.–Canada Free Trade Area has been advocated: Stykolt and Eastman, 1960, pp. 336–47; Eastman, 1964, pp. 437–48; English, 1964; Wonnacott, 1967; Canadian–American Committee, 1963 and 1965.

[41] Grubel, 1967, pp. 375–88. Balassa, 1966, pp. 466–73.

[42] The European Coal and Steel Community provides a representative case. The Canada–United States Automative Agreement is another successful example. The differentiation of motor vehicle types produced in various countries has also been planned by multi-national enterprises. The development of complementary industries in L.A.F.T.A. countries has so far been undertaken mainly by giant American companies. See also Lea, 1966.

[43] See Maxwell Stamp Associates, 1967; English, 1968.

[44] See Kojima, 1968.

has been recommended to less developed countries and is being pushed forward in Latin America. Effective regional integration is also an objective within socialist countries. In the solution of international monetary and financial problems substantial progress has been made towards international co-operation. Why not in the field of international specialization too? The theory of agreed specialization begins to provide a foundation for such international co-operation.

REFERENCES

BALASSA, B., 'Towards a Theory of Economic Integration', *Kyklos*, Vol. XIV, fasc. 1 (1961).

——, *Economic Development and Integration*, Centro de Estudios Monetarios Latinoamericanos (Mexico, 1965).

——, 'Tariff Reductions and Trade in Manufactures among the Industrial Countries', *American Economic Review*, June 1966.

BHAGWATI, J., 'Immiserising Growth: A Geometrical Note', *Review of Economic Studies*, June 1958.

——, 'International Trade and Economic Expansion', *American Economic Review*, December 1958.

——, 'The Pure Theory of International Trade', *Economic Journal*, March 1964.

COOPER, C. A. and MASSELL, B. F., 'A New Look at Customs Union Theory', *Economic Journal*, December 1965.

DELL, S., *A Latin American Common Market* (O.U.P., London, 1966).

DENIAU, J. F., *The Common Market, Its Structure and Purpose* (London, 1960).

EASTMAN, H. C., 'The Canadian Tariff and the Efficiency of the Canadian Economy', *American Economic Review*, Vol. LIV (1964).

ENGLISH, H. E., *Industrial Structure in Canada's International Competitive Position*, Private Planning Association of Canada (Montreal, 1964).

——, *Transatlantic Economic Community: Canadian Perspectives* (University of Toronto Press, Toronto, 1968).

GÓRA, S. and HOKOWSKI, M., 'The Criteria of Intra-branch Specialization among Socialist Countries', *Problems of Economic Theory and Practice in Poland*, Vol. 2 (Polish Scientific Publishers, Warsaw, 1966).

GRAHAM, F. D., 'Some Aspects of Protection further considered', *Quarterly Journal of Economics*, February 1923.

GRUBEL, H. G., 'Intra-industry Specialization and the Pattern of Trade', *Canadian Journal of Economics and Political Science*, Vol. 33 (1967).

HARROD, R., 'Notes on Supply', *Economic Journal*, Vol. XL (1930).

——, 'The Law of Decreasing Costs', *Economic Journal*, Vol. XLI (1931).

——, 'Economic Development and Asian Regional Co-operation', *Pakistan Development Review*, Vol. 2, No. 1, spring 1962.

HIRSCH, S., *Location of Industry and International Competitiveness* (Oxford, 1967).

HUMPHREY, D. D., 'The Effects of a Customs Union in Western Europe', *Southern Economic Journal*, April 1961.

ISARD, W., *Location and the Space Economy* (New York, 1956).

JANSSEN, L. H., *Free Trade, Protection and Customs Union* (H. E. Stenfert Kross N.V., Leiden, 1961).

JOHNSON, H. G., 'The Criteria of Economic Advantage', in G. D. N. Worswick, ed., *The Free Trade Proposals* (Oxford, 1960).

——, 'International Trade Theory and Monopolistic Competition Theory', in R. E. Kuenne, ed., *Monopolistic Competition Theory* (John Wiley and Sons, New York, 1967).

———, 'An Economic Theory of Protectionism, Tariff Bargaining, and the Formation of Customs Union', *Journal of Political Economy*, June 1965.

———, *Comparative Cost and Commercial Policy Theory for a Developing World Economy*, Wicksell Lectures for 1968 (Stockholm, 1968) (i).

———, 'Notes on Some Theoretical Problems posed by the Foreign Trade of Centrally Planned Economies', in A. E. Brown and E. Neuberger, eds., *International Trade and Central Planning* (University of California Press, Berkeley and Los Angeles, 1968) (ii).

KAVÁSZNAI, G. and KOZMA, F., 'Some Problems of Inter-industry Co-operation between the Countries of the Council for Mutual Economic Assistance', Hungarian Academy of Sciences Institute of Economics, *Studies in International Economics* (Akadémiai Kaidó, Budapest, 1966).

KOJIMA, K., ed., *Pacific Trade and Development*, Japan Economic Research Center (Tokyo, 1968).

LARY, H. B., *Imports of Manufactures from Less Developed Countries*, National Bureau of Economic Research (New York, 1968).

LEA, S., 'Free Trade by Sectors', National Planning Association, *Looking Ahead*, September 1966.

LIPSEY, R. G., 'The Theory of Customs Union: A General Survey', *Economic Journal*, September 1965.

LLOYD, P. J., *International Trade Problems of Small Nations* (Duke University Press, Durham, 1968).

MCLACHLAN, D. L. and SWANN, D., *Competitive Policy in the European Community* (Oxford U.P., London, 1967).

MATTHEWS, R. C. O., 'Reciprocal Demand and Increasing Returns', *Review of Economic Studies*, Vol. XVII (1949–50).

MEADE, J. E., *A Geometry of International Trade* (George Allen and Unwin, London, 1952).

MINABE, N., 'The Meanings and the Limitations of a Theory of Agreed Specialisation' (in Japanese), *Keizaigaku Zassi*, February 1968.

MYRDAL, G., *An International Economy, Problems and Prospects* (Harper Bros., New York, 1956).

———, *Economic Theory and Under-Developed Regions* (Duckworth, London, 1957).

———, 'The Efforts toward Integration in Rich and Poor Countries', Paper delivered in Mexico City, 3 October 1966.

NURKSE, R., *Patterns of Trade and Development*, Wicksell Lectures for 1959 (Stockholm, 1959).

OHLIN, B., *Interregional and International Trade*, revised edition (Harvard University Press, Cambridge, 1967).

PREBISCH, R., *Towards a New Trade Policy for Development*, United Nations (New York, 1964).

———, *Towards a Global Strategy of Development*, United Nations (New York, 1968).

ROBINSON, E. A. G., ed., *Economic Consequences of the Size of Nations* (Macmillan, London, 1960).

SCITOVSKY, T., *Economic Theory and Western European Integration* (George Allen and Unwin, London, 1958).

SERGEYEV, V. P., 'Economic Principles of the Foreign Trade of Socialist States', in R. Harrod and D. C. Hague, eds., *International Trade Theory in a Developing World* (Macmillan, London, 1963).

STIGLER, G. J. and BOULDING, K. E., eds., *Readings in Price Theory* (Chicago, 1952).

STYKOLT, S. and EASTMAN, H. C., 'A Model for the Study of Protected Oligopolies', *Economic Journal*, June 1960.

VINER, J., 'Cost Curves and Supply Curves', *Zeitschrift für Nationalökonomies*, Vol. III (1931–2).

———, *The Customs Union Issue*, Carnegie Endowment for International Peace (New York, 1950).

WIONCZEK, M. S., ed., *Latin American Economic Integration* (Praeger, New York, 1966).
WONNACOTT, R. J. and P., *Free Trade between the United States and Canada* (Harvard University Press, Cambridge, 1967).

CANADIAN–AMERICAN COMMITTEE, *A Canada–U.S. Free Trade Arrangement, Survey of Possible Characteristics*, National Planning Association, Washington, D.C., October 1963.
——, *A Possible Plan for Canada–U.S. Free Trade Area, A Staff Report*, February 1965.
E.C.A.F.E., *Economic Bulletin for Asia and the Far East*, December 1963.
G.A.T.T., *International Trade 1959–1960* (Geneva, 1960).
Maxwell Stamp Associates, *The Free Trade Option, Opportunity for Britain*, Atlantic Trade Study (London, 1967).
UNITED NATIONS, *World Economic Survey 1958* (New York, 1959)

21

MODEL CONSTRUCTION IN INTERNATIONAL TRADE THEORY

BERTIL OHLIN

1. In the last century up to the 1950's international trade theory has on the whole concentrated on trade between industrialized countries, or the export of manufactured commodities from such countries in exchange for 'primary goods' from countries which, in the period considered, exported little else. More recently the appearance of industrially 'less developed' countries which aim at a rapid development of manufactures—and to a considerable extent seem to achieve it—has brought a somewhat different setting of the problem. The central task remains, of course, the same: to explain the character and development of the international division of labour and the exchange of commodities and, above all, to explain short-term and long-term *variations* in trade as well as in the production of each country. It is easy to explain in historical terms why for a century economists in this connection talked so much about *trade* and said so little about *production*, except in the simplest terms. The dominating interest was given to comparative efficiencies of labour in different industries in different countries.

It would have brought considerable advantages if an analysis had been made of the international location of industry under the assumption of a limited *international* mobility of commodities—owing to transport costs, tariffs, etc.[1] This might be analysed with the assumption that capital and highly skilled labour are completely mobile, while all other productive factors are not mobile between countries. If their mobility *inside* each country is assumed to be complete, then each country can be regarded as a point. The Thunen–Weber type of location theory can then be used to explain the location of industry at each point and the movements of commodities between them. The international transfer costs are to some extent 'border costs'—like tariffs—but international transport costs are dependent on distance, etc. For goods

---

[1] This approach is different from the ones used by Lösch and Isaac. Around 1927–8 I met Professor Alleyn Young in London and discussed with him the possibility of rewriting my unpublished book on 'Interregional and International Trade' following the pattern indicated in the text above. I also considered working out a 'competing' theory along such lines. He expressed the tentative view that 'imperfect competition' would complicate matters at an early stage of such a theory more than with the conventional approach.

that are heavy and bulky in relation to value, or which are for other reasons difficult to transport, international trade is influenced by the geographical distribution of the different countries. Vicinity still plays some role. Hence, the utilization of a simple location theory model of this sort may throw some light on the importance of two sets of circumstances: (1) the geographical distribution in the world of raw material resources and of 'ordinary' labour; (2) the costs of transfer of different commodities between different countries. One would come even closer to the Thunen–Weber type of location theory by means of a first assumption that ordinary labour also is completely mobile between nations and receives the same real wage everywhere, but a model based on this assumption would not be helpful.

2. Let me return now to the more usual basis of trade theory. Conditions of production are different in different countries. The supply and quality of productive factors and transport conditions differ, e.g., between industrially underdeveloped and developed countries, which I below call u-countries and i-countries respectively. There are also differences in the 'infrastructure', in the size of markets and in political risks. *How are we to 'formalize' as many essential aspects of these differences as possible and do it in such a way that quantitative theoretical models can be constructed?* They should be used in a comparative *static analysis*, i.e., a comparison between the state of a model at one time and its state at some other time when some 'basic' circumstances have changed. Secondly, how can we obtain useful *growth models* which throw some light on the process of change in these basic conditions and thereby also on the influence of economic and social policy on the development of production and trade?

I confine myself below chiefly to comments on the first question, the comparative static model analysis. The two most common very simple international trade models are the theory of *comparative costs*—real costs—and the *factor proportions* theory, which runs in terms of money costs. Both have their merits and weaknesses. None of them can serve as more than a general introduction, as the simplifications made are far reaching. The tendency to stress 'precision' in theory through exercises with simple models—e.g., two countries and two commodities—and the application of the conclusions to concrete problems has sometimes led to unrealistic results, e.g., about the small effects of exchange rate depreciation or capital exports on the volume and above all the value of commodity exports. A country which is economically only a small part of the world may—after a few years—more than double its exports of many commodities as a result of a 10 per cent price reduction. After all, even first-year students are taught to make a distinction between the demand curve from the point of view of the individual firm and the elasticity of demand in the market as a whole.

Should we, then, make the models more complicated and thereby more realistic, but also more difficult to handle? Or is it preferable to use many separate models to illuminate different aspects of international economic relations? Both procedures can, I think, be useful. It must be an advantage if a model can easily be 'expanded' and made more realistic through the introduction of neglected elements, e.g., the consideration of special production costs like taxes, etc. This is an argument in favour of a consistent analysis in terms of *money* costs, not real costs. But if the real cost reasoning is regarded only as a method of simplifying the description of the basic conditions of production in the countries concerned, and if money wage rates are introduced at an early stage of the exposition, the neo-classical approach becomes a simplified *money* cost model, which may be easier to handle than the factor proportions model in cases where there are large differences in the quality of labour in different countries.

In the factor proportions model it is necessary either to regard common labour in countries at different stages of industrial development as different factors of production, or to introduce different production functions. Whatever method is used, the simple conclusions concerning the equalization of factor prices are to some extent impaired.

3. It is relatively easy to introduce international transfer costs for commodities in a theoretical model, i.e. transport costs, extra trade costs, and tariffs minus export subsidies. Internal transport costs are a more complicated story. It is well known that some countries import bricks over one frontier for use nearby, while they export the same quality of bricks over another frontier. In the absence of tariffs—in free trade areas and customs unions—similar cases will, no doubt, become more numerous and important. Much of this can, however, be more easily explained and understood without the use of quantitative models, which may lose more through unrealistic assumptions than they gain in precision. After all they often cannot do more than create an understanding of the character of the problem—something which an exposition of the 'essay writing' type can also do. Let us not carry the enthusiasm for quantitative models too far.

4. *The size of the market* for a certain commodity in a world with tariffs, differences in language, cultural traditions, taste, and living standards may exercise a considerable influence on the conditions of production of that commodity in different countries. The size of the geographical area is another element, as the costs of internal transportation may affect prices and quantities sold. Furthermore, the demand for capital goods inside the tariff area—and thus the size of the market—depends on the degree of industrialization. All these circumstances affect the possibility of obtaining economies of large scale in the production of goods the cost of which is too high to make considerable exports possible. An analysis of the trade between large and small countries can probably more profitably be directed to such phenomena than

to the not unusual discussion of the assumptions under which in 'two-commodity and two-country cases', one nation may reap the whole benefit from the trade between them. Fortunately, the recent discussion of tariff unions and free trade areas is devoting growing attention to market size.

It goes without saying that dumping and other aspects of imperfect competition can play a substantial role in international trade, the more so the more the world is divided into markets that are separated from each other by tariffs, transport costs, firm control of the market under imperfect competition, etc.

5. In this paper I shall now concentrate my observations on some special sets of conditions which influence the international division of labour. They have, as far as I know, been given relatively little attention in international trade theory. They can almost certainly be advantageously analysed with the aid of theoretical models.

That *taxes and social payments*, which enter into costs of production or take away a part of the profit otherwise obtained, affect trade is obvious. However, the prices of factors of production are not unaffected. This too affects supply prices of producers as well as the profitability and volume of investment in different lines of output. Thereby, the volume of production and sales are influenced. Consequently, the tax systems used in different countries can affect the international division of labour. A special group of tax cases—tariffs and export subsidies—has been extensively analysed. The rest has been almost ignored until recent years. A great deal of thought has been given to the problem in the E.E.C. during the last decade, as a basis for the political 'follow up work' after the signing of the Rome Treaty. These reports are not at present available to me. Their scientific contents have not, as far as I know, found their way into the academic journals.[2]

I here refer to the structure of the tax system and not to the effects on foreign trade of changes in the sum total of public expenditure and in budget balances. The latter question, regarded as a part of the international aspects of expansionary or deflationary processes, has been extensively dealt with in connection with monetary policy, business cycles, and financial policy. The neglected part is the effect of differences and changes in the structure of tax systems—apart from the much debated structure of tariff and subsidy systems.[3]

It may be objected that the analysis of the shifting and incidence which follow changes in the tax structure in 'an isolated country'—by means of a

[2] The most recent survey of post-war international trade theory (Krueger, 1969), which covers much more than its title indicates, makes no reference to taxation aspects. See also well-known surveys by Bhagwati, Caves, and Chipman.

[3] Some aspects of my own views have been presented (in a somewhat sketchy manner) in Ohlin, 1956. See also Ohlin (1933 and 1968), Chapter VI, Section 10, and the new Appendix II in the revised edition.

one-market theory—has been found to offer extremely great difficulties. Must not such an analysis serve as a basis for a theoretical analysis of the same sort in a 'many markets theory' for trading countries? While this would generally speaking be desirable, it is probable that the effects of certain tax changes and tax differences between countries can be analysed in a simpler way, e.g., a consistent double taxation of corporation profits in country A but no such double taxation, or a small one, in country B will tend to keep back the development in A of industries which need to use the legal corporation form. More generous depreciation rules in taxation in country B, which lead to larger 'hidden' internal corporation savings, will stimulate investment and expansion of productive capacity in industries for which B has in general reasonably favourable opportunities. It seems probable that simple theoretical models can be used advantageously for the analysis of such questions.

Let me add that policies to affect the location of industry *inside a country*— like the Mezzo Giorno project in Italy and the British policies to foster industrial development in Scotland and in the northern half of England— use tax rebates, generous depreciation rules, and subsidies (i.e., negative taxes). There can be no doubt that such policies have had a considerable influence on the location of industry and thus on *inter-regional* trade.

Similarly, tax advantages offered to foreign firms by Ireland and by some u-countries have brought results in the form of foreign owned factories and farms. In these cases the effect of the 'artificially' more favourable conditions of production is to bring about an influx of foreign capital and know-how and to speed up industrial development. Tax policies and railroad rebates have often been a supplement to tariff policy with the intention of stimulating industrial development—with or without an influx of foreign capital.[4]

6. Before the middle of the 1950's and the preparation for the E.E.C., the influence of international differences with regard to *social policies* was not much discussed in a 'scientific' manner. The fact that trade adapted itself to existing differences in social policy was taken more or less for granted. However, some of the experts and politicians, who had to work out the details of the economic relations of the member countries, advanced a view which had long been influential in most sections of the International Labour Office in Geneva. To avoid 'unfair' competition, all social regulations that affect production and trade must be 'harmonized'. Only wages must be allowed to differ as a consequence of inequalities in productivity. The ironical question by a French expert why one should not start with 'harmonizing' the climate just as much as 'the social *milieu*' was not well received in governing circles. However, over-simplified and partly misleading though

---

[4] It seems to me that the International Economic Association could render a great service, if it devoted one of its annual sessions to 'Tax structures in their relation to international trade and the movement of capital, labour and know-how'.

some of the official views no doubt were, they had the merit of demonstrating the need for a more thorough analysis.[5]

As an introduction to a discussion of suitable methods of analysis, I want to make some observations on the different aspects of social policies. Some social insurance payments are made by employers. They affect production costs largely in the same way as taxes that are proportional to payroll. Another type of social policy regulates the utilization of labour: the length of the working week, the number of holidays, the amount of 'over-time' permitted, the use of two or three shifts during each 24-hour period, special restrictions for the use of female labour, etc. Apart from compulsory public regulation, there may be agreements and fixed behaviour patterns which exercise a similar influence. Industries that require large quantities of capital per worker—not only a relatively great fixed capital but also large inventories—can make considerable economies through work in two or three shifts. The right to use a continuous production process during weekends in one country but not in another can, of course, tend to keep costs per unit down in the former. The productivity curve is affected by such rules. The more efficient utilization of capital—during more hours per year—means a saving of capital. If a proportional or more than proportional expansion of the relevant industries is not brought about, an increased supply of capital for other kinds of economic activity will follow, with some tendency to lower interest rates.

If the term social policy is widened to include habits and traditions and attitudes, much needs to be added on that account. In some u-countries workers regard it as natural to stay away from the job when they 'feel like it'. It is an example of costly behaviour patterns.

7. It is not easy to indicate briefly how a formalized model treatment of international differences and changes in productivity conditions can be handled, except in special cases. I recommend it as a task for young economists. There is, however, a group of circumstances which—although they are very different in character—can all be treated as *risk elements* and handled by means of simple models.

I am thinking of a varied group of risks due to new legislation and other kinds of *political* interference as well as to certain traditions and cultural inhibitions. Investments—particularly by foreign citizens—in enterprises in u-countries may be successful so far as the building up of production is concerned, but may nevertheless prove to be a partial or total loss owing to a later nationalization, accompanied by little or no compensation. Any rational investment appraisal calculations must allow for such risks. Furthermore, there is the possibility of government interference and regulations on the

---

[5] The head of the I.L.O. research section, Mr. Roberts, was critical of the old I.L.O. doctrine and took the initiative to the expert committee report of the I.L.O., published in 1956, which is mentioned in the list of references (Ohlin, 1956).

commodity, labour, or capital markets, in such a way that the effectiveness of production and the size of various cost items is affected. A special case is the risk of new or tougher exchange regulations which can make 'repatriation' of amortisation and profits to the investors in the home country impossible. Lack of tradition and leadership in trade unions may bring about erratic labour conflicts. The risk of such negative effects on output cannot be overlooked. Even without labour conflicts, workers may stay at home now and then, being unaccustomed to the regularity of work in industrialized countries. To some extent all these risks may be insurable and their economic importance estimated by the individual firm or government agencies. Anyway, somehow these risks are an item on the prospective cost account, and, therefore, affect investment, production, and trade. It seems safe to say that reforms in the u-countries, whereby such risks are reduced, can serve as a powerful stimulus to their industrial development. If governments in the i-countries take over the political risks, e.g., through a national or international insurance system, the influx into the u-countries of capital, know-how, and initiative will be increased.

In economic calculations it is, of course, in principle possible to introduce, for example, the risk of increased labour costs per unit or the risk of a lower total output than one could otherwise obtain from a certain input. It should not be difficult to construct simple models that take into account changes in such risks. The difficulty is to estimate the size of the risk in concrete cases.

This leads to the question of how an exercise with more or less complicated theoretical models contributes to knowledge, once certain fundamental characteristics of trade and the location of industry have been made clear with simple models. In this simple group I include some that illuminate international capital movements. But what about further complications? In the last few years I have become more sceptical about the fruitfulness of the application of so much scientific energy to a refined and detailed analysis of models based on violent abstractions. Is it perhaps more fruitful to use *several* new models, and to admit that they all, taken together, can do little more than increase our understanding of the problem. I am inclined to think that the influence of some forms of taxation and risk elements, and the size of the market, could be profitably illuminated with the use of new models. One could also, as indicated above, utilize location theory models to illustrate the influence of 'border costs' and international transport costs on the division of labour, particularly with regard to the division of the productive process and the location in different countries of raw material production and different stages of the manufacturing process. Exports and imports of capital goods would then receive much needed attention.

8. Without denying that other new models in comparative statics can be useful, I should like to put the following question. Would it not be fruitful to

concentrate attention from the beginning on *the cost account* and its com-ponents—adding, of course, a consideration of price and sales policies under imperfect competition? Anything that figures on the cost account of the producers and traders belongs to the more or less essential 'conditions of production'.

In brief, the above reasoning seems to lend some support to the view that the international aspect of price theory might be chiefly a *theory of the cost account and its constituents*. A consistent analysis, step by step, of the econo-mic importance of each of its constituents in different countries could be accompanied by the analysis of price and sales policies and, of course, various aspects of demand—all within the framework of the mutual interdependence type of reasoning. It goes without saying that international demand consists not only of demand for consumer goods but also of demand for semi-manufactured and other capital goods. An explanation of the location of industry is hence, at the same time, an explanation of the demand for capital goods.[6]

9. Every economist dreams of the time when the comparative statics theory will be supplemented by, to some extent substituted by, a dynamic theory. Roy Harrod belongs to the great pioneers, who have laid several stones in the foundation of such a dynamic theory—although this is only one of the several lasting contributions made by him to economic science. Simple growth models have already increased our insight into the conditions necessary for industrial development not only in 'isolated' but also in trading countries.[7] The basic or fundamental conditions of production cannot be described in static terms alone. For example, the effects of trade variations and tariff policy on the supply and quality of labour may be more important than many immediate benefits or damages, as the protectionists of the last century were already insisting. Investment may be based on the expected *future* growth of the demand for some commodities and not so much on the present more limited market. Models may be used in a study of the effects of different rates of growth of domestic capital, skilled labour, influx of capital, etc., as well as in an analysis of the influence of such growth on the balance of pay-ments in well chosen typical cases. I mention all these obvious things for one reason only: to use them to support a plea for some redistribution of interest in favour of dynamic models. It would, I think, bring greater marginal utility than continued exercises with the basic very simple comparative statics models in international trade theory. The latter are useful, probably necessary, for the teaching of such theory to young students. They need supplements in the form of *new* static models, rather than refinements of the old ones, as I have

---

[6] Some observations on this approach are made in a paper written by me for the *Swedish Economic Journal*, 1970.

[7] At the symposium on international economic relations in Brissago, 1961, Roy Harrod presented an important paper illuminating the growth process. See Harrod, 1963.

tried to demonstrate above. But it goes without saying that growth models deserve our attention even more.

REFERENCES

HARROD, R. F., 'Desirable International Movements of Capital in Relation to Growth of Borrowers and Lenders and Growth of Markets', in Harrod and Hague, eds., *International Trade Theory in a Developing World* (London, 1963).

KRUEGER, A. O., 'Balance of Payments Theory', *Journal of Economic Literature*, March 1969.

OHLIN, B., *Interregional and International Trade* (Harvard, 1933 and revised edition 1968).

——, *Social Aspects of European Economic Co-operation*, Appendix I, 'Taxation and International Trade' (International Labour Office, Geneva, 1956).

22

COMPARATIVE ADVANTAGE AND THE USE OF HOME-PRODUCED VERSUS IMPORTED MATERIALS

M. FG. SCOTT

SIR ROY HARROD's exposition of the theory of comparative advantage is 'based on the idea that each commodity requires for its production one or more factors that are specific to it: trade is profitable when, as between two countries, the amounts of each specific factor with which they are endowed are not in proportion to their respective demands for the commodity to which each relates'.[1] He lists the main differences between countries in regard to their endowments of specific factors as being due to natural resources (e.g., minerals, climate, soil), numbers of people in relation to natural resources, human capacity (partly innate, partly the result of history), and the legacy of the past (e.g., equipment, factories, railways, organization, knowledge, habit).[2]

It is clear that many factors determine comparative advantage. Nevertheless, a theory which credits each commodity with its own specific factor appears, at first sight, unpromising. One asks of a theory that it should simplify the variety and complexity of the world so that one can make some general statements about it. It is not surprising that others have attempted such generalizations, and that Professor Ohlin's model in which differences in comparative advantage are explained by differences in the proportions of non-specific factors (labour and capital) required to make different goods, combined with differences in countries' endowment of these factors, has been popular.[3]

This essay is, in one sense, a generalization about comparative advantage. Nevertheless, in another sense the main lesson I draw from this example is

---

[1] Harrod, 1957, p. 35. [2] *Ibid.*, pp. 10, 11.

[3] Sir Roy believes 'that it will be found that the unequal endowment with non-specific factors will never give rise to very big differences of comparative cost—to differences big enough, for example, to cover substantial international transport costs. This is not to impugn the theory as such, but only to cast doubt on the quantitative importance of the phenomena to which it relates. Accordingly it does not seem suitable to make the unequal endowment of countries with non-specific factors the main foundation of the theory of international trade.' *Ibid.*, p. 36.

that some simple theories can lead one dangerously astray in this field. It is profoundly true that the attempt to single out particular industries for encouragement on the basis of some simple criteria can result in economic waste on a large scale. If one interprets Sir Roy's specific factor for each commodity as standing for the complex of factors which influence its cost of production, then it is certainly true that this complex varies from commodity to commodity (or even process to process), and that whether a particular process is viable or not can only be determined by the most detailed and careful examination.

The generalization I wish to examine is, in fact, also Sir Roy's. 'Countries with a population dense in proportion to the capacity of the soil would naturally employ their surplus on the processes which do not have to be undertaken in close conjunction with the soil, and exchange manufactured goods for the raw products of more sparsely peopled regions.'[4]

Sir Roy probably had his own country, amongst others, in mind when he wrote this. It certainly fits the bill. I shall confine my attention to poorer countries—those for whom 'the legacy of the past' is insufficient to compensate for their meagre endowment of natural resources.

The outstanding example of exporting manufactures based on imported materials is Hong Kong. Before and after the war, she relied heavily on entrepôt trade. In 1952, over 80 per cent of her exports were re-exports. The Korean War, however, led to restrictions being placed on trade with the Chinese mainland, so this trade suffered. Instead, Hong Kong rapidly developed her manufacturing industry. Domestic exports multiplied in value about twelve times from 1952 to 1966, an average compound rate of growth of 19 per cent p.a. This high rate of growth in exports was accompanied by a rapid growth in Hong Kong's real net output per head of population of more than 5 per cent p.a. over the decade ending in 1964 and led to a level of output per head which was probably second in Asia, outside the Middle East, only to Japan (and possibly Singapore).

Various factors explain this success: the inflow of skilled immigrants from the mainland; access to capital from Hong Kong's banks; the excellent infrastructure; and the services of export merchants, and insurance and shipping companies. An important part of the explanation, however, is that Hong Kong's businessmen have been able to buy their materials and machinery in the cheapest markets. With Hong Kong's good port facilities, transport costs on raw cotton and textiles are relatively small; and although cotton yarn and cloth are both manufactured in the colony, there has been no attempt to protect these industries; indeed, large quantities of yarn and cloth are imported as well as exported. Consequently, the weavers can buy their yarn and the clothing manufacturers their cloth at the best prices, and can pick

[4] *Ibid.*, p. 11.

and choose the qualities and quickly adapt them to changes in fashions and techniques.

Another example is Taiwan. Her success in increasing her exports of manufactures, many of them consisting of processed imported materials, dates from the end of the 1950's, and has been phenomenal. From 1958 to 1966 her exports of manufactures grew by 40 per cent a year in dollar terms, and rose from a ninth to a half of her total exports. Again, many factors help to explain this achievement, notably the large amount of aid she received. But an essential ingredient was the series of measures taken to rebate duties levied on imported materials and to improve the import licensing system so that manufacturers who wished to export did not have to pay exorbitant prices for their materials to import licence holders. The simplification of the multiple exchange rate system, coupled with some devaluation of the rates, was also important. All these measures meant that, as in Hong Kong, exporters could buy their materials at world prices and so could compete with other exporters of the processed products on world markets.

A particularly striking example of the kind of activity I have in mind is provided by the Kaohsiung Export Processing Zone, situated in a good harbour at the south of Taiwan. The manufacturers who have set up in this Zone are allowed to import duty-free any materials or equipment they need with the minimum of administrative formalities. They can export freely too, but if they wish to sell to Taiwan they are treated as if they were foreigners, and their goods are subject to tariffs and import restrictions just like goods imported from anywhere else. In practice, they mostly export all their output elsewhere. There is an electronics firm, a subsidiary of a large Western company, which flies in parts for computers, employs young women to process them, and then flies them back to the parent company or to other subsidiaries. In this way they take advantage of the low local labour costs in a labour-intensive process. In terms of efficiency, the local women are as good as in the West, but their wages are much lower.

One may ask 'But what does Taiwan get out of this?' The main advantage is the extra employment, and the income earned by workers in the Zone. This has been secured without calling on Taiwan's own supplies of capital or land to any significant extent, since the capital mostly comes from abroad (and even the small amount of land required has been reclaimed from the sea!). In addition, local labour receives some training in factory and managerial skills. After a five-year tax holiday, the companies in the Zone will have to pay income tax. In a country where labour is abundant, and capital and land are scarce, these gains are significant.

Pakistan's exports of manufactures have grown very rapidly, like those of Hong Kong and Taiwan. From 1953 to 1965 they increased on average at 36 per cent p.a., and this growth represented 35 per cent of Pakistan's exports of all merchandise in 1965. Like Taiwan, therefore, Pakistan was able to increase her exports of manufactures from negligible quantities to an amount which represented a sizeable contribution to her total foreign exchange earnings.

Unlike Hong Kong and Taiwan, however, Pakistan's exports of manufactures have been very largely based on home-produced materials: raw jute and raw cotton. While her manufactured exports have increased, her exports of primary products have fallen, and the result has been a much slower growth in her total exports than in those of Hong Kong and Taiwan.[5] Furthermore, the rise in exports of manufactures has been at least in part the *cause* of the fall in exports of primary products, and economic policy has helped to bring both about.

Exports of jute and cotton textiles have been encouraged by what are, in effect, very substantial subsidies. There is no need to go into details here.[6] Suffice to say that there has been the equivalent of a nominal subsidy of 20 per cent on jute goods and around 35 per cent on cotton textiles in recent years. These nominal rates of subsidy give rise to much higher *effective* rates of subsidy (i.e., in relation to value added), since manufacturers of jute and cotton buy their materials at below world prices because of export taxes on them. There are various ways of calculating this effective rate of subsidy (or protection). Using the 'Corden' method,[7] which tends to give a lower figure than other methods, Professor Lewis estimates the rate of protection for jute textiles in 1963/4 at 183 per cent, and for cotton textiles at 213 per cent.

While exports of processed jute and cotton have been encouraged in this way, exports of raw jute and cotton have been actively discouraged by export taxes of up to 10 per cent in recent years.

Economic policy in Pakistan has discouraged industries based on imported materials. The discouragements have taken several different forms. Import licences for materials have usually been based on one-shift capacity, and have sometimes been insufficient even for this. Hence, while the textile industries have been able to work two or three shifts, industries using imported materials have usually been forced to work only one shift, and even on this basis have had spare capacity. In addition, there have been high tariffs on many imported intermediate goods. The planners have also looked with disfavour on industries using imported materials, and this has affected the attitude of the investment licensing authorities and probably credit institutions as well.

In principle, if a manufacturer wishes to export some item containing an imported material or component, he can claim a rebate of the duty paid on it. But it can be a lengthy and difficult process, especially if the exported item

[5] From 1953 to 1965, Hong Kong's total exports increased in dollar terms by 211 per cent, Taiwan's by 252 per cent, and Pakistan's by only 20 per cent.

[6] For a detailed analysis, and references to other studies, see Lewis, 1970, on which much of the following is based.

[7] See Corden, 1966.

is a new one so that no standard formula for the calculation of the rebate has been worked out. Similarly, import licences should, in principle, be more easily obtained for materials used to make exports, but in practice there can be delays and difficulties in getting them. Requests have to be made well in advance, and unexpected needs cannot easily be met. There is already a disadvantage in having to order one's materials from abroad, and this is compounded by the bureaucratic delays of the licensing system.

The same firm that had set up an electronics subsidiary in the Taiwan Export Processing Zone had previously set up one in Pakistan. Their experience had been less favourable. They had hardly started before their licence to import components had been cut severely because of a foreign exchange crisis.

The attitude of the Pakistan authorities towards industries based on imported materials is understandable. The official exchange rate is overvalued, and access to imports at that rate, via import licences, is a privilege which is worth a lot of money. There is therefore a built-in incentive to use imported materials which has to be countered in other ways. Unfortunately, as a by-product of the system, and because the apparatus of control cannot in practice make the fine discrimination required, some activities using imported materials are discouraged too much.

While this largely explains the discouragement given to industries based on imported materials, it does not explain the sharp discrimination in policy between exports of raw jute and cotton and exports of jute and cotton manufactures. Part of the explanation for this is the belief that manufacturing must be encouraged relatively to agriculture—the infant industry argument applied to exports. Even this, however, is not the whole story.

Pakistan is the world's largest exporter of raw jute. In 1965 its exports accounted for 69 per cent of world exports of jute and kenaf. The authorities probably believed that demand for these exports was not highly elastic, so that Pakistan could exploit its monopoly position by taxing them. On the other hand, Pakistan's exports of jute manufactures were a much smaller proportion of world exports of these manufactures in 1959, when the policy of subsidizing their exports began. Even by 1965 they only represented 15 per cent of world exports of jute manufactures. Hence, on straightforward terms of trade grounds there seemed to be a case for discriminating in favour of exports of jute manufactures relatively to exports of raw jute.

For cotton and cotton textiles the case was not so clear, since Pakistan provided a small proportion of world exports of each. However, even here the same line of reasoning may have been employed.

But this reasoning (if indeed it was employed) overlooked the fact that additional exports of jute or cotton manufactures tend to depress the price of the country's exports of raw jute and cotton in just the same way as do additional exports of the raw products themselves. If there is good reason to tax the export of raw jute and cotton, then, for exactly the same reason, one should tax the export of the raw jute and cotton contained in exports of manufactures. On certain simplifying assumptions, the export tax in each case should be the same. A more rigorous proof is given in the Appendix, but it is worth sketching the main reasons here, since some may find this result surprising.

Suppose that the export price of raw jute is Rs. 1 per ton (the figures are chosen for simplicity, not reality). Suppose that if an extra ton is exported by Pakistan (while Pakistan's exports of jute manufactures are constant) the world price of raw jute is reduced by Rs. k. Suppose, furthermore, that 1 ton of raw jute makes 1 ton of jute manufactures, and that value added per ton in the rest of the world is constant. If an extra ton of raw jute is exported it will therefore reduce the world price of jute manufactures by Rs. k. Suppose Pakistan exports altogether x tons of raw jute and jute manufactures. Then, if an extra ton of raw jute is exported, the increase in the value of Pakistan's exports of jute and jute manufactures is Rs. $(1-xk)$. This is therefore the country's marginal revenue from exporting raw jute and so, on well-known assumptions, the correct export tax is Rs. xk per ton, since this makes the price received by the exporter equal to the country's marginal revenue.

Now consider an extra ton of exports of jute manufactures (exports of raw jute from Pakistan being constant). This must have exactly the same effect on the export prices of raw jute and jute manufactures, i.e., it must reduce them by Rs. k per ton. For a reduction of this amount will increase the rest of the world's consumption of jute manufactures and reduce its output of raw jute by amounts which are exactly the same as in our first case. And in that case, just as in this, the gap between consumption and production of jute in the rest of the world widens by the extra 1 ton exported from Pakistan. Since the reductions in price are the same, the loss of export revenue from this cause is also the same, namely, Rs. xk. Hence the correct export tax is also the same, namely, Rs. xk per ton.

Of course, the various simplifying assumptions made in this argument may not hold in reality, and their failure could mean that the correct export tax on jute manufactures should be more or less than that on raw jute.[8] Furthermore, the argument is *only* concerned with terms of trade reasons for taxing or subsidizing exports, and ignores the infant industry argument (for example) for favouring jute manufactures. Despite these limitations,[9] the

---

[8] If value added per ton in jute manufacture in the rest of the world tended to fall when Pakistan increased its exports of jute manufactures, and to rise when it increased its exports of raw jute (so that the 'supply of value added' in the rest of the world was less than infinitely elastic), then the export tax on jute manufactures should be higher, and that on raw jute lower, than the above argument suggests.

[9] There are better ways of promoting infant industries than providing them with export subsidies. See Little, Scitovsky and Scott, 1970, Chapters IV and IX.

case analysed here may have a fairly wide applicability. Another example is the export of instant coffee from Brazil.

It is interesting to push the argument a little further, at the risk of discrediting it in the eyes of some because of its surprising conclusions! If it is right to restrict exports of jute, or coffee, to keep up their prices in world markets, then it must also be right to encourage imports of manufactures containing these products beyond the amounts which would come in under *laissez faire*. Hence Pakistan ought to put a subsidy on imports of jute manufactures [10] and Brazil one on imports of instant coffee. Of course, the subsidy might be inoperative in many cases, since imports might be unable to compete with domestic production. Where they could compete, however, extra imports would raise demand in the rest of the world for exports of the primary product and so improve the country's terms of trade.

Although I have taken Pakistan as my chief example, there are undoubtedly other countries in which economic policy has discriminated unduly in favour of industries based on domestic materials and against those based on imported materials. The opportunity to export the country's labour services without having to draw on its scarce supplies of natural resources has thereby been neglected. I do not imply by this that such opportunities are necessarily widespread, nor that good, or even better, opportunities of exploiting domestic natural resources are not neglected as well. I am not proposing a simple recipe for choosing industries to develop. Rather, in keeping with Sir Roy's insistence on the importance of specific factors in creating comparative advantage, I am warning against policies which, by pushing along particular avenues, shut off others which are promising.

APPENDIX

This Appendix gives the model used in the text to analyse the optimum tax on exports of a material and of a manufacture made from it. For simplicity's sake, they are called jute and jute manufactures.

The rest of the world's demand for jute manufactures, Q_f, depends on their export price, P_f, and on other factors which are assumed constant, so

$$(1) \qquad Q_f = Q_f(P_f).$$

The rest of the world's supply of jute, Q_r, depends on its export price, P_r, and on other factors which are assumed constant, so

$$(2) \qquad Q_r = Q_r(P_r).$$

---

[10] Since Pakistan's currency is overvalued at the official exchange rate, a subsidy might not be needed—merely freedom to import.

The units of Q_f and Q_r are chosen so that one unit of Q_r is required to make one unit of Q_f, and this relationship is assumed to be fixed.

Consequently, if the country's exports of jute are X_r and of jute manufactures are X_f, measured in the same units,

$$(3) \qquad\qquad Q_r + X_r = Q_f - X_f.$$

The supply of value added in jute manufacturing in the rest of the world is infinitely elastic, so that

$$(4) \qquad\qquad P_f = P_r + \text{a constant.}$$

The value of the country's total exports of jute and jute manufactures is

$$(5) \qquad\qquad V = P_r \cdot X_r + P_f \cdot X_f.$$

By differentiating (5) with respect to X_r and X_f respectively we can find the country's marginal revenue from exporting more jute and jute manufactures respectively.

Keeping X_f constant we have:

$$\frac{dV}{dX_r} = P_r + X_r \cdot \frac{dP_r}{dX_r} + X_f \cdot \frac{dP_f}{dX_r}.$$

But from (4)

$$\frac{dP_r}{dX_r} = \frac{dP_f}{dX_r},$$

hence

$$\frac{dV}{dX_r} = P_r + (X_r + X_f) \cdot \frac{dP_r}{dX_r}.$$

Likewise

$$\frac{dV}{dX_f} = P_f + (X_r + X_f) \cdot \frac{dP_r}{dX_f}.$$

In each of these last two equations, the second term (which is negative) shows the difference between marginal revenue and price. This difference is the correct export tax (specific, per unit of export quantity) to levy, if the aim of the tax is to equalize the price received by the exporter and the country's marginal revenue. It is the same for jute as for jute manufactures, since

$$\frac{dP_r}{dX_r} = \frac{dP_r}{dX_f}.$$

The value of each can be worked out. It is

$$\frac{dP_r}{dX_r} = \frac{dP_r}{dX_f} = -\frac{1}{\dfrac{Q_r}{P_r} \cdot e_r - \dfrac{Q_f}{P_f} \cdot e_f},$$

where e_r is the elasticity of supply of jute in the rest of the world, derived from (2), and e_f is the elasticity of demand for jute manufactures (defined so as to be negative), derived from (1).

REFERENCES

CORDEN, W. M., 'The Structure of a Tariff System and the Effective Protective Rate', *The Journal of Political Economy*, June 1966.

HARROD, R. F., *International Economics*, Fourth Edition (Cambridge, 1957).

LEWIS, S. R., Jr. *Pakistan: Industrialization and Trade Policies* (London, 1970).

LITTLE, I. M. D., SCITOVSKY, T., and SCOTT, M. FG., *Industry and Trade in Some Developing Countries* (London, 1970).

23

INTERNATIONAL ECONOMIC CO-OPERATION AND THE OBSTACLES CONFRONTING MONETARY POLICY IN SMALL COUNTRIES

JEAN WEILLER

W E present here some reflections on the difficulties encountered by *small countries* who follow, more or less faithfully, the prescriptions of *monetary policy* as practised in Western countries.

The problems do not appear to be exactly the same in socialist economies—at least at first sight, and if one believes that there is a marked difference between the two types of economies in regard to their international economic relations.[1] One can, in fact, argue that the dangers we mention are precisely those inherent in any neoclassical policy for *capitalist* countries in which the price mechanism plays the major role. Furthermore, we are concerned with credit policy in relation to private enterprise dependent on a Western-type banking system.

Without wishing to enter into a whole series of considerations which would be appropriate were we making a systematic comparison, we must mention, first, that the analysis is at a certain level of abstraction—one where comparisons and generalizations are most useful since we are attempting to shed light, not on the working of an automatic mechanism, but rather on the decision processes of monetary authorities.[2] Secondly, we are not concerned with fully industrialized countries, but with the monetary policy of developing countries more or less integrated into the international trading system.

When a small country of this kind, dependent on foreign trade, begins to develop, it encounters serious balance of payments problems. Its demand for imports presses on its capacity to import, which is determined by its exports, receipts of aid, and foreign capital. The small country must then limit its absorption so as to import only essentials and to free sufficient domestic production for export.

Reducing absorption poses policy problems even for large developed countries, since one no longer believes in the existence of automatic adjustment

---

[1] cf. Perroux, 1958.   [2] cf. Johnson, 1967, Fellner, Machlup, and Triffin, 1966.

23—I.G.T.

mechanisms. In every developing country today the question is what policy to adopt. We shall show that *global* monetary policies, which have been so often blessed by many writers, are useless for small countries, even if they are strictly orthodox.

1. In general, for large industrial countries, modern theory approves of monetary policy, supplemented as necessary by fiscal policy.[3] The efficacity of these policies in curing internal or external (fundamental) imbalances does not depend, so it seems, on the size or development of the country concerned.

On this view, the efficacity of monetary policy is only limited by the possible conflict between the objectives of growth and full employment, on the one hand, and equilibrium in the balance of payments, on the other.[4] An external deficit may require a restrictive credit policy which is often incompatible with full employment.

A conflict arises when:

(i) there is an external deficit combined with under-employment; or
(ii) there is an external surplus combined with over-employment.

This shows that one cannot rely solely on short-term interest-rate policy. Nevertheless, monetary policy retains its privileged position.

Two ways of resolving this conflict of objectives have been attempted, notably in the United States since 1960:

First, the '*twist policy*' begun by the Kennedy Administration. This was intended to correct both disequilibria simultaneously by *changing the structure of interest rates*: changes in short-term rates maintaining external balance through their influence on international capital movements, and changes in long-term rates maintaining internal balance through their effects on investment. Short-term interest rates had to be increased when there was an external deficit and long-term rates lowered if there was under-employment [case (i) above and *vice versa* in case (ii)].

Secondly, the '*mixed policy*'. This attempted to resolve the conflict by using monetary policy to maintain external balance and budgetary policy to maintain internal balance. The basic idea was to correct internal disequilibrium by altering public expenditure or receipts, while the effects on the external balance could be corrected by influencing international capital movements through monetary policy. Thus, if there was simultaneously an external deficit and under-employment, one needed tight credit, higher interest rates, and an expansionary budgetary policy.

It is noteworthy that leading orthodox opinion seems to prefer the 'mixed policy' to the 'twist policy', and that the former is deemed suitable for every

---

[3] cf. Mundell, 1962.
[4] See the round-table discussion of the Conference of the International Economic Association held in Brissago, in Harrod and Hague, 1963, pp. 403–33 and 522–50.

situation. Whatever the stage of development, monetary policy must be the king-pin of compensatory policies.

2. It is their *neutrality* which explains this preference for monetary measures. True, they are not neutral as regards growth. But, according to orthodox opinion, their global nature means that they do not distort the economy, whether from the internal or external aspect. Competition is supposed to maintain the optimum allocation of resources. The structure of the economy is merely the result of the forces of competition, according to neo-classical theory, and monetary policy is neutral with regard to structure. Selective measures inevitably affect the allocation of resources, and thus destroy the virtue of monetary policy.

The inappropriateness of a *global* monetary policy in a small developing country does not imply that all monetary measures are inappropriate, but only that global measures are. Their aim is to maintain the balance of the economy by means of automatic mechanisms. But these are acceptable only if they are *universal*, *symmetrical*, and *reversible*. Since the very opposites of these three characteristics are to be found in developing countries, it is clear that automatic mechanisms have no part to play in such a context.

The kinds of *selective* monetary measures which ought to be taken depend upon the circumstances of each case. One cannot discuss them without knowing the exact nature of the problem. The monetary experience of developed Western countries is only relevant to a small developing country if their financial institutions are similar, and if the considerations governing the structure of their assets are the same (profitability and security, after taking into account priority lending).[5] Many of the disadvantages of global monetary policy may apply whatever the level of development, but they are especially severe where there are marked structural inequalities. On the other hand, some partial, well adapted, *specific* measures are worthy of serious consideration, particularly for countries with adequate international reserves.

It follows that international economic co-operation should encourage—not the classical type of international economic integration—but the adoption of specific measures designed to overcome the particular problems of small countries. In theory, the Common Market economists who do not generally accept development planning nevertheless emphasize that certain planning priorities must be respected. We would not need to do so in discussions with economists familiar with development planning. But we would need to draw attention to the uncertainties which arise when one seeks to improve international economic relations.

More precisely, recognizing that cyclical fluctuations particularly affect the balance of payments of an open economy, we have often sought for adjustment mechanisms which will respect the desires of some countries to

[5] cf. Goldsmith, 1966.

industrialize. Some recent international agreements have, as we fully appreciate, minimized the dangers mentioned above. But methods of international monetary co-operation have still to be worked out, and it may therefore be useful to draw attention to some new aspects of the problems involved, since discussion is so often confined to the future of the reserve currencies and to the Western monetary system.[6]

Finally, two points which must not be overlooked:

(1) Although we have confined our attention to small developing countries, of which there are many and which are of great theoretical interest, one should not forget the problems faced by the small, fully industrialized, countries, especially in Western Europe.[7]

(2) Unless international co-operation can be strengthened, one cannot exclude the possibility of sudden changes in restrictions in trade. We must, however, avoid the usual exaggerations about the effects of such changes, which, in fact, often help to smooth out the trade cycle.[8]

REFERENCES

FELLNER, W. J., MACHLUP, F., TRIFFIN, R., and eleven others, *Maintaining or Restoring Balance in International Payments* (Princeton, 1966).

GOLDSMITH, R., *The Determinants of Financial Structure* (O.E.C.D., Paris, 1966).

HARROD, R. F. and HAGUE, D. C. (eds.), *International Trade Theory in a Developing World.* Proceedings of a conference held by the International Economic Association (London, 1963).

JOHNSON, H. G., *Essays in Monetary Economics* (London, 1967).

MUNDELL, R. A., *The Appropriate Use of Monetary and Fiscal Policy for Internal and External Equilibrium*, International Monetary Fund Staff Papers (March 1962).

OHLIN, G., *'Trade in a "Non-Laissez-Faire" World'*, Report to the International Congress on the Future of International Economic Relations, Montreal, September 1968. To be published by the International Economic Association.

PERROUX, F., *La Coexistence Pacifique*, Vol. II. *Pôles de développement ou Nations* (Paris, 1958).

ROBINSON, A. E. G. (ed.), *The Economic Consequences of the Size of Nations*, International Economic Association (London, 1960).

SALETTE, G., *La Flexibilité de l'économie, croissance et transformation des échanges* (Paris, 1968).

[6] Of course, once the problem has been approached along this line, the debate starts anew very soon, and traditional protectionist arguments are put forward. But clearer formulations have been considered. Cf. Myint in Harrod and Hague, 1963, and Weiller, 1965. However, our discussion was placed at a different level: what impressed us most was the long-term continuity emerging through slowly processing structural changes. Cf. Weiller, 1969; Ohlin, 1968; and Salette, 1968.

[7] The most appropriate way in which to classify countries is discussed in Robinson, 1960.

[8] Cf. some considerations presented 'in order to try to identify the moment when, in France, for example, collective preferences regarding national economic structure and domestic development modified the real effects of trade policy'. Weiller, 1950 and 1969.

WEILLER, J., *Problémes d'Économie Internationale*, Vol. I—*Les échanges du capitalisme libéral* (Paris, 1946); Vol. II—*Une Nouvelle Expérience: l'organisation internationale des échanges* (Paris, 1950).

——, *L'Économie Internationale depuis 1950* (Paris, 1965).

——, *Commerce mondial et conditions internationales de la croissance* (Cahiers de l'Institut de Science Économique Appliquée—I.S.E.A.—Paris, P Séries, from 1957 to 1969). The last numbers are published under the title: "*Économies et Societies*", Droz (Geneva, 1968–69).

——, 'Anti-cyclical policies. . .' *Economia Internazionale*, Vol. XXII, N2 (Genoa, 1969).

24

THE FIRM WITH INELASTIC DEMANDS

WILLIAM J. BAUMOL*

THE received theory of monopoly tells us that equilibrium will be established at the point of maximum profits, an assumption which for many purposes has served us well. Yet, as my colleague Professor Lewis has recently reminded me, this view of the matter seems to fly in the face of experience, which suggests that the demands for many of the monopolist's (and the quasi-monopolist's) products are inelastic, at least over the relevant range. Since, as is well known, profits cannot possibly be at a maximum at any positive output level at which demand is inelastic, something is obviously amiss—either the alleged facts or the basic assumption must be false.

In this paper I examine the basis for our impressionistic conclusions about the inelasticity of demand for a variety of products, and consider the consequences for the model of the firm. As we shall see, these issues affect not only theoretical matters, but are significant also for regulatory policy and for decision making in real business enterprises.

1. Basis for the Empirical Allegations

Unfortunately, dependable estimates of elasticities of demand are not easily come by. The econometric problems of simultaneity in the relationships and all the related materials are all too familiar to bear repetition. In the case of products sold under conditions of oligopoly or monopoly these difficulties are often compounded by the infrequency of price changes, which means that the number of pertinent observations is likely to be unusually small. For all these reasons our views on the elasticity of demand for products sold in this sector of the economy are, by and large, unavoidably impressionistic. They are, unhappily, based on rather superficial observation of responses to particular price changes, on reports by those engaged in the industries in question, or on our intuition as to the nature of the products and their markets.

For these reasons it is impossible to document the materials presented in

* The author wishes to thank the National Science Foundation whose grant greatly facilitated completion of this paper. He is grateful for their very helpful comments to David Bradford, W. Arthur Lewis, Jesse Markham, Robert Solow, and Ralph Turvey.

this section. Even in several cases where the discussion is based on the results of rather careful studies, their sources cannot be given because they are based on proprietary materials which will not be released by the firms to whom they belong.

It is interesting that even where several competing firms sell the same or very similar items, provided these are consumer goods rather than industrial products, their demand often does not appear to be very elastic. I will return to this point presently. First let me mention a few specific cases.

Medicines are often cited in the literature as items whose demands are plausibly taken to be inelastic. We have no statistical evidence for this view, but the nature of the product suggests to us that a lowering of the price of some proprietary drug will produce no influx of new customers, while people who need it will generally manage somehow to meet any likely increase in its price.

But if we are to go beyond such extreme cases we are forced to rely on quasi-empirical evidence. A typical case of a pertinent industry study was provided by the manufacturer of hunting rifles. All his experience suggested to him that any reasonable change in any of his prices would make no noticeable difference to his sales. He reported that this view was confirmed by results of a market survey in which the consumer was asked to rank product characteristics in the order of their importance to him as elements which entered into his purchase decision. Here price generally ranked very low. Scepticism as to the results provided by such a questionnaire is thoroughly justified, but much stronger evidence was provided by another set of questions. Customers, including many who had recently made substantial purchases, were asked to rank in terms of price a number of the most popular products of this firm and of its leading competitors, indicating which were the more expensive and which were cheaper, and most of the respondents were simply unable to do so. Moreover, they were unaware of a recent price change in one of the company's best selling products. Now, it is nevertheless possible that customers will react instinctively to a price reduction of which they are not conscious, but at this point the plausibility of the relationship becomes rather tenuous.

In the study of the performing arts conducted by Professor Bowen and myself we came across a number of cases which suggested that the demand for tickets is inelastic. Various managers reported no noticeable change in volume in response to reductions in ticket prices. At the opera or at theatrical performances in heavy demand, expensive tickets are often harder to obtain than are low- and medium-priced seats. In at least one case (which was meant by the man who described it to typify the workings of the market) a theatrical management found itself unable to sell out its least expensive balcony seats though the rest of the theatre was filled. The management promptly raised the balcony prices and suddenly found the theatre sold out.

Presumably, judgement of quality by price and snob appeal both enter into this manifestation, but, whatever the reason, such experiences certainly do not suggest that demand is very elastic.

A more convincing and systematic set of data was accumulated and analysed by a major public utility. Over the post-war period it had instituted less than a dozen major changes in the prices of its products. For each of these price changes data were collected on sales volume and total revenues for a substantial period after each rate variation. These figures were compared with the trend values of the same series, i.e., with the sales and revenues which might have been expected in the absence of the price changes. In every case the results were unambiguous in direction. When company prices rose, there was a very clear subsequent fall in volume (below its predicted value) but total revenue rose well above its trend, and where there was an unambiguous price decline the reverse occurred—sales increased but revenues fell, precisely as one would expect of an item whose demand is inelastic.[1]

2. *Price Consciousness*

Let me return briefly to the case of the rifles in which the consumers showed that they had very incomplete price information. There is considerable evidence that this is not an isolated phenomenon. A noteworthy case in point was provided by the much publicized price reduction in evening telephone rates in the United States. When a few years ago it was announced by the company that after 9 p.m. one could now call anywhere in the United States for no more than one dollar (for the first three minutes), there was a significant increase in evening calls (though the net percentage increase in volume seems to have been less than the percentage reduction in price). But when, some time later, the lower rates were extended to 8 p.m., the bulk of the added traffic continued to occur after nine.[2] And, on Sundays, though the lower rates apply throughout the day, calls continue to bunch between 9 p.m. and 10 p.m., though this was never a particularly popular hour before the rate reduction!

Here, then, is a case where every attempt was made to publicize the reduction and yet few people understood its terms thoroughly.[3] Even in cases where

---

[1] Some admittedly crude tests of significance were also conducted. The trend lines for sales and revenues were determined by least squares, and, after the price changes, sales and revenues generally departed from the trend lines by more than two standard errors.

[2] Indeed, according to testimony presented before the Federal Communications Commission, it seems to occur precisely at 9.15 during the first set of television advertisements after 9 p.m.

[3] At one meeting of consultants to the telephone company it transpired that a substantial proportion of the group did not know that the lower rates went into effect at 8 p.m. Moreover, several of them did not know that the one dollar rate was a maximum figure and that for calls between most pairs of locations in the United States the charge was lower than this.

one expects very sharp pencils to be used, knowledge is sometimes strikingly imperfect. I have seen two neighbouring Swiss banks that offered significantly different rates of exchange on the dollar. It is not surprising, then, in fields where one expects information to be imperfect, and where obfuscation is even sometimes deliberate, that such phenomena will be encountered. I can easily demonstrate very considerable dispersion in the price of a given wine. I have seen two liquor stores located cheek by jowl in one of which a wine sold for three dollars while in the other shop the same wine for the same year handled by the same shipper sold for five dollars. Even on items whose purchases are often repeated, goods such as washing machine soaps, we are told by surveys that the consumer does not know much about price. But, then, how could he be expected to know when packages seem designed to create illusions about the magnitudes of their contents, where 'giant economy sizes' have been found to sell at a price per pound higher than that for smaller packages? It is noteworthy that for such products, while there may be little response to a real price reduction, experience seems to show that sales volume may react materially to a very visible sticker on the package that proclaims 'Five cents off' (off what?).

As far as major purchases are concerned, the situation does not seem much different. A survey of purchasers of such items as automobiles and washing machines suggested that often price was only a minor consideration in the purchase decision and that comparison shopping at different outlets was rare. The preponderance of purchasers bought their refrigerators and other appliances at the first shop they visited. Automobile purchasers usually did not visit more than two dealers, while house buyers most frequently purchased the third house they were shown.

All of this is in sharp contrast with markets where firms buy from other firms, where a little competition can introduce a lot of demand elasticity. I can list a number of cases ranging over fuels, machine tools, modes of transportation and communications equipment in which each competitor knew that he could not exceed by any significant amount the prices offered by his rivals without a major loss in his industrial sales, and where a price reduction which could not be matched by competitors effectively drove them out of the pertinent sector of the industrial market.

3. *Equilibrium of the Firm with Some Inelastic Demands*

While the preceding discussion is far from conclusive it does suggest that the case of inelastic demand should not be ignored by our theory. I turn, therefore, to the model of the firm and its equilibrium under these circumstances, that is, where *some* of its products face an inelastic demand.

As a matter of fact the basic issues are easily dealt with. The problem, to be specific, is to explain why firms some of whose demands are inelastic do not raise the prices of the inelastic items to a point where they enter an elastic segment of their demand functions or, if the demands are inelastic throughout, why they do not raise their prices beyond any pre-assigned limits. As a practical matter, one can very probably exclude the latter possibility—presumably for any commodity there is some price at which it will find no takers simply because no one can afford it. But this does not get to the heart of the matter. One assumes that most firms whose demands are inelastic at present prices do have an elastic portion to their demand curves but that they simply choose not to move to it.

For such a self-denying decision there are several handy explanations: regulation, the threat of regulation, and, to the extent that entry is possible and likely, potential competition.[4] These three elements probably suffice to resolve the issue. In the case where prices are established by a regulatory agency this is obvious. And the firm which is not regulated is all too well aware that very high prices and very high profits are likely to produce the entry of new rivals and of new investigators who represent the government.

We may note that this resolution of the pricing problem really represents no essential departure from the profit-maximization model. It only involves a minor but necessary broadening of the concept of the profit function, to take account of reductions in profit which are likely to result from the activities of the regulators and of competitors. It is easy but pointless to formalize the matter and to describe the requisite modifications in the first- and second-order maximum conditions. Our profit function need merely be assigned terms representing the respective probabilities of regulation and of new entry and the corresponding expected costs (each as a function of our company's prices) and the rest is simply a trivial matter of elementary manipulation.

4. *Discretion in Prices and Profits*

But there is more to the story than that. The preceding discussion is unsatisfactory in a number of respects. While it offers a plausible explanation of the firm's willingness to restrain itself in its quest for short-run profits it leaves other matters so subjective that we really are given no handle with which things can be determined. First, we have no idea what profit rate the firm will feel it can get away with. Second, even given such a profit ceiling, it is not clear how the firm will select the relative prices of its various outputs. After all, if it supplies several items, more than one of whose demands are inelastic, it may be able to earn what it considers its profit quota by charging a sufficiently high price for any one of them or for any of a variety of combinations of sufficiently high prices.

---

[4] The last of these was forcefully brought to the attention of the profession by Sir Roy Harrod, albeit in a slightly different connection—in his discussion of full cost pricing (Harrod, 1952).

This is no mere abstract problem. It is a practical issue that worries both managements of individual firms and regulatory agencies. For the regulator it raises some very obvious issues. When he, instead of the businessman, imposes a ceiling on company profit he is left with the uncomfortable feeling that this limitation alone still leaves management with too much room for manœuvre. He still suspects that somehow, even within the limits imposed on profit, the company may end up setting some prices too high and some too low. He just does not know how to judge the propriety of prices and as a result is sometimes driven to extremely crude and arbitrary rules of thumb which serve as his standards.

Management, in turn, has similar worries. It is not quite sure how to distribute its unrealized profit potential among its various inelastic demand outputs. This is, for example, a concern of producers of medicines. Moreover, the decision not to realize all its potential short-run profits leaves management the option of pursuing alternative goals, objectives which are less likely to provoke competitive or regulatory countermeasures. It thus finds itself with room for what Oliver Williamson has described as 'discretionary behaviour'.

We will see that in both cases—that of regulatory control and that of company profit limitation policy, pricing decisions can be rationalized by the adoption of supplementary maximands—the social welfare function or some approximation to it in the one case, and some additional managerial objective in the other. But, before turning to a more careful analysis of the pricing decision in these circumstances, I will offer only a few casual observations on the other decision problem—the choice of maximum profit level. I would surmise that this figure, though rather vague, would tend to be somewhat in excess of the literature's standard 'normal profit'. First, this is so because of the competitive relationship. Normal profit, after all, is what can be earned by capital elsewhere in the economy, and, if entry is possible at all, the difference between our firm's profits and the normal profit level constitutes the incentive for new competitors to arise. Obviously, the more difficult and costly it is for rivals to establish themselves in the field the less will be the pressure from this source to drive company profits down to the normal profit level.

The relationship between regulatory standards and the normal profit level is, of course, not so automatic. But there is evidence that in setting profit ceilings for public utilities the governmental agencies grope toward such a standard. They would appear to be willing to permit the company to earn just enough 'to make it possible to attract new capital' and that is, of course, what constitutes normal profit. Whether or not they succeed in estimating this figure very closely may be a moot question, but there is considerable reason to believe that this is, typically, their standard. If this is so it means that the unregulated firms which stick close to the profit rate that is permitted the public utilities are not courting regulatory troubles, at least on this score. The further they are prepared to raise their earnings beyond this level the more dangerously they must be deciding to live. On all of these scores one might expect the inelastic demand firm to earn somewhat more than can be obtained by capital in the economy generally, but substantial and sustained departures from this level may well be uncommon.

5. *Price Setting: Regulatory Standards*

There are two separate matters to be taken up in a discussion of the price setting process. First, how should relative prices for the firm's different outputs be set from the viewpoint of the interests of society? Second, what relative prices will most effectively serve the purposes of the firm?

Any attempt to determine society's pricing needs and standards will, of course, run afoul of the theory of the second best. Even if we can determine how the company should price if it were operating in a world in which everyone else was acting ideally, in our imperfect economy the Lipsey–Lancaster theorem reminds us that behaviour in accord with these same rules may conceivably make things worse. Nevertheless, since most of us are unprepared to be forced into total inaction it is of interest to see what can be said if the second-best problem is put to one side.

One's first instinct is to recommend that prices be set proportionate to marginal costs, each exceeding marginal cost by a ratio adequate for the achievement of the permitted profit level. For such prices might well induce customers to allocate their expenditures among the company's products in accord with their relative resource costs, and will therefore make for something resembling an efficient allocation of resources.

A number of limitations besetting this rule of thumb have long been recognized[5] and there is no point in rehashing them here. What is less well known is a very ingenious result, provided independently by a number of authors.[6] In its crudest and simplest form the theorem states that to maximize

[5] See, e.g., McKenzie, 1951, pp. 785–803.

[6] The earliest source to which the mathematical argument has been traced is Ramsey's classic article, 'A Contribution to the Theory of Taxation' (Ramsey, 1927, 47–61). The first simple proof of the theorem is found in Manne (1952, 322–6). See also Flemming (1953, 215–36), and for a really sophisticated analysis disposing of a number of problems previously left unsettled (including issues arising out of the theory of the second best) see Boiteux (1956, 22–40).

The earlier intuitive arguments in favour of a similar proposition rested not so much on considerations of resource allocation as on grounds of Pareto efficiency. In the words of Professor Lewis, '... it is possible in some cases that the net result may be that everyone pays a lower price for the commodity than he would if there were no discrimination. ... If the undertaking is out merely to cover its costs and could cover them without discrimination [by charging a uniform percentage over marginal cost] since reducing the price to some persons with elastic demands may increase the surplus over marginal cost which they contribute, and thus allow the price to others also to be reduced' (Lewis, 1949, 21–2).

Marshallian consumers' and producers' surplus, where the former is defined as the area under the demand curve, any of the following three virtually equivalent rules should be followed by the firm whose profits are limited: (a) let the excess of each item's price over its marginal cost be proportionate to the difference between its marginal revenue and marginal cost; (b) let the ratio $(P - MC)/P$ be inversely proportionate to the item's elasticity of demand; and (c) let all outputs be restricted proportionately from the levels that equate P and MC. Though Boiteux has long ago replaced the argument with an analysis and a result that is far more sophisticated, since the proof of this noteworthy theorem is so simple it bears repetition here.

Let us use the following mnemonic notation:

TC = total cost,

P_i = price of item i,

x_i = output of item i,

TR_i = total revenue of item i,

MC_i = marginal cost of item i,

MR_i = marginal revenue of item i,

E_i = elasticity of demand of item i.

Then the objective is to maximize consumers' and producers' surplus

$$\sum_{i=1}^{n} \int_{0}^{x_i} P_i \, dx_i - TC,$$

subject to the profit limitation

$$\sum_{i=1}^{n} TR_i - TC \leq M.$$

These yield the Lagrangian

$$L = \sum \int_{0}^{x_i} P_i \, dx_i - TC + \lambda(M - \sum TR_i + TC),$$

which in turn give us the Kuhn–Tucker conditions[7]

$$\frac{\partial L}{\partial x_i} = P_i - MC_i - \lambda(MR_i - MC_i) \leq 0, \qquad (i = 1, 2, \ldots, n).$$

For all outputs that are actually produced these inequalities become equations and they immediately constitute rule (a): the excess of price over

[7] Note that if $\lambda = 0$ these conditions yield $P_i = MC_i$ for $x_i > 0$, i.e., in that case for any output that is produced price will equal marginal cost and our entire problem does not arise. We therefore assume $\lambda \neq 0$.

marginal cost should be proportionate to the excess of marginal revenue over marginal cost. Rule (b) follows when we write $MR_i = P_i + x_i\,dP_i/dx_i = P_i - P_i/E_i$. Substituting this into the preceding equation (on the premise $x_i > 0$) we have

(1) $$(1 - \lambda)(P_i - MC_i)/P_i = -\lambda/E_i,$$

which is our rule (b). Finally, to obtain rule (c) write the 'excess price', $P_i - MC_i$, as ΔP_i and assume that this quantity is small. The preceding equation then becomes

$$(1 - \lambda)\,\Delta P_i/P_i = \lambda(x_i/P_i)(dP_i/dx_i),$$

or

$$x_i \frac{\lambda}{1 - \lambda} = \frac{dx_i}{dP_i}\,\Delta P_i = \Delta x_i \quad \text{(approximately).}$$

That is, all outputs should be restricted in the same proportion, $\lambda/(1 - \lambda)$, which is rule (c).

These three rules constitute a rather interesting result. They suggest that the firm serves society best when it does what comes naturally, i.e., when it raises prices most sharply on the items whose demand is most inelastic! A moment's thought suggests why this should be so—by definition, a given price rise causes a smaller departure from ideal output the less responsive the demand for that item to the price change. This analysis should, of course, be taken with a grain of salt, given the second best problem, the argument's crude definition of consumer's surplus, its ignoring of interdependence among the demands for the various company outputs and other difficulties. There exists work which has improved the analysis in each of these respects. But even as it stands the argument is highly suggestive and, I believe, casts considerable illumination on the nature of the problem.

6. *Price Setting and the Firm's Objectives*

For the management of the individual firm issues are also raised by the room for manœuvre provided by the combination of inelastic demands and a limitation on profits. Since the company's profit potential is not completely utilized it becomes possible to employ the unrealized profits as a resource for the pursuit of supplementary goals. Such a course may also serve to dispose of the other decision problem that arises in these circumstances, the choice of relative product prices. That is, the firm may in these conditions select arbitrary prices for its various outputs by convention or rule of thumb, so long as their total yield adds up to the allowable profit level. For example, a uniform percentage mark-up on variable costs of sufficient magnitude may serve this purpose. But supplementary company goals may provide a more rational approach to the pricing decision.

Suppose, for example, that the firm produces n goods whose outputs are $x_1, \ldots, x_n$. Then, using the notation employed in the previous section, we may easily describe the optimal decision process of a firm which seeks to maximize its total revenue (sales) $\sum P_i x_i$, subject to the profit constraint

$$\sum TR_i - TC \le M.$$

To avoid paradoxical results it is assumed that while the firm produces output levels that lie in the inelastic demand range, at zero output levels these demands are elastic—otherwise, any commodity which is not produced by the firm would have to command an infinite price.[8] Hence $MR_i > 0$ for $x_i = 0$.

Our Lagrangian becomes

$$L = \sum TR_i + \lambda(M + TC - \sum TR_i),$$

which yields the Kuhn–Tucker conditions

(2) $\qquad\qquad (1 - \lambda)MR_i + \lambda MC_i \le 0 \qquad (i = 1, 2, \ldots, n).$

We know that if $\lambda = 0$ then by (2) $MR_i \le 0$. This means, in turn, that all $x_i > 0$ by our assumption that $MR_i > 0$ at $x_i = 0$ (elastic demand at zero output). Therefore by the Kuhn–Tucker condition $x_i \, \partial L/\partial x_i = 0$, we must have $MR_i = 0$ for all i, i.e., we will have the case of pure total revenue maximization. This case will occur only if with pure revenue maximization the profit constraint is precisely satisfied, for if this does not enable the firm to obtain M dollars in profits presumably management will simply seek to maximize profits and come as close to the M dollar profit ceiling as possible.

Consider now the alternative possibility, $\lambda > 0$, so that, by the Kuhn–Tucker condition $\lambda \, \partial L/\partial \lambda = 0$, the profit constraint $\partial L/\partial \lambda = M + TC - \sum TR_i \ge 0$ must be satisfied as an equation. In this case, for any $x_i > 0$ the Kuhn–Tucker condition (2) is satisfied as an equation[9]

(3) $\qquad\qquad MR_i/(MR_i - MC_i) = \lambda.$

This states that, for the revenue maximizing firm, prices and outputs will be adjusted so that for all produced outputs marginal revenues bear a constant proportion to marginal profits. For any commodity, j, whose equilibrium outputs are zero, we have by (2)

$$MR_j/\lambda \le (MR_j - MC_j),$$

and since at $x_j = 0$, $MR_j > 0$ it follows that $MR_j - MC_j > 0$ so that by (2), for $x_j = 0$

(4) $\qquad\qquad MR_j/(MR_j - MC_j) \le \lambda.$

---

[8] For if $x_i = 0$ at any finite price we have $1/E_i = -(x_i/P_i)(dP_i/dx_i) = 0$ so that elasticity of demand must be 'infinite', i.e., demand certainly cannot be inelastic.

[9] This confirms $\lambda > 0$ since, by assumption, $MR_i < 0$, $MC_i > 0$.

Thus, comparing this result with (3) we see that j will not be produced if its marginal revenue is disproportionately small (or at least not disproportionately large) relative to its marginal profit yield, as is to be expected.

Conditions (3) and (4) together with the profit constraint then suffice to determine output levels and prices, subject to the usual reservations.

Condition (3), or, more directly, (2) in its equality form, can also usefully be rewritten by substituting for MR_i its equivalent in terms of price and elasticity to obtain

$$(1 - \lambda)[P_i - P_i/E_i] = -\lambda MC_i,$$

or

(5) $$MC_i = P_i(1 - 1/E_i)[(\lambda - 1)/\lambda].$$

Now, by the equality case of (2), i.e., by (3) and with demand inelastic, $(\lambda - 1)/\lambda = MC_i/MR_i < 0$, and $1 - 1/E_i < 0$. We see at once that the equilibrium ratio of price to marginal cost will vary inversely with the elasticity of demand of the item.[10]

It is, of course, not seriously proposed that the illustrative supplementary objective utilized in this section will be the solution adopted by all business firms. Rather, the revenue maximization case was employed to show how the inelastic demand company that is prevented by a profit constraint from setting its prices in accord with the principles described in the usual analysis finds itself with the opportunity to pursue further objectives, and how these supplementary or subsidiary goals may provide the pricing decision mechanism that is required for these circumstances.[11]

---

[10] Indeed, there is a curious resemblance between (5), which characterizes the behaviour of the self-seeking firm with the objectives specified and the condition (1) of the previous section which is intended to approximate the socially ideal pricing decisions of the firm under a profit constraint. For (1) can be rewritten as

$$1 - (MC_i/P_i) = \lambda/[E_i(1 - \lambda)]$$

or

(6) $$MC_i = P_i[1 - (1/E_i)\lambda/(1 - \lambda)].$$

Since, in fact, (1), and hence (6) can, as they stand, at best be treated as third-best-rule-of-thumb approximations to the desired optimality conditions, then (3) or (5) may perhaps serve as fairly good approximations for the purpose. Of course, not too much should be made of the resemblance.

[11] One particular reason for choosing the revenue maximization goal as our illustration is that it may not be obvious how this objective can determine prices in the inelastic demand case. For with inelastic demands a rise in prices adds *both* to profits and to revenues, so that it may not be clear immediately how any non-zero output levels for the firm's inelastic demand products can be consistent with maximal revenues. We see easily how, say a *physical* output maximization objective, because its pursuit cuts down on profits, solves the pricing decision problem: i.e., it calls for prices to be cut until profits are reduced to the constraint level. But with revenue maximization it is only because the firm is in no position to accept *more* than its permitted profits that a solution is possible.

Ralph Turvey has suggested to me that repose and good fellowship are attractive

7. *Profit Maximization* vs. *Sales Maximization Once More*

Though the particular secondary goals that were described in the preceding section were intended merely to be illustrative, the discussion may shed some light on the plausibility of the sales (revenue) maximization hypothesis and some of the other alternatives that have been offered as competitors to the view that companies seek to maximize their profits. In a carefully qualified statement, Professor Solow has recently suggested that the empirical evidence seems to favour the latter.[12] In particular he has asked, if firms do not want to maximize profits, how does one explain the apparent fact that profits tend to be higher in industries in which entry is more difficult? In reply, one is tempted to ask why, if firms really maximize profits, are so many prices set in the range of inelastic demand. Of course, this paper has attempted to provide the answer, and in doing so it may have contributed to a reconciliation of the apparently conflicting empirical hypotheses.

Specifically, I have suggested that firms with inelastic demands in effect set themselves a profit constraint as a means to avoid the dangers of new entry and regulation, and in this very fundamental sense they remain profit maximizers—maximizers who recognize the long-run costs of short-run greed. But I have noted also that the difference between this profit ceiling and the level of normal profit is likely to vary inversely with the immediacy of these threats and hence is likely to correlate inversely with freedom of entry, as the Solow observation requires.

But once having set the ceiling on profits, the firm is free to pursue other goals, in a venture that is, in effect, financed by the company's unrealized short-run profits. This latitude is almost a necessary consequence of inelastic demands in a real world. And once having this latitude and being effectively precluded from the pursuit of further short-run profits, it is hard to believe that management will not find some other combination of objectives which it will wish to adopt. This would then account for all the observed examples of business behaviour which would appear to conflict with a profit maximization goal.[13]

candidates as supplementary goals, noting that while they are non-quantifiable they may go far in explaining Professor Leibenstein's X inefficiency. For an excellent discussion and further references to the extensive literature relating to supplementary maximands see Williamson (1964).

[12] Solow, 1967, pp. 106–7.

[13] In a letter, Professor Solow points out that the operation of firms on the inelastic portion of their demand curves is sufficient but not necessary for the existence of unused short-run monopoly power, so that the case can stand but need not fall on the validity of the hypothesis about demand elasticity.

However, he asks, if there is ample unused monopoly power, why do profits fluctuate so sharply in minor recessions and booms? Wouldn't one expect firms to use and disuse their leeway to stabilize profits as an important subsidiary goal? He supplies what I believe to be part of the answer—the difficulty of making rapid changes in decisions in

Thus, harmony would appear to reign once more—the provision of alternative objectives creating no necessary conflict, either among themselves or with the observed facts. This resolution of these issues also encompasses regulatory matters. We have seen that the imposition of a ceiling on profits, either voluntarily or by governmental coercion, leaves the decision process with too many degrees of freedom. Prices still remain indeterminate. Only a supplementary maximand can supply the required decisions. In the case of government the appropriate maximand is the social welfare, however defined and measured. In the case of private firms, a variety of alternatives—growth, market share, sales, etc., are possible and plausible. For even if potential competition and the threat of regulation do generally serve to impose a profit constraint, there is no way to judge in advance how the firm will deal with the latitude that still remains to it. Having no choice but to leave some profits unrealized, the company is unavoidably left with a costless opportunity to pursue some alternative objectives of its choice not because management necessarily prefers them to profits but because circumstances effectively prevent profit maximization. What the supplementary objectives will be is surely an empirical matter and the answer may well vary from firm to firm and from time period to time period.

REFERENCES

BOITEUX, M., 'Sur la gestion des monopoles publics astreints à l'équilibre budgétaire', *Econometrica*, Vol. 24, No. 1, January 1956, pp. 22–40.

FLEMMING, M., 'Optimal Production with Fixed Profits', *Economica*, N.S. Vol. 20, August 1953, pp. 215–36.

HARROD, R. F., 'Theory of Imperfect Competition Revised', *Economic Essays* (Harcourt, Brace, New York, 1952).

LEWIS, W. A., *Overhead Costs* (George Allen & Unwin, London, 1949), pp. 21–2.

MANNE, A. S., 'Multiple-Purpose Public Enterprises—Criteria for Pricing', *Economica*, N.S. Vol. 19, August 1952, pp. 322–6.

MCKENZIE, L., 'Ideal Output and the Interdependence of Firms', *Economic Journal*, Vol. 61, December 1951, pp. 785–803.

RAMSEY, F., 'A Contribution to the Theory of Taxation', *Economic Journal*, Vol. 37, March 1927, pp. 47–61.

SOLOW, R., 'The New Industrial State, or Son of Affluence', *The Public Interest*, No. 9, Fall 1967, pp. 106–7.

WILLIAMSON, O., *The Economics of Discretionary Behavior* (Prentice-Hall, Englewood Cliffs, N.J., 1964).

large, conglomerate firms. In addition, firms often adopt price stability (what we would call sticky prices) as an avowed objective and are very reluctant to change prices in response to changing circumstances. It is possible to provide some documentation of both of these explanatory hypotheses.

BIBLIOGRAPHY OF THE WORKS OF SIR ROY HARROD

BOOKS
(IN ORDER OF PUBLICATION)

International Economics (Cambridge University Press, 1933). Cambridge Economic Handbooks, 8, first rev. ed. 1939, second rev. ed. 1957.

The Trade Cycle: An Essay (Oxford, The Clarendon Press, 1936).

Britain's Future Population (Oxford Pamphlets on Home Affairs, No. H.4, 1943).

Liberal Plan for Peace (anonymous; introduction by Lord Crewe) (London, Victor Gollancz, 1944).

A Page of British Folly (London, Macmillan & Co. Ltd., 1946).

Are These Hardships Necessary? (London, Rupert Hart-Davis, 1947).

Towards a Dynamic Economics; Some Recent Developments of Economic Theory and Their Application to Policy (London, Macmillan & Co. Ltd., 1948).

The Life of John Maynard Keynes (London, Macmillan & Co. Ltd., 1951).

And so it goes on: Further Thoughts on Present Mismanagement (London, Rupert Hart-Davis, 1951).

Economic Essays (London, Macmillan & Co. Ltd., 1952).

The Pound Sterling (Princeton, 1952). Princeton University International Finance Section, Essays in International Finance, No. 13, February 1952.

The Dollar. Sulgrave Manor Board Lectures by Occupant of Watson Chair (London, Macmillan & Co. Ltd., 1953; 2nd edn. with new introduction, the Norton Library, 1963).

Foundations of Inductive Logic (London, Macmillan & Co. Ltd., 1956).

The Pound Sterling, 1951–1958 (Princeton, 1958). Essay No. 30.

Policy against Inflation (London, Macmillan & Co. Ltd., 1958).

The Prof.: A Personal Memoir of Lord Cherwell (London, Macmillan & Co. Ltd., 1959).

Topical Comment: Essays in Dynamic Economics Applied (London, Macmillan & Co. Ltd.; New York, St. Martin's Press, 1961).

The British Economy (New York, McGraw-Hill Book Co. Inc., 1963).

Growth Policy for Europe (Brussels and London, European League for Economic Co-operation, 1963).

Plan to Increase International Monetary Liquidity (Brussels and London, European League for Economic Co-operation, 1964).

Reforming the World's Money (London, Macmillan & Co. Ltd., New York, St. Martin's Press, 1965).

Towards a New Economic Policy. Lectures given in the University of Manchester by Sir Roy Harrod (Manchester University Press, 1967).

Dollar–Sterling Collaboration (Atlantic Trade Study, Moor House, London Wall, 1968).

Money (London, Macmillan & Co. Ltd.; New York, St. Martin's Press, 1969).

CONTRIBUTIONS TO BOOKS
(IN ORDER OF PUBLICATION)

Editor—Hutchinson's University Library of Economics (1950–1969).

'Appendix, foreign exchanges and their relation to unemployment', in *Unemployment: Its Cause and Cure*. An inquiry authorized by the General Federation of Trades Unions. Summarized by W. A. Appleton (London, P. Allen & Co., 1928).

Separate Report in *Library Provision in Oxford*, Report of Commission Appointed by the Congregation of Oxford (1931).

'Currency and Central Banking', in *What Everybody wants to know about Money* (London, Victor Gollancz, 1933).

Report of the Proceedings of the Meeting of Economists (Antwerp Chamber of Commerce, 1935).

'Examination in the Final Honour School of P.P.E.', in *The Purposes of Examinations*. A symposium with an introductory survey by Sir Philip Hartog (London, Evans Bros. Ltd., 1938). Reprinted from the *Year Book of Education*.

'Vers une théorie dynamique', in *Mélanges économiques et sociaux, offerts a Emile Witmeur* (Paris, Librairie du Recueil Sirey, 1939).

Contribution in *Consumers' Co-operation in Great Britain—An Examination of the British Co-operative Movement*, by Carr-Saunders, A. M. and others (London, George Allen & Unwin, 1942, rev. edn.).

Memorandum to the *Royal Commission on Equal Pay for Men and Women*, Appendix IX in the Fourth Volume of Memoranda of Evidence (London H.M.S.O., 1945).

'Financial Position of Great Britain and the Balance of Payments', in *Current Financial Problems*. Institute of Bankers, International Banking Summer School (Oxford, 1948).

'The Economic Consequences of Atomic Energy', in *The Atomic Age*. Sir Halley Stewart Lectures, 1948 (George Allen and Unwin, London).

'Capital Formation in an Expanding Economy', in *International Thrift Institute, Address and Lectures*, First International Summer School for Savings Bankers (Oxford, July 1950).

Memoranda (submitted in August and December, 1944), *Papers of the Royal Commission on Population*, Vol. 5 (London, H.M.S.O., 1950).

Contributions (several) in *Defence, Controls and Inflation* (Chicago Law School Conference, 1951).

'Developments in Europe', in *The World Payments Situation*, I.M.F. Meeting (Mexico City, September 1952).

The Next 50 Years, Golden Jubilee booklet of The Association of Certified and Corporate Accountants (November/December 1954).

'Retiring Age for University Teachers', *Report of the Proceedings of the Conference of the Universities of Great Britain and Northern Ireland* (University of London, December 1954).

'Keynes', in *Handwörterbuch der Sozial-Wissenshaften* (Göttingen, Vandenhoeck & Ruprecht, 1956).

'The Common Market and Economic Depressions', in *The Common Market to Promote Social Prosperity*. Introductory Report to the Third International Conference of the European League for Economic Co-operation (Brussels, European League for Economic Co-operation, 1956).

'Economics, 1900–1950', *The New Outline of Modern Knowledge* (Victor Gollancz, 1956).

'Possibility of Economic Satiety; Use of Economic Growth for improving the Quality of Education and Leisure', *Problems of U.S. Economic Development*, Vol. 1 (Committee on Economic Development, 1958); reprinted in *Topical Comment* (London, 1961), q.v.

'Inflation and Investment in Underdeveloped Countries', in *Ekonomi, Politik, Samhalle: en bok Tillagnad Bertil Ohlin*, ed. John Bergvall (Stockholm, Bokförlaget Folk och samhälle, 1959).

Contributor—Worswick, Geo., David Norman, ed., *The Free Trade Proposals* (Oxford, Basil Blackwell, 1960).

Evidence submitted to Radcliffe Committee on the Working of the Monetary System, May 1958 (Vol. 3 of *Principal Memoranda of Evidence*, London, H.M.S.O., 1960).

'Inflation in Dynamic Theory', in *Stabile Preise in Wachsender Wirtschaft ...*, Festschrift for Erich Schneider, ed. G. Bombach (Tübingen 1960).

'The Dollar Problem and the Gold Question', in *The Dollar in Crisis ...*, ed. S. E. Harris (New York and Burlingame, Harcourt, Brace & World, 1961).

Preface to *The Export of Capital*, by C. K. Hobson (London, Constable, 1963).

'Sales Proceeds Funds and Inflation. Remarks on Prof. S. Naggar's Speech; 'Economic and Capital Investment'; 'Summary of the Third Week'; in *Capital Formation and Investment in Industry*, a Report of the International Conference on Problems of Capital Formation and Investment in Industry held at Istanbul, August 1962, sponsored by the Economic and Social Studies Conference Board (Istanbul, Economic and Social Studies Conference Board, 1963).

Editor (assisted by Douglas Hague), *International Trade Theory in a Developing World*. Proceedings of a conference held by the International Economic Association (London & New York, Macmillan & Co. Ltd., 1963).

Contribution to above: 'Desirable International Movements of Capital in Relation to Growth of Borrowers and Lenders and Growth of Markets'.

Statement in *The United States Balance of Payments—Statements by Economists, Bankers and Others on the Brookings Institution Study* 'The United States Balance of Payments in 1968', Joint Economic Committee of Congress, 88th Congress, First Session (Washington D.C., U.S. Government Printing Office, 1963).

'Liquidity', in *World Monetary Reform*, ed. H. C. Grubel (Stanford University Press, 1963).

'Comparative Analysis of Policy Instruments', in *Inflation and Growth in Latin America* (Economic Growth Centre, Yale and Richard D. Irwin, Homewood, Ill., 1964).

'Mr. Keynes and Traditional Theory (1937). Retrospect on Keynes (1963)', in *Keynes' General Theory . . .*, ed. R. Lekachman (New York and London, Macmillan & Co. Ltd., 1964).

Note in Appendix B, *International Monetary Arrangements. The Problem of Choice* (International Finance Section, Princeton University, August 1964).

'J. M. Keynes', in *Lebensbilder grosser nationökonomen*, ed. H. C. Rechtenwald (Köln, Kiepenheuer and Witsch, 1965).

'Comment', in *International Payments Problems*; a Symposium sponsored by American Enterprise Institute (Washington, American Enterprise Institute, 1965).

'Saving and Economic Growth', in *Saving in Contemporary Economic Research*, Transactions of a Congress organized by General Savings Bank and Pension Fund of Belgium (1965).

'International Reserves and Domestic Economic Policies', in *Gold and World Monetary Problems*. Proceedings of the National Industrial Conference Board Convocation, Tarrytown, New York, 6–10 October 1965 (New York, Macmillan & Co. Ltd., 1966).

Contribution in *Maintaining and Restoring Balance in International Payments*, by William Fellner, Fritz Machlup, Robert Triffin, and 11 others (Princeton University Press, 1966).

'Optimum Investment for Growth', in *Problems of Economic Dynamics and Planning*, Essays in Honour of Michael Kalecki (Oxford, Pergamon Press, and Warsaw, Polish Scientific Publications, 1966).

Reprint of Statement to the Joint Economic Committee of Congress, in *Monetary Theory and Policy*, ed. R. A. Ward (Scranton, Pa., International Textbook Co., 1966).

Reprint of 'Domar and Dynamic Economics', *Economic Journal*, September 1959, in *Readings in Macro-Economics*, ed. M. G. Mueller (New York, Holt, Rinehart & Winston & Co., June 1966).

'Increasing Returns', in *Monopolistic Competition Theory: Studies in Impact*, Essays in honour of Edward H. Chamberlain, ed. Robert E. Kuenne (New York, etc., John Wiley & Sons, Inc., 1967).

Statement in *Testimony on Special Drawing Rights* (I.M.F.), International Sub-Committee of the Joint Economic Committee of Congress (Washington D.C., U.S. Government Printing Office, 22 November 1967).

Contributions (several) in *Economic Development for Eastern Europe*. Proceedings of a Conference held by the International Economic Association, ed. M. C. Kaser (Macmillan, 1968).

Contribution to *Brian Howard, Portrait of a Failure*, ed. M. J. Lancaster (London, Antony Blond, January 1968).

'What is a Model?' in *Value, Capital and Growth: Papers in honour of Sir John Hicks*, ed. J. N. Wolfe (Edinburgh University Press, 1968).

Contributions in *Monetary Problems of the International Economy*, ed. Robert A. Mundell and Alexander K. Swoboda (University of Chicago Press, 1969).

'Doctrines of Imperfect Competition', *Quarterly Journal of Economics*, 48, May 1934. Reprinted in *Readings in Micro-Economics*, ed. S. M. Blumner (Scranton, Pennsylvania, International Textbook Company, 1969).

Editor, new English translation of *Geometry in the Sensible World* and *The Logical Problem of Induction* by Jean Nicod (Routledge & Kegan Paul, 1970).

ARTICLES
(INCLUDING REVIEWS, IN ORDER OF PUBLICATION)

The 'popular' titles of some of the articles in non-academic periodicals were composed by the editors. Despite them, most of the articles contain strictly economic, and often quantitative, analysis.

'An Early Exposition of "Final Utility"; W. F. Floyd's Lecture on "The Notion of Value" (1833) reprinted', *Economic History*, 1, May 1927.

'Mr. Robertson's Views on Banking Policy', in *Economica*, 7, June 1927.

'Notes on Supply', *Econ. J.*, 40, June 1930.

'Progressive Taxation and Equal Sacrifice', *Econ. J.*, 40, December 1930.

'The Law of Decreasing Costs', *Econ. J.*, 41, December 1931.

'Decreasing Costs: An Addendum', *Econ. J.*, 42, September 1932.

'A Further Note on Decreasing Costs', *Econ. J.*, 43, June 1933.

'Professor Pigou's Theory of Unemployment', *Econ. J.*, 44, March 1934.

'Doctrines of Imperfect Competition', *Quarterly Journal of Economics*, 48, May 1934. Reprinted in *Readings in Micro-Economics*, ed. S. M. Blumner, 1969.

'The Equilibrium of Duopoly', *Econ. J.*, 44, June 1934.

'The Expansion of Credit in an Advancing Community', *Economica*, N.S. 1, August 1934.

Rejoinder to Mr. Robertson, *Economica*, N.S. 1, November 1934.

[Monetary Equilibrium and the Price Level in a Progressive Economy], Rejoinder to Drs. Haberler and Bode, *Economica*, N.S. 2, February 1935.

'Utilitarianism revised', *Mind*, April 1936.

'Another Fundamental Objection to Laissez-Faire,' *Econ. J.*, 46, March 1936.

'Imperfect Competition and the Trade Cycle', *Review of Economics and Statistics*, May 1936.

'Renseignement économique en Grande Bretagne, l'Université d'Oxford, l'enseignement économique en France et à l'étranger, *Revue d'économie politique*, 1937.

'Mr. Keynes and Traditional Theory', *Econometrica*, 5, January 1937.

'Studies in the Theory of Economic Expansion', *Zeitschrift für Nationalökonomie*, 8, August 1937.

'Lord Nuffield's Foundation in Oxford', *Econ. J.*, 47, December 1937.

'The Future of Gold', *The Banker*, March and April 1938 (2 parts).

'Population and the Future', *The Political Quarterly*, April/June 1938.

'Scope and Method of Economics', *Econ. J.*, 48, September 1938.

'Modern Population Trends', *Manchester School of Economics and Social Studies*, 10, 1939.

'Population Trends and Problems', *Lloyds Bank Review*, January 1939.

'Price and Cost in Entrepreneurs' Policy', *Oxford Economic Papers*, 2, May 1939.

'An Essay in Dynamic Theory', *Econ. J.*, 49, March 1939; Errata, June 1939.

'Value and Capital by J. R. Hicks', *Econ. J.*, 49, June 1939.

'The Conscription of Wealth', *Political Quarterly*, July/September 1939.

'Peace Aims and Economics', *Horizon*, March 1940.

'The Population Problem: A Rejoinder', *Manchester School of Economics and Social Studies*, 11, April 1940.

'Memory', *Mind*, January 1942.

'Full Employment and Security of Livelihood', *Econ. J.*, 53, December 1943.

'Price Flexibility and Employment by Oscar Lange', *Econ. J.*, 56, March 1946.

'Kelly, Aquinas and Interest-taking', *Econ. J.*, 56, June 1946.

(With Robinson, E. A. G.) John Maynard Keynes (announcement of death), *Econ. J.*, 56, June 1946.

'Anglo-American Co-operation', *The Banker*, June and July 1946 (2 parts).

'Consequences of Nationalising the Bank of England', *The Political Quarterly*, July/September 1946.

'Professor Hayek on Individualism', *Econ. J.*, 56, September 1946.

'John Maynard Keynes', *Review of Economics and Statistics*, 28, November 1946.

'A Comment [on R. Triffin's 'National Central Banking and the International Economy'], *Review of Economic Studies*, 14, 1947.

'Anglo-American Economic Co-operation', *University Observer*, University of Chicago, May/June 1947.

'The Dollar Problem', *The Banker*, December 1947.

'John Maynard Keynes', *Economie Appliquée*, Archives de l'Institut de Science Economique Appliquée, April/September 1948.

'The Fall in Consumption', *Bulletin of the Oxford University Institute of Statistics*, 10, May 1948.

'Problèmes économiques de la co-operation internationale', *Aussenwirtschaft* (Zürich), June 1948.

'European Union', *Lloyds Bank Review*, 9, July 1948.

'The Fall in Consumption: A Rejoinder', *Bulletin of the Oxford University Institute of Statistics*, 10, July–August, September 1948.

'The Way to Recovery', *District Bank Review*, December 1948.

'Disinflation', *The Secretary*, January 1949.

'The Outlook for 1949', *World Review*, London, January 1949.

'Measures to prevent a Slump', *Foreign Affairs*, July 1949

'Wesley Mitchell in Oxford', *Econ. J.*, 59, September 1949.

'Britain under a Labour Administration', *I.P.A. Review* (Australia), November/December 1949.

'European Economic Co-operation: A British Viewpoint', *Public Finance*, 5, 1950.

'Sargeant and Smedley', *The Trifler*, Westminster School, 1950.

'Our Economic Prospects', *World Review*, January 1950.

'La cooperation économique internationale', *Economie Appliquée*, January/March 1950.

'The Dollar Problem', *The Accountant*, April 1950.

'The Dollar Sterling Problem', *International Affairs*, Royal Institute of International Affairs, April 1950.

'The Problem of Sterling Convertibility', *Three Banks Review*, 6, June 1950.

'The Problem of Employment Stabilisation by Bertil Ohlin', *Econ. J.*, 60, September 1950.

'E. G. Dowdell 1902–1950 (obit.)', *Econ. J.*, 60, December 1950.

'The Tight-Rope Year', *The Director*, February 1951.

'The Economic Prospect', *The World Review*, March 1951.

'An Atlantic Payments Union', *The Director*, April 1951.

'Clearing the Air on Inflation', *The Director*, June 1951.

'Notes on Trade Cycle Theory', *Econ. J.*, 61, June 1951.

'U.S. Defence Effort and Inflation', *The Director*, August 1951.

'Britain's Economic Problem', *World Review*, August 1951.

'Keynes' General Theory by A. C. Pigou', *American Economic Review*, September 1951.

'A Plan to Control Inflation', *The Director*, October 1951.

'Hands and Fists across the Sea', *Foreign Affairs*, New York, October 1951.

'More or Less Controls', *The Director*, December 1951.

'Britain's Balance of Trade Problems', *Quarterly Survey of Banque de Bruxelles*, 1952, no. 1/2.

'The Tasks for 1952', *The Secretary*, February 1952.

'Currency Appreciation as an Anti-Inflationary Measure; Comment', *Quarterly Journal of Economics*, 66, February 1952.

'The Butler Remedies—and After', *The Director*, February 1952.

'The Drive against Inflation', *District Bank Review*, March 1952.

'The Role of Gold in Modern International Trade', *Optima*, South Africa, March 1952.

'This Year of Trial', *The Director*, April 1952.

'The Narrow Road', *The World Review*, April 1952.

'Monetary Policy: A Symposium' (Comment), *Bulletin of the Oxford University Institute of Statistics*, 14, April–May 1952.

'The Two Balances', *The Director*, June 1952.

'Conservative Policy and Modern Economics', *Réalités*, Paris, June 1952.

'What I think of British Management', *The Manager*, March 1953.

'Imbalance of International Payments.' *International Monetary Fund Staff Papers*, 3, April 1953.

'Now the Accent is on Demand', *The Director*, April 1953.

'Foreign Exchange Rates: A Comment', *Econ. J.*, 63, June, 1953.

'Sir Hubert Henderson, 1890–1952', *Oxford Economic Papers*, N.S. 5, suppl., June 1953.

'Towards a Simpler Economy', *The Director*, June 1953.

'British Economy at the Cross-Roads', *Revue de la Banque de Bruxelles*, Nos. 2–3, June 1953.

24*

'Getting Ready for a Recession', *The Director*, August, 1953.

'Self-Help and "Helpfulness" in British–American Trade', *Foreign Affairs*, New York, October 1953.

'Industry gets the Green Light', *The Director*, October 1953.

[Full Capacity vs. Full Employment Growth.] A Comment on Pilvin', *Quarterly Journal of Economics*, 67, November 1953.

'Industry must be Equipped to Fight', *The Director*, December 1953.

'Free-er Trade and Britain's Strategy', *The Director*, February 1954.

'What is Convertibility?', *Société Belge d'Etudes et d'Expansion*, March–April, 1954.

'Economic Change' (a review note on Simon Kuznets, 'Economic Change'), *Journal of Political Economy*, 62, April 1954.

'American Recession and British Business', *The Director*, April 1954.

'A more Flexible Investment Allowance?', *The Director*, June 1954.

'When Pound meets Dollar on Level Terms', *The Director*, August, 1954.

'What is Convertibility?', *Rivista di Politica Economica*, October 1954.

'Lending an Ear to the Man on the Job', *The Director*, October 1954.

'Convertibility Problems', *The Bankers' Magazine*, October 1954.

'A Holiday for Trade Restrictions', *The Director*, December 1954.

'Convertibility Problems', *Economia Internazionale*, 8, February 1955.

'Post-Mortem on a Crisis', *The Director*, February 1955.

'The Bank Rate', *The Bankers' Magazine*, March 1955.

'Budgetary Proposals', *Local Government Finance*, March 1955.

'Convertibility Problems: Reply to Dr. Erhard,' *The Bankers' Magazine*, April 1955.

'Time for Revision', *The Director*, April 1955.

'Will the Bank Rate Work?', *Purchasing Journal*, April 1955.

'Investment and Population', *Revue Economique*, May 1955.

'Putting Brakes on the Boom', *The Director*, June 1955.

'The Broken Promise of Nationalization', *The Director*, August 1955.

'Prospects for Convertibility', *Optima*, September 1955.

'Assisting Under-developed Regions', *Confluence*, October 1955.

'The Truth about the Crisis', *The Director*, October 1955.

'The Credit Squeeze—and after', *The New Commonwealth*, November 1955.

'Current Problems and their Impact on 1956', *The District Bank Review*, December 1955.

'The Economic Outlook', *The Secretary*, December 1955.

'Sterling and the Second Budget', *The Director*, December 1955.

'Limits of Government Intervention in Economic Matters', *Freedom First*, Winter Issue 1956.

'Expansion without Boom', *Steel*, January 1956.

'How Tight is the Credit Squeeze?', *The Director*, February 1956.

'The British Boom, 1954–55', *Econ. J.*, 66, March 1956.

'Talking Ourselves into Trouble', *The Director*, April 1956.

'Can Sterling take the Strain?', *The New Commonwealth*, May 1956.

'Walras: A Re-appraisal', *Econ. J.*, 66, June 1956.

'Tripped up by the Printing Press', *The Director*, June 1956.

'The Government's Responsibility for the Nation's Economy', *Progress*, Summer 1956.

'On Lord Keynes', *Indian Journal of Economics*, 37, July 1956.

'Britain and her Competitors', *The New Commonwealth*, July 1956.

'When the Boom Ends', *The Director*, August 1956.

'Measures against Inflation', *Vie Economique et Sociale*, 5, 1956.

'Future of Sterling', *Economics* (Journal of the Economics Association), Autumn 1956.

'Time to Slacken the Reins', *The Director*, October 1956.

'Concluding Phase of the Credit Squeeze', *Bankers' Magazine*, November 1956.

'World Bank and the Commonwealth', *The New Commonwealth*, November 1956.

'A National Wages Policy—the Problem', Institute of Municipal Treasurers & Accountants. Joint Committee of Students' Societies, November 1956.

'Policy for the Next Two Years', *The Director*, December 1956.

'Great Britain and Inflation (1954–56)', *Vie Economique et Sociale* (Antwerp), 1–2, 1957.

'Professor Fellner on Growth and Unemployment', *Kyklos*, 10 Fasc. 1, 1957.

'Britain and the Common Market', *Foreign Affairs*, January 1957.

'Time Ripe for an Easier Credit Policy', *Times Review of Industry*, January 1957.

'What the Credit Squeeze won't do', *The Director*, February 1957.

'The Common Market in Perspective' (the free trade proposals), *Bulletin of Oxford University Institute of Statistics*, 19, February 1957.

'British Experience of Disinflationary Policy in 1955–56', *Nationalekonomiska Föreningen Förhandlingar* (Stockholm), March 1957.

Review article on *Financial Policy, 1939–45*, by R. S. Sayers, *The Bankers' Magazine*, April 1957.

'First Signs of a Recession', *The Director*, April 1957.

'Domestic Activity and External Balance', *The Bankers' Magazine*, May 1957.

Review of *Logic and Knowledge*, by Bertrand Russell, *Nature*, 18 May 1957.

'Encouraging Selective Investment', *The Director*, June 1957.

Review of *International Economic Policy*, vol. ii, by J. E. Meade, *Econ. J.*, 67, June 1957.

'Gilbert Murray: A Personal Recollection', *National & English Review*, July 1957.

'The Gilt-Edged Surplus', *The Director*, August 1957.

Review article on United Nations '*The World Economic Survey, 1956*', *Times Review of Industry*, August 1957.

'European Common Market and the Commonwealth', *Optima*, September 1957.

'These Directives should go', *The Director*, October 1957.

'Clive Bell on Keynes', *The Econ. J.*, 67, December 1957.

'The Mis-directed Squeeze', *The Director*, December 1957.

[Trade Fluctuations and Buffer Policies of Low-income Countries.] Comments on Professor Nurkse's paper, *Kyklos*, 11, 1958.

'Recent Movements of Expansion and Recession in the British Economy', *Rivista di Politica Economica*, January 1958.

'The Role of Sterling', *South African Bankers' Journal*, February 1958.

'Britain must Plan for Investment', *The New Commonwealth*, February 1958.

'Last Sterling Crisis', *The Director*, February 1958.

Review of *Prosperity through Competition* by L. Erhard, *Books of the Month*, March 1958.

'The Role of Gold To-day', *The South African Journal of Economics*, 26 March 1958.

'Co-ordination of Currency and Trade Cycle Policy in a European Community', *Aussenwirtschaft* (Zürich), March/June 1958.

'Questions for a Stabilization Policy in Primary Producing Countries', *Kyklos*, 11, Fasc. 2, 1958.

'How Wise were the Three Wise Men?', *The Director*, April 1958.

'Factor-Price Relations under Free Trade', *Econ. J.*, 68, June 1958.

'Britain's Attitude to the Free Trade Area', *Revue Internationale du Marché Commun*, June 1958.

'World Recession', *The Director*, June 1958.

'A New Policy for Britain', *Journal of the Advertising Association*, August 1958.

'Why we should back Japan', *The Director*, August 1958.

Review of *Europe and the Money Muddle*, by Professor Triffin, *Econ. J.*, 68, September 1958.

'Why the Dollar Price of Gold must Rise', *Optima*, September 1958.

'World Recession and the United States', *International Affairs* (Royal Institute for International Affairs), October 1958.

'What the Cohen Report left out', *The Director*, October 1958.

'Marx', *Parsons' Pleasure*, October 1958.

'"Expansion" is the Key Word', *The New Commonwealth*, November 1958.

'Sterling Convertibility', *The Bankers' Magazine*, November 1958.

'Britain's Responsibility now', *The Director*, December 1958.

'Case for a Budget Deficit', *The Director*, February 1959.

Review of the *History of the Dollar*, by Dr. G. Nussbaum, *Econ. J.*, 69, March 1959.

[The Role of Gold Today.] Rejoinder to Mr. Katzen, *South African Journal of Economics*, 27 March 1959.

'World Monetary Liquidity', *Irish Banking Review*, March 1959.

'Capitalism—Interview with Polish Marxist', *Dialogue*, ed. Alasdair Clayre and Peter Jay, Vol. I, No. 1, March 1959.

'Possibilities of European Cooperation in a World Recession', *Aussenwirtschaft* (Zürich), March/June 1959.

'Keynes, Keynesians, and Mr. Jacobsson: A Note', *Kyklos*, 12, Fasc. 2, 1959.

'The Abbot', *Cornhill*, Spring 1959.

'Why not Easy Money?', *The Director*, April 1959.

'Britain's Economy needs Planning', *The New Commonwealth*, April 1959.

'Investment and Inflation', *F.B.I. Review*, April 1959.

'The Current Economic Situation', *The Purchasing Journal*, May 1959.

'Policy for Expansion and the Money Weapon', *The District Bank Review*, June 1959.

'Should we have a Target for Expansion?', *The Director*, June 1959.

'Atlantic Policy for Economic Growth', *European–Atlantic Review*, Summer 1959.

Review of *The Long and the Short View* by J. Viner, *Economica*, August 1959.

'Forward Foreign Exchange', *The Director*, August 1959.

'Domar and Dynamic Economics', *Econ. J.*, 69, September 1959.

Review of *Trends in International Trade* by panel of experts (Chairman: Professor Haberler), G.A.T.T., *Econ. J.*, September 1959.

'The Trade Cycle and Public Buying Policy', *Journal of the Institute of Public Supplies*, September 1959.

'Preparing to meet a Crisis', *The Director*, October 1959.

'Is the Money Supply Important?' (Review of the Radcliffe Report), *The Westminster Bank Review*, November 1959.

'Making Good the U.S. Deficit', *The Director*, December 1959.

'Economic Impact of Changing Needs', *Bacie Journal*, December 1959.

'New Arguments for Induction: Reply to Professor Popper', *British Journal for the Philosophy of Science*, February 1960.

'The German Dilemma', *The Director*, February 1960.

'Keynes' Attitude to Compulsory Military Service: A Comment', *Econ. J.*, 70, March 1960.

'Re-thinking the Radcliffe Report', *The Director*, March 1960.

'The U.S. Overall Deficit—a British View', *Moorgate & Wall Street Review*, Spring 1960.

'The Right Weapon at the Right Time', *The Director*, April 1960.

'Industry can do more for the Commonwealth', *The New Commonwealth*, 1960.

'More Income, More Consumption, More Investment', *The Director*, 1960.

'Second Essay in Dynamic Theory', *Econ. J.*, 60, June 1960.

Comment. *Econ. J.*, 70, December 1960.

'The Restraining Measures' and 'Sir Roy Harrod Replies' (letter), *The Director*, August 1960.

Review of *Canadian Commercial Policy* by J. H. Young, *Canadian Journal of Economic and Political Science*, August 1960.

'Return to Normal?', *The Director*, October 1960.

'Lindemann's Spinning Experiments', *Aeronautics*, November 1960.

'Gold—the American Dilemma', *The Director*, December 1960.

'The General Structure of Inductive Argument', *Proceedings of the Aristotelian Society*, 1960–1.

'Prosperity without Inflation, a Time to Shed Old Ideas', *The Director*, February 1961.

'Memo. on Gold Question', *Mining World*, March 1961.

'Real Balances: A Further Comment', *Econ. J.*, 71, March 1961.

'The D Mark', *The Director*, April 1961.

'A Plan for Increasing Liquidity: A Critique', *Economica*, N.S. 28, May 1961.

'Facts about Industrial Growth' (review of *Patterns of Industrial Growth, 1938–58*, U.N., N.Y.), *Nature*, May 1961.

'Mutual Credit and False Hopes', *The Director*, June 1961.

'The "Neutrality" of Improvements', *Econ. J.*, 71, June 1961.

'Liquidity', *Rivista di Politica Economica*, July 1961.

'Priorities', *The Director*, August 1961.

'Monetary Policy and Economic Growth', *National Bank of Belgium Bulletin*, October 1961.

'The Three Strands in the Chancellor's Policy', *The Director*, October 1961.

'The Government Clouds the Crystal Ball', *Business*, November 1961.

'The Significance of "Planning"', *District Bank Review*, December 1961.

'The British Performance', *The Director*, December 1961.

Review of Sraffa's *Production of Commodities by Means of Commodities*, *Econ. J.*, 71, December 1961.

'Control of Hire Purchase', *Credit* (Quarterly Review of Finance Houses Association), December 1961.

'The Squeeze on Profits', *Esso Magazine*, Winter 1961/2.

'The Pound at Home and Abroad', *Kyklos*, 15, 1962.

'Economic Development and Asian Regional Cooperation', *Pakistan Development Review*, 2, 1962.

'The British Balance of Payments', *Weltwirtschaftliches Archiv*, 88, Heft, 2 1962.

'Economic Analysis for the New Year', *Times Review of Industry*, January 1962.

'New Thinking in Europe', *European–Atlantic Review*, January–February, 1962.

'Dynamic Theory and Planning', *Kyklos*, 15, February 1962.

'Internationalism and the Common Market', *The Director*, February 1962.

'Enlargement of the Common Market?', *Caractère et Culture de l'Europe* (Fondation Européenne de la Culture), February 1962.

'A.B.C. of the Present Situation', *The Director*, April 1962.

'Britain and the Balance of Payments', *The Purchasing Journal*, April 1962.

'Inflation and Investment in Under-Developed Countries', *Rassegna Economica* (Bank of Naples), April 1962.

'Where the Authorities went wrong', *The Director*, June 1962.

'Great Britain and the Common Market', *The South African Bankers' Journal*, August 1962.

'Gold: What the Problem is', *The Director*, August, 1962.

'Growth and Liquidity', *Rivista di Politica Economica*, October 1962.

'When the Next Crisis comes', *The Director*, October 1962.

'El Problema de la Incorporacion de Gran Bretaña al Mercado Común', *De la Revista di Economia y Estadistica* (Cordoba), November 1962.

'A Reply to Mr. Bilkey', *Econ. J.*, 72, December 1962.

'The Case against Signing the Treaty of Rome', *The Director*, December 1962.

Review of *Studies in an Inflationary Economy*, by F. W. Paish, *Economica*, February 1963.

'What is the Next Step?', *The Director*, February 1963.

'World Trade and Development', *World Economic Conference*, 11–15 March 1963.

'Taking Stock after Brussels', *The Purchasing Journal*, May 1963.

'Policy for Growth', *Rivista di Politica Economica*, May 1963.

'Mid-year Outlook', *F.B.I. Review*, June 1963.

'Sense and Sensibilia', Review article on Austin's work, *Philosophy*, July 1963.

'The Influence of Erhard on German Recovery' (Review of his *Economics of Success*), *The Purchasing Journal*, September 1963.

'Personal Saving and Business Profit', *The Investment Analyst*, September 1963.

'Creation of Credit and Dearer Gold', *European Review*, Autumn 1963.

'Changing Pattern', *Civilta delle Macchine*, November/December 1963.

Reviews of *Trade Blocs and Common Markets* by S. Dell, and *The Economics of Banking Operations* by J. A. Galbraith, *Econ. J.*, 73, December 1963.

'Themes in Dynamic Theory', *Econ. J.*, 73, September 1963. Corrigendum, December 1963.

'How the Basel Club works', *European Review*, Winter 1963/4.

'Are we really all Keynesians now?', *Encounter*, January 1964.

'Value Judgements', *Rivista di Politica Economica*, Rome, February 1964.

'New Tools for the Treasury', Review of Lord Bridges' *The Treasury*, *Times Review of Industry*, June 1964.

'Neddy and Growth: A Theoretical Question', *The Bankers' Magazine*, June 1964.

'Economic Prospects', *The Purchasing Journal*, July 1964.

Review of *Sunshades in October*, by N. Macrae, *Kyklos*, Fasc. 3, September 1964.

'Balm for the I.M.F.', *Times Review of Industry*, September 1964.

'New Thinking needed on International Liquidity', *Optima*, September 1964.

'Sir Roy Harrod's View of the British Economy', *Economica*, 31, November 1964.

'Are Monetary and Fiscal Policies Enough?' *Econ. J.*, 74, December 1964.

'World Reserves', *List Gesellschaft*, March 1965.

'The Financial Position and Prospects', *The Purchasing Journal*, March 1965.

'Advice for the Chancellor', *Times Review of Industry*, April 1965.

Review of Culbertson's *Full Employment or Stagnation*, *Econ. J.*, 75, June 1965.

'Report on the Economy', *The Purchasing Journal*, June 1965.

'The Present Position of Sterling', *Weltwirtschaftliches Archiv* (Kiel), July 1965.

Review of S. Brittan, *The Treasury under the Tories, 1951–1964*, *Econ. J.*, 75, September 1965.

'Appreciation des mouvements internationaux des capitaux en liaison avec la croissance des pays emprunteurs et prêteurs', *Cahiers de l'I.S.E.A.*, 167, November 1965.

'The British Problem', *The Bankers Magazine*, November 1965.

'International Balance of Payments Problem', *Studies*, Deutsche Bank AG, Autumn 1965.

Review of *Essays on Economic Policy* by N. Kaldor, *Econ. J.*, 73, December 1965.

Review of *The Pressure on the Dollar* (proposal for a long-term solution), by M. Negreporti-Delivanis, *Econ. J.*, 76, March 1966.

'Financial Conditions and Budget Prospects', *The Purchasing Journal*, March 1966.

'International Monetary Fund, Yesterday, Today and Tomorrow', *Bernard Harms Vorlesungen*, ed. E. Schneider, June 1966 (lecture at Kiel on the occasion of the award of the Bernard Harms Prize).

'International Liquidity', *The Bankers' Magazine*, June 1966.

'International Liquidity', *Scottish Journal of Political Economy*, 13, June 1966.

'British Policy. The Role of Sterling', *District Bank Review*, December 1966.

'Prices and Incomes Freeze', 'Status of Sterling and International Liquidity', *Dun's Review* (Dun and Bradstreet), December 1966.

'Recent Events in the British Economy', *Weltwirtschaftliches Archiv*, Band 97, Heft 2, 1966.

'The Bitter Squeeze', *Scotland*, January 1967.

'Harrod on Rueff', *European Review*, Winter 1966/67.

'Methods of Securing Equilibrium', *Kyklos*, February 1967.

'When can the Squeeze be ended?' *Management Accounting*, February 1967.

Review of Heller, *New Dimensions of Political Economy* (The New Economist in Action), *Challenge* (Magazine of Economic Affairs), March 1967.

'World Reserves and International Liquidity', *South African Journal of Economics*, June 1967

'Prospects for the British Economy', *The Purchasing Journal*, July 1967.

Review of *National Economic Policy*, by J. Tobin, *National Banking Review* (U.S.), June 1967.

'Assessing the Trade Returns', *Econ. J.*, 77, September 1967.

Review of volume of *Collected Wicksell Lectures*, *Journal of Political Economy*, 1967.

Review of *Europe and the Dollar* by C. P. Kindleberger, *Econ. J.*, 77, December 1967.

'British Economy and Prospects for Sterling', *The Bankers Magazine*, January 1968.

'Rio Agreement', *The Bankers Magazine*, March 1968.

'World Monetary Problems since Rio', *Bancaria*, March 1968.

'The Devaluation of Sterling', *Weltwirtschaftliches Archiv*, Heft 1, 1968.

Review of *Essays in Monetary Economics* by Harry Johnson, *Economica*, February 1968.

Review of Shackle, *Years of High Theory*, and M. Lipton, *Assessing Economic Performance, Econ. J.*, 78, September 1968.

Review of Brookings Report on U.K., *The Bankers' Magazine*, October 1968.

'Atlantic Free Trade Area', *Three Banks Review*, December 1968.

'Devaluation—The Year After', *The Bankers' Magazine*, December 1968.

'State of the Economy', *Purchasing Journal*, January 1969.

'The British Economy in 1969–70', *Scotland*, January 1969.

'Problemi Monetari d'Oggi', *Bancaria*, July 1969.

Review of *Why Growth Rates Differ* by Edward F. Denison, *Economica*, August 1969.

'Euro-Dollars and Balances of Payments', *Euromoney*, October 1969.

'Sterling in the International Monetary System', *Cadres Roma*, October 1969.

'What is Inflation?', *Wharton Quarterly*, Fall, 1969.

OTHER

Monthly memoranda on current economic situation prepared for Philips and Drew since 1955. These are available up to 1967 in sets of three bound volumes, in the Libraries of Oxford (Institute of Economics and Statistics), Yale, and the University of Pennsylvania.

NEWSPAPERS, ETC.
PRE-WAR LETTERS AND ARTICLES (SEE PREFACE)

'Monetary policy' (letter), *The Economist*, 4 June 1932 (see also 18 June 1932).

'Restoration of prices; fresh money for spending' (this letter was written by Sir Roy Harrod and privately printed by him for circulation, in order to collect signatures. As published, it was signed by 42 economists, including Keynes), *The Times*, 5 July 1932.

'The dilemma in the economy; how to restore demand; a case for limited reflation' (article described as 'from a correspondent', and referring to another by Arthur Salter on 'Reflation' which had appeared on 3 June 1932), *The Times*, 4 November 1932.

'More money in circulation' (letter written by Sir Roy Harrod and signed by 37 economists), *The Times*, 10 March 1933.

'Trade of the world; British policy of expansion' (letter), *The Times*, 21 April 1933.

'Banking and trade recession' (letter), *The Economist*, 9 July 1938.

'Meeting on trade recession; the case for monetary reflation', *The Times*, 11 August 1938 (see also 17, 26 August and 14 September 1938).

'Expanding the credit base' (letter), *The Economist*, 10 September 1938.

'Credit, growth and trade', *The Financial Times*, 12 September 1938.

'Appeal for Liberal–Labour Agreement at Oxford' (this open letter initiated the idea that the Liberal and Labour candidates for the Oxford by-election should withdraw in favour of an independent anti-Munich candidate, which they subsequently did. The independent candidate, A. D. Lindsay, did not get in, but the idea was taken up at Bridgewater shortly afterwards, where the independent anti-Munich candidate, Vernon Bartlett, was victorious), *The Oxford Mail*, 10 October 1938.

'Sir Stafford Cripps's campaign. The clear duty of Labour Associations' (letter), *The Manchester Guardian*, 19 January 1939.

'Expenditure on defence: good out of evil' (letter), *The Times*, 22 February 1939.

'National economic policy' (anonymous), *The Times*, 2 and 3 March 1943.

REGULAR CONTRIBUTOR AT VARIOUS PERIODS TO

Bank of Tokyo Review
The Financial Times
The Liverpool Post
Nihon Keizai Shimbun
Soundings
Times Literary Supplement (anonymous reviews)

OCCASIONAL CONTRIBUTIONS TO

The Birmingham Post
The Daily Telegraph
The Economist
The Listener
Mercurio
The Sydney Morning Herald
Time and Tide
The Times